OXFORD STUDIES IN EUROPEAN LAW

Series Editors

PAUL CRAIG

Professor of English Law at St John's College, Oxford

GRÁINNE DE BÚRCA

Professor of Law at New York University School of Law

Business Freedoms and Fundamental Rights in European Union Law

OXFORD STUDIES IN EUROPEAN LAW

Series Editors:
Paul Craig, Professor of English Law at St John's College, Oxford and
Gráinne de Búrca, Professor of Law at New York University School of Law

The aim of this series is to publish important and original research on EU law. The focus is on scholarly monographs, with a particular emphasis on those which are interdisciplinary in nature. Edited collections of essays will also be included where they are appropriate. The series is wide in scope and aims to cover studies of particular areas of substantive and of institutional law, historical works, theoretical studies, and analyses of current debates, as well as questions of perennial interest such as the relationship between national and EU law and the novel forms of governance emerging in and beyond Europe. The fact that many of the works are interdisciplinary will make the series of interest to all those concerned with the governance and operation of the EU.

OTHER TITLES IN THIS SERIES

Compliance with European Consumer Law
The Case of E-Commerce
Felix Pflücke

Legislative Authority and Interpretation in the European Union
Martijn van den Brink

Secession and European Union Law
The Deferential Attitude
Núria González Campañá

Fiscal State Aid Law and Harmful Tax Competition in the European Union
Dimitrios Kyriazis

The Abuse of Constitutional Identity in the European Union
Julian Scholtes

Judging European Democracy
The Role and Legitimacy of National Constitutional Courts in the EU
Nik de Boer

EU Values Before the Court of Justice
Foundations, Potential, Risks
Luke Dimitrios Spieker

Postnational Constitutionalism
Europe and the Time of Law
Paul Linden-Retek

The Legislative Priority Rule and the EU Internal Market for Goods
A Constitutional Approach
Eadaoin Ní Chaoimh

The Jurisprudence of Constitutional Conflict in the European Union
Ana Bobić

Reflexive Governance in EU Equality Law
Emma Lantschner

Enhanced Cooperation and European Tax Law
Caroline Heber

Legal Pluralism in European Contract Law
Vanessa Mak

Europe's Passive Virtues
Deference to National Authorities in EU Free Movement Law
Jan Zglinski

Accountability in EU Security and Defence
The Law and Practice of Peacebuilding
Carolyn Moser

Accountability in the Economic and Monetary Union
Foundations, Policy, and Governance
Menelaos Markakis

Business Freedoms and Fundamental Rights in European Union Law

NIALL O'CONNOR

Senior Lecturer, University of Essex, Colchester, Essex, UK

OXFORD
UNIVERSITY PRESS

OXFORD
UNIVERSITY PRESS

Great Clarendon Street, Oxford, OX2 6DP,
United Kingdom

Oxford University Press is a department of the University of Oxford.
It furthers the University's objective of excellence in research, scholarship,
and education by publishing worldwide. Oxford is a registered trade mark of
Oxford University Press in the UK and in certain other countries

Published in the United States of America by Oxford University Press
198 Madison Avenue, New York, NY 10016, United States of America

British Library Cataloguing in Publication Data

Data available

Library of Congress Control Number: 2024944351

ISBN 9780192888020

DOI: 10.1093/9780191982132.001.0001

Printed and bound by
CPI Group (UK) Ltd, Croydon, CR0 4YY

MIX
Paper | Supporting
responsible forestry
FSC® C013604

For Thomas

Preface

This book provides a critical and reconstructive account of the freedom to conduct a business in EU law, a freedom which is now contained in Article 16 of the EU Charter of Fundamental Rights and Freedoms.

While aspects of the freedom to conduct a trade or business had previously been articulated by the Court of Justice in pre-Charter case law, and was said to derive in part from various provisions of national constitutions, the articulation of freedom to conduct a business in Article 16 has generated extensive litigation as well as some important—and controversial—rulings of the Court on the meaning and scope of that right. Seen by some as a natural and reasonable codification of earlier jurisprudence of the Court of Justice on the general principles of EU law, and by others as the insertion of a novel and disruptive provision of neoliberal intention and effect, Article 16 of the Charter has already generated a lively scholarly debate.

The author of this book adds to those debates by arguing that the freedom to conduct a business under Article 16 needs to be understood not as a self-standing economic freedom or right, but in its relationship to a range of other dimensions and provisions of EU law. Focusing in particular on the domain of employment law, he argues that Article 16 should be interpreted and developed in relation to existing general principles of EU law and to other provisions of the Charter, and in relation to EU and national legislation governing the issues. Freedom to conduct a business should be considered, he argues, not just in its relationship to other social rights under EU law, but also as itself reflecting a dimension of social rights.

The book should be of relevance to all of those interested in the impact of the Charter of Rights on employment law, as well as those interested more broadly in the Court of Justice's interpretation of Charter rights, and in the place of the freedom to conduct a business within the framework of EU social rights and social law.

Paul Craig and Gráinne de Búrca

Acknowledgements

I first became interested in exploring the topic of the freedom to conduct a business as a fundamental right in 2013, while completing my LLM dissertation at the College of Europe, Bruges. It was at this time that Dr Síofra O'Leary (my thesis supervisor, and latterly the President of the European Court of Human Rights) directed me towards the then recently delivered Opinion of Advocate General Cruz Villalón in *Alemo-Herron*, which would provoke an ongoing academic curiosity concerning the tensions between economic and social aspects of European Union integration.[1]

The eventual PhD thesis, on which this book is partly based, was completed at the University of Cambridge in 2018 on the topic of the 'Impact of EU Fundamental Rights on the Employment Relationship', with the United Kingdom employment law context providing a rich backdrop against which to evaluate competing EU-derived economic and social rights concepts within a concrete domestic contractual setting. The intervening Brexit referendum of 2016, while undoubtedly disruptive, has since formed the focus of much of my subsequent academic work.

I remain grateful to Professor Catherine Barnard and Professor Louise Merrett for their supervision and encouragement, and to Professor Simon Deakin and Professor Virginia Mantouvalou for their thoughtful examination of the original thesis. The resultant book is undoubtedly more EU (fundamental rights) law and less (domestic) employment law focused, though the employment rights context remains the regulatory field against which the normative and legal value of the freedom to conduct a business as a fundamental right is assessed.

I also want to thank my colleagues at Essex Law School for providing such a welcoming and collegial environment in which to pursue legal scholarship. In particular, I want to acknowledge the support of the University of Essex's open access fund. Thanks are also due to the series editors, the editorial and production teams at Oxford University Press (particularly Lindsay Glick), as well as the three anonymous reviewers for their guidance and support from

[1] AG Opinion in Case C–426/11 *Mark Alemo-Herron v Parkwood Leisure Ltd* ECLI:EU:C:2013:82.

the outset of the process, which began at the height of the Covid-19 pandemic. Finally, I want to acknowledge the role of my family and friends who have made the—at times challenging—process of writing a book that much more enjoyable.

Colchester, April 2024

Contents

Table of Cases

I. EUROPEAN UNION CASE LAW

A. Judgments of the Court of Justice of the European Union

B. Opinions of the Court of Justice of the European Union

C. Judgments of the General Court

D. Opinions of the Advocates General

II. INTERNATIONAL CASE LAW

A. Judgments of the European Court of Human Rights

B. Judgments of the European Free Trade Association Court

III. DOMESTIC CASE LAW

A. Germany

B. United Kingdom

C. United States

Table of Treaties and Legislation

B. International Treaties and Instruments

II. LEGISLATION

A. European Union

B. Domestic Legislation and Constitutions

I. UNITED KINGDOM

II. UNITED STATES

III. GERMANY

IV. ITALY

V. IRELAND

List of Abbreviations

CFR	European Union Charter of Fundamental Rights
CJEU	Court of Justice of the European Union
CLS	Critical Legal Studies
DCFR	Draft Common Frame of Reference
EAT	Employment Appeal Tribunal
ECHR	European Convention on Human Rights
ECSC	European Coal and Steel Community
ECtHR	European Court of Human Rights
EEA	European Economic Area
EFTA	European Free Trade Association
ESC	European Social Charter
EU(W)A	European Union (Withdrawal) Act 2018
ICESCR	International Covenant on Economic Social and Cultural Rights
ILO	International Labour Organization
REULA	Retained EU Law (Revocation and Reform) Act 2023
TCA	Trade and Cooperation Agreement
TEU	Treaty on European Union
TFEU	Treaty on the Functioning of the European Union
TUD	Transfer of Undertakings Directive
TUPE	Transfer of Undertakings (Protection of Employment) Regulations 2006
UKSC	United Kingdom Supreme Court
USSC	United States Supreme Court
WA	Withdrawal Agreement
WF	Windsor Framework
WTD	Working Time Directive

Introduction

Exploring the Constitutional and Social Dimensions of a Contested Fundamental Right

> One can sometimes get the impression that freedom of contract is the elephant in the room. In my opinion it has not yet found its rightful place in the system of EU law. However, it underpins its framework, above all in the context of the operation of fundamental freedoms.[1]
>
> Advocate General Szpunar, *Thelen Technopark*

The Freedom to Conduct a Business as a Contested Fundamental Right

At first glance, the freedom to conduct a business found within Article 16 of the European Union Charter of Fundamental Rights (CFR) appears rather innocuous, providing succinctly that 'the freedom to conduct a business in accordance with Union law and national laws and practices is recognised'.[2] The Explanations attached to the Charter further clarify that the freedom to conduct a business is composed of a number of distinct elements, notably for present purposes: (1) the freedom to exercise an economic or commercial activity; and (2) freedom of contract.[3] Rarely, however, has such a seemingly harmless provision provoked such controversy, with Article 16 CFR now lying at the centre of debates surrounding the precise place of business freedoms, particularly freedom of contract, within the Union's wider economic constitution. Particularly problematic are a number of controversial judgments delivered in the employment context, in which the Court of Justice of the European Union (CJEU) relied on freedom of contract—as a component of

[1] AG Opinion in Case C-261/20 *Thelen Technopark Berlin GmbH v MN* ECLI:EU:C:2021:620, para 76.
[2] Charter of Fundamental Rights of the European Union [2012] OJ C326/391.
[3] Explanations Relating to the Charter of Fundamental Rights [2007] OJ C303/17.

Business Freedoms and Fundamental Rights in European Union Law. Niall O'Connor, Oxford University Press.
 DOI: 10.1093/9780191982132.003.0001

the freedom to conduct a business as a fundamental right—in order to undermine the protections granted within EU-derived employment legislation.[4]

Of particular note is the decision of the CJEU in *Alemo-Herron*, which represents a turning point in the CJEU's treatment of freedom of contract as a component of the wider freedom to conduct a business. In that case, the CJEU controversially relied on freedom of contract as a constitutional fundamental right in order to negate the legislative protections granted to workers in the context of a transfer of a business from one employer to another, despite the purported purpose of that legislation in preserving employment terms and conditions.[5] It is argued here that *Alemo-Herron* and its progeny are emblematic of wider deficiencies within the Union's fundamental rights regime, with the freedom to conduct a business as a fundamental right disrupting existing understandings of foundational fundamental rights concepts such as the relationship between the unwritten general principles and the codified Charter of Fundamental Rights, and indeed the relationship between 'rights' and 'principles' within the Charter itself.

At the same time it will be shown that, understood within its proper constitutional and social dimensions, there is nothing *inherently* deregulatory in the recognition of business freedoms as fundamental rights, with those freedoms also capable of encapsulating social rights, interests, and values. The CJEU's jurisprudence on the freedom to conduct a business thereby sits at the forefront of discussions concerning the potentially diverging value to be attributed to the Charter's economic freedoms and social rights provisions. In this regard, it should also be noted that the precise jurisprudential, legal, normative, political, or social consequences of (deregulatory) judgments may not be understood for years or perhaps even decades after they have been handed down. For example, the highly controversial decision of the United States Supreme Court (USSC) in *Lochner*, in which freedom of contract was recognized as a constitutional right, was only viewed with disapproval in light of the New Deal, after which 'the historical *Lochner* was transformed into the normative *Lochner*—that is, into this symbol of judges usurping legislative authority by basing decisions on policy preferences rather than the law'.[6]

[4] Case C-426/11 *Mark Alemo-Herron v Parkwood Leisure Ltd* ECLI:EU:C:2013:521; Case C-201/15 *Anonymi Geniki Etairia Tsimenton Iraklis (AGET Iraklis)* ECLI:EU:C:2016:972.

[5] Directive 2001/23/EC on the approximation of the laws of the Member States relating to the safeguarding of employees' rights in the event of transfers of undertakings, businesses or parts of undertakings or businesses [2001] OJ L82/16.

[6] *Lochner v New York* 198 US 45 (1905); Howard Gillman, 'De-Lochnerizing *Lochner*' (2005) 85 BULRev 859, 861.

Within the EU context, Barnard has identified four stages of academic response to the controversial and highly deregulatory *Viking* and *Laval* line of cases, in which internal market freedoms were relied on to the detriment of fundamental (collective) employment rights.[7] The first stage constitutes 'the initial reaction: understanding the decision and framing the debates'. The second stage necessitates 'exploration: deepening and reframing the debate'. The third stage involves 'concept and theory building'. Finally, the fourth step calls for a response 'to subsequent developments and reassessment of the situation'. The existing literature on the consequences of the CJEU's decision in *Alemo-Herron* has tended to focus on the first and fourth steps, namely reacting to that decision while considering its potential effects within particular regulatory fields.

This book aims to conduct a deeper exploration of the theoretical implications of the CJEU's interpretation and application of the freedom to conduct a business as a fundamental right within the context of the legal reasoning of the CJEU. Particular consideration is given to the normative interdependence of the freedom to conduct a business with fundamental 'social rights' concepts, allowing for an exploration of the 'essence' of competing economic and social rights while also developing a social (functional) and critical understanding of the freedom to conduct a business as a fundamental right, through a re-evaluation of that concept's interpretation and application within existing CJEU case law. Moreover, the space granted by a monograph necessarily allows for a more comprehensive assessment of the consequences of 'problematic' judgments.

Of course, the 'significance' of particular judgments is also open to various interpretations. First, there is the question of whether a topic covered by a judgment is 'of particular significance and controversy in a specific regulatory domain of EU law, be that due to the development of a novel legal point or due to a change in tack in existing approaches'.[8] Secondly, 'whether the decision has caused particular upheaval or controversy in at least some of the Member States' domestic systems'.[9] Finally, a vital measure of a judgment's importance is its value as a source of law, that is to say as precedent, and 'understood in this way, an important judgment establishes a legal rule or principle that is employed to resolve future issues, thereby distinguishing itself from judgments

[7] Catherine Barnard, 'The Calm after the Storm: Time to Reflect on EU (Labour) Law Scholarship Following the Decisions in *Viking* and *Laval*' in Alan Bogg, Cathryn Costello, and Anne Davies (eds), *Research Handbook on EU Labour Law* (Elgar 2016) 337.

[8] Mark Freedland and Jeremias Prassl, *Viking Laval and Beyond* (Hart 2015) 3.

[9] ibid.

doomed to spend eternity on the ash heap of legal history'.[10] As explored throughout this book, *Alemo-Herron*—and related judgments—score in all three respects, albeit to differing degrees and depending on the constitutional or legislative context in question.

There is no doubt that decisions such as *Alemo-Herron* have had the effect of rendering the assessment of the relationship between business freedoms and other fundamental rights within the Charter more difficult, given that these sources are of nominally equal weight. It has been said that the constitutional architecture of the EU is deeply entwined with the idea of economic integration, with the internal market providing 'the very foundation of the autonomous interpretation of fundamental rights'.[11] The Charter, with its—at least formal—emphasis on the indivisibility of civil and political rights on the one hand, and economic and social rights on the other, has the potential both to reinforce but also to disrupt existing understandings of a market-led approach to the development of EU fundamental rights. At the same time, this book's proposed reconceptualization of the freedom to conduct a business in relation to both its constitutional and social (rights) functions provides for an understanding of that freedom that does not *necessarily* imply deregulatory consequences, with this ambiguity also being reinforced by the open-ended nature of the freedom to conduct a business, including in its component parts.

Indeed, this book opened with remarks from Advocate General Szpunar in the case of *Thelen Technopark*, which highlight an ongoing and significant gap at the heart of the CJEU's jurisprudence concerning the freedom to conduct a business, namely that court's reluctance to elucidate the precise meaning, content, and effects of freedom of contract as a component of wider business freedoms within Union law. In *Thelen Technopark*, the CJEU did not accede to the Advocate General's request 'to take a closer look at freedom of contract and clarify its place in the system of EU law'.[12] The challenge taken up by this book is therefore to evaluate the role of freedom of contract as a fundamental right, but within its wider constitutional and (social) rights context. It is argued that a fundamental rights conceptualization of freedom of contract can only properly be understood by considering its place in relation to: (1) the various dimensions of business freedoms as fundamental rights; (2) the Union's wider

[10] Mattias Derlén and Johan Lindholm, 'Goodbye *van Gend en Loos*, Hello *Bosman*? Using Network Analysis to Measure the Importance of Individual CJEU Judgments' (2014) 20 ELJ 667, 668.

[11] Sybe de Vries, 'The Charter of Fundamental Rights and the EU's "Creeping" Competences: Does the Charter Have a Centrifugal Effect for Fundamental Rights in the EU?' in Sionaidh Douglas-Scott and Nicholas Hatzis (eds), *Research Handbook on EU Law and Human Rights* (Edward Elgar 2017) 58, 72–73.

[12] AG Opinion in *Thelen Technopark* (n 1) para 77.

fundamental rights regime, including the relationship between general principles and the Charter, as well as between business freedoms and potentially competing social rights; and, perhaps most significantly, (3) the social dimensions of freedom of contract itself, including its proposed reconceptualization in 'social' rights terms.

The book could also readily have borne the title *Business Freedoms as a Fundamental Right in European Union Law*, that is to say that the freedom to conduct a business has itself been entrenched as a fundamental right within both the general principles of European Union (EU) law and the Charter of Fundamental Rights. Instead, the focus on *Business Freedoms* and *Fundamental Rights in European Law* is intended to emphasize the core argument made throughout this book that it is only through examining the relationship between the freedom to conduct a business and fundamental social rights that the nature and the implications of the former freedom can be ascertained.

In other words, an understanding of freedom of contract as encapsulated within the freedom to conduct a business as a fundamental right will only ever remain *partial* in the absence of a consideration of its relation to wider fundamental (social) rights concepts within the Union legal order. Assessing the relationship between business freedoms and social rights also contributes to our understanding of core (constitutional) rights concepts within the Union's wider fundamental rights regime, notably the relationship between 'rights' and 'principles', the horizontal application of fundamental rights, the relationship between general principles and the Charter, and finally the relationship between the Charter and the fundamental economic freedoms of the EU internal market.

It is argued that the relationship between business freedoms and fundamental social rights is composed of (interrelated) internal and external dimensions. The 'external' dimension recognizes that there are potentially competing social rights concepts that contour the scope and reach of the freedom to conduct a business as a fundamental right. The analysis here goes beyond the traditional conception of the relationship between economic freedoms and social rights as a 'clash' or 'conflict' of rights, to instead emphasize the legal and normative weight granted to the freedom to conduct a business relative to the Charter's social rights provisions, which underscores the normative and practical interdependence between economic freedoms and social rights.[13]

[13] Phil Syrpis and Tonia Novitz, 'Economic and Social Rights in Conflict: Political and Judicial Approaches to their Reconciliation' (2008) 33 ELRev 411; Sacha Garben, 'Balancing Social and Economic Fundamental Rights in the EU Legal Order' (2020) 11 ELLJ 364.

Understanding this relationship thereby necessitates a re-evaluation of the fragmented 'values', 'rights', 'freedoms', and 'principles' that underpin the Charter, including the role of Union legislation in articulating such concepts in practice. It will be shown that there are 'social' dimensions of the freedom to conduct a business—including freedom of contract—as a fundamental right which inhere within—that is, are 'internal' to—that freedom itself, including the long-recognized but underexplored 'social function' of such freedoms, albeit that this internal dimension must also now be *informed* by external conceptions of fundamental social rights found elsewhere within the Charter.

The particular focus of this book remains on the implications of the freedom to conduct a business within the context of the *legal reasoning* of the CJEU, for the reason that the Court enjoys a pre-eminent role within the Union fundamental rights context, given that the 'whole foundations' of EU fundamental rights law were largely the work of that court.[14] As the EU's competence in the fundamental rights field—or at least in areas with fundamental rights implications—has expanded, so too has the importance of the CJEU as a fundamental rights actor grown.[15] Given the complexity of the Union's fundamental rights architecture, courts in particular are charged with both generating and protecting those rights, with the CJEU also enjoying the exclusive power to *interpret* Union law.[16] Although not the only actors involved in the protection of fundamental rights, courts—including the courts of the Member States—have a role not merely in 'applying' fundamental rights norms, but also in navigating the various instruments, delineating the precise role of different fundamental rights actors, and ensuring that fundamental rights—including fundamental *social* rights—considerations are represented.[17]

The freedom to conduct a business as a Union fundamental right is the subject of an ever-expanding academic literature, which is reflective of the contested nature of this now codified fundamental right.[18] Much of the (early) literature is largely constituted of extended case notes reacting to controversial judgments of the CJEU, but with a recognition of the wider regulatory and

[14] Francis G Jacobs, 'Human Rights in the European Union: The Role of the Court of Justice' (2001) 26 ELRev 331, 340.

[15] Janneke Gerards, 'Who Decides on Fundamental Rights Issues in Europe? Towards a Mechanism to Coordinate the Roles of the National Courts, the ECJ and the ECHR' in Sybe de Vries, Ulf Bernitz, and Stephen Weatherill (eds), *The EU Charter of Fundamental Rights as a Binding Instrument: Five Years Old and Growing* (Hart 2015) 51; Sionaidh Douglas-Scott, 'The Court of Justice of the European Union and the European Court of Human Rights after Lisbon' in Sybe de Vries, Ulf Bernitz, and Stephen Weatherill (eds), *The Protection of Fundamental Rights in the EU After Lisbon* (Hart 2013) 153.

[16] AG Toth, 'Human Rights as General Principles of Law, in the Past and in the Future' in Ulf Bernitz and Joakim Nergelius (eds), *General Principles of European Community Law* (Kluwer 2000) 73, 76.

[17] Mark Dawson, *The Governance of EU Fundamental Rights* (CUP 2017) 20.

[18] With the caveat that the focus here remains on the literature produced in English.

constitutional challenges posed by those judgments.[19] Particular attention has been paid to the CJEU's recognition of the freedom to conduct a business, including freedom of contract in such a way as to overturn existing approaches to the interpretation and application of such concepts.[20] Other contributions have examined the relationship between the freedom to conduct a business as a fundamental right and substantive areas of EU law.[21] The 'dual' nature of the freedom to conduct a business as both an *individual* right but also a concept of wider significance for the Union's *economic* constitution has been recognized.[22]

The consequences of the Charter for national regulatory autonomy have been addressed, including in the context of an assessment of the role of the freedom to conduct a business as a fundamental right in particular areas of EU regulatory influence, including the employment sphere.[23] More recent

[19] Charles Wynn-Evans, 'TUPE, Collective Agreements and the Static-Dynamic Debate' (2010) 39 ILJ 275; Jeremias Prassl, 'Freedom of Contract as a General Principle of EU Law? Transfers of Undertakings and the Protection of Employer Rights in EU Labour Law' (2013) 42 ILJ 434; Stephen Weatherill, 'Use and Abuse of the EU's Charter of Fundamental Rights: On the Improper Veneration of "Freedom of Contract"' (2014) 10 ERCL 167; Ilektra Antonaki, 'Collective Redundancies in Greece: *AGET* Iraklis' (2017) 54 CMLRev 1513; Menelaos Markakis, 'Can Governments Control Mass Layoffs by Employers? Economic Freedoms vs Labour Rights in Case C-201/15 *AGET Iraklis*' (2017) 13 EuConst 724; Justin Lindeboom, '*Thelen Technopark* and the Legal Effects of the Services Directive in Purely Internal and Horizontal Disputes' (2022) 7 European Papers 305.

[20] Prassl (n 19); Weatherill (n 19); Peter Oliver, 'What Purpose Does Article 16 of the Charter Serve?' in Ulf Bernitz, Xavier Groussot, and Felix Schulyok (eds), *General Principles of EU Law and European Private Law* (Kluwer 2013) 281; Xavier Groussot, Gunnar Thor Pétursson, and Justin Pierce, 'Weak Right, Strong Court—The Freedom to Conduct Business and the EU Charter of Fundamental Rights' in Sionaidh Douglas-Scott and Nicholas Hatzis (eds), *Research Handbook on EU Law and Human Rights* (Edward Elgar 2017) 326.

[21] Markakis (n 19); Andrea Usai, 'The Freedom to Conduct a Business in the EU, its Limitations and its Role in the European Legal Order: A New Engine for Deeper and Stronger Economic, Social, and Political Integration' (2013) 14 Ger Law J 1867; Nils Wahl, 'The Freedom to Conduct a Business: A Right of Fundamental Importance of the Future of the European Union' in Fabian Amtenbrink and others (eds), *The Internal Market and the Future of European Integration* (CUP 2019) 273; Rufat Babayev, 'Duality of Economic Freedom Protection in the Interplay of Article 16 CFR and Article 102 TFEU' (2020) 45 ELRev 694.

[22] Wahl (n 21); Dagmar Schiek, 'Towards More Resilience for a Social EU—The Constitutionally Conditioned Internal Market' (2017) 13 EuConst 611; Michelle Everson and Rui Correia Gonçalves, 'Article 16' in Steve Peers and others (eds), *The EU Charter of Fundamental Rights: A Commentary* (2nd edn, Hart 2021) 463.

[23] Markakis (n 19); Marija Bartl and Candida Leone, 'Minimum Harmonisation after *Alemo-Herron*: The Janus Face of EU Fundamental Rights Review' (2015) 11 EuConst 140; Niall O'Connor, 'The Impact of Positive Action on Private Law Freedoms—Proposed EU Directive on Gender Balance in the Boardroom' (2015) 18 TCLR 128; Jeremias Prassl, 'Business Freedoms and Employment Rights in the European Union' (2015) 17 CYELS 189; Rebecca Zahn, 'The Court of Justice of the European Union and Transfers of Undertakings: Implications for Collective Labour Rights' (2015) 6 ELLJ 72; Anne Davies, 'Has the Court of Justice Changed its Management and Approach towards the Social Acquis?' (2018) 14 EuConst 154; Stefan Giubboni, 'Freedom to Conduct a Business and EU Labour Law' (2018) 14 EuConst 172; Femke Laagland, 'Member States' Sovereignty in the Socio-Economic Field: Fact or Fiction? The Clash between the European Business Freedoms and the National Level of Workers' Protection' (2018) 9 ELLJ 50; Bruno Veneziani, 'Article 16—Freedom to Conduct a Business' in Filip Dorssemont and others (eds), *The Charter of Fundamental Rights of the European Union and the Employment Relation* (Hart 2019) 351; Niall O'Connor, 'Whose Autonomy is it Anyway? Freedom

attention has also turned to tracing the 'origins' of the freedom to conduct a business as a fundamental right partly due to the consolidation of the Charter's *travaux préparatoires*, which provide an insight into the rationale behind the inclusion within the Charter of this most unusual of fundamental rights, at least by international standards, with the freedom to conduct a business (and freedom of contract) not usually being found within international fundamental rights instruments.[24] In a similar vein, the potentially diverging legal meanings of (economic) 'freedom' or 'autonomy' have begun to be explored.[25]

This book re-evaluates existing understandings of the freedom to conduct a business as a fundamental right in two broad—and interrelated—ways, namely by: (1) assessing the place of the freedom to conduct a business within the Union's *fundamental (constitutional) rights* framework, thereby addressing the role (and value) of freedom of contract within the wider fundamental (social) rights context, including the inconsistencies engendered by the differing understanding of freedom to conduct a business depending on the relevant constitutional or 'rights' setting; and (2) reconceptualizing the freedom to conduct a business through a fundamental social rights lens, thereby emphasizing the hitherto underappreciated 'social' aspects of that freedom, including in its guise as freedom of contract. With this dual approach, it is argued that a proper understanding of the meaning and consequences of the freedom to conduct a business as a fundamental right requires that freedom to be situated within its wider constitutional and social rights dimensions.

Constitutional Dimensions of the Freedom to Conduct a Business as a Fundamental Right

The EU now has a significant and well-developed (constitutionalized) system for the protection of fundamental rights, with the Union enjoying not only the

of Contract, the Right to Work and the General Principles of EU Law' (2020) 49 ILJ 285; Berdien van der Donk, 'Restricting Access to Legal Content in House Rules: The Platform's Freedom to Conduct a Business as a Counterargument to Limit Users' Freedom of Expression' in Steffen Hindelang and Andreas Moberg (eds), *YSEC Yearbook of Socio-Economic Constitutions 2021: Triangulating Freedom of Speech* (Springer 2022) 33.

[24] Hilary Hogan, 'The Origin and Development of Article 16 of the Charter of Fundamental Rights' (2023) 2 European Law Open 753.

[25] Rufat Babayev, 'Private Autonomy at Union Level: On Article 16 CFREU and Free Movement Rights' (2016) 53 CMLRev 979; Eduardo Gill-Pedro, 'Freedom to Conduct a Business in EU Law: Freedom from Interference or Freedom from Domination?' (2017) 9 European Journal of Legal Studies 103; Eduardo Gill-Pedro, 'Whose Freedom is it Anyway? The Fundamental Rights of Companies in EU Law' (2022) 18 EuConst 183.

power to prohibit the violation of fundamental rights, but also the ability to elaborate a positive vision of such rights through its political institutions.[26] In fact, it has been said that it is precisely because of the role of fundamental rights within the EU legal order that it can be described as a 'union of values'.[27] This has not always been the case and there continues to be academic scepticism surrounding the strength of the EU as a fundamental or human rights actor, and the retrospectively developed 'myth' that the Union has always been constructed on a foundation of fundamental rights protection.[28]

The field of fundamental rights continues to be a complex and contested area of EU law. This is despite the further constitutionalization of Union fundamental rights within the Charter, with 'constitutionalization' here understood as the entrenchment of legal norms which have thereby been endowed with higher legal status.[29] The fundamental rights architecture of the EU is currently multi-layered, fragmented, and difficult to navigate, deriving as it does from a number of interrelated and overlapping sources.[30] The European system for the protection of fundamental rights can therefore be characterized by a plurality of constitutional sources, a plurality of constitutional actors, and a plurality of constitutional views on rights.[31]

This pluralism creates a 'crowded' or 'fractured' normative and institutional space within an unclear hierarchy of sources.[32] Indeed, the 'heterarchical' vision espoused by the constitutional pluralism approach sits somewhat uneasily with a 'hierarchical' rights framework through which Union and national instruments must comply with EU-derived rights concepts found within the Charter and the general principles. Within the EU context, 'plurality' usually

[26] Mark Dawson, 'Fundamental Rights in European Union Policy-Making: The Effects and Advantages of Institutional Diversity' (2020) 20 HRLRev 50.

[27] Šejla Imamović, *The Architecture of Fundamental Rights in the European Union* (Hart 2022) 1; Case C-621/18 *Andy Wightman v Secretary of State for Exiting the European Union* ECLI:EU:C:2018:999, para 63.

[28] Imamović (n 27) 39–43; Gráinne de Búrca, 'The Drafting of the EU Charter of Fundamental Rights' (2001) 26 ELRev 214; Stijn Smismans, 'Fundamental Rights as a Political Myth of the EU: Can the Myth Survive?' in Sionaidh Douglas-Scott and Nicholas Hatzis (eds), *Research Handbook on EU Law and Human Rights* (Edward Elgar 2017) 13, 18.

[29] For different understandings of the term 'constitutionalization' in the social rights context, see Niall O'Connor, '"UnChartered" Waters: Fundamental Rights, Brexit and the (Re)Constitution of the Employment Law Hierarchy of Norms' (2021) 12 ELLJ 52, 57–63.

[30] Federico Fabbrini, *Fundamental Rights in Europe* (OUP 2014); Lorenza Violini and Antonia Baraggia (eds), *The Fragmented Landscape of Fundamental Rights Protection in Europe: The Role of Judicial and Non-Judicial Actors* (Edward Elgar 2018).

[31] Fabbrini (n 30) 14.

[32] ibid 30; Dawson (n 17) 2; Nico Krisch, 'The Open Architecture of European Human Rights Law' (2008) 71 MLR 183. For a discussion on the competing accounts of pluralism in the EU legal order, see Kaarlo Tuori, 'The Pluralism of European Fundamental Rights Law' in Sionaidh Douglas-Scott and Nicholas Hatzis (eds), *Research Handbook on EU Law and Human Rights* (Edward Elgar 2017) 35.

characterizes the relationship between Union law and the laws of the Member States, ie plurality at the level of the legal order or legal 'system' and within the context of multi-level constitutionalism.[33] In other words, EU law and domestic law should be considered together (holistically) when determining the relationship between them.[34]

The interest of this book instead lies primarily in the relationship between 'internal' Union sources of fundamental rights, namely the Charter, and the general principles given that these sources are of most direct relevance to a consideration of the relationship between fundamental economic freedoms and social rights. Both of these sources also enjoy the status of primary law and thus bind the EU in all its activities, as well as binding the Member States when they are acting within the scope of EU law. This is not to deny that the precise contours of the internal sources may be influenced by sources extraneous to the Union legal order strictly speaking, namely: (1) the common constitutional traditions of the Member States; and (2) international sources such as the European Convention on Human Rights (ECHR), as well as social rights instruments such as the European Social Charter (ESC).

Since Brexit, the United Kingdom (UK) legal order remains similarly permeable to external sources interacting with internal legal norms, with Union rights sources thereby likely to remain influential in that country, even if only indirectly. Brexit thereby adds a novel layer to the constitutional context against which business freedoms as fundamental rights can be understood, albeit through a process of 'deconstitutionalization', and which compounds the fragmentary constitutionalization of fundamental rights concepts already found within Union law. There is a particularly complex relationship between Union fundamental rights and Union values, for example through the reliance on the values espoused in Article 2 of the Treaty on European Union (TEU) in determining the core content or essence of Charter rights.[35]

There is also a more immediate connection between the values embodied at the level of the *Charter* and the rights and principles contained therein, which pursue potentially conflicting—or even contradictory—aims and objectives. As such, the relationship between Charter 'rights' and 'values' adds

[33] Neil Walker, 'The Idea of Constitutional Pluralism' (2002) 65 MLR 317; Franz C Mayer and Mattias Wendel, 'Multilevel Constitutionalism and Constitutional Pluralism' in Matej Avbelj and Jan Komárek (eds), *Constitutional Pluralism in the European Union and Beyond* (OUP 2012) 127.

[34] Dana Burchardt, 'The Relationship between the Law of the European Union and the Law of its Member States—A Norm-based Conceptual Framework' (2019) 15 EuConst 73, 78.

[35] Consolidated version of the Treaty on European Union [2012] OJ C326/13; Francesco de Cecco, 'The Trouble with Trumps: On How (and Why) Not to Define the Core of Fundamental Rights' (2023) 60 CMLRev 1551, 1563.

an additional layer of complexity to the traditional understanding of rights as an 'intermediary' facilitating the 'operationalization' or 'concretization' of values.[36] It will be argued that the values encapsulated by the Charter notably 'freedom' and 'solidarity', can also be utilized in ascertaining the *relationship* between (economic and social) rights as well as in determining their competing *normative* weight. There also remains particular uncertainty surrounding the relationship between the general principles and the Charter. This uncertainty affects the application and interpretation of fundamental rights concepts, notably where sources intersect or overlap, which thereby creates potential normative gaps in the relative level of protection granted to economic and social aspects of Union fundamental rights.

Social Dimensions of the Freedom to Conduct a Business as a Fundamental Right

Of particular relevance to the present discussion advocating an understanding of the freedom to conduct a business in relation to its social dimensions are the Charter's 'Freedoms' and 'Solidarity' Titles, which are themselves reflective of the already mentioned values of 'freedom' and 'solidarity'.[37] The intention is not to conduct a provision-by-provision examination, but rather to focus on the potentially competing 'values', 'freedoms', 'rights', and 'principles', that it is suggested lie at the foundation of the conceptual, legal, and normative tensions that exist between business freedoms and fundamental social rights, including the extent to which there is cross-fertilization between the Charter's values, which leads to potentially competing (social) conceptions of the freedom to conduct a business as a fundamental right, notably in relation to its 'social function'. Moreover, 'social' rights themselves can be constructed around the normative foundation of 'freedom' or 'autonomy' in the sense of the positive freedom to make choices, which reinforces the argument that business freedoms and contractual autonomy concepts can themselves be (re)conceived in social (rights) terms.

With regard to the first point that business freedoms must be understood in relation to their 'social function', this is a concept that has long been deployed

[36] ibid 1564, 1565; John Gardner, '"Simply in Virtue of Being Human": The Whos and Whys of Human Rights' (2008) 2 JESP 1.

[37] Niilo Jääskinen, 'Fundamental Social Rights in the Charter—Are They Rights? Are They Fundamental?' in Steve Peers and others (eds), *The EU Charter of Fundamental Rights: A Commentary* (2nd edn, Hart 2021) 1855.

in the case law of the CJEU, but without any genuine explanation of the meaning or content of that concept as applicable to business freedoms. It will be argued that competing fundamental social rights provide for compelling 'counterweights' to liberal or economic conceptions of the freedom to conduct a business, including freedom of contract. Of particular relevance in this regard are: (1) the right to collective bargaining and action in Article 28 CFR due to the competing protections granted to 'individual' and 'collective' autonomy within the context of the freedom to conduct a business as a fundamental right; and (2) the right to fair and just working conditions in Article 31(2) CFR as this provision constitutes a 'right' rather than a 'principle', and thereby acts as a potent corollary to the CJEU's treatment of the freedom to conduct a business as a fundamental right.

With regard to the second (and related) point that freedom of contract as a component of the freedom to conduct a business can be reconceived in social terms, particular reliance will be placed on the right to work found in Article 15 CFR given its connection to the freedom to pursue a trade or profession as a general principle. As such, it will be argued that the common origin of the freedom to conduct a business and the right to work within the general principles provides for potential mutual normative interdependence between those concepts, despite their diverging personal and material scopes, and which is also illustrative of the mutual reinforcement between the proposed internal and external social dimensions of business freedoms.

The main thrust of the present discussion unfolds against the legislative and regulatory context of the *employment* relationship for a number of reasons. First—and perhaps least convincingly—this is the substantive field of EU (and domestic) law most familiar to the author. Secondly, the CJEU's most controversial (deregulatory) judgments in relation to the freedom to conduct a business as a fundamental right have concerned the employment context. Thirdly, the employment rights found within the Charter's Solidarity Title readily lend themselves to being conceived as 'social' rights, in both the 'legal' and 'moral' senses of that concept.[38] The legal concept attributes the 'social rights' label to: (1) international social rights, ie rights found within international social rights instruments; (2) legislative social rights, ie rights embedded in legislation; and (3) constitutional social rights, ie rights that have been granted a

[38] Also relevant in this regard are art 27 CFR (worker information and consultation), art 29 CFR (right of access to placement services), art 30 CFR (protection from unjustified dismissal), art 32 CFR (prohibition of child labour and protection of young people at work), and art 33 CFR (the right to family and professional life).

privileged place among sources of norms, though without necessarily implying 'justiciability'.[39]

All three attributes are applicable to the employment rights found in the Solidarity Title and which also merit the characterization of 'social' due to their connection to the Social Title of the Treaty on the Functioning of the European Union (TFEU).[40] The Charter's employment provisions can also be connected to moral conceptions of social rights, which include their recognition as 'social human rights' as well as their role in creating a more 'egalitarian' notion of social citizenship. As argued here, the moral conception of employment rights as 'social rights' can most forcefully be seen in their connection to the right to (decent) work. Fourthly, the right to 'work' bridges the 'economic' (liberal) and the 'social' dimensions of freedom of contract.

Fifthly and finally, the employment relationship is somewhat unusual in that, despite being constructed on the foundation of a 'contract', it is also heavily influenced by competing social (solidarity) rights concepts, with the protection of fundamental (human) rights also constituting a continued marker of the 'autonomy' of employment law from other (commercial) legal fields.[41] At the same time, employment rights are a distinct form of social rights in that they do not (necessarily) involve the allocation or redistribution of (public) resources.[42] In this way, the employment relationship is characterized by the tensions surrounding the appropriate role for business freedom concepts within the context of social regulation.

Employment legislation has certainly encroached significantly into the principle of freedom of contract, in part due to the recognition of the inequality of bargaining power that pertains between employers and employees. Nevertheless, general principles of contract law including freedom of contract continue to provide the background rules against which protective employment legislation must be interpreted and applied. Indeed, unlike other international rights courts, for example the European Court of Human Rights, the

[39] Jeff King, *Judging Social Rights* (CUP 2012) 18, 19.

[40] Consolidated Version of the Treaty on the Functioning of the European Union [2012] OJ C326/47; eg art 31(2) CFR has been recognized as 'a fundamental social right in itself': AG Opinion in Joined Cases C-569/16 and 570/16 *Stadt Wuppertal v Maria Elisabeth Bauer and Volker Willmeroth v Martina Broßonn* ECLI:EU:C:2018:337, para 51.

[41] Hugh Collins, 'Theories of Rights as Justifications for Labour Law' in Guy Davidov and Brian Langille (eds), *The Idea of Labour Law* (OUP 2011) 137; Alan Bogg and others (eds), *The Autonomy of Labour Law* (Hart 2015); Hugh Collins and Virginia Mantouvalou, 'Human Rights and the Contract of Employment' in Mark Freedland and others (eds), *The Contract of* Employment (OUP 2016) 188; Joe Atkinson, 'Human Rights as Foundations for Labour Law' in Hugh Collins, Gillian Lester, and Virginia Mantouvalou (eds), *Philosophical Foundations of Labour Law* (OUP 2018) 122; Philippa Collins, *Putting Human Rights to Work: Labour Law, The ECHR, and the Employment Relation* (OUP 2022).

[42] King (n 39) 18.

CJEU does have a 'legislative will' to consider in the interpretation of Union law and in assessing its compatibility with fundamental rights.[43] Moreover, legislation frequently has rights implications even if the Union itself lacks general competence to act in the human rights field.[44]

It will be shown in particular that the social rights found within the Solidarity Title of the Charter are especially dependent on underlying legislative sources for their legal (and normative) content, which has profound implications for their relative weight when compared with the freedom to conduct a business as a fundamental right, with the latter freedom instead deriving from the constitutional general principles rather than being dependent on further legislative elucidation. This is despite the fact that the freedom to conduct a business in Article 16 CFR is explicitly stated to be recognized (only) 'in accordance with Union law and national laws and practices', which suggests that this provision constitutes a 'principle' rather than a 'right', the former of which does indeed require further legislative concretization. This requirement poses particular problems within the employment context due to the rather piecemeal adoption of Union legislation in this field, derived essentially from the historical prioritization of the Union's economic constitution at the expense of the protection of (fundamental) social rights.[45]

Structure and Outline of Chapters

The book is structured around three main themes through which the social and constitutional functions of the freedom to conduct a business as a fundamental right—notably in its relationship with competing fundamental social rights—are evaluated, with these themes being addressed in each of the book's three parts, namely: 'The Constitutional Contours of Business Freedoms and Fundamental Rights' (Part I), 'The Reconstitution of the Freedom to Conduct a Business as a Fundamental Right' (Part II), and 'The Entrenchment of the Freedom to Conduct a Business as a Fundamental Right' (Part III). The

[43] Iain Cameron, 'Competing Rights' in Sybe de Vries, Ulf Bernitz, and Stephen Weatherill (eds), *The Protection of Fundamental Rights in the EU After Lisbon* (Hart 2013) 181, 188.

[44] Elise Muir, 'The Fundamental Rights Implications of EU Legislation: Some Constitutional Challenges' (2014) 51 CMLRev 219; Tobias Mast and Christian Ollig, 'The Lazy Legislature: Incorporating and Horizontalising the Charter of Fundamental Rights through Secondary Union Law' (2023) 19 EuConst 462.

[45] Mark Bell, 'Constitutionalization and EU Employment Law' in Hans W Micklitz (ed), *Constitutionalization of European Private Law* (OUP 2014) 137; Catherine Barnard, 'The Protection of Fundamental Social Rights in Europe After Lisbon: A Question of Conflicts of Interest' in Sybe de Vries and others (eds), *The Protection of Fundamental Rights in the EU After Lisbon* (Hart 2013) 37.

employment law context provides the legal and normative backdrop against which these themes are addressed, both due to the already disruptive effect of the freedom to conduct a business within that context, but also due to tension within employment law between its contractual and (legislative) rights-based underpinnings.

Part I explores the 'constitutional contours' within which the freedom to conduct a business, as well as Union fundamental rights more broadly, must operate and suggests that business freedom concepts have had the effect of distorting existing understandings concerning the normative value of—and relationship between—sources of Union fundamental rights, notably in the relationship between that freedom and competing fundamental social rights. Chapter 1 reassesses the foundations of the fundamental rights architecture of the Union and argues that the general principles continue to represent the 'cornerstone' of the Union's fundamental rights edifice despite their purported '(re)constitutionalization' within the Charter. Particular emphasis is placed on the 'fragmentary' nature of the sources of Union fundamental rights. It is suggested that this fragmentation can be seen in the selective development of fundamental rights as general principles; the constitutional and legal constraints that have been placed on the personal and material scope of the Charter; and, perhaps most significantly, the competing normative, legal, and particularly constitutional, weight that has been assigned to the freedom to conduct a business relative to the 'social' rights found within the Charter's Solidarity Title.

It is certainly difficult to comprehend the relative weight of business freedoms and (potentially competing) fundamental (social) rights without first unpacking the now labyrinthine interrelationship between rights, freedoms, and (general) principles within the Union's fundamental rights order. Moreover, it is suggested that understanding the ambiguous ongoing relationship between the general principles and the Charter is key to addressing the apparent inconsistencies and contradictions that lie within the CJEU's interpretation and application of the freedom to conduct a business as a fundamental right.

Chapter 2 explores the consequences of the UK's withdrawal from the EU in creating additional layers of fragmentation and variability to the competing weight of the Charter's economic freedoms and fundamental social rights, both within the UK but also within the wider framework of EU law. It is argued that despite the Charter's purported exclusion from the category of 'retained EU law' post-Brexit, Union social rights concepts have an ongoing (albeit indirect) influence within domestic law as well as those legal provisions governing the UK's departure from—and new relationship with—the EU.

It is suggested that the Union's reaction to Brexit, both in its navigation of legal relations with the UK but also in its consideration of the competing weight of economic and social objectives within EU law, has demonstrated a recommitment to the protection of labour standards. Perhaps more significantly, Brexit provides an avenue for exploring the 'deconstitutionalization' of (former) Union fundamental rights concepts, which is illustrative of the relative 'embeddedness' of business freedoms and fundamental social rights within domestic law. Brexit thereby exposes deeper divergences between economic freedoms and fundamental social rights within the Charter, including the relationship between those provisions and the general principles of EU law.

Part II argues that there has been a 'reconstitution' of the freedom to conduct a business as a fundamental right, by charting the evolution of that freedom from its initial emergence as a general principle of EU law. It is suggested that the reconstitution of the freedom to conduct a business has tended to obfuscate its 'constitutional' origins, which has led to further fragmentations and the development of 'competing conceptions' of business freedoms as fundamental rights. Chapter 3 demonstrates that this reconstitution of the freedom to conduct a business results from the fact that, despite its origins within the concept of business freedoms as general principles, it is also distanced from those concepts in large part due to the CJEU's inconsistency in its treatment of the freedom to conduct a business as a 'constitutionalized' fundamental right. In particular, it will be shown that the earliest case law on business freedoms as general principles is grounded in the concept of the 'social function' of such freedoms, albeit that the CJEU has yet to provide a satisfactory definition of the meaning of that concept. A deeper understanding of the social function of business freedoms is offered by drawing from the theoretical foundations of that concept within property theory, while also applying critical approaches to conceiving the relationship between the individual (freedom or autonomy) and the community (social rights).

The argument is that the social function of business freedoms acts as an internal restriction on those freedoms, which creates space for the consideration of social values and interests. In this way, the chapter reassesses the pre-existing limitations on business freedoms as general principles in order to facilitate an evaluation of the Charter's disruption of these preconceived understandings. The origins, content, and status of the freedom to conduct a business within Article 16 CFR are then assessed, notably through an exploration of the contrasting intended functions of that freedom and the potentially competing social rights found within the Charter's Solidarity Title.

It will be shown that Article 16 CFR distorts the relationship between rights, freedoms, and principles as understood both within and beyond the confines of the Charter itself. Finally, the chapter reassesses the relationship between broader constitutional concepts, namely the general principles, and codified Charter rights and argues for a parallel (autonomous) application of those concepts within the CJEU's fundamental rights reasoning, with the aim of rationalizing the relationship between the various sources of business freedoms as fundamental rights within Union law.

Chapter 4 builds on this re-evaluation of the evolution of the freedom to conduct a business as a fundamental right by assessing the strength of that freedom in the CJEU's early case law following the enactment of the Charter. It is explained that an initial period of relative continuity, with pre-existing business freedoms as general principles, was interrupted by the CJEU's expansive approach to the interpretation of the freedom to conduct a business in the case of *Alemo-Herron*. It is argued that this case is emblematic of more foundational ambiguities concerning the meaning and core content of the freedom to conduct a business, notably in the form of freedom of contract, whether as a fundamental right or within Union law more generally.

These ambiguities are exacerbated by the absence of in-depth engagement with the potential legal counterweights to business freedoms as fundamental rights, notably those social provisions found within the Solidary Title of the Charter, which are argued here to shape the 'essence' of business freedoms as fundamental rights. It is the very open-ended nature of freedom of contract as a (contested) regulatory concept that constitutes such a potentially disruptive force within the fundamental rights context, including in the distortions caused to traditional understandings of the distinction between rights, freedoms, and principles both within and outside the context of the Charter. The suggestion here is that the existing inconsistencies in the CJEU's conceptualization of the freedom to conduct a business are also representative of wider deficiencies in the Court's fundamental rights reasoning, including the structural imbalances that exist between the relative weight granted to economic and social interests, which forms the focus of Part III.

More particularly, Part III evaluates the potential 'entrenchment' of the CJEU's competing conceptions of the freedom to conduct a business within the jurisprudence of that court and considers in particular the systemic deregulatory implications of the expansive interpretation of freedom of contract as a component of the freedom to conduct a business as a fundamental right. Chapter 5 assesses the materiality and significance of the freedom to conduct a business as a fundamental right in the judicial reasoning of the CJEU, with a particular focus on tracing the Court's expansive conception of that freedom in its relationship with protective social legislation. It is shown that the CJEU continues to oscillate between the reinforcement of—and retrenchment from—this expansive approach to business freedoms, which is suggested here to represent a more profound reflection of that court's approach to the interpretation and application of Union (fundamental rights) law.

In particular, it is argued that the constitutional value of the freedom to conduct a business is reinforced through its connection to the fundamental freedoms of the Union's internal market, which thereby risks the importation of deregulatory values in the absence of genuine consideration for competing social rights and interests. Moreover, the recognition of the fundamental constitutional status of those same internal market freedoms leads to the mutual reinforcement of deregulatory (rights) concepts.

The CJEU's jurisprudence concerning the freedom to conduct a business is characterized by its inconsistency and incoherence, both of which are argued to derive from the absence of effective engagement with the normative value of that freedom within EU law more generally, including in its relationship to competing social rights. The latter deficiency in the CJEU's fundamental rights reasoning is argued to compound existing gaps in the application of the already recognized 'social function' of business freedoms, hence the necessity of reconceptualizing the freedom to conduct a business in relation to its social dimensions.

Chapter 6 advances such a 'socialized' conception of the freedom to conduct a business through the argument that the 'right to work', itself a fundamental right found within Article 15 CFR, constitutes a potential entryway to social rights reasoning within the context of business freedoms. The freedom to pursue a trade or occupation and business freedoms have been deeply interconnected since the earliest case law of the CJEU recognizing fundamental rights as general principles, which is demonstrative of the competing economic and social values that inhere in the freedom to conduct a business as a fundamental right. Coupled with the legislative expression of social rights, notably in the employment context, a deeper understanding of the animating values underpinning the freedom to conduct a business allows for a reconsideration of the deregulatory potential of that freedom. In this way, it is suggested that existing literature comparing the CJEU to the *Lochner*-era USSC has overlooked the real value of *Lochner* discourse within the EU context.

There is no doubt that *Lochner* is a highly deregulatory judgment, and indeed it has become a watchword for ideologically charged judicial activism. But also evident in that judgment—as well as subsequent USSC judgments—is judicial engagement with competing constitutional values, with the *Lochner* jurisprudence thereby providing insights into how liberty or autonomy-based constitutional arguments can be reconceived in social terms. *Lochner* also certainly provides lessons as to how deregulatory constitutional concepts can become judicially embedded and with potentially systemic implications for the protection of competing (legislative) social rights. Within the EU context such an assessment is rendered all the more difficult by ongoing ambiguities concerning the value of—and relationship between—the Charter's substantive provisions, which remain grounded in the language of (conflicting) 'rights', 'freedoms', and 'principles' and which are of potentially diverging legal and normative value. It is to the challenge of unpacking these interrelated concepts and fragmented sources of Union fundamental rights that the first chapter of this book now turns.

PART I

THE CONSTITUTIONAL CONTOURS OF BUSINESS FREEDOMS AND FUNDAMENTAL RIGHTS

1
The Fragmentary Constitutionalization of Rights, Freedoms, and (General) Principles

1.1 Introduction

The overarching purpose of this chapter is to reassess the foundations of the fundamental rights architecture of the European Union (EU), with the aim of grounding the discussion on the competing legal and normative value granted to (economic) business freedoms and fundamental (social) rights within the EU Charter of Fundamental Rights (CFR). Indeed, economic freedoms and general principles have been intertwined since the very foundation of the Union's fundamental rights regime, and as argued here, business freedom concepts have the capacity both to enhance but also to disrupt our pre-conceived understandings of the origin, nature, structure, and function of the Union fundamental rights, particularly the relationship between sources of rights, as well as their relative normative weight.

The chapter therefore begins by re-evaluating the role of the general principles of EU law as the constitutional cornerstone of the Union's fundamental rights edifice (Section 1.2).

Overall, it is suggested that the general principles represent a fragmentary, albeit enduring, foundation upon which to construct the Union's fundamental rights regime, a fragmentation which derives from the (selective) sourcing of the general principles from the common constitutional traditions of the Member States. It is argued that this fragmentation not only paved the way for the emergence of the freedom to conduct a business as an expansive and unpredictable fundamental right within Article 16 CFR, but also engendered the inconsistencies that would later emerge in the application of that freedom, including in its uncertain relationship to other fundamental economic and social rights. At the same time, general principles remain a significant constitutional intermediary of the relationship between the various sources of rights found within Union law. This is despite their purported 'codification' within

Business Freedoms and Fundamental Rights in European Union Law. Niall O'Connor, Oxford University Press.
 DOI: 10.1093/9780191982132.003.0002

the Charter, a process which embodies—but is also embodied by—the fragmentary constitutionalization of Union fundamental rights, freedoms, and principles.

First, it is argued that the Charter represents a 'constrained' source of fundamental rights given its limited scope of application and interrelationship, indeed interdependence, with other sources of Union fundamental rights, both external and internal to the Union legal order, and which continue to act as constraints on the Court's fundamental rights jurisprudence (Section 1.3). Secondly, the Charter is a 'heterogenous' source of fundamental rights in that its provisions carry different normative weight, in part depending on their classification as 'rights', 'freedoms', or 'principles', with some provisions, but not others, also capable of application to disputes between private parties (Section 1.4). Section 1.5 concludes that the Charter, which is now the Union's pre-eminent fundamental rights instrument, has led to the emergence of ambiguities and divergences among its provisions, thereby opening unexpected pathways for both contestation and convergence between the freedom to conduct a business and at least some of the social rights found within the Charter's Solidarity Title. Ongoing uncertainties surrounding the precise status of certain Charter provisions, despite that instrument having binding legal effect since 2009, have had the (unintended) consequence of strengthening the role of business freedoms, notably in the guise of freedom of contract, in the face of competing economic and social rights.

1.2 General Principles as the Constitutional Cornerstone of the Fundamental Rights Edifice

1.2.1 The development of fundamental rights as general principles

The general principles are among the primary sources of EU law, alongside the Treaties and the Charter and consist of a set of largely unwritten rules that have been developed over time by the Court of Justice of the European Union (CJEU).[1] They have been defined as 'fundamental propositions of law which

[1] Paul Craig, 'General Principles of Law: Treaty, Historical and Normative Foundations' in Katia S Ziegler, Päivi J Neuvonen, and Violeta Moreno-Lax (eds), *Research Handbook on General Principles of EU Law* (Edward Elgar 2022); Matthias Herdegen, 'General Principles of EU Law—The Methodological Challenge' in Ulf Bernitz and others (eds), *General Principles of EC Law in a Process of Development* (Kluwer 2008); Stefan Vogenauer and Stephen Weatherill (eds), *General Principles of Law: European and Comparative Perspectives* (Hart 2017) 343; Takis Tridimas, *The General Principles of EU Law* (2nd edn, OUP 2006).

underlie a legal system and from which concrete rules or outcomes may be derived'.[2] Initial attempts by litigants to invoke national fundamental rights, for example constitutional rights to free choice of trade, occupation or profession, were resisted by the CJEU, which declined to recognize these rights as part of the Union legal order.[3] This reluctance to apply domestic rights standards stemmed from the need to preserve the autonomy and primacy of EU law.[4] As such, the CJEU rejected the very idea of fundamental rights as general principles of EU law as a limit on Union action.[5] This has been described as the initial 'indifference' or 'impermeability' of EU law towards national constitutional law.[6]

Consequently, there was a fear that those rights found in national constitutions would be undermined if their application could be avoided through the adoption of measures at Union level.[7] This concern was addressed in the seminal *Stauder* case in which the CJEU 'discovered' the general principles of EU law, including the protection of fundamental rights such as human dignity.[8] In other words, EU law contained its own catalogue of 'fundamental rights enshrined in the general principles'.[9] The CJEU did not, however, provide a clear definition of what might constitute such a fundamental right, thereby exposing normative and interpretative gaps in the protection of fundamental rights, and, as argued here, providing for ambiguities at the foundation of such rights, deriving essentially from the unclear relationship between general principles and written sources of rights, notably the Charter.[10]

[2] Tridimas (n 1) 1.

[3] Case C–1/58 *Friedrich Stork & Cie v High Authority of the European Coal and Steel Community* ECLI:EU:C:1959:4.

[4] Tomi Tuominen, 'Reconceptualizing the Primacy-Supremacy Debate in EU Law' (2020) 47 LIEI 245, 249; Joseph HH Weiler, 'Eurocracy and Distrust: Some Questions Concerning the Role of the European Court of Justice in the Protection of Fundamental Human Rights Within the Legal Order of the European Communities' (1986) 61 Wash L Rev 1103, 1108.

[5] Joined Cases C–36, 37, 38, and 40/59 *Geitling Ruhrkohlen-Verkaufsgellschaft v High Authority of the European Coal and Steel Community* ECLI:EU:C1960:36; Case C–40/64 *Marcello Sgarlata v Commission of the European Economic Community* ECLI:EU:C:1965:36.

[6] Oreste Pollicino, 'Common Constitutional Traditions in the Age of the European Bill(s) of Rights: Chronicle of a (Somewhat Prematurely) Death Foretold' in Lorenza Violini and Antonia Baraggia (eds), *The Fragmented Landscape of Fundamental Rights Protection in Europe: The Role of Judicial and Non-Judicial Actors* (Edward Elgar 2018) 42, 43.

[7] William Phelan, 'The Role of the German and Italian Constitutional Courts in the Rise of EU Human Rights Jurisprudence: A Response to Delledonne & Fabbrini' (2020) TRiSS Working Paper Series TRiSS-WPS-02-2020; Giacomo Delledonne and Federico Fabbrini, 'The Founding Myth of European Human Rights Law: Revisiting the Role of National Courts in the Rise of EU Human Rights Jurisprudence' (2019) 44 ELRev 178.

[8] Case C–29/69 *Erich Stauder v City of Ulm* ECLI:EU:C:1969:57.

[9] ibid para 7.

[10] Stijn Smismans, 'Fundamental Rights as a Political Myth of the EU: Can the Myth Survive?' in Sionaidh Douglas-Scott and Nicholas Hatzis (eds), *Research Handbook on EU Law and Human Rights* (Edward Elgar 2017) 13, 19.

In *Internationale Handelsgesellschaft*, the CJEU clarified that recourse could not be had to national law to assess the validity of EU measures as to do otherwise would be to undermine the uniformity and efficacy of Union law, but that fundamental rights protection at Union level would be inspired by national constitutional law.[11] In that case, the relevant rights were the fundamental rights to free expression and free choice in commercial decisions, both of which were to be found in the German Basic Law. According to the CJEU, while guarantees analogous to national constitutional rights may exist within Union law, as is the case with the protection of fundamental rights, which 'forms an integral part of the general principles of law protected by the Court of Justice', the protection of such rights 'whilst inspired by the constitutional traditions common to the Member States, must be ensured *within the framework of the structure and objectives of the [Union]*' [emphasis added].[12] This approach was not readily accepted by the superior courts of all Member States. The German Constitutional Court, in particular, reserved the right to exercise its own jurisdiction where the level of rights protection fell below that guaranteed under German law.[13]

In addition to the common constitutional traditions of the Member States, the CJEU has also relied on international sources to inspire the development of general principles, notably international treaties for the protection of human rights to which the Member States are signatories, for example the European Convention on Human Rights (ECHR), subject to the clarification that non-absolute rights may be limited in order to protect the interest of the Union.[14] The CJEU has also looked to relevant case law of the European Court of Human Rights (ECtHR) when interpreting the Charter in specified areas.[15] Reference to external human rights sources—particularly sources other than the ECHR—is not made routinely by the CJEU.[16] Article 6(3) of the Treaty on European Union (TEU) only contains reference to the ECHR and national constitutional traditions, without referring to other international rights sources. The Charter's Explanations do, however, refer to social rights sources

[11] Case C–11/70 *Internationale Handelsgesellschaft mbH v Einfuhr- und Vorratsstelle für Getreide und Futtermittel* ECLI:EU:C:1970:114.

[12] ibid para 4.

[13] *Solange II* [1987] 3 CMLR 225.

[14] Case C–4/73 *J. Nold, Kohlen- und Baustoffgroßhandlung v Commission of the European Communities* ECLI:EU:C:1974:51, para 13.

[15] eg Case C–400/10 PPU *J McB v LE* ECLI:EU:C:2010:582.

[16] Vasiliki Kosta and Bruno de Witte, 'Human Rights Norms in the Court of Justice of the European Union' in Martin Scheinin (ed), *Human Rights Norms in Other International Courts* (CUP 2019) 263; Opinion 2/94 Accession by the Community to the European Convention for the Protection of Human Rights and Fundamental Freedoms ECLI:EU:C:1996:140, para 33.

such as the Community Charter of Fundamental Social Rights of Workers and the European Social Charter. The CJEU has also referred to these other sources in its case law, albeit infrequently.[17]

A clear articulation of the CJEU's approach to the recognition of fundamental rights as general principles can be seen in *Hauer*.[18] First, the CJEU highlighted once again that 'the question of a possible infringement of fundamental rights by a measure of the [Union] institutions can only be judged in the light of [Union] law itself'.[19] The reason being that to introduce 'special criteria for assessment stemming from the legislation or constitutional law of a particular Member State would, by damaging the substantive unity and efficacy of [Union] law, lead inevitably to the destruction of the unity of the Common Market and the jeopardizing of the cohesion of the [Union]'.[20] Secondly, the CJEU reaffirmed that 'fundamental rights form an integral part of the general principles of the law', the observance of which the Court ensures.[21] In so doing, the CJEU is 'bound to draw inspiration from constitutional traditions common to the Member States' with the consequence that 'measures which are incompatible with the fundamental rights recognized by the constitutions of those States are unacceptable in the [Union]'.[22] Similarly, 'international treaties for the protection of human rights on which the Member States have collaborated or of which they are signatories, can supply guidelines which should be followed within the framework of [Union] law'.[23]

1.2.2 The function of fundamental rights as general principles

Despite ongoing conceptual and methodological uncertainty, the broad purposes of the general principles are particularly relevant for their 'constitutional' role in the protection of fundamental rights. First, they can act as an aid to the interpretation of EU measures, ie measures must be interpreted insofar as

[17] eg Case C-149/77 *Gabrielle Defrenne v Société anonyme belge de navigation aérienne Sabena* ECLI:EU:C:1978:130, para 28. Olivier de Schutter and Israel de Jesús Butler, 'Binding the EU to International Human Rights Law' (2008) 27 YEL 277; Tawhida Ahmed and Israel de Jesús Butler, 'The EU and Human Rights: An International Law Perspective' (2006) 17 EJIL 771.

[18] Case C-44/79 *Liselotte Hauer v Land Rheinland-Pfalz* ECLI:EU:C:1979:290.

[19] ibid para 14.

[20] ibid.

[21] ibid para 15.

[22] ibid.

[23] ibid.

possible in accordance with the general principles.[24] Secondly, fundamental rights as general principles can be used as a ground for reviewing the validity of EU measures or Member State measures falling within the scope of EU law. Measures which are incompatible with the general principles will be void. This is due to the place of the general principles within the hierarchy of norms, which as primary sources rank higher than secondary sources such as Union legislation.[25] Although the hierarchy of sources within EU law is now relatively clear, there continues to be overlap between primary and secondary sources, with the latter often being used to define the content of the former.[26] Moreover, increased reference to fundamental rights standards can be found within secondary legislation, and which may sit uneasily with the scope of application of the Charter itself, thereby compounding existing fragmentations in the protection of fundamental rights.[27]

EU legislation can, thus, be reviewed for compatibility with the protection of fundamental rights as a general principle.[28] Limitations on non-absolute rights are permissible if they are shown to be a proportionate means of achieving a legitimate Union objective. The CJEU now views the Charter as the principal basis on which to build the protection of EU fundamental rights, particularly in its review of the validity of legislation, but the general principles remain significant, for example in the interpretation of those Charter provisions that derive from the general principles. It is suggested here that the enactment of the Charter does not preclude the further development of the general principles, including where both sources overlap, and despite the additional complexity this causes. This argument is advanced further when considering the relationship between the freedom to conduct a business as a fundamental right in Article 16 CFR and business freedoms as general principles.[29]

The CJEU can also review the acts of Member States for their compatibility with the general principles whenever the Member State is acting within the

[24] See eg Joined Cases C-201/85 and 202/85 *Marthe Klensch v Secrétaire d'État à l'Agriculture et à la Viticulture* ECLI:EU:C:1986:439.

[25] AG Toth, 'Human Rights as General Principles of Law, in the Past and in the Future' in Ulf Bernitz and Joakim Nergelius (eds), *General Principles of European Community Law* (Kluwer 2000) 73, 76; Case C-709/20 *CG v The Department for Communities in Northern Ireland* ECLI:EU:C:2021:602; Case C-333/13 *Elisabeta Dano and Florin Dano v Jobcenter Leipzig* ECLI:EU:C:2014:2358.

[26] Phil Syrpis, 'The Relationship Between Primary and Secondary Law in the EU' (2015) 52 CMLRev 461.

[27] Tobias Mast and Christian Ollig, 'The Lazy Legislature: Incorporating and Horizontalising the Charter of Fundamental Rights through Secondary Union Law' (2023) 19 EuConst 462; Elise Muir, 'The Horizontal Effects of Charter Rights Given Expression to in EU Legislation, from *Mangold* to *Bauer*' (2019) 12 Review of European Administrative Law 185.

[28] See eg Case C-236/09 *Association belge des Consommateurs Test-Achats ASBL v Conseil des ministres* ECLI:EU:C:2011:100.

[29] Section 3.4.

scope of EU law.[30] The latter concept has been defined as including situations in which the Member States are either implementing or applying EU law, or when national measures derogate from EU law.[31] When Member States are implementing EU law, they are considered 'agents' of the Union and so are expected to comply with Union fundamental rights in the same way that the underlying EU legislation must itself be compatible with fundamental rights.[32] When it comes to derogation from EU law, the CJEU made its rationale clear in *ERT* where it noted that where a Member State relies on an exception or derogation from EU law—in that case, the freedom to provide services—the Member State's justification for the derogation must be reviewed and interpreted 'in the light of the general principles of law and in particular of fundamental rights' and that a national rule will only fall within an exception to EU law to the extent to which it is 'compatible with the fundamental rights, the observance of which is ensured by the Court'.[33] It is therefore difficult for Member States to escape the reach of Union fundamental rights review, even where Union law itself ostensibly provides for derogations and exceptions.[34] If the matter falls outside the scope of Union law, the general principles will not be applicable regardless of the importance of the fundamental rights at issue.[35]

The CJEU has also recognized that the protection of fundamental rights—whether deriving from the general principles or the Charter—can constitute a legitimate aim allowing the Member States to justify a restriction on Treaty rights to free movement, and which may eventually lead to reliance on the freedom to conduct a business as a fundamental right to justify such derogation.[36] At the same time, the horizontal application of free movement rights

[30] Joined Cases C-411/10 and 493/10 *NS v Secretary of State for the Home Department and M E v Refugee Applications Commissioner and Minister for Justice, Equality and Law Reform* ECLI:EU:C:2011:865.

[31] Case C-5/88 *Hubert Wachauf v Bundesamt für Ernährung und Forstwirtschaft* ECLI:EU:C:1989:321; Case C-260/89 *Elliniki Radiophonia Tiléorassi AE and Panellinia Omospondia Syllogon Prossopikou v Dimotiki Etairia Pliroforissis and Sotirios Kouvelas and Nicolaos Avdellas* ECLI:EU:C:1991:254.

[32] Tridimas (n 1) 320.

[33] *Elliniki Radiophonia Tiléorassi* (n 31) para 43.

[34] Francis G Jacobs, 'Human Rights in the European Union: The Role of the Court of Justice' (2001) 26 ELRev 331, 337–39.

[35] Case C-299/95 *Kremzow v Republik Österreich* ECLI:EU:C:1997:254.

[36] Case C-438/05 *International Transport Workers' Federation and Finnish Seamen's Union v Viking Line ABP and OÜ Viking Line Eesti* ECLI:EU:C:2007:772; Case C-341/05 *Laval un Partneri Ltd v Svenska Byggnadsarbetareförbundet, Svenska Byggnadsarbetareförbundets avdelning 1, Byggettan and Svenska Elektrikerförbundet* ECLI:EU:C:2007:809; Case C-36/02 *Omega Spielhallen- und Automatenaufstellungs-GmbH v Oberbürgermeisterin der Bundesstadt Bonn* ECLI:EU:C:2004:614; Case C-112/00 *Eugen Schmidberger, Internationale Transporte und Planzüge v Republik Österreich* ECLI:EU:C:2003:333; Rufat Babayev, 'Private Autonomy at Union Level: On Article 16 CFREU and

might constitute a limitation of the freedom to conduct a business as a fundamental right.[37] As explored in Chapter 4, business freedoms as fundamental rights and the fundamental freedoms of the Union's internal market are mutually reinforcing (deregulatory) concepts. The CJEU has also long been engaged in a balancing act between the economic objectives of the Union's internal market and the protection of wider fundamental rights considerations.

In *Schmidberger*, for example, there was a conflict between the right of an environmental group to protest (freedom of association and assembly) and the free movement of goods, when the former caused the closure of the Brenner motorway in Austria.[38] The CJEU found that the failure of the Austrian authorities to prevent the closure of the motorway represented a measure having equivalent effect to a quantitative restriction on goods. Nonetheless, the CJEU concluded that this restriction could be justified given that fundamental rights protection 'is a legitimate interest which, in principle, justifies a restriction of the obligations imposed by [Union] law, even under a fundamental freedom guaranteed by the Treaty'.[39] A balance had to be struck between these two competing interests which were of equal constitutional weight.[40]

The 'fundamental' constitutional status of the free movement provisions potentially affects the manner in which they might be balanced with the more 'traditional' rights provisions in the Charter, particularly when the former are reinforced with reference to the freedom to conduct a business in Article 16 CFR. Indeed, business freedoms are at the core of early EU human rights law and, as just seen, the development of fundamental rights as general principles within the Union legal order stemmed from challenges from businesses which attempted to invoke business freedoms within national law to limit the application of EU law. Business freedoms at Union level thereby derive from a rather piecemeal interpretation of the same concepts found within domestic constitutions, thus obscuring their foundational normative and constitutional value.

Free Movement Rights' (2016) 53 CMLRev 979, 992; Niamh Nic Shuibhne, 'Settling Dust? Reflections on the Judgments in *Viking* and *Laval*' (2010) 21 EBLR 681; Norbert Reich, 'Free Movement v Social Rights in an Enlarged Union—the *Laval* and *Viking* Cases before the ECJ' (2008) 9 Ger Law J 125; Catherine Barnard, 'Social Dumping or Dumping Socialism' (2008) 67 CLJ 262.

[37] Babayev (n 36) 1005. eg Case C-281/98 *Roman Angonese v Cassa di Risparmio di Bolzano SpA* ECLI:EU:C:2000:296.

[38] *Schmidberger* (n 36).

[39] ibid para 74.

[40] Tridimas (n 1) 338.

1.2.3 The horizontal application of the general principles

From the very inception of fundamental rights as general principles of Union law, the question has arisen as to the extent of their application to disputes between private parties.[41] The possible horizontal direct effect of the general principles raises issues of profound constitutional significance within the EU legal order, but also has practical implications for the enforcement of fundamental rights by individual litigants.[42] Two broad issues arise in connection with the potential horizontal application of general principles. First, whether they are *capable* of being invoked between private parties and secondly, the wider normative question as to whether general principles, which are inherently vague, imprecise, and usually of a constitutional or administrative law character, *should* be applicable to private disputes.[43] Although these two issues are interrelated in that a vague general principle may not be capable of meeting the criteria for direct effect, the present concern lies more with the narrower question of whether the general principles have the capacity for horizontal direct effect. The wider question concerning the 'intrusion' of fundamental rights concepts into private contractual relations is addressed when assessing the horizontality of the Charter's provisions, and the related distinction between 'rights' and 'principles' contained therein.

In order to be relied on in a dispute between private parties, ie 'horizontally', the general principles would first have to be raised in a dispute falling within the scope of EU law and be capable of direct effect. Direct effect is here understood as the capacity of a provision of EU law to be invoked by individual litigants before national courts.[44] In order to be directly effective, the relevant measure must be sufficiently clear, precise, and unconditional.[45] 'True' horizontal direct effect, ie the ability of an individual to enforce a right against another individual, can also be contrasted with 'incidental' direct effect, whereby

[41] Eleanor Spaventa, 'The Horizontal Application of Fundamental Rights as General Principles of Union Law' in Anthony Arnull and others (eds), *A Constitutional Order of States? Essays in EU Law in Honour of Alan Dashwood* (Hart 2011) 199.

[42] Nicole Lazzerini, 'The Horizontal Application of the General Principles of EU Law: Nothing Less than Direct Effect' in Katia S Ziegler, Päivi J Neuvonen, and Violeta Moreno-Lax (eds), *Research Handbook on General Principles of EU Law* (Edward Elgar 2022) 173.

[43] Michael Dougan, 'The General Principles of EU Law and Private Relationships' in Dorota Leczykiewicz and Stephen Weatherill (eds), *The Involvement of EU Law in Private Relationships* (Hart 2013) 71, 74.

[44] Michael Dougan, 'When Words Collide! Competing Visions of the Relationship between Direct Effect and Supremacy' (2007) 44 CMLRev 931.

[45] Michael Dougan, 'In Defence of Mangold?' in Anthony Arnull and others (eds), *A Constitutional Order of States? Essays in EU Law in Honour of Alan Dashwood* (Hart 2011) 219, 227.

a measure is set aside due to a conflict with a superior source of law—such as general principles—with *subsequent* consequences for private parties.[46]

A national rule falling within the scope of EU law must comply with the general principles, including fundamental rights. This rule is equally applicable when the dispute concerns two private parties. When a dispute involves compatibility of a national measure with the Treaties, the relevant Treaty provision must itself be capable of direct effect in order to trigger the application of the general principles, as otherwise there would be no underlying provision of EU law to invoke in the dispute.[47] When Treaty provisions are themselves applicable horizontally, the general principles can also be relied on by a private party to resist the application of the Treaty.[48] The situation is more complicated with regard to cases in which the application of the general principles in a horizontal situation is triggered by secondary legislation rather than a provision of the Treaties. For example, in the *Mangold* and *Kücükdeveci* cases, it is well known that the CJEU applied the (itself contested) general principle of non-discrimination on the grounds of age in a private dispute, with the underlying equality legislation being found to give 'expression' to the general principle.[49]

The confirmation of the relevance of fundamental rights concepts for inter-individual disputes has been described as 'testament to the constitutionalizing force of the fundamental rights protected in the EU legal order, as unwritten general principles or as codified provisions of the Charter'.[50] It is argued here that this approach has the consequence of increasing variability among—and thereby the *divisibility* of—the Charter's provisions, notably in the diverging legal effects granted to economic (business) freedoms and social rights respectively. This is despite the fact that at least one of the intentions behind the Charter's drafting was to emphasize the indivisibility of political, economic, and social rights within the Union legal order.[51]

[46] Spaventa (n 41).
[47] ibid 206; Michael Dougan, 'Judicial Review of Member State Action under the General Principles and the Charter: Defining the "Scope of Union Law"' (2015) 52 CMLRev 1201.
[48] eg *Viking* (n 36); and *Laval* (n 36).
[49] Case C-144/04 *Werner Mangold v Rüdiger Helm* ECLI:EU:C:2005:709; Case C-555/07 *Seda Kücükdeveci v Swedex GmbH & Co KG* ECLI:EU:C:2010:21; Pedro Cabral and Ricardo Neves, 'General Principles of EU Law and Horizontal Direct Effect' (2011) 17 EPL 437; Mirjam de Mol, 'The Novel Approach of the CJEU on the Horizontal Direct Effect of the Principle of Non-Discrimination' (2011) 18 MJ 109; Elise Muir, 'Of Ages in—and Edges of—EU Law' (2011) 48 CMLRev 39; Marek Safjan and Przemysław Mikłaszewicz, 'Horizontal Effect of the General Principles of EU Law in the Sphere of Private Law' (2010) 18 ERPL 475.
[50] Lazzerini (n 42) 185.
[51] Łukasz Bojarski, Jane A Hofbauer, and Natalia Mileszyk (eds), 'The European Charter of Fundamental Rights as a Living Instrument: Guidelines for Civil Society' (Facultas 2014) 9.

1.3 The Charter as a Constrained Source of Fundamental Rights

As with the general principles, the Charter performs a number of functions in the fundamental rights field. It can be relied on in the interpretation of EU measures and can act as a ground for the review of both EU rules and national measures falling within the scope of EU law. That such EU and Member State measures should be interpreted consistently with the Charter itself constitutes a 'general principle of interpretation'.[52] In addition, EU measures that breach the Charter will be declared invalid while national implementing legislation that contravenes the Charter's provisions will be set aside.[53] Finally, the Charter is a potential source of inspiration for the discovery of new general principles, demonstrating the continued autonomous role for the latter as sources of EU fundamental rights.

The ongoing relevance of the general principles is in part due to the fact that the Charter is rather laconic as rights instruments go, with the content of its individual rights failing to match the lofty and aspirational language of its preamble, which refers to 'indivisible', 'universal', and 'common' 'values'. Instead, the Charter contains a series of carefully delimited and perfunctory provisions, divided into several substantive Titles headed 'Dignity', 'Freedoms', 'Equality', 'Solidarity', 'Citizens' Rights', and 'Justice', some of which are again said in the preamble to represent 'indivisible, universal values', upon which the Union is founded but with an unclear relationship or hierarchy between them, save to the extent that the Dignity provisions have been suggested as the 'core protection standard for the effective guarantee of any other right'.[54]

The Charter's Explanations also recognize that '[t]he dignity of the human person is not only a fundamental right in itself but constitutes the real basis of fundamental rights'. The concept of 'human dignity', while relevant, does not necessarily represent a convincing normative foundation for the most important Titles for the present consideration of the relationship between business freedoms and fundamental rights within EU law, namely the Freedoms Title (Title II) and the Solidarity Title (Title IV). It is suggested that far from undermining the effectiveness of social rights, which is the traditional (judicial) view of the dependency of such rights on legislative elucidation, the clear

[52] Case C–579/12 *RX-II - Réexamen Commission v Strack* ECLI:EU:C:2013:570, para 40.

[53] Koen Lenaerts and José Antonio Gutiérrez-Fons, 'The Place of the Charter in the European Legal Space' in Steve Peers and others (eds), *The EU Charter of Fundamental Rights: A Commentary* (2nd edn, Hart 2021) 1711.

[54] Bojarski, Hofbauer, and Mileszyk (n 51) 14.

articulation of the purpose and value of social rights in Union legislation actually reinforces its normative content and value.

The Solidarity Title therefore represents the most prominent internal source (ie internal to the Charter) of counterweights to the freedom to conduct a business as a fundamental right given its close connection to protective legislation, but also through the fact that at least some of its provisions are of nominally equivalent weight to the freedom to conduct a business. The relative normative weight of these provisions is again explored further in Part III, through the analytical lens of the 'values' and 'principles' underpinning the freedom to conduct a business, while this chapter considers some of the limitations placed by the Charter on the invocability of the provisions in the Solidarity Title, and thereby their potential to circumscribe the freedom to conduct a business as a fundamental right.

The substantive provisions of the Charter are also supported by accompanying Explanations which refer to other pre-existing and more precise sources to which 'due regard' must be given in the interpretation of the Charter according to Article 52(7) CFR. As explored in Chapter 3 in the context of the emergence of the freedom to conduct a business as a fundamental right from the concept of business freedoms as general principles, the Explanations also reveal the incomplete nature of the Charter's purported codification of pre-existing general principles through their rather selective and at times inaccurate reference to underlying case law. This process might be described as one of 'double fragmentation' in that the general principle which has now been selectively codified in the Charter was likely itself developed from a rather selective amalgamation of constitutional traditions from the then Member States of the Union.

The Explanations nevertheless emphasize the idea that the Charter did not create any new rights, but merely recognized existing rights deriving from the Treaties, legislation, the general principles, the ECHR, and other international sources. The very desirability, potential impact, or even need for the Charter in the first place had thereby been questioned.[55] Despite this, the Member States, perhaps anxious about the Charter's ability to extend the reach of EU law into the realm of national regulatory autonomy, insisted on the inclusion of a number of limitations to the Charter's scope, interpretation, and field of application within Articles 51–54 CFR, which can be found within Title VII of

[55] Lammy Betten, 'The EU Charter of Fundamental Rights: A Trojan Horse or a Mouse?' (2001) 17 Int J Comp LLIR 151; Joseph Weiler, 'Does the European Union Truly Need a Charter of Rights?' (2000) 6 ELJ 95.

the Charter. As will be seen, none of these measures preclude the dynamic evolution of the Charter, including in its relationship with other sources of fundamental rights, but they do constitute the bounded framework within which Union fundamental rights, freedoms, and principles must now be construed.

1.3.1 The limited scope of application of the Charter

Article 51(2) CFR once again emphasizes continuity and clarifies that the Charter 'does not extend the field of application of Union law beyond the powers of the Union or establish any new power or task for the Union, or modify powers and tasks as defined in the Treaties'.[56] Article 51(1) CFR addresses the scope of application of the Charter and specifies that it applies to the Union's institutions and agencies as well as the Member States when they are 'implementing'—as opposed to 'acting within the scope of'—EU law, the latter phrase being used to describe the scope of the general principles. The Charter always applies to the EU institutions, even when they act outside the framework of EU law.[57] Despite some initial doubts as to whether the Charter and the general principles were intended to have the same scope of application with regard to the Member States, the CJEU in *Åkerberg Fransson*—a tax case that did not obviously involve any implementation of EU law—noted that the Charter applies whether the Member States are acting or have failed to act in an area governed by a substantive rule of EU law.[58] As the CJEU put it, 'in essence [. . .] the fundamental rights guaranteed in the legal order of the European Union are applicable in all situations governed by European Union law, but not outside such situations'.[59] The Court held that the imposition of tax penalties in national criminal proceedings in the context of Value Added Tax, which is harmonized at EU level, did constitute 'implementation' of EU law and thus triggered the application of the Charter. The CJEU relied on the fact that the Explanations to the Charter use the broader term 'in the scope of Union law'.[60]

[56] Piet Eeckhout, 'The EU Charter of Fundamental Rights and the Federal Question' (2002) 39 CMLRev 945.

[57] Case C–8/15 P *Ledra Advertising Ltd v European Commission and European Central Bank (ECB)* ECLI:EU:C:2016:701.

[58] Case C–617/10 *Åklagaren v Hans Åkerberg Fransson* ECLI:EU:C:2013:105; Dougan (n 47); Emily Hancox, 'The Meaning of "Implementing" EU Law under Article 51(1) of the Charter: *Åkerberg Fransson*' (2013) 50 CMLRev 1411; Daniel Sarmiento, 'Who is Afraid of the Charter? The Court of Justice, National Courts and the New Framework of Fundamental Rights Protection in Europe' (2013) 50 CMLRev 1267.

[59] *Åkerberg Fransson* (n 58) para 19.

[60] ibid para 21.

In addition to its interpretative role, the Charter can, therefore, be used to review both EU measures and acts of the Member States falling within the scope of EU law.[61] In the same way as for the general principles, acting 'within the scope' of EU law includes the implementation or application of EU law by the Member States as well as Member State derogation from EU law. It would certainly add unnecessary complexity to the Union's fundamental rights order if the Charter, which was intended to codify existing rights, had a narrower scope than the general principles, but the term 'within the scope of EU law' remains nebulous as evidenced by *Åkerberg Fransson* itself. Advocate General Cruz Villalón, in that case, had found, for example, that the connection to EU law was too remote for the Charter to be applicable.[62]

Member States are therefore unlikely to have much success, following *Åkerberg Fransson*, in using Article 51 CFR to shield largely internal Member State law from the application of the Charter.[63] It is not, however, enough for a national measure merely to be adopted in a field in which the EU has competence to act. Rather, what is required is a specific connection between the national measure and obligations arising from EU law. As the CJEU put it in *Siragusa*, it is necessary to establish a 'degree of connection above and beyond the matters covered being closely related or one of those matters having an indirect impact on the other'.[64] Criteria to consider in determining whether this sufficient connection exists include whether the national rule is intended to implement EU law; the nature of the rule and whether it pursues an objective other than those covered by EU law, even if it is capable of affecting EU law indirectly; and whether there are specific EU law rules on the matter, or whether there are EU rules that are capable of having an effect on the matter.[65] It seems that where the exercise of discretion or a derogation by a Member State is determined by EU law, this will be a sufficient connecting factor.[66]

In *TSN*, the CJEU also determined that Member States are not 'implementing' EU law when they go beyond the minimum requirements of a directive.[67] That case involved national provisions falling within the powers

[61] eg Case C–293/12 *Digital Rights Ireland v Minister for Communications* EU:C:2014:238.
[62] *Åkerberg Fransson* (n 58).
[63] Mark Dawson, 'Fundamental Rights in European Union Policy-Making: The Effects and Advantages of Institutional Diversity' (2020) 20 HRLRev 50, 56.
[64] Case C–206/13 *Cruciano Siragusa v Regione Sicilia—Soprintendenza Beni Culturali e Ambientali di Palermo* ECLI:EU:C:2014:126, para 24.
[65] Case C–198/13 *Víctor Manuel Julian Hernández v Reino de España (Subdelegación del Gobierno de España en Alicante)* ECLI:EU:C:2014:2055; *Siragusa* (n 64).
[66] *Hernández* (n 65).
[67] Joined Cases C–609/17 and 610/17 *Terveys- ja sosiaalialan neuvottelujärjestö (TSN) ry v Hyvinvointialan liitto ry and Auto- ja Kuljetusalan Työntekijäliitto AKT ry v Satamaoperaattorit ry* ECLI:EU:C:2019:981.

granted by Article 15 of the Working Time Directive (WTD), which allows Member States to introduce more favourable provisions, for example by providing entitlements to annual leave going beyond the minimum of four weeks required by Article 7 WTD.[68] According to the CJEU, neither that provision nor Article 31(2) CFR, which provides for the fundamental right to paid annual leave, could preclude national measures preventing the carrying over of paid leave beyond the minimum four weeks, where that leave overlapped with periods of sick leave.

The reason for this conclusion was that these provisions were not applicable to national rules—including collective agreements—going beyond the minimum leave period provided for in the Directive, with the latter instead falling outside the scope of EU law and thereby being governed entirely by national law.[69] This approach could be contrasted with a situation whereby EU law itself grants Member States some choice as to how to implement Union measures, or where they are granted some margin of discretion forming an integral part of the underlying legal regime, or, finally, where the EU instrument authorizes the adoption of specific national measures.[70] In any case, more favourable measures adopted or permitted by the Member States must not undermine the coherence of the underlying EU measures.[71] In addition, the CJEU, in its assessment of the Charter's applicability, will consider the extent to which the relevant field has been harmonized at Union level, as well as the nature of the Union's competence in that field.[72]

In *TSN*, the CJEU paid particularly close attention to the legal basis of the Working Time Directive in Article 153(4) of the Treaty on the Functioning of the European Union (TFEU), which reiterates that measures adopted under Article 153 TFEU do not affect the Member States' ability to maintain or introduce 'more stringent protective measures compatible with the Treaties'.[73] The salient issue, therefore, is not whether the situation is within the *scope* of the Charter as such, but rather to identify the existence of a *right* flowing from a *specific* provision of EU law, which would trigger the protections granted by

[68] Directive 2003/88/EC of the European Parliament and of the Council of 4 November 2003 concerning certain aspects of the organisation of working time [2003] OJ L299/9.

[69] *TSN* (n 67) para 35.

[70] ibid para 50; Angela Ward, 'Article 51—Field of Application' in Steve Peers and others (eds), *The EU Charter of Fundamental Rights: A Commentary* (2nd edn, Hart 2021) 1553, 1590.

[71] AG Opinion in Joined Cases C–609/17 and 610/17 *Terveys- ja sosiaalialan neuvottelujärjestö (TSN) ry v Hyvinvointialan liitto ry and Auto- ja Kuljetusalan Työntekijäliitto AKT ry v Satamaoperaattorit ry* ECLI:EU:C:2019:459, paras 47–51.

[72] AG Opinion in Case C–826/18 *LB v College van burgemeester en wethouders van de gemeente Echt-Susteren* ECLI:EU:C:2020:514.

[73] *TSN* (n 67) para 48.

the Charter.[74] The consequence of this approach is that even where a legislative provision falls 'within the scope of EU law' as broadly defined, Union law (including the Charter) does not necessarily govern the situation in question due to the regulatory space left to the Member States in areas of shared competence. In other words, 'the division of powers as regards the protection of fundamental rights ultimately hinges upon the degree of regulatory autonomy available to the member states in the relevant policy area'.[75]

There continue to be uncertainties surrounding the applicability of the Charter to measures going beyond the minimum requirements provided for in Union legislation, and indeed in *TSN,* Advocate General Bot had come to the conclusion that the national measures in that case did amount to the 'implementation' of EU law for the purposes of Article 51(1) CFR, thereby engaging the Charter.[76] The Advocate General found that 'a national measure adopted in the application of a provision of a directive that authorizes enhanced national protection is *closely linked* to that directive and therefore must be regarded as implementing EU law' [emphasis added].[77] In other words, Article 15 WTD granted the Member States the discretion to go beyond the minimum protections afforded by Article 7 of the same directive, a discretion that is thereby explicitly authorized by the Directive itself, thus falling within the scope of EU law.[78] This was described as the 'domestic extension' of the Directive's provisions, with the enhanced national law protections constituting the 'implementation' of EU law.[79]

The case of *Alemo-Herron* was relied on to support this conclusion, but, as argued in Chapter 3, the CJEU in that case chose to review the relevant national legislation more *indirectly*, by interpreting the applicable EU directive instead, thereby essentially avoiding the question as to whether the Charter applies to Member State discretion when going beyond the minimum protection found in the relevant directive.[80] That case, which arose in the context

[74] AG Opinion in *LB* (n 72) para 112.
[75] Maxime Tecqmenne, 'Minimum Harmonisation and Fundamental Rights: A Test-Case for the Identification of the Scope of EU Law in Situations Involving National Discretion?' (2020) 16 EuConst 493, 498.
[76] AG Opinion in *TSN* (n 71) para 89. Eleanor Spaventa, 'Should we "Harmonize" Fundamental Rights in the EU? Some Reflections About Minimum Standards and Fundamental Rights Protection in the EU Composite Constitutional System' (2018) 55 CMLRev 997; Benedikt Pirker, 'Mapping the Scope of Application of EU Fundamental Rights: A Typology' (2018) 3 European Papers 133.
[77] AG Opinion in *TSN* (n 71) para 90.
[78] ibid para 82.
[79] ibid para 86.
[80] Case C-426/11 *Mark Alemo-Herron v Parkwood Leisure Ltd* ECLI:EU:C:2013:521; Richard Král and Petr Mádr, 'On the (In)Applicability of the EU Charter of Fundamental Rights to National Measures Exceeding the Requirements of Minimum Harmonisation Directives' (2021) 46 ELRev 81, fn 18.

of Article 16 CFR, is also illustrative of the fact that the applicability of the Charter does not always entail 'protective' effects, with fundamental rights in the guise of business freedoms capable of eroding—as much as enhancing—legislative protections.

The final limitation is that Charter rights are not absolute but can be limited as set out in Article 52(1) CFR. Article 52(1) CFR provides that any such limitation must be provided by law, respect the essence of the right, and be subject to the proportionality principle. The concept of the 'essence' or 'core content' is explored further within the particular context of examining the reach of the freedom to conduct a business as a fundamental right.[81] Limitations must also be necessary and genuinely meet 'objectives of general interest recognized by the Union or the need to protect the rights and freedoms of others.[82] Similarly, Article 52(2) CFR provides that Charter rights which are also recognized in the Treaties 'shall be exercised under the conditions and within the limits defined by those Treaties'. In other words, Charter rights deriving from the Treaty must be granted the same scope as the corresponding Treaty provision. In addition, Article 54 CFR prohibits the abuse of rights, including the destruction of any of the rights and freedoms recognised in this Charter or at their limitation to a greater extent than is provided for by the Charter. Essentially, this provision is aimed at ensuring that Charter rights cannot be used in order to deprive individuals of rights which are themselves conferred by the Charter.

1.3.2 The relationship between the Charter and other sources of fundamental rights

Given the Charter's close relationship to other rights sources both internal (general principles) and external to EU law strictly speaking (common constitutional traditions of the Member States and the ECHR), it was also necessary to provide rules governing those relationships in order to avoid potential conflict. This is particularly important due to the complex interconnection between the external sources and the general principles, which can lead to an indirect 'internalization' of the former. Article 6(3) TEU provides that the fundamental rights guaranteed by the ECHR and the common constitutional

[81] Section 4.5.

[82] Takis Tridimas and Giulia Gentile, 'The Essence of Rights: An Unreliable Boundary?' (2019) 20 Ger Law J 794; Koen Lenaerts, 'Limits on Limitations: The Essence of Fundamental Rights in the EU' (2019) 20 Ger Law J 779; Maja Brkan, 'The Concept of Essence of Fundamental Rights in the EU Legal Order: Peeling the Onion to its Core' (2018) 14 EuConst 332.

traditions of the Member States shall constitute general principles, suggesting an ongoing role for those principles, although in practice, where the two do overlap, the CJEU is more likely to rely on the Charter.[83]

While it is now evident—and largely unsurprising—that the CJEU uses the Charter as the starting point in its discussion of fundamental rights issues, Article 6(3) TEU itself preserves the pre-Lisbon approach to fundamental rights protection, giving both the ECHR and the common constitutional traditions a 'paramount role' in the interpretation of legal instruments and in ensuring a minimum level of protection.[84] The CJEU has also demonstrated its willingness to preserve the 'independent normative input' of the general principles, even though their concrete added value may, at times, be difficult to discern.[85] The continued autonomy of the general principles as a source of EU fundamental rights is necessary for a number of reasons.

First, the Charter, as a written source, although more precise, is also necessarily more circumscribed than the unwritten general principles and so cannot preclude the independent development of the latter. For example, the material, personal, and institutional scope of certain Charter provisions differs from the corresponding general principle developed in the case law of the CJEU.[86] On the other hand, certain Charter provisions are also deliberately left open-ended and use non-exhaustive phrases such as 'this right *includes*', thereby necessitating reliance on other rights sources, such as the general principles.[87] Secondly, it is the general principles and not the Charter that have been granted a gap-filling function, ie to remedy lacunae in EU law. As also mentioned, the Charter can itself act as a source of inspiration for general principles in the same way that common constitutional traditions and international rights sources always have.[88] Finally, the general principles have continued—albeit

[83] AG Opinion in Case C-398/13P *Inuit Tapiriit Kanatami v European Commission* ECLI:EU:C:2015:190, para 69; Case C-398/13P *Inuit Tapiriit Kanatami v European Commission* ECLI:EU:C:2015:535, para 47.

[84] Sara Iglesias Sánchez, 'The Court and the Charter: The Impact of the Entry into Force of the Lisbon Treaty on the ECJ's Approach to Fundamental Rights' (2012) 49 CMLRev 1565, 1599.

[85] eg Case C-604/12 *H.N. v Minister for Justice, Equality and Law Reform* ECLI:EU:C:2014:302, para 49; Lady Arden and Takis Tridimas, 'Limited But Not Inconsequential: The Application of the Charter by the Courts of England and Wales' in Michal Bobek and Jeremias Adams-Prassl (eds), *The EU Charter of Fundamental Rights in the Member States* (Hart 2020) 331, 347.

[86] Herwig CH Hofmann and Bucura C Mihaescu, 'The Relation between the Charter's Fundamental Rights and the Unwritten General Principles of EU Law: Good Administration as the Test Case' (2013) 9 EuConst 73, 74.

[87] ibid 79.

[88] Bruno de Witte, 'The Legal Status of the Charter: Vital Question or Non-Issue?' (2001) 8 MJ 81, 84; Lenaerts and Gutiérrez-Fons (n 53) 1726; Koen Lenaerts and José A Gutiérrez-Fons, 'The Constitutional Allocation of Powers and General Principles of EU Law' (2010) 47 CMLRev 1629, 1660.

curtailed—relevance in the UK post-Brexit, while the Charter no longer represents a formal source of law within the UK legal order.

These considerations suggest that a pluralistic rather than a hierarchical relationship exists between the Charter and the general principles even if, in practice, the Charter will serve as the primary reference point in the CJEU's discussion of fundamental rights.[89] The relationship between the Charter and the general principles, where they cover the *same* right, is addressed in Chapter 3, given the continued relevance of both sources as conduits for business freedoms as fundamental rights.[90] In particular, it is suggested that the confused relationship between the Charter and the general principles goes some way to explaining apparent divergences in the CJEU's treatment of the freedom to conduct a business as a fundamental right and the same concept found within the general principles of EU law.

It has been seen that in its initial discovery and development of EU fundamental rights as general principles, the CJEU borrowed heavily from existing sources such as the ECHR and national constitutional traditions.[91] This relationship is not static and continues to develop despite the concretization of the Union's fundamental rights acquis in the Charter.[92] Article 6(3) TEU recognizes the continued role of the ECHR—in the absence of EU accession to the Convention—not as an independent source of EU fundamental rights, but as a source of inspiration for the discovery of general principles. Where rights in the ECHR and the Charter correspond, Article 52(3) CFR provides that without prejudice to a more extensive protection being provided for in EU law, 'the meaning and scope of those rights shall be the same as those laid down by [the ECHR]'. In other words, the CJEU must ensure that the Charter is interpreted in such a way that it aligns with the interpretation given by the ECtHR to the corresponding provision of the ECHR. Where a provision of the Charter reflects a right also found in the ECHR, the Explanations specify this.

The ECHR thereby continues to act as a floor of fundamental rights, but above which EU law is permitted to provide enhanced protection. The CJEU will look to the relevant ECtHR jurisprudence to guide its application of the Charter in areas also covered by the ECHR.[93] The ECHR has been especially

[89] Hofmann and Mihaescu (n 86) 79; Emily Hancox, 'The Relationship Between the Charter and General Principles: Looking Back and Looking Forward' (2020) 22 CYELS 233.

[90] Section 3.4.

[91] Katja S Ziegler, 'Autonomy: From Myth to Reality—or Hubris on a Tightrope? EU Law, Human Rights and International Law' in Sionaidh Douglas-Scott and Nicholas Hatzis (eds), *Research Handbook on EU Law and Human Rights* (Edward Elgar 2017) 267, 268.

[92] Hofmann and Mihaescu (n 86).

[93] eg Case C–279/09 *DEB Deutsche Energiehandels- und Beratungsgesellschaft mbH v Bundesrepublik Deutschland* ECLI:EU:C:2010:811; Amalie Frese and Henrik Palmer Olsen, 'Spelling It

influential in particular substantive areas, for example the right to privacy.[94] The ECtHR will also have jurisdiction over a provision of EU law where the protection afforded by EU law is not equivalent to the protection found in the ECHR or where the CJEU lacks jurisdiction to review the measure.[95] There is a presumption of equivalence which can be rebutted where the protection of the relevant right has been manifestly deficient.[96]

In a similar way, Article 52(4) CFR governs the interpretative relationship between the Charter and the common constitutional traditions of the Member States and provides that '[i]n so far as [the Charter] recognises fundamental rights as they result from the constitutional traditions common to the Member States, those rights shall be interpreted in harmony with those traditions'. Article 52(6) CFR further provides that '[f]ull account shall be taken of national laws and practices as specified in this Charter'. In addition to the interpretative obligations set out in Article 52(3) CFR and Article 52(4) CFR, Article 53 CFR, which governs the level of protection granted by the Charter, provides that:

> [n]othing in this Charter shall be interpreted as restricting or adversely affecting human rights and fundamental freedoms as recognised [...] by Union law and international law and by international agreements to which the Union or all the Member States are party, including the [ECHR], and by the Member States' constitutions.

The question was whether this provision allowed Member States to apply the fundamental rights found in national constitutions instead of the Charter, where these provided a higher level of rights protection than the Charter, or whether such an approach would undermine the primacy of EU law.[97] In *Melloni*, the CJEU held that this was not permissible, as to do otherwise would be to undermine the primacy and uniform application of EU law in that it 'would allow a Member State to disapply EU legal rules which are fully in

Out—Convergence and Divergence in the Judicial Dialogue between the CJEU and ECtHR' (2019) 88 Nord J Intl L 429; Barrett Jizeng Fan, 'Convergence, Compatibility or Decoration: The Luxembourg Court's References to Strasbourg Case Law in its Final Judgments' (2016) Pécs Journal of International and European Law 38.

[94] Joined Cases C–465/00, 138, and 139/01 *Rechnungshof v Österreichischer Rundfunk and Christa Neukomm and Joseph Lauermann v Österreichischer Rundfunk* ECLI:EU:C:2003:294.

[95] *Matthews v UK* (1999) 28 EHRR 361.

[96] *Bosphorus Hava Yolları Turizm ve Ticaret Anonim Şirketi v Ireland* (2006) 42 EHRR 1.

[97] Jonas Bering Liisberg, 'Does the EU Charter of Fundamental Rights Threaten the Supremacy of Community Law?' (2001) 38 CMLRev 1171.

compliance with the Charter where they infringe the fundamental rights guaranteed by that State's constitution'.[98] The CJEU did, however, go on to say that:

> [i]t is true that Article 53 of the Charter confirms that, where an EU legal act calls for national implementing measures, national authorities and courts remain free to apply national standards of protection of fundamental rights, provided that the level of protection provided for by the Charter, as interpreted by the Court, and the primacy, unity and effectiveness of EU law are not thereby compromised.[99]

Where EU law is completely determinative of Member State action, the Charter applies. Where EU law only partially determines Member State action, national fundamental rights can instead be used as the standard of legality, unless the Charter provides a higher level of protection. Finally, in areas where Member State action is not entirely determined by EU law, for example where the Member State is exercising a derogation, the Member State courts can apply the higher standard found in national fundamental rights instruments as long as this does not undermine the primacy, unity, and effectiveness of EU law.[100] In any event, the level of protection cannot fall below that required by the ECHR, with Article 53 CFR thereby acting as a form of non-regression clause.

It is clear that the purpose of the horizontal provisions of the Charter is to constrain the Charter's potential reach into national legislative and regulatory autonomy, but also to ensure that the enactment of the Charter does not jeopardize the floor of rights that it was intended to codify. Perhaps the most significant horizontal provision for the present purpose of examining the differing impact of the business freedoms and fundamental economic and social rights found within the Charter is the distinction drawn in Article 52(5) CFR between rights and principles and which is illustrative of broader divergences amongst the provisions found within the Charter, despite their purported 'indivisibility'.

[98] Case C-399/11 *Stefano Melloni v Ministerio Fiscal* ECLI:EU:C:2013:107; Xavier Groussot, Laurent Pech, and Gunnar Thor Petursson, 'The Reach of EU Fundamental Rights on Member State Action' in Sybe de Vries, Ulf Bernitz, and Stephen Weatherill (eds), *The Protection of Fundamental Rights in the EU After Lisbon* (Hart 2013) 97; Nik de Boer, 'Addressing Rights Divergences Under the Charter: *Melloni*' (2013) 50 CMLRev 1083.

[99] *Melloni* (n 98) para 60.

[100] *Åkerberg Fransson* (n 58).

1.4 The Charter as a Source of Fundamental Rights Heterogeneity

1.4.1 The distinction between rights and principles

Despite the rhetoric of indivisibility surrounding the Charter's inclusion of economic and social rights alongside civil and political rights, a clear limitation on the invocability of the Charter's social rights can be seen in the distinction drawn between rights and principles.[101] Rather confusingly, the Treaties and the CJEU use the term 'principles' in a number of different contexts and to mean different things. In addition to the general principles of EU law, the CJEU has also used terms such as 'fundamental principles', 'essential principles', and importantly for the discussion in Part III on the role of social rights as potential counterweights to business freedoms as fundamental rights, 'particularly important principle of EU social law'.[102] Moreover, the CJEU has specified the existence of 'general principles of civil law', which has been found to include the binding nature of contractual obligations, but without clarifying whether this constitutes a *distinct* category of general principle.[103]

While in general it may be difficult to place an EU rule within the rights and principles dichotomy, the Charter makes it clear that such a division exists among its provisions. This distinction is important, as unlike the general principles, the 'principles' in the sense used by the Charter necessarily depend on further concretization in legislation.[104] This distinction is provided for in Article 52(5) CFR which stipulates that:

> [t]he provisions of this Charter which contain principles may be implemented by legislative and executive acts taken by the institutions, bodies, offices and agencies of the Union, and by acts of Member States when they are implementing Union law, in the exercise of their respective powers. They shall be judicially cognisable only in the interpretation of *such acts* and in the ruling on their legality. [emphasis added]

[101] Síofra O'Leary, 'The Charter and the Future Contours of EU Social and Employment Law' in Pascal Cardonnel, Allan Rosas, and Nils Wahl (eds), *Constitutionalising the EU Judicial System: Essays in Honour of Pernilla Lindh* (Hart 2012) 317.

[102] eg Case C–214/16 *Conley King v The Sash Window Workshop Ltd, Richard Dollar* ECLI:EU:C:2017:914.

[103] Case C–277/05 *Société thermale d'Eugénie-les-Bains v Ministère de l'Économie, des Finances et de l'Industrie* ECLI:EU:C:2007:440, para 24.

[104] Dorota Leczykiewicz, 'Prohibition of Abusive Practices as a "General Principle" of EU Law' (2019) 56 CMLRev 703, 733.

Article 51(1) CFR further emphasizes the distinction, providing that rights must be 'respected' whereas principles must merely be 'observed'. The role of the principles is confined to that of interpreting implementing acts and for the assessment of the validity of measures that disregard the Charter's principles.

It remains unclear whether the role of the principles as a ground of review is confined merely to those acts which give specific expression to the underlying principle, or whether principles can be used more broadly in the review of other acts not intended to give direct expression to the underlying principle.[105] The former approach risks undermining the effectiveness of the Charter as a rights instrument by allowing for some of its provisions, but not others, to be used in the review of EU and Member State measures, despite the fact that all Charter provisions enjoy the formal status of fundamental rights. Moreover, from a 'functionalist' perspective, it is the very use of a provision as a ground for assessing the validity of other norms that renders that provision 'fundamental'.[106] In practice, such a narrow approach can usually be avoided by assessing the question of whether an act 'implements' a Charter principle broadly, and with reference to the subject matter of the underlying rule.[107]

The distinction within the Charter between rights and principles stems ultimately from disagreement within the Convention which drafted the Charter, as to the enforceability of social rights. The solution was that these social rights should take the form of 'principles' which, 'whilst common to Member States, are implemented differently in their national laws and practices'.[108] The latter term, 'national laws and practices', is used frequently throughout the Charter as an indication that a particular provision represents a principle rather than a

[105] Jasper Krommendijk, 'Principled Silence or Mere Silence on Principles? The Role of the EU Charter's Principles in the Case Law of the Court of Justice' (2015) 11 EuConst 321, 347; Case C–356/12 *Wolfgang Glatzel v Freistaat Bayern* ECLI:EU:C:2014:350; AG Opinion in Case C–176/12 *Association de médiation sociale (AMS) v Union locale des syndicats CGT* ECLI:EU:C:2013:49; Case C–571/10 *Servet Kamberaj v Istituto per l'Edilizia Sociale della Provincia autonoma di Bolzano (IPES)* ECLI:EU:C:2012:233; Steve Peers and Sacha Prechal, 'Article 52' in Steve Peers and others (eds), *The EU Charter of Fundamental Rights: A Commentary* (2nd edn, Hart 2021) 1611, 1663.

[106] Orlando Scarcello, 'Preserving the "Essence" of Fundamental Rights under Article 52(1) of the Charter: A Sisyphean Task?' (2020) 16 EuConst 647, 655; John Gardner, '"Simply in Virtue of Being Human": The Whos and Whys of Human Rights' (2008) 2 Journal of Ethics and Social Philosophy 1.

[107] Tobias Lock, 'Rights and Principles in the EU Charter of Fundamental Rights' (2019) 56 CMLRev 1201, 1224.

[108] Lord Goldsmith QC, 'A Charter of Rights, Freedoms and Principles' (2001) 39 CMLRev 1201, 1212; Krommendijk (n 105) 326.

right, as has also been reinforced in later cases concerning the Charter's horizontal direct effect.[109]

The Charter's distinction between rights and principles broadly follows the traditional—if contested—dichotomy between civil and political rights on the one hand, and economic and social rights on the other, with the latter requiring legislative intervention.[110] In other words, in the absence of implementing legislation, the Charter's principles cannot be relied on to create positive obligations. Overall, the rights and principles distinction appears to map onto this contentious division between negatively oriented civil and political rights, and more positively oriented economic and social rights, the latter often being classed as non-justiciable.[111] The dichotomy between rights and principles is to an extent also reflective of the distinction in legal theory between 'rules' and 'principles', the latter being no more than starting points and lacking the precision and definitiveness of the former which may also affect their binding nature.[112]

Different levels of 'generality' are at play in the distinction between rights and principles in the same way as between rules and principles. The more general the principle, the more readily it may be distinguished from legal rules. However. this distinction is not necessarily determinative in the EU context, given that at least some (general) principles are binding and can be used in both the interpretation and review of legislation, although the absence of implementation may affect their 'justiciability'.[113] As such, principles that are of a lesser degree of generality might be commensurate with legal rules that are formulated in a very general way.[114] In the same vein, the traditional distinction within legal theory between the 'will' and 'interest' theories of fundamental

[109] eg Joined Cases C–569/16 and 570/16 *Stadt Wuppertal v Maria Elisabeth Bauer and Volker Willmeroth v Martina Broßonn* ECLI:EU:C:2018:871, para 84.

[110] Lock (n 107); Krommendijk (n 105); Dóra Guðmundsdóttir, 'A Renewed Emphasis on the Charter's Distinction between Rights and Principles: Is a Doctrine of Judicial Restraint More Appropriate?' (2015) 52 CMLRev 685; Jeff Kenner, 'Economic and Social Rights in the EU Legal Order: The Mirage of Indivisibility' in Tamara Hervey and Jeff Kenner (eds), *Economic and Social Rights under the EU Charter of Fundamental Rights* (Hart 2003) 3.

[111] Sybe de Vries, 'The Charter of Fundamental Rights and the EU's "Creeping" Competences: Does the Charter Have a Centrifugal Effect for Fundamental Rights in the EU?' in Sionaidh Douglas-Scott and Nicholas Hatzis (eds), *Research Handbook on EU Law and Human Rights* (Edward Elgar 2017) 58, 76.

[112] Ronald Dworkin, *Taking Rights Seriously* (Duckworth 1977) 22–25.

[113] Päivi J Neuvonen and Katja S Ziegler, 'General Principles in the EU Legal Order: Past, Present and Future Directions' in Katia S Ziegler, Päivi J Neuvonen, and Violeta Moreno-Lax (eds), *Research Handbook on General Principles of EU Law* (Edward Elgar 2022) 7, 11.

[114] Joxerramon Bengoetxea, *The Legal Reasoning of the European Court of Justice: Towards a European Jurisprudence* (OUP 1993) 72.

'rights' is not of much assistance in distinguishing between Charter rights and principles.

The will theory provides that a right is enjoyed where the rights-holder has the power to alter the duty of another person. According to the interest theory, a right exists where it aims at furthering the interests of the individual.[115] The latter approach goes beyond a 'symmetrical' Hohfeldian understanding of rights by positing that rights are grounded in interests, but that duties are grounded in rights.[116] The difficulty lies in the fact that many of the Charter's provisions, which are expressly stated in the Explanations to be 'principles', nevertheless appear to promote specific interests.[117] The freedom to conduct a business as a fundamental right also poses particular challenges in this regard, in that various models for restricting freedom of contract are predicated on the assumption either that parties are unable to identify their own preferences (social model), or that their preferences are mistaken (perfectionist model), thereby negating the interest in 'personal choice'.[118]

A Hohfeldian understanding of rights may also be applied to the distinction between the Charter's rights and principles, in that rights can be characterized as 'relational', that is entailing a correlative *duty* and, 'intersubjective' in that they define the relationship between the right bearer and the addressee. In other words, rights are subjective entitlements which may evolve over time depending on the underlying societal conditions, and which are further dependent on clusters of 'fundamental legal relations' composed of correlatives and opposites, and which guide the practical application of rights.[119] The Charter's principles can be classed as 'objective law', meaning that although they may impose *duties* on the Union or the Member States to comply with their provisions, this duty does not entail a corresponding subjective claim-right that might be invoked by an individual.

In other words, principles are one-sided and non-relational duties, which, as mentioned, impedes their justiciability (in the absence of legislative implementation), but not their 'binding' nature (on the Member States).[120] Finally, there is a potential connection between the Charter's use of the term 'principle' and the wider concept of (directive) principles found within international

115 Jeremy Waldron, *The Right to Private Property* (OUP 1990) 79–94.
116 Andrei Marmor, 'On the Limits of Rights' (1997) 16 Law & Phil 1, 4.
117 Lock (n 107) 1206.
118 Section 4.4; Marmor (n 116) 5.
119 Lock (n 107) 1207; Scarcello (n 106); Wesley N Hohfeld, 'Some Fundamental Legal Conceptions as Applied in Judicial Reasoning (1913) 16 Yale LJ 16; Wesley N Hohfeld, 'Fundamental Legal Conceptions as Applied in Judicial Reasoning' (1917) 26 Yale LJ 710.
120 Lock (n 107) 1215.

social rights law. The latter concept connotes the idea of a norm (right) that is to be realized as far as possible given the legal and factual context (duty), but without rendering the underlying goal merely 'aspirational'.[121]

It will, however, be argued in Part III that there is actually a need for a more principled differentiation between the Charter's various provisions due to their competing normative weight, but which constitutes a *new* divisibility, and one that is constructed around the Charter's underpinning values rather than on a formalist distinction between rights and principles, or between civil and political, and economic and social, rights. Indeed, it is not uncontested that the Charter's social rights—or, as argued here, the freedom to conduct a business—should be classified as fundamental 'rights' in the more orthodox sense, ie beyond the rights and principles distinction found within the Charter itself.[122] In other words, there is a need to address the question as to whether the Charter's provisions can be classed as 'fundamental rights' simply by virtue of their inclusion therein.

The EU Agency for Fundamental Rights has described Article 16 CFR in the following terms: '[t]he freedom to conduct a business *is* a fundamental right, and *as such* is first and foremost justiciable for that very reason-for being a right' [emphasis added].[123] Even accepting the Charter's division between rights and principles on its own terms, it is not at all obvious whether the freedom to conduct a business falls on the 'rights' side of the rights and principles dichotomy, let alone whether business freedom concepts attract the status of a fundamental (human) right, whether as a stand-alone right or through its derivation from more traditional rights concepts such as the right to work and property rights. Additional difficulty is caused in relation to the rights and principles distinction by the fact that some provisions, which may well be rights, use the descriptor 'principle'—for example Article 23 CFR on the principle of equality—while other provisions which contain rights may previously have been classed as 'general principles' in the CJEU's case law concerning fundamental rights as general principles.[124]

The first opportunity for the CJEU to address the distinction between rights and principles came in the case of *AMS*.[125] Advocate General Cruz Villalón

[121] Robert Alexy, *A Theory of Constitutional Rights* (OUP 2004) 45–57.
[122] John Tasioulas, 'On the Nature of Human Rights' in Gerhard Ernst and Jan-Christoph Heilinger (eds), *The Philosophy of Human Rights* (De Gruyter 2012) 17.
[123] European Agency for Fundamental Rights, 'Freedom to Conduct a Business: Exploring the Dimensions of a Fundamental Right' (2015) 2.
[124] Peers and Prechal (n 105) 1659.
[125] Case C-176/12 *Association de médiation sociale (AMS) v Union locale des syndicats CGT* ECLI:EU:C:2014:2.

noted that in order to be effective, principles require further concretization through implementing legislation.[126] The Advocate General concluded that Article 27 CFR governing worker information and consultation was a principle rather than a right. The first reason for this conclusion was the limited scope of that provision, which was granted 'under the conditions provided for by Union law and national laws and practices', without specifying how the objective was to be achieved.[127] This 'textual' argument was coupled with a more 'systemic' argument to deny the status of a right to Article 27 CFR.

The Advocate General noted that the rights found within the Charter's Solidarity Title are largely social rights and that provisions are usually designated as 'social' in order to indicate that no subjective or directly enforceable right is to be derived from them and which indicates a 'strong presumption' that those provisions are principles.[128] Social rights could therefore be described as 'rights' by their nature and content, but 'principles' in terms of their operation.[129] The Advocate General then linked the distinction between rights and principles to the question of horizontal direct effect and held that 'it is evident [. . .] that its wording very implicitly but unequivocally excludes the possibility of directly relying on a "principle" so as to exercise an individual right based on that principle'.[130]

The CJEU in its judgment held that some Charter provisions may have horizontal direct effect if they meet the necessary tests of being sufficiently clear, precise, and unconditional, ie they are concrete enough to be relied on by themselves. The CJEU did not, however, link the question of horizontal effect to that of the distinction between rights and principles, noting that '[i]t is therefore clear from the wording of Article 27 of the Charter that, for this article to be fully effective, it must be given more specific expression in European Union or national law'.[131] Article 27 CFR can thus be contrasted with other Charter provisions such as Article 21(1) CFR which is 'sufficient in itself to confer on individuals an individual right which they may invoke as such'.[132]

The crucial distinction, therefore, seems to be between those provisions that are capable of direct effect and those that are not, rather than necessarily a distinction between rights and principles as such.[133] In other words, Article 27

[126] AG Opinion in *AMS* (n 105) para 45.
[127] ibid para 54.
[128] ibid para 55.
[129] ibid para 45.
[130] ibid para 68.
[131] *AMS* (n 125) para 45.
[132] ibid para 47.
[133] cf Lock (n 107) 1226; Krommendijk (n 105) 322.

CFR constitutes either a principle, or a non-directly effective right, with this classification having attendant and potentially significant consequences for the relative weight of Charter provisions, particularly in their relationship to legislative protections.[134] As Advocate General Bot in *Bauer* put it, 'it is possible to take the view that, in *Association de médiation sociale*, the Court respected, without a clear statement to that effect, the *summa divisio* between the principles proclaimed by the Charter, the enforceability of which is limited and indirect, and the rights recognised by the Charter, which, for their part, are fully and directly enforceable'.[135]

The CJEU more explicitly addressed the distinction between rights and principles in case of *Glatzel*.[136] In that case, the question was whether conditions set out under EU legislation governing physical ability to drive amounted to discrimination contrary to Article 21 CFR on non-discrimination and Article 26 CFR on the integration of persons with disabilities.[137] The CJEU addressed each of these provisions separately for the reason that Article 26 CFR—in contrast to Article 21 CFR—was a principle rather than a right. The reason for this conclusion was that Article 26 CFR 'does not require the EU legislature to adopt any specific measure' and that 'in order for that article to be fully effective, it must be given more specific expression in EU or national law'.[138]

The CJEU appears to have adopted two different approaches to dealing with the rights and principles distinction in *AMS* and *Glatzel*. In *AMS*, the CJEU very much focused on the text of Article 27 CFR to find that it was not sufficiently clear to be relied on by an individual. In *Glatzel*, on the other hand, the CJEU concentrated on Article 26's *status* as a principle, which is largely facilitated by the Explanations to the Charter which specify that Article 26 CFR is indeed a principle.[139] In *Dominguez*, the CJEU did not specify whether the right to paid annual leave might constitute a general principle, nor did the Court engage with Article 31(2) CFR which provides for the same right. The CJEU's then reticence to engage in the classification of the right to paid annual leave can be contrasted with the Opinion of Advocate General Trstenjak, who stipulated that the 'right' to paid annual leave in Article 31(2) CFR represents

[134] Krommendijk (n 105) 346.

[135] AG Opinion in Joined Cases C-569/16 and 570/16 *Stadt Wuppertal v Maria Elisabeth Bauer and Volker Willmeroth v Martina Broßonn* ECLI:EU:C:2018:337, para 70.

[136] *Glatzel* (n 105).

[137] Directive 2006/126/EC of the European Parliament and of the Council of 29 December 2006 on driving licences [2006] OJ L403/18.

[138] *Glatzel* (n 105) para 78.

[139] Petra Herzfeld Olsson, 'Possible Shielding Effects of Article 27 on Workers' Rights to Information and Consultation in the EU Charter of Fundamental Rights' (2016) 32 Int J Comp LLIR 251, 260.

a 'social fundamental right' and not a principle. According to the Advocate General:

> the very wording of this provision immediately suggests the conclusion that entitlement to paid annual leave was designed to be a 'fundamental right', whereupon inclusion in the 'principles' referred to in Article 51(1) of the Charter, which do not create any direct subjective rights and indeed need to be given expression by the entities to which it addressed, can instantly be ruled out.[140]

A right without direct effect would, nonetheless, be capable of being relied upon in the review of any EU act as well as any situation falling within the scope of EU law.[141]

The consequences of the classification of a provision as a principle for its role in the interpretation and review of legislation remains unclear, particularly given continued doubts surrounding the concept of 'implementing' found within Article 52(5) CFR.[142] It is, however, to be welcomed that the CJEU has provided some guidance for the determination of whether a Charter provision is a right or a principle. The first step is usually to examine the wording (literal approach) of the relevant Charter provision itself, which may use the term 'right', or may grant rights to individuals, although the language used will not always be determinative, in that some provisions which purport to be principles also use the label 'right'—Article 25 CFR on the rights of the elderly, for example—while some rights are themselves inherently vague and require further elaboration.[143] As such, the degree of generality of a particular provision may well be an approximating, but not a definitive criterion for distinguishing between rights and principles, at least in a formal, as opposed to a normative, sense.[144]

The use of the proviso, 'rules laid down by Union law and national laws and practices' may suggest that the relevant provision is a principle, but, as will be seen in Chapter 3, the same proviso is found within Article 16 CFR on the freedom to conduct a business, and yet that provision appears to be treated as a right in the case law of the CJEU even though it is, in fact, described as a

[140] AG Opinion in Case C-282/10 *Maribel Dominguez v Centre informatique du Centre Ouest Atlantique and Préfet de la région Centre* ECLI:EU:C:2011:559, para 76; cf *Bauer* (n 109).

[141] Nicole Lazzerini, '(Some of) the Fundamental Rights Granted by the Charter may be a Source of Obligations for Private Parties: *AMS*' (2014) 51 CMLRev 907, 932.

[142] Krommendijk (n 105) 355.

[143] Peers and Prechal (n 105) 1660.

[144] Bengoetxea (n 114) 73.

'freedom', thereby distorting the conventional understanding of the rights and principles dichotomy. Finally, the inclusion of a provision within the Solidarity Title of the Charter may be an—albeit weak—indicator of its status as a principle rather than a right (contextual approach). Indeed, an earlier version of the Charter made specific reference to 'social principles' in addition to 'social rights', thereby confining the concept of a 'principle' to the social sphere.[145] This is reflective of broader concerns surrounding the potential justiciability and enforceability of the Charter's Solidarity Title and which ultimately led to the rights and principles distinction being introduced within the Charter.[146]

As mentioned, this distinction is also reflective of the traditional dichotomy between justiciable civil and political rights on the one hand, and programmatic (non-justiciable) economic and social rights on the other.[147] Moreover, this distinction has also been employed to deny the 'rights' status of social rights generally, and labour rights more specifically.[148] First, it has been suggested that social rights are not 'rights', by virtue of their resource implications, and with the attendant consequence that the allocation or redistribution of resources is best left to democratically elected institutions rather than the judiciary.[149] Of course, this view overlooks the fact that many civil and political rights, for example the right to vote, have resource implications, and is also based on a rather narrow conception of democracy, which 'properly understood, requires satisfaction of certain basic needs'.[150]

While never particularly convincing, this distinction between negative (civil and political) and positive (economic and social) rights is also essentially undermined with regard to the Charter by the very fact that at least some of the Charter's 'social' provisions are indeed considered (justiciable) 'rights', in accordance with the rights and principles distinction, and which is particularly true for some of the employment rights provisions of relevance to the present discussion, ie those provisions with a particularly close connection to the employment *contract*, notably Article 31 CFR on fair and just working conditions, and likely Article 28 CFR on the right to bargain collectively and to engage in

[145] Art 31 Charte 4383 Convent 41.

[146] Lock (n 107) 1208.

[147] Judy Fudge, 'The New Discourse of Labour Rights: From Social to Fundamental Rights?' (2007) Comparative Labor Law and Policy Journal 29.

[148] Cass Sunstein, 'Against Positive Rights: Why Social and Economic Rights Don't Belong in the New Constitutions of Post-Communist Europe' (1993) 2 EECR 35; Sandra Fredman, 'Scepticism Under Scrutiny: Labour Law and Human Rights' in Tom Campbell, KD Ewing, and Adam Tompkins (eds), *Sceptical Essays on Human Rights* (OUP 2001) 197; Jay Youngdahl, 'Solidarity First Labour Rights Are not the Same as Human Rights' (2009) 18 New Labour Forum 30; Jay Youngdahl, 'Youngdahl Replies' (2009) 18 New Labour Forum 46.

[149] Conor Gearty and Virginia Mantouvalou, *Debating Social Rights* (Hart 2011) 161.

[150] ibid 123.

collective action.[151] Moreover, and as argued throughout this book, civil and political 'freedoms', notably the freedom to conduct a business, also have social dimensions which can act as 'internal' or inherent constraints on (economic) 'liberty' conceptions of those freedoms.

From a 'positivist' perspective, the Charter's Solidarity provisions can also be considered rights on the basis of their inclusion in international rights instruments. The Explanations to the Charter point to pre-existing international (social) rights sources from which the Charter's provisions are drawn, notably the European Social Charter and the Community Charter of the Fundamental Social Rights of Workers. Article 28 CFR, which provides for the right of collective bargaining and action, is somewhat unusual in that the right to bargain collectively is derived in part from the freedom of association found within Article 11 ECHR. Article 28 CFR, despite its inclusion as a 'social' right in the Solidarity Title, can therefore also be conceived in similar terms to a civil and political right, and with different Hohfeldian conceptions of that right existing alongside each other, namely: (1) a 'privilege' that can be exercised without generating a claim on the part of the addressees (the Union and the Member States); (2) a 'duty' on the addressees not to interfere with collective bargaining and action, with the correlative 'claim right' being enjoyed by those acting collectively; and (3) an 'immunity', in the sense that the legislative restrictions on the right to bargain collectively to take collective action must comply with the requirements of Article 52(1) CFR.[152] In a similar vein, the CJEU in *Bauer*, concerning the right to paid annual leave, noted that this right 'entails, by its very nature, a corresponding obligation on the employer'.[153] In other words, there is no compelling reason to exclude 'social' rights from the category of (Hohfeldian) rights, while at the time same time, not *all* social rights will be capable of such classification, with genuinely programmatic social rights continuing to constitute goals to strive towards.[154]

The same is largely true of the freedom to conduct a business which, as argued here, similarly enjoys a 'mixed' status as both a civil liberty and a social right, and which also exhibits elements of: (1) a privilege, in the sense of a freedom or liberty to conduct or not conduct a business; (2) a (potential) claim right on the part of those conducting a business; (3) a corresponding duty on

[151] *Bauer* (n 109); Niilo Jääskinen, 'Fundamental Social Rights in the Charter—Are They Rights? Are They Fundamental?' in Steve Peers and others (eds), *The EU Charter of Fundamental Rights: A Commentary* (2nd edn, Hart 2021) 1855.

[152] Lock (n 107) 1213.

[153] *Bauer* (n 109) para 90.

[154] Wojciech Załuski, 'On Social Rights from an Analytical Perspective' (2016) 2 Archiwum Filozofii Prawa i Filozofii Społecznej 76.

the Union and Member States not to interfere with the conduct of a business; and (4) an immunity, in that all Charter provisions are subject to the same permissible restrictions found in Article 51(2) CFR. The point here is that the distinction between the freedom to conduct a business and the Charter's Solidarity rights is perhaps less stark than it first appears, and regardless of whether those provisions are classed as 'rights' or 'principles' in the sense provided for in the Charter. This is not to suggest that there can be no differentiation between the Charter's provisions, for example in recognition of the fact that the freedom to conduct a business in Article 16 CFR is merely 'recognised' without specifying the rights-holder, and which may well be suggestive of a duty without generating a corresponding right. In other words, the freedom to conduct a business appears to be a 'principle' as reinforced by the reference to 'Union law, national laws and practices', but is essentially treated as a 'right' by the CJEU in the same way as Article 28 CFR.

From a 'normative' perspective, it has also been suggested that employment rights lack the features typically associated with 'human rights', namely: (1) that human rights represent urgent and compelling moral claims; (2) that human rights are *universally* applicable; (3) that human rights represent strict standards; and (4) that human rights embody timeless, fundamental needs.[155] There is nothing particularly controversial in suggesting that certain employment rights, such as the right to paid annual leave, are not as 'compelling' or 'imperative' as, say, the right to life. That some rights may be more 'important' than others does not necessarily detract from the characterization of less important rights as human rights. However, such a view would also be to overlook the fact that many employment rights are underpinned by civil and political rights, notably the right to human dignity.

As mentioned, although Article 1 CFR makes clear that 'the dignity of the human person' constitutes the 'real basis' of all fundamental (Charter) rights, 'dignity' does not constitute the most *immediate*, nor indeed the most *compelling*, normative underpinning for the provisions of the Charter's Freedoms and Solidarity Titles. To focus solely on dignity as a normative underpinning would also be to impede considerations of the relative normative weight of the freedom to conduct a business and competing social rights, save to the extent that the 'connection' to dignitarian notions might vary as between the Charter's provisions. Rather, the focus of this book remains on the potentially competing 'values' that it is suggested lie at the foundation of the conceptual, legal, and normative tensions that exist between business freedoms and fundamental

[155] Virginia Mantouvalou, 'Are Labour Rights Human Rights?' (2012) 3 ELLJ 151, 164.

social rights, including the extent to which there is cross-fertilization between the Charter's 'freedom' and 'solidarity' values, and which leads to potentially competing conceptions of the freedom to conduct a business as a fundamental right.

The second argument against the human rights status of employment rights, namely that they lack universality, is equally uncompelling. It is certainly the case that many employment rights at both EU and national level depend on the existence of an employment relationship, and with potentially diverging entitlement to employment rights being dependent on the precise characterization of that relationship, ie rights may be confined to dependent or subordinate labour as opposed to the self-employed. Of course, this is to overlook that most of us are compelled to work at some point in our lives, as well as to underestimate the value of work to the human experience. In addition, many civil rights are also dependent on gaining some form of status such as citizenship. Moreover, 'social' rights themselves can be constructed around the normative foundation of 'autonomy' in the sense of the positive freedom to make choices, reinforcing the argument that business freedom and contractual autonomy concepts can themselves be (re)conceived in social terms.[156]

As to the argument that employment rights do not embody strict standards, ie they vary from country to country depending on available resources, Mantouvalou points out that many 'universal' rights also have resource implications and that there is a continued obligation to 'strive' to meet these rights requirements.[157] Finally, the idea that employment rights evolve over time whereas human rights are timeless is also easily refuted. Many labour rights can be said to represent 'abstract principles', which themselves represent timeless normative standards.[158] As also argued here, legislation plays a crucial role both within and beyond the EU context in concretizing these abstract principles into practicable rights. Finally, it should be noted that the contract of employment is one of the few categories of contract to require that at least one of the parties be 'human'.[159]

In any event, the preferred term adopted here to refer to the provisions of the Charter is 'fundamental' rather than 'human' rights in recognition of: (1) the equivalent weight, ie regardless of 'justiciability', granted to all Charter provisions, whether civil, political, economic, or social in the interpretation and review of Union law as well as Member State measures falling within the scope

156 Załuski (n 154) 82.
157 Mantouvalou (n 155) 166.
158 ibid 169.
159 Gabrielle Golding, *Shaping Contracts for Work* (OUP 2023) 121.

of EU law, albeit that the use of principles in this regard may be confined to measures *implementing* that principle; and (2) the fact that the freedom to conduct a business—as with the internal market freedoms—is applicable to legal as well as natural persons.

Given these conceptual difficulties surrounding the definition of a 'right', it is perhaps unsurprising that the CJEU, in cases such as *AMS*, has tended to sidestep the distinction between rights and principles, preferring to tread the more familiar—if no less complex—ground of direct effect. In other words, the relevant distinction remains between those Charter provisions that might or might not be capable of invocation in horizontal situations, with principles usually lacking direct effect due to their imprecision and conditionality. This is not to say that some 'rights' might not need further elaboration in legislation, or that they may be too imprecise—or lacking in individual rights conferral—to be granted direct effect.[160]

1.4.2 The horizontal application of the Charter

It has been seen that Article 51(1) CFR governing the Charter's personal scope provides that 'the provisions of the Charter are addressed to the institutions, bodies, offices and agencies of the Union [. . .] and to the Member States only when they are implementing EU law'. As the Charter is not explicitly addressed to private parties, the question had arisen as to whether its provisions could nevertheless be applied horizontally.[161] Other provisions of primary EU law—the status now also enjoyed by the Charter—although not addressed to private parties, have indeed been found to have horizontal direct effect, for example the Treaty provisions governing equal pay.[162] Moreover, the freedom to conduct a business and related internal market freedoms benefit companies as well

[160] Peers and Prechal (n 105) 1663; Guðmundsdóttir (n 110) 698.

[161] Lazzerini (n 141); Eleni Frantziou, 'The Horizontal Effect of the Charter: Towards an Understanding of Horizontality as a Structural Constitutional Principle' (2020) 22 CYELS 208; Eleni Frantziou, *The Horizontal Effect of Fundamental Rights in the European Union: A Constitutional Analysis* (OUP 2019); Aurelia Colombi Ciacchi, 'The Direct Horizontal Effect of EU Fundamental Rights' (2019) 15 EuConst 294; Eleni Frantziou, '(Most of) the Charter of Fundamental Rights is Horizontally Applicable' (2019) 15 EuConst 306; Eleni Frantziou, 'The Horizontal Effect of the Charter of Fundamental Rights of the EU: Rediscovering the Reasons for Horizontality' (2015) 21 ELJ 657; Dorota Leczykiewicz, 'Horizontal Application of the Charter of Fundamental Rights' (2013) 38 ELRev 479.

[162] Case C-43/75 *Gabrielle Defrenne v Société anonyme belge de navigation aérienne Sabena* ECLI:EU:C:1976:56.

as natural persons, hence the necessary use of the term 'fundamental' as opposed to 'human' rights, albeit that the two categories may well overlap.[163]

The CJEU has since confirmed—continuing the approach that it had adopted in relation to the general principles in *Mangold*—that the Charter can be invoked horizontally where the matter has been brought within the scope of EU law due to the presence of a directive which will not itself be horizontally directly effective. This has especially been the case when the directive and the relevant Charter provision govern the same right, as is common in the employment context, for example.[164] There is an added layer of complexity to this line of case law given the distinction between rights and principles and, as such, that distinction and the question of the Charter's horizontal direct effect are closely entwined.

The potential horizontal application of the Charter was addressed in *AMS*, a case concerning one of the social rights found in the Charter's Solidarity Title, namely Article 27 CFR, which provides for a right to worker information and consultation and which was also relevant to the discussion on the rights and principles distinction.[165] AMS was a trade union that sought to rely on Article 27 CFR to challenge a private employer's refusal to establish worker consultation pursuant to Directive 2002/14.[166] Under the relevant national legislation implementing the Directive, the employer was entitled to exclude certain categories of worker when calculating staff numbers for the purpose of collective redundancies. The CJEU found this aspect of the national legislation to be incompatible with the Directive, but since directives cannot be relied on horizontally, it was necessary for the trade union to turn to Article 27 CFR.

First, Advocate General Cruz Villalón rejected the notion that because the Charter is only addressed to the Union and its Member States that it cannot also apply to private parties.[167] According to the Advocate General, the purpose of Article 51(1) CFR was simply to clarify the extent to which EU fundamental rights are binding on the Union's institutions and the Member States and was not intended to address the question of horizontal direct effect. The wording of Article 27 CFR was also influential in that it refers to 'the undertaking', which suggests that '"the undertaking" is in some way involved in the effectiveness of

[163] Gardner (n 106) 4; art 54 TFEU defines 'companies' or 'firms'.

[164] Case C-55/18 *Federación de Servicios de Comisiones Obreras (CCOO) v Deutsche Bank SAE* ECLI:EU:C:2019:402; *Bauer* (n 109); Case C-684/16 *Max-Planck-Gesellschaft zur Förderung der Wissenschaften eV v Tetsuji Shimizu* ECLI:EU:C:2018:874.

[165] *AMS* (n 125).

[166] Directive 2002/14/EC of the European Parliament and of the Council of 11 March 2002 establishing a general framework for informing and consulting employees [2002] OJ L80/29.

[167] AG Opinion in *AMS* (n 105) para 30.

that right'.[168] The CJEU, in its judgment, accepted that the national legislation could be considered an implementing measure of the Directive thus bringing the case within the scope of EU law and engaging the Charter. However, the provision of the Directive prohibiting the exclusion of certain types of contracts from the calculation of the number of employees could not be said to derive from the wording of Article 27 CFR. This case could therefore be contrasted with *Kücükdeveci* in that the latter involved the application of the general principle on the grounds of age that had been given expression in Article 21(1) CFR and could thus be relied on against another individual.[169]

The CJEU in *AMS* implicitly accepted the possibility that a Charter provision might have horizontal direct effect but held that Article 27 CFR was not sufficiently specific to create an obligation on a private employer. Having said this, recent developments have seen the emergence of legislative specification of the horizontal effect of particular provisions on private parties, potentially going beyond the scope of application of the Charter itself, thereby leading to a possible finding of incompatibility with the Charter.[170] It is also argued here that the role of legislation in providing normative content to—as opposed merely to triggering the (horizontal) application of—Charter provisions, has largely been overlooked, with the CJEU's emphasis continuing to be placed on 'justiciability' as the touchstone for Charter 'rights', with 'principles' denied that status due to their dependence on legislative implementation.

The very fact that a particular Charter provision either derives from, or is implemented by, Union legislation signals the democratic significance, indeed legitimacy, of that provision. Moreover, the rights and principles distinction, and the related horizontality (or lack thereof) of Charter provisions overlooks the fact that certain liberty rights such as the freedom to conduct a business, including in the guise of the more specific freedom of contract, lack specificity precisely due to the absence of legislative implementation. Given that the Charter's application is conditional upon the existence of Union or national law falling within its scope, the very application of the Charter is *enabled* by the legislature.[171]

The CJEU has subsequently made it clear that Charter provisions that are sufficiently clear can indeed have horizontal direct effect.[172] In *Egenberger*, the

[168] ibid para 40.
[169] *AMS* (n 125) para 47.
[170] Mast and Ollig (n 27) 3.
[171] ibid 5.
[172] Case C-414/16 *Vera Egenberger v Evangelisches Werk für Diakonie und Entwicklung eV* EU:C:2018:257, para 75; Case C-68/17 *IR v JQ* ECLI:EU:C:2018:696.

CJEU held that '[t]he prohibition of all discrimination on grounds of religion or belief is mandatory as a general principle of EU law. That prohibition, which is laid down in Article 21(1) of the Charter, is sufficient in itself to confer on individuals a right which they may rely on as such in disputes between them in a field covered by EU law.'[173] The Court then drew an analogy between Article 21 CFR and Article 47 CFR—both of which apply horizontally—and those Treaty provisions prohibiting discrimination, which have also been found to be horizontally effective even in the presence of private contractual arrangements, for example the principle of equal pay in Article 157 TFEU, which was found in *Defrenne* to have horizontal direct effect.[174]

Finally, the CJEU noted that it may be called on to balance competing fundamental rights deriving from either the Charter or the Treaty, but that such a need to balance rights using the proportionality principle cannot call into question the very possibility of a private party relying on those rights horizontally.[175] These factors enabled the CJEU to hold that Article 4 of the Framework Equality Directive, providing for religion as an occupational requirement, did not preclude the review of a decision by a religious organization on whom to employ. In addition, the balancing exercise between religious belief and the principle of non-discrimination itself had to be subject to independent review.[176] This case demonstrates that horizontal direct effect may be accorded to Charter rights even when the relevant provision is less detailed than the underlying directive. Nevertheless, it is the Charter and not the directive that is being applied horizontally, even though the directive shapes the contours of the relevant right.

This approach aligns with the CJEU's case law on the general principles and the continued absence of horizontal direct effect of directives, albeit that the Court has now formalized the disjunction between legislative and constitutional versions of the (same) right, despite continuing to rely on both.[177] As suggested here, it should also not be overlooked that it is legislation, notably in the employment context, that both inspired and gave content to a number of Charter provisions themselves. For example, in the context of the Solidarity Title, Article 31 CFR stipulates that its provisions are 'based on' Union

[173] *Egenberger* (n 172) para 76; cf AG Opinion in *Egenberger v Evangelisches Werk für Diakonie und Entwicklung eV* ECLI:EU:C:2017:851, paras 117–23.

[174] *Egenberger* (n 172) para 77; *Defrenne* (n 162).

[175] *Egenberger* (n 172) para 80.

[176] ibid paras 52–53; Council Directive 2000/78/EC of 27 November 2000 establishing a general framework for equal treatment in employment and occupation [2000] OJ L303/16.

[177] Muir (n 27) 193.

legislation aimed at encouraging improvements in the safety and health of workers (Article 31(1) CFR), as well as legislation governing the organization of working time (Article 31(2) CFR), and related wording is used across multiple other provisions found within the same Title.[178]

In *Bauer*, Article 31(2) CFR was itself found capable of being relied on in a dispute between two private parties, which stands in contrast to the CJEU's finding that Article 27 CFR on worker information and consultation lacked such horizontal effect.[179] This was despite the fact that the underlying Working Time Directive could not itself be relied on horizontally. Again, there is a normative circularity in this approach, in that the very reason for Article 31(2) CFR's horizontality is that it specifies a right that has already been sufficiently concretized in Union legislation, namely Article 7 WTD. This legislation is then interpreted in light of Article 31(2) CFR, which itself is interpreted through the lens of the Working Time Directive as interpreted by the CJEU.[180] This is also reminiscent of the complex interplay of legislative and constitutional sources evident in earlier cases such as *Mangold* and *Kücükdeveci* concerning the horizontal application of the general principles in the context of non-discrimination on the grounds of age. There remains, however, a great deal of uncertainty as to the extent to which the Charter can act as an independent source of (workers') rights, and thereby (employers') duties.[181]

In *Bauer*, the issue that arose was whether the former employers of the claimants' deceased husbands were obliged to pay an allowance in lieu of paid annual leave for those leave periods not taken by their husbands before their deaths. The right to paid annual leave can be found in Article 31(2) CFR. One of the claims involved two private parties and so the Working Time Directive was not applicable, as directives do not have horizontal direct effect. The relevant national law implementing the Directive could not be interpreted to grant the requested right. The CJEU found instead that the Directive could be interpreted to confer these benefits and that the relevant provision, namely Article 7 WTD, was capable only of vertical direct effect. Nevertheless, the claimant could rely directly on the same right found in Article 31(2) CFR. The CJEU noted that:

[178] ibid 214.

[179] *Bauer* (n 109); *Max-Planck-Gesellschaft* (n 164).

[180] Niall O'Connor, 'Interpreting Employment Legislation through a Fundamental Rights Lens: What's the Purpose?' (2017) 8 ELLJ 193, 203.

[181] Dorota Leczykiewicz, 'The Judgment in *Bauer* and the Effect of the EU Charter of Fundamental Rights in Horizontal Situations' (2020) 16 ERCL 323, 332.

> [t]he right to a period of paid annual leave, affirmed for every worker by Article 31(2) of the Charter, is thus, as regards its very existence, both mandatory and unconditional in nature, the unconditional nature not needing to be given concrete expression by the provisions of EU or national law.[182]

The CJEU also settled the argument that private parties are not addressed by the Charter and so its provisions may not be relied on in horizontal disputes. According to the CJEU, the Charter has nothing to say on the issue of whether individuals 'may, where appropriate, be directly required to comply with certain provisions of the Charter and [Article 51(2) CFR] cannot, accordingly, be interpreted as meaning that it would systematically preclude such a possibility'.[183]

Finally, the CJEU raised the same point that had been addressed in relation to Article 27 CFR concerning that provision's use of the term 'undertaking', that the right to paid annual leave necessarily entails a corresponding obligation on employers to grant such leave.[184] As with the general principles, the CJEU reiterates that the Directive reflects rights that also exist within the Charter, with the Directive merely providing for the conditions for the exercise of that right, for example on the duration of the right to paid annual leave. Of course, in reality, the Directive predates the Charter, although similar rights can also be found in the common constitutional traditions as well as international social rights instruments.[185]

Once again, it is evident that the Charter's social provisions are interlaced with, and dependent on, legislative instruments for both their content and normative value, which, as will be explored in Chapter 3, contrasts with the freedom to conduct a business as a fundamental right. The latter is almost entirely dependent on the pre-existing general principles for its normative and legal content. As is also the case for the general principles, the Charter can be relied on in the interpretation of EU law as well as Member State law implementing EU law, regardless of whether the dispute arises in a horizontal context.[186] The CJEU's confirmation that the Charter's provisions are in principle capable of horizontal direct effect, provided that they meet the criteria of being sufficient in and of themselves to confer rights, ie they are unconditional

[182] *Bauer* (n 109) para 85.
[183] ibid para 87; cf AG Opinion in *Dominguez* (n 140) paras 80–83.
[184] *Bauer* (n 109) para 90.
[185] Arts 6 and 7 of the International Covenant on Economic, Social and Cultural Rights (1966) 993 UNTS 3; arts 2–4 of the European Social Charter (revised) European Treaty Series 163.
[186] Ward (n 70) 1602.

and mandatory, has been reiterated in subsequent case law of the CJEU.[187] At the same time, despite the CJEU's holding in *Bauer* that Article 31(2) CFR was 'sufficient in itself to confer on workers a right that they may actually rely on', that right would be rendered essentially meaningless without reference to the underlying legislative protections that have themselves been elaborated in the previous case law of the CJEU.[188]

Cases such as *Bauer* concerning the horizontal direct effect of Article 31(2) CFR also have wider significance in (re)affirming the 'indivisibility' of the Charter's provisions, in the sense of their formal constitutional status, even if they do not always enjoy direct effect. This is not to say, however, that all of the Charter's provisions are, or should be, endowed with equivalent normative or legal value. Although the freedom to conduct a business and the provisions in the Solidarity Title may enjoy formally equivalent status as fundamental Charter rights, they are nevertheless endowed with differing normative value, as evidenced in part through their differing relationships with—indeed capacity to influence the effectiveness of—Union legislation.

1.5 Conclusion

This chapter has had the purpose of re-evaluating the origins of fundamental rights within the EU legal order for the reason that the freedom to conduct a business as a fundamental right continues to be composed of diverse sources, with its origins intimately linked to the emergence of the very concept of fundamental rights within EU law, and with the uncertain relationship between sources of Union fundamental rights also continuing to contour the relative constitutional weight of economic freedoms and social rights. The Union's fundamental rights order now consists of a complex and intricate web of interrelated sources, with the general principles representing the underpinning of the entire fundamental rights edifice, including the fragmentations which lie at its foundation. It was shown that from its earliest case law on fundamental rights as general principles, the CJEU has been engaged with concepts of business freedoms and has recognized their status as fundamental rights, largely drawing inspiration from the common constitutional traditions of (some of) the then Member States.

[187] eg Case C–193/17 *Cresco Investigation GmbH v Markus Achatzi* EU:C:2019:43.
[188] *Bauer* (n 109) para 85.

Perhaps due to the recognition that national constitutional provisions have no direct application at Union level, the CJEU neither fully engages in discussion on the origins, limitations, or value of business freedoms in national law, nor does it clearly articulate a Union-level vision for those freedoms. This is the methodological lacuna at the heart of the development of fundamental rights as general principles, and which continues to undermine coherence and consistency in the Court's fundamental rights reasoning. These gaps are exacerbated by a more recent failure properly to consider the place of the general principles within the Union's fundamental rights edifice, particularly in disputes involving private parties, where legal certainty is of particular importance.

The enduring value of the general principles derives in part from the emerging interpretative gaps between the general principles and the equivalent provisions found within the Charter, with the latter thereby representing no more than a 'fragmentary' (re)constitutionalization of the pre-existing general principles, with particular consequences for the relationship between business freedoms and fundamental social rights. As such, some of the methodological and normative ambiguities surrounding the status of fundamental rights sources within the Union legal order do not stem exclusively, or even predominantly, from the vagaries of unwritten general principles as such, but rather from the unstable relationship between those principles and their written counterparts within the Charter.

It was shown that the Charter has a rather limited scope of application and continues to enjoy an uncertain relationship to the general principles that it purports to replace, and which is argued in Chapter 3 to have particular consequences for our understanding of the precise content and value of the freedom to conduct a business as a fundamental right. Furthermore, the Charter's horizontal provisions, which include the distinction between rights and principles, as well as the related issue of the Charter's applicability to private parties, essentially impede the effectiveness of the Charter's social rights, both in and of themselves, but also, as argued here, in their relationship to competing business freedoms. It is only by understanding the origins of and relationship between the various sources of EU fundamental rights, including the flaws inherent in the Union's existing fundamental rights architecture, that the relative weakness of the protection granted to social rights—in contrast to economic freedoms—can truly be appreciated.

In other words, the potential scope, application, and interpretation of business freedoms and fundamental rights concepts found within the Charter are bounded by the wider fundamental rights framework within the Union legal order, which both modulates—and is modulated by—those concepts. It was demonstrated that Union law contains a number of deficiencies in its protection of economic and social rights, which may undermine the capacity of such concepts to counteract the freedom to conduct a business as a fundamental right. It was argued that the Charter is a 'fragmentary' rights instrument in the sense that (1) it continues to rely on the underlying support of other rights instruments both internal and external to the EU legal order; and (2) in the granting of differing normative and legal value to its provisions, particularly through the distinction drawn within the Charter between rights and principles and the attendant consequences for the horizontal application of Union fundamental rights.

That the Charter is, in principle, capable of application in the context of disputes between private parties is now beyond doubt, although precisely which of its provisions might enjoy such effect remains to be determined. Much of the recent activity in this field has concerned the Solidarity Title of the Charter, particularly Article 31(2) CFR which grants the right to paid annual leave. Despite the Solidarity Title's restrictive formulation and relative lack of enforceability, certain Member States, but particularly the UK, were always antagonistic towards the inclusion in the Charter of social rights such as Article 31(2) CFR, fearing that the provisions of the Solidarity Title might be used to extend the powers of the CJEU over sensitive fields of national social concern, notably employment law and the regulation of the labour market.

The UK has long been ambivalent in its relationship with the Charter, first seeking an opt-out from some of its effects and later in the context of Brexit, excluding—or at least attempting to exclude—the influence of the Charter from domestic law altogether, thereby compounding the 'variability' of the Charter as a fundamental right source, while re-emphasizing the general principles as an autonomous source for the protection of EU-derived fundamental rights. Brexit is also a useful lens through which to analyse the competing relationship between business freedoms and fundamental (social) rights by exploring the potential longevity of EU fundamental rights concepts within the UK legal order and within a context of particular Charter (social) rights scepticism. It is therefore useful to assess the UK's role in the development of EU fundamental rights and the immediate consequences of the UK's withdrawal from the EU for the ongoing relevance of Union-derived rights in that country, but also the consequences of Brexit for the relationship between economic freedoms and social rights within EU law more generally.

2
The Deconstitutionalization of European Union Fundamental Rights in the United Kingdom

2.1 Introduction

If the first chapter had the purpose of re-evaluating the constitutional status of the European Union's (EU) fundamental rights framework, notably the (increasing) divergence between the economic and social provisions found within the European Union Charter of Fundamental Rights (CFR), the present chapter assesses the particular consequences of Brexit, not only for the protection of EU-derived fundamental rights concepts in the United Kingdom (UK), but also for the composition and future trajectory of the fundamental rights regime of the Union itself, including the competing relationship between economic freedoms and fundamental social rights. First, it is argued that the UK's long-standing antipathy towards the Charter exposes deeper divergences between the Solidarity Title and the Charter's other (more 'traditional') fundamental rights provisions (Section 2.2). The chapter then turns to assessing the legal status of EU-derived fundamental rights concepts within the UK legal order following Brexit (Section 2.3). In particular, it is suggested that the Withdrawal Agreement (WA) governing the UK's departure from the Union exhibits a degree of continuity with existing EU constitutional and fundamental rights arrangements. It is further argued that the UK's traditional Charter-scepticism, coupled with the deregulatory thrust of Brexit itself, contributed to the Union's insistence upon strong protections for social rights, notably labour rights, in the new arrangements governing the UK's relationship with the EU. While framed in the language of trade implications and competitiveness, the measures contained in the Level Playing Field provisions of the Trade and Cooperation Agreement (TCA) represent a recognition of the constitutional value attributed to at least some of these social rights within the Union legal order.

Business Freedoms and Fundamental Rights in European Union Law. Niall O'Connor, Oxford University Press.
 DOI: 10.1093/9780191982132.003.0003

All of this is despite the fact that the Charter—but not the general principles—was denied the status of 'retained' EU law in the domestic legislative regime designed to facilitate the disentanglement of the Union and UK legal systems. The formal (and gradual) 'deconstitutionalization' of EU-derived fundamental rights concepts within UK law is beginning to concretize, with the enactment of recent legislation also converting 'retained' EU law into 'assimilated' EU law, with potential significant consequences for the ongoing relevance of—and level of protection granted to—economic freedoms and social rights within domestic law. This assimilation process thereby raises profound constitutional questions as to the nature, legal status, and extent of the reach of (former) EU law concepts in the UK legal order. Section 2.4 concludes that the further fragmentation of the Charter provoked by Brexit has significant consequences for the ongoing relationship between business freedom concepts and social rights not only within the UK, but also in the EU legal order, despite the newly deconstitutionalized status of both the Charter and now the general principles within domestic UK law.

2.2 The Role of the Charter During the United Kingdom's Membership of the European Union

While the UK was a member of the EU, it had often shown resistance to the increasing influence of the Union over sensitive areas of social law, which were perceived as the proper domain of national sovereignty, perhaps most famously in its initial opt-out from the Social Chapter of the Maastricht Treaty.[1] The UK was similarly sceptical towards the codification of social rights within the Charter and therefore secured a so-called 'opt-out' from the Charter through Protocol No. 30.[2] Although no longer applicable to the UK, the Protocol is illustrative of the UK's attempts to avoid the application of the Charter, which culminated in the latter's purported exclusion from domestic law post-Brexit. Furthermore, the Protocol provides an indication of the differing normative and legal weight to be granted to various Charter provisions, notably those rights and principles found within the Solidarity Title, which has ongoing relevance in ascertaining the relative strength of fundamental rights sources within EU law more generally.

[1] European Commission, 'Facts About the "Social Chapter"', MEMO/97/13, 5 February 1997.

[2] Protocol No. 30 on the application of the Charter of Fundamental Rights to Poland and to the United Kingdom [2007] OJ C306/157.

Article 1(1) of the Protocol provides that the Charter does not *extend* the ability of the Court of Justice of the European Union (CJEU)—or courts of the UK and Poland—to make a finding of inconsistency between national law and the rights found within the Charter. This provision, which addresses the ability of litigants to invoke the Charter to challenge national measures, amounts to no more than a restatement of the horizontal provisions of the Charter itself, which, as has already been noted, affirms at Article 51(2) CFR that the Charter does not create any new powers or extend the existing competences of the Union. Article 1(1) of the Protocol specifies that the Charter does not 'extend' the CJEU's ability to review national measures for fundamental rights compatibility but, as seen in the case law on fundamental rights as general principles, this is precisely a role that the CJEU has long performed in relation to Member State acts falling within the scope of EU law. As such, Article 1(1) could not constitute an 'opt-out' from the Charter, particularly given that this provision—along with Article 1(2)—would have been rendered redundant if the Charter did not apply to the UK at all.[3]

Article 1(2) of the Protocol seemed to go further and provides that 'nothing in Title IV [...] creates justiciable rights applicable to [...] the United Kingdom except in so far as [...] the United Kingdom has provided for such rights in its national law'. This appears to be the only provision of the Protocol capable of constituting a true opt-out in that it purports to exclude reliance on the Solidarity Title to derive enforceable 'rights' insofar as such rights have not already been provided for in domestic law.[4] This opt-out was particularly relevant for Article 28 CFR on the right of collective bargaining and action, but which also at least partially exists as a general principle, and for Article 30 CFR on the prevention of unjustified dismissal, both of which are couched in the language of 'rights', but operate in fields over which the EU lacks competence, thus making the application of the Charter less likely.[5] It has already been noted that Article 31(2) CFR on paid annual leave is also a right found within the Solidarity Title, but that provision has been further implemented in national

[3] Paul Craig, *The Lisbon Treaty: Law, Politics and Treaty Reform* (OUP 2010) 237; House of Commons European Scrutiny Committee, 'The Application of the EU Charter of Fundamental Rights in the UK: A State of Confusion' HC 979, 2 April 2014; Ministry of Justice, 'Government Response to the House of Commons European Scrutiny Committee Report 43rd Report, 2013–2014, HC 979, The Application of the EU Charter of Fundamental Rights in the UK: a state of confusion' CM 8915, July 2014.

[4] Catherine Barnard, 'The "Opt-Out" for the UK and Poland from the Charter of Fundamental Rights: Triumph of Rhetoric over Reality?' in Stefan Griller and Jacques Ziller (eds), *The Lisbon Treaty: EU Constitutionalism Without a Constitutional Treaty* (Springer 2008) 257.

[5] cf Case C–438/05 *International Transport Workers' Federation and Finnish Seamen's Union v Viking Line ABP and OÜ Viking Line Eesti* ECLI:EU:C:2007:772, para 40.

law, for example through the provisions of the Working Time Regulations in the UK, which implemented the EU Working Time Directive.[6]

Article 2 of the Protocol provides that where reference is made in the Charter to 'national laws and practices', those provisions should only apply to the UK to the extent that the rights or principles contained therein have already been recognized in the law or practices of the UK. It has been suggested that this provision merely reflects Article 52(6) CFR, which requires full account to be taken of national laws and practices where specified in the Charter, as well as Article 52(5) CFR, which, as has been seen, seeks to limit the legal effects of 'principles'.[7] Where EU legislation exists governing a particular issue, for example a directive giving expression to a fundamental right, these rights will apply to all Member States, regardless of the operation of the Protocol.[8]

Overall, then, the opt-out may not have had anything other than declaratory effect, for the benefit of *all* Member States, with the CJEU confirming—as the UK government had itself conceded—in *NS*, that the Charter was applicable to the UK.[9] In that case, the CJEU noted that Article 1(1) of the Protocol 'does not call into question the applicability of the Charter [to the UK and Poland]'.[10] Rather, Article 1(1) of the Protocol merely restates the provisions of Article 51 of the Charter governing its field of application.[11] The CJEU did not address Article 1(2) of the Protocol, but Advocate General Trstenjak had found that provision to represent a clarification of the validity or enforceability of individual (social) provisions within the Charter in the UK.[12] The very purpose underlying the opt-out from the Charter was to assuage fears that 'the economic and social rights contained in Title IV of the Charter would provide the basis for a judicial assault upon the UK's (neo-) liberal employment legislation'.[13] For Dougan, the Protocol's primary purpose was thus to 'serve as an effective political response to a serious failure of public discourse. Indeed,

[6] Working Time Regulations 1998 (SI 1998/1833); Directive 2003/88/EC of the European Parliament and of the Council of 4 November 2003 concerning certain aspects of the organisation of working time [2003] OJ L299/9.

[7] Steve Peers, 'The "Opt-Out" that Fell to Earth: The British and Polish Protocol Concerning the EU Charter of Fundamental Rights' (2012) 12 HRLR 375, 381.

[8] Vojtech Belling, 'Supranational Fundamental Rights or Primacy of Sovereignty? Legal Effects of the So-Called Opt-Out from the EU Charter of Fundamental Rights' (2012) 18 ELJ 251, 267.

[9] Joined Cases C–411/10 and 493/10 *NS v Secretary of State for the Home Department* EU:C:2011:865; cf *R (on the application of AB) v Secretary of State for the Home Department* [2013] WLUK 177 [14].

[10] *NS* (n 9) para 119.

[11] ibid para 120.

[12] AG Opinion in Joined Cases C–411/10 and 493/10 *NS v Secretary of State for the Home Department* ECLI:EU:C:2011:611, paras 171, 172.

[13] Michael Dougan, 'The Treaty of Lisbon 2007: Winning Minds, Not Hearts' (2008) 45 CMLRev 617, 666.

the Charter emerges as a fantasy solution to a fantasy problem.'[14] In any case, EU legislation, including legislation in the social field, must be interpreted in the light of the Charter, including the Solidarity Title, and so those provisions always had an indirect impact in the UK. The (pre-Brexit) relevance of the Charter in the UK was also confirmed through its—albeit limited—use in subsequent domestic case law as well as in preliminary references from the UK to the CJEU.[15]

In *Benkharbouche*, for example, the United Kingdom Supreme Court (UKSC) referred to Article 47 CFR on the right to an effective remedy and to a fair trial, albeit briefly and only to highlight its role in relation to Article 6 of the European Convention on Human Rights (ECHR), with Lord Reed holding that '[t]he only difference that it makes is that a conflict between EU law and English domestic law must be resolved in favour of the former, and the latter must be disapplied; whereas the remedy in the case of inconsistency with article 6 [ECHR] is a declaration of incompatibility'.[16] It is therefore clear that the Charter (at least outside of the devolved context) provided a much more effective remedial regime than that found with the Human Rights Act 1998 or at common law, including the possible disapplication of national legislation. Similarly, the UKSC in *UNISON* recognized the importance of underlying EU fundamental rights, including Article 47 CFR, in its finding that the UK's existing employment tribunal fees regime was incompatible with the right to effective judicial protection and thereby constituted a breach of EU law.[17] Reliance on the Charter in that case—which was delivered after the Brexit referendum—was somewhat tempered by the more extensive references to the same rights found in the ECHR and at common law.

The final impediment to the Protocol's potential potency in the UK was the continued applicability of the general principles which remain a source of fundamental rights protection within the EU—and at the time, the UK—legal order, and which thereby mitigated any purported opt-out from the Charter. A similar situation arose in the immediate wake of the UK's departure from the EU, with the general principles, but not the Charter, having been granted the status of retained EU law. This status grants a limited—and as we now know temporary—form of supremacy for

[14] ibid 670.

[15] Richard Clayton and Cian C Murphy, 'The Emergence of the EU Charter of Fundamental Rights in UK Law' (2014) 5 EHRLR 469; Catherine Barnard, 'So Long, Farewell, Auf Wiedersehen, Adieu: Brexit and the Charter of Fundamental Rights' (2019) 82 MLR 350, 358.

[16] *Benkharbouche v Secretary of State for Foreign and Commonwealth Affairs and Secretary of State for Foreign and Commonwealth Affairs and Libya v Janah* [2019] AC 777.

[17] *R (on the application of UNISON) v Lord Chancellor* [2020] AC 869 [117].

EU-derived legal and constitutional concepts within the UK legal order. Despite more recent changes to the formal constitutional status of retained EU law within domestic law, Union fundamental rights concepts continue to enjoy an indirect legacy effect, thereby necessitating a clearer understanding of their precise relationship to the domestic fundamental rights regime. As suggested here, this renewed arrangement also provides insights into our understanding of the relationship between the general principles and written fundamental rights sources within the Union legal order, and thereby the relationship between business freedoms and social rights within both UK and EU law.

2.3 The Status of European Union Fundamental Rights in the United Kingdom After Brexit

2.3.1 Fundamental rights and the United Kingdom's withdrawal from the European Union

The UK was evidently at the vanguard of those Member States seeking to limit the potential legal effects of the Charter, whether through supporting the distinction between rights and principles in Article 52(5) CFR or seeking—however unsuccessfully—to opt out of the Charter's application altogether.[18] Even while the UK was a Member State of the EU, it was the Human Rights Act 1998 that represented the principal point of reference for domestic fundamental rights protection, which is entirely unsurprising given the Charter's more limited scope of application. Nevertheless, the Charter constituted an important supplementary source of rights in cases falling within the scope of EU law, with domestic courts referring to the Charter with increasing frequency right up until the UK's departure from the Union.[19] In addition, the common law constitutes a further important source of rights protection, with particular relevance for economic or 'freedom'-based rights, notably economic liberties such as freedom of contract.[20]

[18] Barnard (n 15) 351.

[19] Lady Arden and Takis Tridimas, 'Limited But Not Inconsequential: The Application of the Charter by the Courts of England and Wales' in Michal Bobek and Jeremias Adams-Prassl (eds), *The EU Charter of Fundamental Rights in the Member States* (Hart 2020) 331, 332.

[20] ibid.

After an initial period of post-referendum silence on the matter, the UK government presented the Charter's demise in the UK as something of an inevitable consequence of the decision to withdraw from the EU, with the Great Repeal Bill White Paper noting that '[t]he Charter only applies to member states when acting within the scope of EU law, so its relevance is removed by our withdrawal from the EU'.[21] This argument is somewhat contradicted in the same White Paper, which states that '[m]any of these underlying rights exist elsewhere in the body of EU law which we will be converting into UK law'.[22] The removal of the Charter from domestic law therefore represented a deliberate choice, and moreover a choice that went against the general thrust of domestic withdrawal legislation, which aimed for (at least temporary) continuity rather than divergence.

Both the Charter and the general principles applied to the UK during the transition period that ended on 31 December 2020, and during that time the UK was bound by new rulings of the CJEU, including case law applying the Charter. The Charter will also remain of direct relevance for those areas of the Withdrawal Agreement that continue to be determined by EU law, for example the Citizens' Rights provisions of the Agreement which refer to EU law sources, and which will continue to be interpreted in light of the Charter.[23] Within the context of citizens' rights, the CJEU essentially continues to enjoy a similar jurisdiction to that which pertained before Brexit, with the possibility of UK courts continuing to refer preliminary questions to the CJEU in relation to the Citizens' Rights provisions of the Withdrawal Agreement for eight years after the end of the transition period.[24]

In *AT*, the Charter was found by the domestic courts to be applicable to benefits claims post-transition.[25] This was due to the temporary right of residence found in Article 13 WA for those holding pre-settled status, and which is essentially a modified form of the residence rights found in Article 21 TFEU. Article 4(3) WA provides that EU law concepts found within the Withdrawal Agreement are to be 'interpreted and applied in accordance with the methods and general principles of Union law', which includes the Charter, thereby

[21] Department for Exiting the European Union, 'Legislating for the United Kingdom's Withdrawal from the European Union' CM 9446, March 2017, para 2.23.

[22] ibid para 2.25.

[23] Agreement on the withdrawal of the United Kingdom of Great Britain and Northern Ireland from the European Union and the European Atomic Energy Community [2020] OJ L29/7 (Withdrawal Agreement); Case C-709/20 *CG v The Department for Communities in Northern Ireland* ECLI:EU:C:2021:602; *AT v SSWP* [2023] 1 WLR 2669.

[24] Art 158 WA.

[25] *AT* (n 23); *Fratila v Secretary of State for Work and Pensions* [2022] 3 All ER 1045.

granting it a continued role in the interpretation of domestic measures within the scope of (aspects of) the Withdrawal Agreement.[26]

This does not, however, come close to the full applicability and effect of the Charter that prevailed prior to the UK's departure from the Union, with the Court of Appeal in *AT* addressing the essential transformation of the status of EU law in the UK, first through the adoption of international law instruments, and then through the domestication of these instruments in national law, given the dualist nature of the UK legal order. This meant that only those provisions of EU law that had specifically been preserved in the Withdrawal Agreement would now apply in the UK, and only then to the extent permitted by that Agreement.[27] As the Court of Appeal put it, '[t]he Charter only applies if and insofar as it can attach to rights brought into domestic law *via* the implementation of the Withdrawal Agreement. This is a limited category of rights.'[28]

The Charter (and the general principles) thereby enjoy a much more restricted scope of application within domestic UK law, ie narrower than 'within the scope of EU law', but the Court of Appeal's judgment nevertheless constitutes a clear recognition of the Charter's potential ongoing relevance in domestic disputes. Similarly to the situation existing in EU law, the Charter remains only a secondary source in the sense that it must 'attach' to an underlying provision or right which triggers the Charter's applicability.[29] The Charter thereby constitutes a 'provision of Union law made applicable by the Agreement', in accordance with Article 4(1) WA, with that same provision mandating the reciprocal and identical effect of the Withdrawal Agreement within the UK and Union legal orders. The Charter is an integral part of the Union's fundamental rights regime and would clearly be applicable to any Union interpretation of Article 13 WA, thereby entailing its applicability in the UK context in order to ensure the same legal outcome or effects.[30]

The Trade and Cooperation Agreement also contains provisions preventing, or at least mitigating, potential regulatory competition between the EU and the UK, notably in the field of labour rights. Although not specifically concerned with the preservation of 'fundamental rights', these Level Playing Field provisions also have clear implications for the ongoing (albeit indirect) relevance of the rights found in the Charter's Solidarity Title—as well as other international

[26] Art 2 WA.
[27] *SSWP v AT* [2023] 11 WLUK 104 [48].
[28] ibid [103].
[29] ibid [84].
[30] ibid [85].

social rights instruments.[31] The Level Playing Field essentially constrains the UK's ability to diverge from the social protections granted by EU labour law, with the overall purpose of this instrument being to ensure 'fair' competition between the two parties, which includes 'non-regression' and 'rebalancing' mechanisms to prevent labour rights divergences from adversely affecting trade or investment, and with the labour protections in place at the end of the transition period constituting a floor of protection.[32]

The TCA further contains obligations on the Parties to respect the core International Labour Organization (ILO) principles as set out in the 1998 Declaration on Fundamental Principles and Rights at Work, in addition to ongoing obligations to respect European Social Charter provisions as well as ILO Conventions as ratified by the parties. The core obligations found within international social rights instruments are largely consonant with the provisions of the Charter's Solidarity Title. For example, Article 7 of the International Covenant on Economic, Social and Cultural Rights includes an obligation on States parties to '[i]ntroduce and enforce minimum standards in relation to rest, leisure, reasonable limitation of working hours, paid leave and public holidays', which is reflective of the content of Article 31 CFR despite not being listed as a direct source of those rights in the Charter's Explanations.[33]

The Withdrawal Agreement also has continued—and more precise—rights implications through the Ireland/Northern Ireland Protocol, now known as the Windsor Framework (WF), which secures the ongoing relevance of the Charter for that part of the UK. Article 2(1) WF, which is directly effective, stipulates that '[t]he United Kingdom shall ensure that no diminution of rights, safeguards or equality of opportunity, as set out in that part of the 1998 Agreement entitled Rights, Safeguards and Equality of Opportunity results from its withdrawal from the Union'. Within the social law context, this provision may necessitate the ongoing application in Northern Ireland of important EU (social) legislative measures, for example those rules governing part-time work and maternity leave, which can be said to constitute the 'underpinnings' of Good Friday Agreement rights such as 'the right to equal opportunity in all social and economic activity, in both the public and private sectors, regardless

[31] Trade and Cooperation Agreement between the European Union and the European Atomic Energy Community, of the one part, and the United Kingdom of Great Britain and Northern Ireland, of the other part [2021] OJ L149/10 (Trade and Cooperation Agreement), arts 8.3, 399.

[32] Arts 386, 387, 411 TCA. Phil Syrpis, 'The Influence of the EU on UK Labour Law – Before and After Brexit' (2022) 51 ILJ 802.

[33] United Nations Committee on Economic, Social and Cultural Rights, 'General Comment No 23 on the Right to Just and Favourable Conditions of Work', E/C.12/GC/23, 27 April 2016.

of class, creed, disability, gender or ethnicity'.[34] There remain complex questions as to whether a particular EU law provision can be said to 'support' the rights found within the Good Friday Agreement and whether the diminution of such rights might have 'resulted' from the UK's withdrawal from the Union.[35] Similarly, it is difficult to maintain that there is a continued commitment on the UK to remain party to the ECHR on the *basis* of EU law, with Article 2 WF thereby unlikely to be of application to maintaining the status of the ECHR in Northern Ireland.[36]

Article 2 WF's 'non-diminution' commitment in relation to unspecified EU-derived rights existing at the end of the transition period is also accompanied by dynamic alignment requirements, which guarantee the continued protection of certain EU-derived equality rights in Northern Ireland as specified in Article 2(1) WF and contained in Annex 1 WF.[37] The Withdrawal Agreement thereby ensures a continued role for the Charter and general principles in the interpretation of the legislation of relevance to Article 2 WF, albeit that the precise scope of the dynamic alignment obligations remains unclear, for example the extent to which CJEU case law interpreting EU legislation falling within the scope of the non-diminution requirements should be tracked.[38] Article 13(3) WF provides for the application to Northern Ireland of any updates to the directives listed in Annex 1 WF.[39]

Article 13(2) WF also provides for ongoing dynamic interpretation of its provisions in accordance with changes to CJEU case law, notwithstanding the more limited interpretative obligations found in Article 4(4) WA, which relates to case law handed down prior to the end of the transition period, albeit that the UK courts must continue to have 'due regard' to subsequent CJEU case law when interpreting and applying the Withdrawal Agreement in accordance

[34] Christopher McCrudden, 'Human Rights and Equality' in Christopher McCrudden (ed), *The Law and Practice of the Ireland—Northern Ireland Protocol* (CUP 2022) 143, 152; Agreement between the Government of the United Kingdom of Great Britain and Northern Ireland and the Government of Ireland (with annexes) (1998) 2114 UNTS 473, Multi-Party Agreement, Rights, Safeguards and Equality of Opportunity, para 1.

[35] ECNI and NIHRC, 'Working Paper: The Scope of Article 2(1) of the Ireland/Northern Ireland Protocol', December 2022 11.

[36] McCrudden (n 34) 148.

[37] Lisa Claire Whitten, 'Post-Brexit Dynamism: The Dynamic Regulatory Alignment of Northern Ireland Under the Protocol on Ireland/Northern Ireland' (2022) 73 NILQ 37; Eleni Frantziou and Sarah Craig, 'Understanding the Implications of Article 2 of the Northern Ireland Protocol in the Context of EU Case Law Developments' (2022) 73 NILQ 65.

[38] Arts 4(4), (5) and 13(2) WA; NIHRC and ECNI, 'Submission of the NIHRC and ECNI to "Retained EU Law: Where Next?"—An Inquiry by the European Scrutiny Committee', 11 April 2022, para 6.5; Frantziou and Craig (n 37).

[39] ECNI and NIHRC (n 35) 20.

with Article 4(5) WA.[40] Finally, there may be ongoing obligations on the UK to maintain alignment with EU rules to ensure equivalence in rights protection on both sides of the Irish border.[41]

Both the Citizens' Rights provisions and the Windsor Framework, thereby constitute significant contributions to the protection of EU-derived fundamental rights, including the Charter, albeit that these rights may not be applicable across the entire UK, and with Brexit also having particular (negative) rights implications for Northern Ireland, with the Windsor Framework already having been used to 'disapply' provisions of domestic legislation, itself a feature of fundamental constitutional rights.[42] Furthermore, Article 2 WF has potentially significant implications for the ability of the UK to depart from retained or assimilated EU law, at least as it applies to Northern Ireland, although it is the substance not the form of the relevant rights protections that is protected by Article 2 WF, which does not prescribe the existence of 'retained EU law' as such.[43]

2.3.2 The retention of European Union law within the domestic legal order

Retained EU law is a new category of domestic law introduced at the end of the Brexit transition period, with the purpose of providing legal certainty and continuity. This new body of law, which has ongoing (direct) relevance for cases arising before the end of 2023, consists of: (1) EU-derived domestic legislation, for example domestic legislation implementing directives, but without the directives themselves becoming retained EU law; (2) 'direct' EU legislation, for example UK versions of EU regulations which did not require domestic implementation, ie they were directly applicable; and finally (3) EU-derived rights, powers, liabilities, obligations, restrictions, remedies, and procedures, which include any directly effective EU rights of a kind recognized at the end of the

[40] These provisions complement art 4(1) and (2) WA which apply to the Withdrawal Agreement and any EU law made applicable by the Agreement.

[41] Art 13(4) WF; art 166 WA.

[42] CRG Murray and Clare AG Rice, 'Beyond Trade: Implementing the Ireland/Northern Ireland Protocol's Human Rights and Equalities Provisions' (2021) 72 NILQ 1; NI Office, 'UK Government Commitment to "No Diminution of Rights, Safeguards and Equality of Opportunity" in Northern Ireland: What Does it Mean and How Will it Be Implemented?' (NIO 2020), para 29. *Re Spuc Pro-Life Ltd* [2022] NIQB 9 [77]; *Angesom's Application* [2023] NIKB 102 [94].

[43] NIHRC and ECNI (n 38) paras 2.4 and 2.5; *Dillon and In the Matter of the Northern Ireland Troubles (Legacy and Reconciliation) Act 2023 and the Secretary of State for Northern Ireland* [2024] NIKB 11.

transition period, for example those deriving from directives or the Treaties.[44] In addition, the European Union (Withdrawal) Act 2018 preserves some of the constitutional 'features' of pre-existing EU law, notably the principle of 'primacy', which applies to retained EU law deriving from categories (2) and (3), ie retained direct EU legislation and directly effective rights, which thereby enjoy priority over any provision of domestic law enacted before the end of the transition period, but not for prospective legislation.[45]

In addition, the Explanatory Notes to the 2018 Withdrawal Act make clear that retained EU law must be interpreted consistently with EU law, albeit that the precise extent of that obligation is unspecified.[46] There is a continued lack of clarity as to the types of retained EU law to which the supremacy principle applies. For example, the principle appears not to apply to EU law retained under section 2 EU(W)A 2018, which includes implementing legislation embedding rights in domestic law even prior to Brexit, but this is not made explicit in the Explanatory Notes, nor is it clear the extent to which EU-derived concepts such as 'supremacy' are to be guided by the pre-existing treatment of such concepts by the CJEU, despite their domestication. The overarching purpose lying behind the retention of EU law was to provide legal certainty by essentially replicating (with exceptions) the institutional and legal position that prevailed during the UK's membership of the Union, thereby preserving, on a more limited basis, the constitutional value of Union fundamental rights within the domestic legal order.

Despite these elements of continuity, the category of 'retained EU law' is not static, with EU-derived legislation already having been subject to domestic interpretation and modification, leading to the creation of a complex and rather inaccessible body of law.[47] Modified retained EU law also enjoys supremacy over pre-transition domestic law, so long as the application of the supremacy principle would not be inconsistent with the intention behind the modification.[48] This causes potential confusion between a situation in which a legal provision has merely been modified and thereby continues to constitute retained EU law, and a situation in which a modification creates entirely new domestic law.

[44] EU(W)A 2018, ss 2–4.
[45] ibid s 5.
[46] Explanatory Notes to the European Union (Withdrawal) Act 2018, para 104.
[47] EU(W)A 2018, s 6(3) and (6) provides that retained—and thereby, assimilated—EU law includes post-transition interpretations applied by domestic courts.
[48] ibid s 5.

Retained direct *principal* EU legislation as well as EU law retained by virtue of section 4 EU(W)A 2018 were to be treated in a similar way to domestic primary legislation for the purposes of amendment, and would thereby be subject to greater parliamentary scrutiny.[49] Retained direct principal EU legislation, which includes (former) EU regulations, was also treated as primary legislation for the purpose of review under the Human Rights Act 1998, meaning that it was immune from being declared invalid due to incompatibility with the ECHR. This status can be contrasted with the wider powers granted to ministers to amend remaining retained EU law, ostensibly to ensure its effective operation, but which may in practice be used to affect substantive policy changes.[50]

More significantly for the present discussion on the ongoing role of EU-derived fundamental rights concepts, section 5(4) EU(W)A 2018 provides that '[t]he Charter of Fundamental Rights is not part of domestic law on or after exit day', a provision that can be criticized for creating an 'uncertain legal landscape'.[51] Unsuccessful attempts had been made by the House of Lords to retain the Charter during the passage of the then Withdrawal Bill, with the Lords Constitutional Committee also questioning the purpose of the Charter's exclusion from the category of retained EU law:

> If, as the Government suggests, the Charter of Fundamental Rights adds nothing to the content of EU law which is being retained, we do not understand why an exception needs to be made for it. If, however, the Charter does add value, then legal continuity suggests that the Bill should not make substantive changes to the law which applies immediately after exit day.[52]

This passage exposes the contradiction that lies at the heart of the UK government's approach to the post-Brexit effect of the Charter. Despite its purported exclusion, the Charter nevertheless continues to have an indirect influence through the interpretative effect of 'retained case law', that is case law handed down prior to the end of the transition period, and which relates to the three categories of retained EU law already set out, whether deriving from the CJEU (retained EU case law) or domestic courts (retained domestic case law).[53] Judgments of the CJEU delivered prior to the end of the transition

[49] ibid s 7 and Sch 8.

[50] ibid s 8.

[51] Joint Committee on Human Rights, *Legislative Scrutiny: The EU (Withdrawal) Bill: A Right by Right Analysis, First Report of Session 2017–2019* (24 January 2018, HL Paper 70, HC 774) 4; Barnard (n 15) 350.

[52] House of Lords Constitution Committee, *European Union (Withdrawal) Bill* (HL Paper 69, 29 January 2018) para 119.

[53] EU(W)A 2018, ss 5(4) and 6.

period are binding on UK courts when considering unmodified retained EU law, while judgments handed down after that date may be relied on by the courts if relevant to the case at hand.[54]

Section 6(6) EU(W)A 2018 also grants discretion to the UK courts to decide whether to follow CJEU case law when interpreting modified retained EU law insofar as such an interpretation remains consistent with the intention of the modifications. Section 5(5) EU(W)A 2018 further qualifies the exclusion of Union-derived fundamental rights from retained EU law by adding that '[s]ubsection 4 does not affect the retention in domestic law [. . .] of any fundamental rights or principles which exist irrespective of the Charter', in other words, the general principles. For this purpose, references to the Charter in case law should therefore be read as references to corresponding general principles already recognized by the CJEU.[55]

This provision does not apply to general principles that are subsequently recognized by the CJEU, and as Schedule 1 of the EU(W)A 2018 makes clear, the role of the general principles has been curtailed. The interpretative function of the general principles has been maintained, but they can no longer be relied on as a ground for review. In other words, legislation that is incompatible with the general principles can no longer be disapplied and, as such, the already limited form of supremacy of retained EU law provided for in section 5(2) EU(W)A 2018 does not extend to the general principles.[56] It is likely that not all of the Charter's provisions benefit from characterization as general principles of EU law, thereby undermining in particular the post-Brexit status of the rights and principles found within the Charter's Solidarity Title. This is despite the (somewhat ambiguous) suggestion in the Explanatory Notes to the 2018 Act that a broad interpretation should be given to section 5(5) EU(W) A 2018 to the effect that *all* Charter rights and principles exist as general principles outside—ie 'irrespective' of—the Charter, with the Charter merely having codified those general principles.[57]

The Charter will also have continued indirect effect through other provisions of retained EU law, the interpretation of which may have been influenced by the Charter. For example, national legislation implementing a directive can be interpreted in light of the Charter—although now anchored in the language of general principles—in accordance with sections 6(7) and 5(5) EU(W)A

[54] ibid s 6(1) and (2).

[55] Department for Exiting the European Union, 'Charter of Fundamental Rights of the EU: Right by Right Analysis' (5 December 2017).

[56] EU(W)A 2018, s 6(3); *Walker v Innospec* [2018] AC 545.

[57] Explanatory Notes to the European Union (Withdrawal) Act 2018, paras 106, 107.

2018. Indeed, there is a co-dependence between the Charter and EU legislative provisions, as made clear by the Explanations to the Charter, with Charter rights thereby also being replicated within other instruments of retained EU law. To some extent, this mitigates the fact that the same rights may not have explicitly been found to be general principles before the end of the transition period, and so preserves the protection of those rights within retained EU law despite their demotion from the status of 'fundamental' or 'constitutional' rights.

Given the close relationship between the Charter and the general principles, the former is also likely to continue to influence the interpretation of the latter even in the context of retained EU law.[58] Section 6 EU(W)A 2018 further requires the UK courts to interpret retained EU law in light of the retained general principles and CJEU case law handed down before the end of the transition period, which itself includes case law applying the Charter and the general principles (retained case law). The higher courts do have the power to depart from existing CJEU case law and they may also continue to have 'regard' to future judgments of the CJEU, which could include cases applying and interpreting the Charter and general principles.[59] Retained EU law as a category was, however, abolished as of 31 December 2023, with the supremacy of (former) retained EU law (to be known as 'assimilated law') ending on the same date.[60]

2.3.3 The assimilation of retained European Union law

The overall purpose of the Retained EU Law (Revocation and Reform) Act (REULA) 2023 is to remove the distinct (constitutional) status granted to retained EU law within the domestic legal order. The changes to the status and function of retained EU law brought about by the REULA 2023 are largely implemented through the amendment of the European Union (Withdrawal) Act 2018, although the pre-existing provisions will continue to apply to legal proceedings relating to events occurring prior to the end of 2023, while certain provisions of the 2023 Act will not come into force until a date specified by the relevant commencement regulations. Schedule 1 REULA 2023 specifies those provisions of retained EU law (both subordinate legislation and retained

[58] Barnard (n 15) 363.
[59] EUWA 2018, s 6(2) and (5).
[60] REULA 2023, ss 3 and 5.

direct EU legislation) that are not to be assimilated, and which will thereby be repealed, unless preserved.[61]

The status of retained direct EU legislation under section 3 EU(W)A 2018 (which includes post-transition modifications to such laws) has been further downgraded to that of secondary rather than primary law for the purposes of amendment, with such legislation now subject to domestic legislation, and with the government also being granted the (temporary) power to alter the hierarchy between retained direct EU legislation and other provisions of domestic law.[62] Provision has also been made for domestic courts to issue an incompatibility order where it is not possible to interpret domestic legislation and assimilated EU law consistently, ie (1) where a provision of retained direct EU legislation is subject to, and incompatible with, any domestic enactment; and (2) where a domestic enactment is subject to, but incompatible with, a provision of direct EU legislation.[63] Section 2 REULA 2023 further provides for the repeal of (directly effective) rights deriving from section 4 EU(W)A 2018 by revoking the retention rule itself, although the precise content of this category of retained EU law remains unspecified.

Section 5(5) EU(W)A 2018 has also been repealed, with the general principles of EU law no longer forming part of domestic law after the end of 2023, and which will thus no longer act as an interpretative tool for (former) retained EU law, ie assimilated law from the date of the commencement of the relevant provisions, unless their effect was removed earlier by virtue of section 11 REULA 2023.[64] Assimilated EU case law will, however, continue to provide an indirect role for both the general principles and the Charter, but with the 2023 Act also containing provision for reference procedures to higher courts in order to facilitate departure from retained (assimilated) EU case law in cases of 'general public importance'.[65] Section 6(3) REULA 2023 provides a list of non-exhaustive relevant factors to which the higher courts must have regard when considering a departure from assimilated EU case law, namely: (1) the fact that decisions of foreign courts are not usually binding; (2) any changes of circumstances which are relevant to retained EU case law; and finally, (3) the extent to which that case law restricts the 'proper development' of domestic law.[66]

[61] REULA 2023, s 1.
[62] REULA 2023, ss 7, 9, and 21(3).
[63] REULA 2023, s 8.
[64] REULA 2023, s 4.
[65] REULA 2023, s 6(8).
[66] *TuneIn Inc v Warner Music UK Ltd & Anor* [2022] All ER 35.

Similar factors are to be considered when departing from assimilated domestic case law.[67] These provisions replace the pre-existing rules allowing specified higher courts to depart from retained EU case law by applying the test adopted by the UKSC when departing from its own judgments, ie 'when it appears right to do so'.[68] The relevant appeal courts are also not bound by retained EU case law, save to the extent that such case law has been modified or applied by 'relevant domestic case law' which is binding on those courts.[69] The irony of this approach is that while the 2023 Act provides for clearer mechanisms for departure from retained (assimilated) EU case law, legislation enacted since Brexit has simultaneously concretized the (albeit diminished) role of the CJEU within domestic primary law, which signals the importance and ongoing relevance of the CJEU among 'foreign' courts influencing the domestic jurisprudence of the UK.

The 2023 Act grants powers to government ministers and, where relevant, the devolved administrations, to modify assimilated law via Statutory Instrument by restating, replacing, revoking, or updating the relevant provisions up until 23 June 2026, which replaces the now expired powers to amend retained EU law in accordance with the provisions of the 2018 Withdrawal Act.[70] These provisions will have particular implications for areas of domestic law which were largely derived from EU law as implemented into secondary domestic law, notably in the employment context. For now, it can be noted that the purpose of the REULA 2023 is essentially deregulatory, with that legislation operating within the context of the then government's policy of seeking to reduce the regulatory burden on businesses, which may well exacerbate the deprioritization of social rights within the domestic legal order.[71]

The power to 'restate' represents a (limited) counterweight in this regard, in that it enabled UK and devolved authorities (until 31 December 2023) to preserve the effect of: (1) secondary retained EU law (while removing it from that category); (2) secondary assimilated EU law from 31 December 2023 onwards (again, thereby removing it from that category); and (3) any 'sunsetted' rights, powers, and liabilities.[72] For these purposes, secondary retained or assimilated EU law is defined as any EU-derived domestic legislation that is not primary legislation as well as any EU-derived domestic legislation that is

67 REULA 2023, s 6(4).

68 European Union (Withdrawal) Act 2018 (Relevant Court) (Retained EU Case Law) Regulations 2020 (SI 2020/1525); EU(W)A 2018, s 6(5).

69 REULA 2023, s 6(2) and (6).

70 REULA 2023, ss 9 and 11–16.

71 Explanatory Notes to the Retained EU Law (Revocation and Reform) Act 2023, para 3.

72 REULA 2023, s 11 (for retained EU law) and s 12 (for assimilated EU law).

primary legislation, but which was inserted by subordinate legislation. Draft regulations have already been adopted which have the dual effect of departing from pre-existing EU-derived employment and equality law protections, such as information and consultation requirements in the context of business transfers, while simultaneously restating the effects of retained EU case law, notably in the field of paid annual leave provisions.[73]

Where the power to restate retained or assimilated EU law has been exercised, this has the consequence of disapplying the effect of retained general principles as they relate to that legislation, but with the 2023 Act also providing for the possible codification of the *effects* of Union-derived interpretative principles so long as such codification does not lead to substantive policy changes, and without reintroducing concepts such as supremacy or EU general principles per se.[74] This is similar to the way in which section 4 EU(W)A 2018 retained certain directly effective 'rights', rather than the text of the relevant provision (for eg a directive) itself. Section 12(8) REULA 2023 also allows for the stand-alone—ie outside of the context of restatement—reproduction of the effects of what used to constitute retained EU law by virtue of sections 4, 6(3), and 6(6) EU(W)A 2018, including the general principles.

There are also broader limitations on the extent to which retained EU law can be amended or repealed. For example, section 7C EU(W)A 2018 provides for the interpretation in conformity with the Withdrawal Agreement of relevant separation agreement law, such as legislation implementing that Agreement, which ensures a continued role for the general principles, relevant CJEU case law, as well as the principle of supremacy in the interpretation of such law.[75] In other words, any EU-derived law applicable in the UK by virtue of the Withdrawal Agreement must continue to be interpreted in light of the general principles of EU law, which includes the protection of fundamental rights.[76] Similarly, retained EU case law must be interpreted subject to relevant separation agreement law which will thereby influence any decision to depart from assimilated case law.[77]

In certain respects, this interpretative obligation is reflective of similar obligations that apply to those countries which are members of the European Free Trade Association (EFTA) or the European Economic Area (EEA), where EU

[73] The Equality Act 2010 (Amendment) Regulations 2023; The Employment Rights (Amendment, Revocation and Transitional Provision Regulations) 2023.

[74] Explanatory Notes to the Retained EU Law (Revocation and Reform) Act 2023, para 52; REULA 2023, s 13.

[75] REULA 2023, s 3(3).

[76] Explanatory Notes to the Retained EU Law (Revocation and Reform) Act 2023, para 30.

[77] EU(W)A 2018, s 6(6A).

law—inclusive of the Charter—has a more indirect effect through the medium of the 'homogeneity' principle found in Article 6 of the EEA Agreement, governing the relationship between EU and EEA law, and which provides that:

> [w]ithout prejudice to future developments of case-law, the provisions of this Agreement, in so far as they are identical in substance to corresponding rules of [the EU Treaties] and to acts adopted in application of [those Treaties], shall, in their implementation and application, be interpreted in conformity with the relevant rulings of the [CJEU] given prior to the date of signature of this Agreement.

Article 3(2) of the Surveillance and Court Agreement further provides that '[i]n the interpretation and application of the EEA Agreement and this Agreement, the EFTA Surveillance Authority and the EFTA Court shall pay due account to the principles laid down by the relevant rulings by the [CJEU] given after the date of signature'. In practice, the EFTA Court has not distinguished between EU case law arising prior to and after the adoption of the EEA Agreement.[78] The Court has, in fact, stated that 'the objective of establishing a dynamic and homogenous EEA can only be achieved if EFTA and EU citizens, as well as economic operators enjoy—in reliance on EEA law—the same rights in both the EU and EFTA pillars of the EEA'.[79] The homogeneity principle extends to fundamental rights, with the Court referring to judgments of both the European Court of Human Rights (ECtHR) and the CJEU as well as Opinions of Advocates General in fundamental rights cases.[80] As Wahl remarks, '[f]rom the absence of incorporation one cannot just assume that the Charter does not have any effects of a secondary and/or indirect nature. Such ancillary effects can be significant and should in any event not be underestimated.'[81]

[78] Agreement on the European Economic Area [1994] OJ L1/3; Agreement between the EFTA States on the Establishment of a Surveillance Authority and a Court of Justice [1994] OJ L344/3; Carl Baudenbacher, 'The Relationship Between the EFTA Court and the Court of Justice of the European Union' in Carl Baudenbacher (ed), *The Handbook on EEA Law* (Springer 2016) 179, 184.

[79] Case E-18/11 *Irish Bank Resolution Corporation Ltd v Kaupþing hf* [2012] EFTA Ct Rep 592, para 122.

[80] Case E-2/03 *Ákæruvaldið (The Public Prosecutor) v Ásgeir Logi Ásgeirsson, Axel Pétur Ásgeirsson and Helgi Már Reynisson* [2003] EFTA Ct Rep 185, para 23; Case E-8/97 *TV 1000 Sverige AB v The Norwegian Government* [1998] EFTA Ct Rep 68, para 26; Case E-2/02 *Technologien Bau- und Wirtschaftsberatung GmbH and Bellona Foundation v ESA* [2003] EFTA Ct Rep 52.

[81] Nils Wahl, 'Uncharted Waters: Reflection on the Legal Significance of the Charter under EEA Law and Judicial Cross-Fertilisation in the Field of Fundamental Rights' in The EFTA Court (ed), *The EEA and the EFTA Court: Decentred Integration: To Mark the 20th Anniversary of the EFTA Court* (Hart 2014) 281, 282.

Within the social rights context specifically, the EEA Agreement incorporates all of the EU's directives on health and safety, equality law, and labour law, with the EFTA Court often continuing 'faithfully' to apply social rights principles deriving ultimately from CJEU case law.[82] The EFTA Court has notably shadowed the CJEU's interpretation of employment legislation, including in the context of the transfer of undertakings, an area with particular implications for the freedom to conduct a business.[83] For example, in *Deveci*, the Court relied on CJEU case law concerning the application of the freedom to conduct a business in Article 16 CFR, but without directly applying—or even addressing—that provision itself. According to the Court, '[t]he EEA Agreement has linked the markets of the EEA/EFTA States to the single market of the European Union. The actors of a market are, inter alia, undertakings. The freedom to conduct a business lies therefore at the heart of the EEA Agreement'.[84] As such, the freedom to conduct a business must be recognized in accordance with EEA law and national laws and practices, thereby constituting a general principle of EEA law.

The Trade and Cooperation Agreement governing the new relationship between the EU and the UK, while not generally providing for directly effective rights in accordance with Article 5 TCA, contains specific provisions preserving existing levels of social rights protection through (limited) non-regression and Level Playing Field provisions, albeit that these provisions do not encompass a principle of homogeneity, as such.[85] Section 29 of the European Union (Future Relationship) Act 2020 further provides for the consistent interpretation of existing domestic legislation, including retained EU law, with the UK's obligations under the TCA, which may have implications for the interpretation of assimilated EU law.

Overall, the changes brought about by the 2023 Act are likely to engender considerable legal uncertainty as to the precise future status of particular provisions of (former) retained EU law, with the interpretation of assimilated law—including its relationship to other provisions—also likely to lead to an important role for the judiciary in resolving any ambiguities. Moreover, at least three 'versions' of EU law will now be applicable in the UK, namely: (1) EU

[82] Catherine Barnard, 'Social Policy Law' in Carl Baudenbacher (ed), *The Handbook on EEA Law* (Springer 2016) 809.

[83] Case E-2/95 *Eilert Eidesund v Stavanger Catering A/S* [1995–1996] EFTA Ct Rep 1, para 24; Case E-3/96 *Tor Angeir Ask v ABB Offshore Technology AS and Aker Offshore Partner AS* [1997] EFTA Ct Rep 1.

[84] Case E-10/14 *Enes Deveci v Scandinavian Airlines System Denmark-Norway-Sweden* EFTA Ct Rep 1364, para 64.

[85] Paul Craig, 'Legal Structure, Rights and Enforceability' in Christopher McCrudden (ed), *The Law and Practice of the Ireland—Northern Ireland Protocol* (CUP 2022) 31.

legislation as applicable under the Withdrawal Agreement; (2) retained EU law for those situations arising prior to the end of 2023; and (3) assimilated EU law for events arising after that date. Indeed, there is potential overlap between the categories of retained—and now assimilated—law themselves, with the provisions of EU directives causing particular uncertainty.

It has already been noted that section 2 EU(W)A 2018 retains EU-derived domestic legislation, including legislation implementing EU labour law directives, but without retaining any underlying directive itself. Section 4 EU(W) 2018 similarly retains the rights found in directly effective provisions, including of directives, so long as these are 'of a kind' recognized by the CJEU before the transition period ended, or by UK courts for cases commenced before the end of the transition.[86] The latter may also include provisions that derive from fundamental rights espoused by the general principles and the Charter, despite the Charter never having (directly) enjoyed the status of retained EU law.

2.4 Conclusion

The purpose of this chapter has been to assess the consequences of the UK's departure from the EU both for the ongoing relevance of EU-derived fundamental rights concepts in that country, but also for the wider regime of fundamental rights within the Union itself. The UK has long enjoyed an antagonistic relationship with EU fundamental concepts, and with the Charter in particular, which may be reflective of more widespread scepticism towards codified sources of (international) fundamental rights. Particular antipathy has been directed at Union-derived social rights, which is illustrative of deeper fissures within both the domestic and EU fundamental regimes when it comes to the legal and normative status granted to social rights in comparison to more traditional civil and political rights. Nevertheless, it was argued that, despite Brexit, the measures governing the UK's departure from, and future relationship with, the EU provide for ongoing, albeit constrained, protections for EU-derived fundamental rights, notably in the labour law sphere.

Indeed, it was the deregulatory threat posed by Brexit that encouraged the EU to insist on the inclusion of such measures within the TCA. Although placed within a framework of ensuring a level competitive playing field in relation to trade, the ongoing protections granted to minimum social rights protections are illustrative of a recognition of the constitutional value attributed to those

[86] *Harris v Environment Agency* [2022] 9 WLUK 7.

rights within EU law more generally. Within domestic UK law, the Charter and Union fundamental rights concepts continue to enjoy a more indirect, and constitutionally diminished, status albeit that this 'deconstitutionalization' process has simultaneously led to the—perhaps, 'quasi-constitutional' or at least 'enhanced legislative'—concretization and embedment of such rights concepts within the domestic legal order as either 'retained' or 'assimilated' EU law. Employment law is also a field of substantive social protection which is not *necessarily* dependent on EU law, with employment legislation also embodying clear social aims which reflect wider international social rights commitments. Employment legislation thereby lends itself to an ongoing (EU-derived) 'purposive' approach to interpretation in the absence of Union-derived constitutional concepts, whether to ensure the objectives of the underlying legislation or to maintain regulatory alignment with the Union.[87]

It was then argued that the deprioritization of social rights that may follow the deregulatory thrust not only of Brexit itself, but also domestic legislative arrangements seeking to disentangle EU and UK law, will have implications for the legal and normative value granted to fundamental social rights and thereby the relationship of such rights with potentially competing economic rights and freedoms. Although the Charter continues to have an (indirect) influence over the interpretation and application of domestic legislation, it is clear that the absence of equivalent 'social' rights provisions within domestic law means that the provisions (and effects) of the Charter are not directly replicated. At the same time, Brexit itself may have provoked a renewed interest in the protection of social rights at Union level, both within and beyond the context of the UK's withdrawal and future trading relations.[88]

The ongoing uncertainly surrounding the precise status of certain Charter provisions also highlights the continued interrelationship between the general principles and the Charter. The removal of the Charter as a directly binding source of law following Brexit was motivated by largely political rather than practical or legal reasons, with the consequence that litigants will have to rely on the inherently less concrete general principles and only then insofar as such principles have been recognized prior to the end of the transition period, with their role now limited to the interpretation rather than potential disapplication of domestic law and with the general principles no longer forming part of

[87] Lord Sales, 'EU Retained Law: Purposive Interpretation when the Constitutional Architecture Changes', Annual Lecture of the UK Association for European Law, 20 November 2023, 7, 8.

[88] Simon Deakin, 'Brexit, Labour Rights and Migration: Why Wisbech Matters to Brussels' (2016) 17 Ger Law J 13.

domestic law per se from the end of 2023, ie unless their effects are preserved or restated.

The status of the Solidarity Title provisions as general principles is unclear, although for now their continued protection within the UK is ensured through domestic legislation, including provisions of retained or assimilated EU law, though on a more insecure basis. Aspects of the freedom to conduct a business in Article 16 CFR do constitute general principles, with freedom of contract and the ability to conduct a business also being 'facilitated' by UK law.[89] Indeed, business freedoms as fundamental rights owe their origins to the general principles of EU law, albeit that they have always been rather easily constrained by competing social (rights) considerations. As is now argued in Chapter 3, which explores the emergence of the freedom to conduct a business within EU law, both as a general principle and a Charter right, the latter has had the effect of re-emphasizing and strengthening the role of business freedoms, notably when the latter is incarnated in the more particular, if no less ambiguous, principle of freedom of contract, which is also a principle embodied within the English common law of contract. Understanding the relationship between business freedoms as general principles and the same concepts found within Article 16 CFR is crucial to determining the precise impact of the latter, including in its legal and normative value in the face of competing social rights.

[89] Department for Exiting the European Union, 'Charter of Fundamental Rights of the EU: Right by Right Analysis' (5 December 2017) 35.

PART II

THE RECONSTITUTION OF THE FREEDOM TO CONDUCT A BUSINESS AS A FUNDAMENTAL RIGHT

3

The Evolution of the Freedom to Conduct a Business as a Fundamental Right

3.1 Introduction

This chapter explores the development of the freedom to conduct a business as a fundamental right in European Union (EU) law. It charts the emergence of that concept as a general principle of EU law (Section 3.2) and evaluates the limitations that have been placed on those freedoms, notably through a re-assessment of the concept of the 'social function' of business freedoms. Lessons are drawn from broader theoretical discussion concerning the social function of property rights, while also applying a critical approach to the understanding of the relationship between individual and communitarian interests, in order to provide a more coherent understanding of the social function of the freedom to conduct a business. This approach also assists in addressing the apparent inconsistencies that have emerged through the reconstitution of the freedom to conduct a business as a fundamental right with the enactment of the Charter of Fundamental Rights (CFR) (Section 3.3).

The term 'reconstitution' is used here to connote the fact that although the freedom to conduct a business is constituted on the foundations of business freedoms as general principles, it is also normatively differenced from those principles, thereby also compounding the fragmentations surrounding the codification of Union fundamental rights exposed in Chapter 1. Despite some initial continuity between the two sources of rights, these compounded fragmentations would open up the potential for conceptual inconsistencies in the Court of Justice of the European Union's (CJEU) treatment of the freedom to conduct a business as a newly 'constitutionalized' fundamental right.

It has been noted that business freedoms were recognized as forming part of the Union's fundamental rights acquis from the very inception of the CJEU's development of fundamental rights as general principles of EU law. As such, there may not have been anything particularly unusual about the inclusion of the freedom to conduct a business within Article 16 CFR, despite the fact that the pre-existing general principles were not framed in such terms, and the

Business Freedoms and Fundamental Rights in European Union Law. Niall O'Connor, Oxford University Press.
 DOI: 10.1093/9780191982132.003.0004

freedom to conduct a business is alien to most international fundamental rights instruments. This chapter demonstrates that the early case law on the freedom to conduct a business as a fundamental Charter right is largely consistent with the CJEU's approach to the interpretation and application of business freedoms as general principles in that despite recognition of such freedoms as fundamental rights, they nevertheless tended to give way in the face of competing economic and social rights.

Section 3.4 assesses the CJEU's evolving approach to the relationship between the general principles and the Charter within the specific context of the freedom to conduct a business. The CJEU faces an arduous task in navigating the myriad overlapping sources of fundamental rights within the EU legal order. The argument here is that both the general principles and the Charter continue to provide autonomous—yet intertwined—sources for the protection of EU fundamental rights even if, in practice, they are likely to coincide. This involves addressing the question of the precise relationship between business freedoms as general principles and the freedom to conduct a business as a Charter right.

The CJEU's confused approach to managing this relationship has consequences not only with regard to the relative strength of the freedom to conduct a business as a fundamental right, but also for the coherence of the Union's wider fundamental rights regime. Section 3.5 concludes that there are many outstanding ambiguities surrounding the value of the freedom to conduct a business as a fundamental right, including its status as a 'right' or a 'principle', as well as its relationship to business freedoms as general principles. It was within the context of this ambiguity that the *expansive* conception of the freedom to conduct a business was eventually able to emerge, and which then forms the focus of Chapter 4.[1]

3.2 Business Freedoms as General Principles

3.2.1 The origins of business freedoms as general principles

The concept of the freedom to conduct a business first emerged from the general principles of EU law. The general principles are those unwritten rules of EU law that derive from sources other than the Treaty and secondary legislation,

[1] Case C-426/11 *Mark Alemo-Herron v Parkwood Leisure Ltd* ECLI:EU:C:2013:521.

for example international instruments to which the EU is a party, as well as the national constitutional traditions of the Member States.[2] One such general principle of EU law is the protection of fundamental rights.[3] As has been seen, the CJEU's earliest case law on the protection of fundamental rights as general principles is closely connected to the emergence of business freedoms as fundamental rights. From the case law, and indeed the Explanations attached to Article 16 CFR, it is possible to discern two principal components of business freedom as a general principle, at least from an 'individual' rights perspective, namely: (1) the freedom to pursue an economic activity; and (2) freedom of contract.

The Charter's Explanations point to the case of *Nold* as the source for the freedom to pursue an economic activity as a general principle.[4] In that case, Advocate General Trabucchi found that the freedom to choose and practise a trade or profession and the right to property were protected by the Member State constitutions and that the CJEU was obliged to take these rights into consideration in its reasoning, as they now formed part of the Union's legal order. Nevertheless, Nold's argument that the Commission had infringed these rights was simply too broad, as:

> [t]o impose conditions on the right of direct access to coal supplies implies that, however wide these conditions may be, there might always be an undertaking which is unable to satisfy them and which is consequently deprived of the possibility of carrying on direct trade. In that way, the result would be to deny the [Union] executive any power to intervene in the economy.[5]

In other words, any regulatory intervention in the economy could be viewed as inherently restrictive of the business and commercial freedoms of economic operators. Clearly, the concept of property rights and business freedoms within EU law, as with similar concepts found in other international instruments and domestic constitutions, is not absolute but may be subject to limitations in the public interest.[6] As the Advocate General in *Nold* went on to hold: '[r]ecognition by the Constitution does not mean that the subject matter

[2] Takis Tridimas, *The General Principles of EU Law* (2nd edn, OUP 2006) 1.

[3] Case C-29/69 *Erich Stauder v City of Ulm—Sozialamt* ECLI:EU:C:1969:57.

[4] Case C-4/73 *J. Nold, Kohlen- und Baustoffgroßhandlung v Commission of the European Communities* ECLI:EU:C:1974:51.

[5] AG Opinion in Case C-4/73 *J. Nold, Kohlen- und Baustoffgroßhandlung v Commission of the European Communities* ECLI:EU:C:1974:27.

[6] Albertina Albors-Llorens, 'Edging Towards Closer Scrutiny? The Court of Justice and its Review of the Compatibility of General Measures with the Protection of Economic Rights and Freedoms' in

is no longer subject to any rules.'[7] The CJEU agreed with the findings of the Advocate General, noting that although property rights and business freedoms were part of the general principles of EU law:

> [f]ar from constituting unfettered prerogatives, [they] must be viewed in the light of the social function of the property and activities protected thereunder. For this reason, rights of this nature are protected by law subject always to limitations laid down in accordance with the public interest [. . .] on condition that the substance of these rights is left untouched.[8]

It is clear from *Nold* that although the CJEU recognized the existence of a right to engage in commerce, it was not persuaded by arguments based on this right, nor did it offer any further guidance on what might constitute the 'substance' of the right.

Another striking feature of *Nold* is that this case may not even support the proposition it is held out as doing in the Explanations of the Charter, namely the idea that the freedom to pursue an economic activity *is* a general principle. The CJEU instead referred to the right 'freely to choose and practice their trade or profession', which suggests a much narrower concept than a broader right to pursue an economic activity. Indeed, the CJEU went on in that case to note that, '[a]s regards the guarantees accorded to a particular undertaking, they can in no respect be extended to protect mere commercial interests or opportunities, the uncertainties of which are part of the very essence of economic activity'.[9]

Again, this suggests that the scope of the economic freedom referred to is to be narrowly framed, recognizing that it does not extend to mere commercial or business 'interests'. In subsequent cases, the CJEU was inconsistent in the terminology used to describe the freedom to pursue an economic activity. In some cases, it repeated the 'trade or profession' formula found in *Nold*.[10] Other cases did indeed refer to the 'freedom to pursue an economic activity' whether

Anthony Arnull and others (eds), *A Constitutional Order of States? Essays in Honour of Alan Dashwood* (Hart 2011) 245, 250.

[7] AG Opinion in *Nold* (n 5).
[8] *Nold* (n 4) para 14.
[9] ibid.
[10] Case C-265/87 *Hermann Schräder HS Kraftfutter GmbH & Co KG v Hauptzollamt Gronau* ECLI:EU:C:1989:303, para 15.

alone or alongside a reference to the exercise of a trade or profession.[11] The only other case mentioned in the Charter's Explanations is *Eridania*, which provides that 'the carrying on of economic activities must be guaranteed'.[12]

It is also important to consider the wider context of the CJEU's decision in *Nold*. The 'constitution' under consideration was the European Coal and Steel Community (ECSC) treaty. Advocate General Trabucchi viewed this treaty as being inherently concerned with the organization of—and thereby intervention in—the economy. Article 2 of the Agreement constituting the ECSC set out its objective as being to contribute 'through the common market for coal and steel, to economic expansion, growth of employment and a rising standard of living'. To achieve these aims, the institutions of the then Community were tasked with ensuring the orderly supply to the common market by securing equal access to the sources of production, the establishment of low prices, and improved working conditions.

The modern EU has rather more ambiguous goals, with Article 3 of the Treaty on European Union (TEU), outlining the Union's commitment to 'the establishment of an internal market based on sustainable development, balanced economic growth, price stability and a highly competitive social market economy aimed at full employment and social progress'. Some of these concepts are rather nebulous and perhaps contradictory, and the extent to which they are best achieved through state intervention or deregulation remains unclear.[13] Nevertheless, in cases subsequent to *Nold*, the CJEU has continued to confirm its finding that restrictions on business freedoms could be justified on the basis of reasons in the general interest.

3.2.2 Limitations on business freedoms as general principles

In *Hauer*, a case involving restrictions on wine production, which allegedly infringed the right to property and economic freedom found within the German

[11] Joined Cases C-154/04 and 155/04 *The Queen, on the application of Alliance for Natural Health and Nutri-Link Ltd v Secretary of State for Health and The Queen, on the application of National Association of Health Stores and Health Food Manufacturers Ltd v Secretary of State for Health and National Assembly for Wales* ECLI:EU:C:2005:449, para 126; Case C-210/03 *The Queen, on the application of Swedish Match AB and Swedish Match UK Ltd v Secretary of State for Health* ECLI:EU:C:2004:802, paras 72, 74.

[12] Case C-230/78 *SpA Eridania-Zuccherifici nazionali and SpA Società Italiana per l'Industria degli Zuccheri v Minister of Agriculture and Forestry, Minister for Industry, Trade and Craft Trades, and SpA Zuccherifici Meridionali* ECLI:EU:C:1979:216, para 20.

[13] Catherine Barnard, 'EU "Social" Policy: From Employment Law to Labour Market Reform' in Paul Craig and Gráinne de Búrca (eds), *The Evolution of EU Law* (3rd edn, OUP 2021) 678.

Basic Law (Article 14 of the German Basic Law had also been raised in *Nold*), Advocate General Capotorti set out a rather expansive approach to the permissible restrictions on business freedoms, by drawing a distinction between: (1) property rights; and (2) the right to engage in economic activity:

> It is true that as a result of the prohibition on new plantings of vines the owner of a plot of land is prevented from pursuing wine-making activity by using the resources of his land hitherto not planted with vines, but it is clear that the owner retains the possibility of growing vines on other plots of land, belonging to him or other persons, on which vineyards already exist. Therefore, the limitation imposed affects the exercise of the right to property, not the exercise of the right to undertake economic activity, which is not guaranteed with regard to a particular sphere of application.[14]

The CJEU made a similar distinction in its judgment, holding that the 'right to property is guaranteed in the [Union] legal order in accordance with the ideas common to the constitutions of the Member States, which are also reflected in the first Protocol to the European Convention for the Protection of Human Rights'.[15] The question that then arose was:

> whether the restrictions introduced by the provisions in dispute in fact correspond to objectives of general interest pursued by the [Union] or whether, with regard to the aim pursued, they constitute a disproportionate and intolerable interference with the right of the owner impinging upon the very substance of the right to property.[16]

The CJEU confirmed that although property rights and economic freedoms are distinct concepts, the latter 'far from constituting an unfettered prerogative, must likewise be viewed in the light of the social function of the activities protected thereunder'.[17] The CJEU drew on the fact that the right to property has long existed as a human right at both national and European level. The German Basic Law, for example, has been held not to provide for the enjoyment of 'absolute' economic freedom.[18]

[14] AG Opinion in Case C-44/79 *Liselotte Hauer v Land Rheinland-Pfalz* ECLI:EU:C:1979:254.
[15] Case C-44/79 *Liselotte Hauer v Land Rheinland-Pfalz* ECLI:EU:C:1979:290, para 17.
[16] ibid para 23.
[17] ibid para 32.
[18] *Investment Aid Case* 4 BVerfGE 7 (1954); Daniela Caruso, '*Lochner* in Europe: A Comment on Keith Whittington's "Congress Before the *Lochner* Court"' (2005) 85 BULRev 867.

The importance of this case lies in its recognition that property rights are always amenable to restriction in relation to competing societal concerns as to the use (function) of such property. In this way, societal interests that may compete or even conflict with the right to property do not simply constitute 'limitations' on that right, but rather represent a manifestation of values with comparable or commensurate weight.[19] The right to pursue trade or commerce as a fundamental right is a related but distinct concept, but one that must be subject to similar limitations to those placed on the right to property. Subsequent cases (drawing on concepts derived from the right to property) confirmed the principle that the freedom to pursue an economic activity is not absolute but must rather be considered in relation to its social function and provided that any restrictions are proportionate, in the public interest, and do not impair the substance of the right.[20]

A clear example can be seen in *Spain and Finland*, a case that arose in the context of Directive 2002/15 on the organisation of working time of persons performing mobile road transport activities.[21] Article 1 of the Directive provides that its objective is to establish 'minimum requirements in relation to the organisation of working time in order to improve the health and safety protection of persons performing mobile road transport activities and to improve road safety and align conditions of competition'. Self-employed drivers were initially excluded from these protections, but were subsequently brought within the scope of the Directive.[22] The argument was that the inclusion of the self-employed prevented such drivers 'from devoting all their time and effort to the prosperity of their undertaking and constitutes an impermissible infringement of their freedom to pursue an occupation and their freedom to conduct a business'.[23] The claimant also argued that 'while there is indeed justification for regulating the working time of employees, in view of their subordinate position as regards their employer, no such need for protection exists

[19] Joseph HH Weiler, 'Eurocracy and Distrust: Some Questions Concerning the Role of the European Court of Justice in the Protection of Fundamental Human Rights Within the Legal Order of the European Communities' (1986) 61 Wash L Rev 1103, 1127.

[20] *Alliance for Natural Health* (n 11) para 126; *Swedish Match* (n 11) para 72; Case C-200/96 *Metronome Musik v Music Point Hokamp* ECLI:EU:C:1998:172, para 21; Case C-280/93 *Federal Republic of Germany v Council of the European Union* ECLI:EU:C:1994:367, para 78; Case C-177/90 *Ralf-Herbert Kühn v Landwirtschaftskammer Weser-Ems* ECLI:EU:C:1992:2, para 16; Case C-5/88 *Hubert Wachauf v Bundesamt für Ernährung und Forstwirtschaft* ECLI:EU:C:1989:321, para 18; *Schräder* (n 10) para 15; *Eridania* (n 12).

[21] Directive 2002/15/EC of the European Parliament and of the Council of 11 March 2002 on the organisation of the working time of persons performing mobile road transport activities [2002] OJ L80/35.

[22] Joined Cases C-184/02 and 233/02 *Kingdom of Spain and Republic of Finland v European Parliament and Council of the European Union* ECLI:EU:C:2004:497.

[23] ibid para 46.

for self-employed workers, who must be free to organise their activities as they wish'.[24]

This case is notable for its discussion of the freedom to pursue an occupation alongside the freedom to conduct a business, which suggests a close connection between these two concepts, with the Finnish government arguing that in pursuance of their occupation, the self-employed drivers 'must be able to decide freely on the amount and the organisation of the working time [they] intend to devote to [their] business activities'.[25] The CJEU concluded that 'the regulation of the working time of self-employed drivers envisaged in the contested directive cannot be regarded as a disproportionate and intolerable interference impairing the very substance of the freedom to pursue an occupation and the freedom to conduct a business'.[26]

In addition to the general freedom to pursue an economic activity, the CJEU has also recognized more particular—and equally limited—general principles under the umbrella of business freedoms, notably 'freedom of contract'. In *Sukkerfabriken*, the CJEU found that acts of the Union's institutions, which led to a restriction on freedom *to*—as opposed to *of*—contract, were permissible only to the extent that those acts gave explicit authority for the intervention in question.[27] The freedom 'to' contract suggests a potentially narrower conception of contractual autonomy, ie the freedom to *enter* contractual arrangements, albeit that this freedom also constitutes a component of the more general freedom of contract. In *Sukkerfabriken*, the interference with contractual autonomy was found not to be valid as 'no rules or information are provided on the prescribed procedure, the forms or the competent authorities for the action contemplated, such as would be expected if a restriction were to be placed upon the freedom of contract'.[28] It is not altogether clear whether this was intended to mean that freedom of contract can easily be limited by simply setting out a clear procedure for such limitation, or whether only a detailed articulation of the processes and institutions involved in the restriction of freedom of contract can ever justify such limitations.

In another case, the CJEU held that any act authorizing intervention into freedom of contract must stipulate the exact forms and procedures that the intervening authority must follow. As the CJEU put it, 'the right of parties to amend contracts concluded by them is based on the principle of contractual

[24] ibid para 47.
[25] ibid para 49.
[26] ibid para 50.
[27] Case C–151/78 *Sukkerfabriken Nykøbing Limiteret v Ministry of Agriculture* ECLI:EU:C:1979:4.
[28] ibid para 20.

freedom and cannot, therefore, be limited in the absence of [Union] rules imposing specific restrictions in that regard'.[29] The precise nature of such permissible restrictions remains largely ill-defined, thereby necessitating a reassessment of their potential scope, and which is essential to ground later consideration of the use of business freedom concepts to resist legislative restrictions or derogations.

3.2.3 Reassessing the restrictions on business freedoms as general principles

Despite some inconsistencies in terminology, a number of criteria emerge from the case law on business freedoms as general principles, against which any legislative restrictions on such freedoms must be assessed. First, business freedoms are not absolute but must be considered in relation to their social function. Secondly, any restrictions on business freedoms must be proportionate. Thirdly, restrictions on business freedoms must be in the public interest. Finally, any restrictions must not impair the very substance of business freedoms. The second and third conditions (proportionality and the public interest) are commonly applied to cases dealing with limitations to, or restrictions on, fundamental rights or freedoms and so can be dealt with more briefly here before turning to examine the other criteria further.

3.2.3.1 Proportionality and public interest considerations

With regard to the proportionately assessment, the CJEU in cases such as *Hauer* took as its starting point that restrictions on business freedoms as general principles, whether deriving from the European Convention on Human Rights (ECHR) or national constitutions, and imposed on public interest grounds, were lawful. After finding that restrictions on business freedoms could prima facie be justified, the CJEU then turned to examine whether the restrictions were in fact proportionate:

> It is still necessary to examine whether the restrictions introduced by the provisions in dispute in fact correspond to objectives in the general interest pursued by the [Union] or whether, with regard to the aim pursued, they

[29] Case C-240/97 *Kingdom of Spain v Commission of the European Communities* ECLI:EU:C:1999:479, para 99.

> constitute a disproportionate and intolerable interference with the rights of the owner, impinging on the very substance of the right to property.[30]

This approach has been described as representing 'a very high threshold for full review: only disproportionate and intolerable restrictions that affected the very essence of the right could be found incompatible with EU law'.[31] Subsequent case law continued to demonstrate the CJEU's deferential approach towards the EU legislature, with a finding of invalidity of a general measure following only 'in extreme cases of breach of an economic right or a general principle of law'.[32] In *Alliance for Natural Health*, for example, the CJEU held that:

> the [Union] legislature must be allowed a broad discretion in an area such as that involved in the present case, which entails political, economic and social choices on its part, and in which it is called upon to undertake complex assessments. Consequently, the legality of a measure adopted in that area can be affected only if the measure is manifestly inappropriate having regard to the objective which the competent institution is seeking to pursue.[33]

The proportionately hurdle has similarly been easily cleared in other cases concerning business freedoms as general principles.[34] Essentially, this represents nothing more than a restatement of the CJEU's settled case law on the proportionality principle, which is itself a general principle of EU law and which allows broad discretion to the Union institutions to act within their field of competence.[35]

The CJEU has taken a similarly broad approach to the application of the public interest requirement in its assessment of restrictions on business freedoms as general principles. Justifications that have been found to be in the public interest are wide ranging and include the protection of human health, the satisfactory organization of the wine market, the prevention of the overproduction of milk, the control of transport on inland waterways, the efficient operation of a levy scheme, road safety, and the indication of geographical origins of wines.[36] In other words, restrictions on business freedoms have tended to constitute rather mundane, or day-to-day operations of the (internal) market,

[30] *Hauer* (n 15) para 23.
[31] Albors-Llorens (n 6) 250.
[32] ibid.
[33] *Alliance for Natural Health* (n 11) para 52.
[34] *Metronome Musik* (n 20); *Schräder* (n 10); *Eridania* (n 12).
[35] Case C-233/94 *Federal Republic of Germany v European Parliament and Council of the European Union* ECLI:EU:C:1997:231, para 54.
[36] Respectively: *Swedish Match* (n 11); *Hauer* (n 15); *Kühn* (n 20); Joined Cases C-248/95 and 249/95 *SAM Schiffahrt GmbH and Heinz Stapf v Bundesrepublik Deutschland* ECLI:EU:C:1997:377;

with few obvious implications for the protection of fundamental rights. Of more significance for the application and limitation of fundamental rights concepts as general principles is the fourth condition, namely that restrictions should not impede the 'core' or the 'substance' of those rights.

3.2.3.2 The essence of business freedoms as general principles

The CJEU has consistently found that limitations on business freedoms do not go to the core of those freedoms. Indeed, the case law is notable for the relative ease with which the CJEU determines that measures, which appear on their face to interfere with business freedoms as general principles, can nevertheless be justified.[37] This is despite the often severe financial consequences for the holders of those rights, with the CJEU viewing such interference as restricting the *exercise* of business freedoms rather than an interference with the right itself, ie an interference with the operation of the relevant right, rather than with its substance.

The case law dealing with freedom of contract as a general principle does not specifically refer to the core or substance of that right, but in cases concerning the freedom to conduct a business within Article 16 CFR, which also protects freedom of contract, the CJEU has revisited this notion of the core or substance of a fundamental right, and has adopted a much stricter approach to ensuring that the very essence of business freedoms is not eroded.[38] This condition is therefore addressed in more detail in Chapter 4, when considering the CJEU's treatment of the essence of the freedom to conduct a business as a fundamental right. The focus of the present discussion turns instead to assessing in some detail the meaning of the first condition, which is not typically found in the CJEU's fundamental rights jurisprudence, namely the condition that business freedoms be considered in relation to their 'social function'.

3.2.3.3 A (social) functional approach to the restriction of business freedoms as general principles

In the first instance, the CJEU does not define what is meant by a 'social function', or what it might mean to say that business freedoms should be considered in relation to such a social function, a term that has been described, outside of the EU law context, as 'so pregnant with meaning and promise, yet for many so

Schräder (n 10); *Spain and Finland* (n 22); Case C–306/93 *SMW Winzersekt GmbH v Land Rheinland-Pfalz* ECLI:EU:C:1994:407.

[37] *Alliance for Natural Health* (n 11) para 128; *Swedish Match* (n 11) para 73.
[38] *Alemo-Herron* (n 1).

ill defined'.[39] Indeed, it is unclear how the CJEU's use of this concept might tie in with wider discussions within social theory on the social function or functional purpose of law, ie the law as 'a creature of social relations, serving their institutionalization, legitimation, and reproduction'.[40] Critical approaches to understanding the relationship between competing legal concepts can serve as a useful framework through which to examine seemingly contradictory or incoherent approaches to the treatment of business freedoms, including in their relationship to competing social rights concepts.

Further difficulties arise from the fact that the CJEU often refers to the concept of the social function of business freedoms, but without explaining precisely how those freedoms relate to the social function of property; property rights being the right to which the theory of a social function is usually said to apply, but which also has a connection to wider theoretical debates concerning 'progressive' conceptions of property rights.[41] The absence of explicit engagement with the manner in which the social function of property relates specifically to the freedom to conduct a business is likely a result of the earliest case law on the freedom to conduct a business being closely connected to the property rights found in particular Member State constitutions.[42] Indeed, the CJEU frequently refers to the Charter's three 'economic' rights essentially interchangeably, namely Article 15 CFR (the right to work), Article 16 CFR (the freedom to conduct a business), and Article 17 CFR (the right to property).

This approach may impede consideration of how limitations traditionally placed upon one right, for example the restriction of property rights in relation to their social function, might be applicable to the other economic rights found within the Charter, with the freedom to conduct a business forming the focus of the analysis here. Despite being a relatively innovative right—at least by international standards—the freedom to conduct a business derives additional normative weight and legitimacy through its derivation from the more orthodox—albeit perhaps no less contested—rights to (1) property; and to (2) pursue a freely chosen trade or occupation, ie the right to work, the latter of which has a particularly long pedigree as a fundamental right within the Union legal order, as seen in the discussion on the development of business freedoms as general principles.

[39] Colin Crawford, 'The Social Function of Property and the Human Capacity to Flourish' (2011) 80 Fordham L Rev 1089.

[40] Samuel Moyn, 'Reconstructing Critical Legal Studies' (4 August 2023) Yale Law School, Public Law Research Paper, 5, 9.

[41] eg Lorna Fox O'Mahony and Marc L Roark, 'Operationalising Progressive Ideas About Property: Resilient Property, Scale, and Systemic Compromise' (2024) 10 Tex A&M J Prop L 38.

[42] *Hauer* (n 15).

The most obvious normative connection between the right to property and the freedom to conduct a business is that both concepts are related to the notion of individual autonomy, including the protection of individual economic interests.[43] Indeed, the abstracted concepts of freedom of contract, property rights, and 'liberty', broadly speaking, can be said to form the core of classical (liberal) legal formalism.[44] At a more basic level, the 'expectancy' rights generated by freedom of contract can lead to the generation of 'property' rights over time in the sense that the protection of expectations 'invokes the rhetoric of property doctrine'.[45] The essential difference between the two rights, at least as far as the Charter is concerned, is that the right to property in Article 17 CFR relates largely to 'possessions', while the freedom to conduct a business in Article 16 CFR is more closely connected to 'entrepreneurial activity', 'commercial interests', 'business opportunities', or 'business-related rights'.[46]

The CJEU's approach to the interpretation and application of Article 17 CFR demonstrates the restrictive and constrained nature of the fundamental right to property found within the Charter, despite that right's grounding as a fundamental right in more traditional rights instruments such as the ECHR.[47] In particular, the CJEU has noted that the right to property is not absolute, but may be subject to restrictions in the general interest.[48] The right to property is thereby frequently recognized as being subject to legitimate restrictions in the public interest and with the proportionality doctrine being applied, but without always distinguishing between the various elements of that doctrine, ie the (1) objective; (2) appropriateness; and (3) necessity of the restriction; in addition to (4) the balancing of conflicting interests (proportionality *stricto sensu*), to determine the permissible extent of that interference.[49]

Regardless of the continued ambiguity surrounding the relationship between business freedoms and property rights, it is argued here that the concept of a 'social function' should be interpreted and applied broadly, meaning that the freedom to conduct a business should be subject to similar limitations to those placed on the right to property. Indeed, it has been suggested that the

[43] AG Opinion in Case C-134/15 *Lidl GmbH & Co KG v Freistaat Sachsen* ECLI:EU:C:2016:169, para 21.

[44] Betty Mensch, 'Freedom of Contract as Ideology' (1981) Stan L Rev 753, 759.

[45] ibid 762.

[46] AG Opinion in *Lidl* (n 43) para 26; Ferdinand Wollenschläger, 'Article 17(1) Right to Property' in Steve Peers and others (eds), *The EU Charter of Fundamental Rights: A Commentary* (2nd edn, Hart 2021) 489, 501–02.

[47] Art 1 of the Additional Protocol to the ECHR.

[48] Joined Cases C-8/15–10/15 *Ledra v European Commission and European Central Bank* ECLI:EU:C:2016:701, para 69; Case C-258/14 *Florescu v Sibiu* ECLI:EU:C:2017:448, para 51.

[49] Wollenschläger (n 46) 510.

right to economic initiative serves a social function in its own right, namely to protect the benefits—whether direct or indirect—deriving from a single free and competitive market.[50] The idea that property has a social function also reflects a relativist, as opposed to absolutist, view of property rights. In other words, rather than being exclusionary of others, the general or public interest can legitimately be acknowledged in the delimitation of property rights or, as argued here, business freedoms.[51]

This relativist position allows economic and social rights to be accounted for through the recognition of the social function of property, which has also been linked to broader fundamental rights concepts such as human capability and human flourishing.[52] The idea that property rights might have a 'social' function is also a feature of many domestic European constitutions, which serves to recognize that individuals—and individual rights—are rooted in larger communities, whose societal rights and interests may legitimately be considered in the regulation of property.[53]

Such an expansive approach is not at all apparent from a reading of the CJEU's case law. The idea of a 'social function' of property also has a long history as a critique of the liberal conception of property rights, which views property as a 'subjective and nearly absolute right', and one that 'controls the way in which most of the modern law and politics understands this institution [. . .] It is common for citizens, politicians and academics to view property as an individual right that is limited only by the rights of others and the public interest.'[54] The liberal conception of property, as espoused most forcefully by Locke and Hegel, is thus understood in terms of the agency and autonomy of personal selfhood, not merely in the sense of 'property owner', but also 'ontologically, in the way that ownership operates as a basic category through which we understand ourselves *and our relations with others*' [emphasis added].[55]

[50] Andrea Usai, 'The Freedom to Conduct a Business in the EU, its Limitations and its Role in the European Legal Order: A New Engine for Deeper and Stronger Economic, Social, and Political Integration' (2013) 14 Ger Law J 1867, 1886.

[51] Kevin Gray, 'Land Law and Human Rights' in Louise Tee (ed), *Land Law: Issues, Debates, Policy* (Willan 2002) 211, 221.

[52] Koldo Casla, 'The Right to Property Taking Economic, Social, and Cultural Rights Seriously' (2023) 45 HRQ 171, 196; Crawford (n 39).

[53] eg art 42(2) of the Italian Constitution; art 43(2) of the Irish Constitution; and art 14(2) of the German Basic Law; Michael R Antinori, 'Does *Lochner* Live in Luxembourg? An Analysis of the Property Rights Jurisprudence of the European Court of Justice' (1995) 18 Fordham Int'l L J 1778, 1781, 1785.

[54] Sheila R Foster and Daniel Bonilla, 'Symposium on the Social Function of Property: A Comparative Law Perspective' (2011) 80 Fordham L Rev 101.

[55] Matthew Stone, 'Roberto Esposito and the Biopolitics of Property Rights' (2015) 24 Social & Legal Studies 381, 383.

As such, the interest here lies not so much in the relationship between liberal theories of property and concepts such as 'the subject', 'subjectivity', or 'self-realization', but rather the manner in which the connection between property and the self has been used to justify private property, properly understood in terms of our relations with others. Kant, who explicitly linked the concepts of property and freedom (defined as the absence of 'constraint'), also recognized that property has a social function. As Stone remarks, for Kant 'property is not a pure metaphysical bond between an individual and an object; it concerns a social connection with others'.[56] In other words, our freedoms operate only insofar as they remain consistent with the freedom of others.[57]

Rousseau, on the other hand, thought that property rights could be *subordinated* to community rights to regulate property for the common good, which is analogous to the more recent constitutional conception that property rights can be limited in relation to their social function, a view that is more closely reflective of republican—as opposed to liberal—conceptions of property.[58] The republican tradition views freedom as the absence of 'domination', while liberal conceptions view freedom as the absence of interference.[59] At the same time, at least in the context of the United States, 'liberty' of contract also came to embody assumptions as to how a republican constitutional regime should function, with separate and inviolate 'conceptual spheres' within the political economy, namely the 'public' and the 'private'.[60] The 'pre-political' vision of liberty of contract created a presumption in favour of that liberty, and one that could only be rebutted by measures that were genuinely 'public' and 'general', as opposed to partial or class-based.[61]

This view is perhaps based on an outdated conception of the relationship between the public and the private spheres, and more importantly the relationship between fundamental rights and private law. Indeed, the boundary between the public and the private is no longer a useful conceptual distinction within the fundamental rights context, as evidenced within EU law through the concept of 'horizontality' and perhaps more importantly through the recognition of business freedoms as 'fundamental rights'. In other words, not only are private (contractual) relations increasingly 'infiltrated' by (constitutionalized)

56 ibid 384.
57 ibid 383.
58 Antinori (n 53) 1787, 1808, 1814.
59 Eduardo Gill-Pedro, 'Freedom to Conduct a Business in EU Law: Freedom from Interference or Freedom from Domination?' (2017) 9 European Journal of Legal Studies 103, 107.
60 G Edward White, 'Revisiting Substantive Due Process and Holmes's *Lochner* Dissent' (1997) 63 Brook L Rev 87, 105.
61 ibid 106.

fundamental rights concepts, but they are increasingly underpinned by those very concepts.[62] In a similar vein, the formalist distinction between negatively oriented civil and political rights and positively oriented economic and social rights is no longer particularly useful, given the increased recognition that fundamental rights are multifaceted and interconnected.[63]

For example, property, while a quintessential 'liberty' right, can also be conceived as a 'social right' in the sense that it guarantees 'social access' for individuals.[64] In other words, the right to property can be seen as guaranteeing the individual's ability to 'sell' their labour through participation in the market, thereby generating a 'stake' in society'.[65] Within the employment context, this 'capabilities' conceptualization of 'freedom' is coupled with broader notions of freedom as the absence of 'domination' (as opposed to mere formal 'autonomy' or 'choice').[66] It is argued in Part III that a genuine 'socialization' of property rights or business freedoms necessitates legislative intervention derived from public law or fundamental rights concepts. That is to say that avoiding the commodification of social rights, such as the right to work, ie the right to 'sell' labour, requires a reconceptualization of business freedoms and property rights in such a way as to erode the traditional divide between the public and private sphere, with the aim of allowing the latter to be infused with fundamental (social) rights concepts and 'values', particularly given the absence of a clear hierarchy within the Charter between the ill-defined and potentially contradictory values of 'freedom' and 'solidarity'.

Indeed, it can be argued that the right to property should not be tied to the liberal notion of 'freedom' at all, but should rather be understood in its social and political context, that is to say within the context of social relations and power dynamics.[67] Duguit, for example, suggests that 'property has internal limits—not just external ones as in the case of the liberal right to property'.[68] In other words, property is not itself a right but rather a social function, and one which constitutes an inner limit in the sense of recognizing the potential

[62] Olha O Cherednychenko, 'Rediscovering the Public/Private Divide in EU Private Law' (2020) 26 ELJ 27; Dorota Leczykiewicz and Stephen Weatherill (eds), *The Involvement of EU Law in Private Law Relationships* (Hart 2013); Olha O Cherednychenko, 'Fundamental Rights and Private Law: A Relationship of Subordination or Complementarity?' (2007) 3 Utrecht Law Review 1.

[63] Sandra Fredman, *Comparative Human Rights Law* (OUP 2018) 59.

[64] Joshua D Hawley, 'The Intellectual Origins of (Modern) Substantive Due Process' (2014) 93 Tex L Rev 275, 289.

[65] ibid.

[66] Simon Deakin, 'Contracts as Capabilities. An Evolutionary Perspective of the Autonomy-Paternalism Debate' (2010) 3 Erasmus Law Review 141; Guy Davidov, 'Non-waivability in Labour Law' (2020) 40 OJLS 482, 491, fn 52.

[67] Stone (n 55) 385.

[68] Léon Duguit, *Las transformaciónes del derecho público y privado* (Editorial Heliasta 1975) 179.

burden (eg Hohfeldian 'duties') that the exercise of a right might impose on others.[69] Duguit posits three specific challenges to the liberal conception of property rights. First, he contests the existence of an isolated individual, which constitutes the starting point for the liberal conception of property rights. Secondly, he argues that even if such an isolated individual did exist, this conception would be inconsistent with the right to property, given that were people to 'live separately from other members of society, it does not make sense to speak of a right that imposes negative duties on third parties'.[70] Finally, Duguit objects to the classical notion that property exists solely to serve individual interests, which 'obscures the connections between the economic needs of the community and the wealth that is recognized and protected through the institution we know as property. It should also serve the community'.[71]

It is also clear from Duguit's critique that the liberal conception of property rights recognizes that such rights may be limited in consideration of the competing rights of other individuals or in accordance with the public interest. Indeed, there is not necessarily a contradiction between the liberal and social function theories of property rights as '[t]he idea that property owners owe affirmative obligations to the welfare of others, and to societal welfare more generally, can map onto a number of different ideological orientations, including classical liberalism'.[72] Critical Legal Studies (CLS) goes further, and suggests that there is instead a more 'fundamental contradiction' embedded within the (liberal) conception of property itself, namely the tension or contradiction between individual and communitarian values.[73] The tension between these competing interests or values is particularly acute in the fundamental rights context, which tends to involve the opposition of communal (state or societal) interests and individual interests.[74]

3.2.3.4 A critical appraisal of the restriction of business freedoms as general principles

The concept of 'contradiction' is used within CLS to denote the law's 'simultaneous commitment to opposing discourses, values or dichotomies'.[75] These contradictions manifest as 'problematic' in large part due to the emphasis

[69] Andrei Marmor, 'On the Limits of Rights' (1997) 16 Law & Phil 1.
[70] Duguit (n 68) 178.
[71] ibid 237.
[72] Foster and Bonilla (n 54) 107.
[73] Denise Meyerson, 'Fundamental Contradictions in Critical Legal Studies' (1991) 11 OJLS 439.
[74] Weiler (n 19) 1127.
[75] J Paul Oetken, 'Form and Substance in Critical Legal Studies' (1991) 100 Yale L J 2209, fn 5; Mark Tushnet, 'Some Current Controversies in Critical Legal Studies' (2011) 12 Ger Law J 290, 296.

placed by liberal legalism on consistency and predictability in the law in the sense that legal rules 'yield determinant and predictable results in their application in the juridical process'.[76] The very purpose of the CLS movement is to uncover contradictions in the law in order to demonstrate the erratic, ambiguous, and inconsistent interpretation and application of legal rules, or to demonstrate the law's tilt in favour of the status quo.[77]

Without wishing to engage with (or accept) all of its precepts, it is argued here that the CLS idea of 'fundamental contradiction' as a critique of liberal legalism resonates strongly with the notion that concepts such as liberal property rights are imbued with essentially contradictory principles, which consist of rival social visions (or values, in the language adopted by the Charter) that may be difficult (or impossible) to reconcile. In other words, once business freedoms have been conceptualized as the 'right' to be protected, competing economic and social interests may be framed as 'restrictions' or 'derogations' from that right, which has the consequence of privileging the freedom to conduct a business over competing Charter provisions, which enjoy nominally equivalent status as fundamental rights. This approach ultimately derives from the context of EU free movement law, whereby restrictions and derogations on fundamental freedoms must be interpreted strictly.[78] This approach also demonstrates the importance of the association between the freedom to conduct a business as a fundamental right within Article 16 CFR and the freedom of establishment found within Article 49 of the Treaty on the Functioning of the European Union (TFEU), a connection which is addressed further in Chapter 4 when considering the CJEU's expansive approach to the interpretation of business freedoms as fundamental rights.

The core critique of liberal legalism proffered by the CLS movement is its inherently flawed claim to be able to 'resolve the persistent and systematic conflict between individual and social interests through the mechanism of objective rules within a framework of procedural justice'.[79] Kennedy argued that all legal contradictions follow ultimately from the fundamental contradiction between

[76] Alan Hunt, 'The Theory of Critical Legal Studies' (1986) 6 OJLS 1, 4, 16.

[77] Raymond Wacks, *Understanding Jurisprudence: An Introduction to Legal Theory* (6th edn, OUP 2020) 344; Stefan Sciaraffa, 'Critical Legal Studies: A Marxist Rejoinder' (1999) 5 Legal Theory 201; Mark Tushnet, 'Critical Legal Studies: An Introduction to its Origins and Underpinnings' (1986) 36 J Legal Educ 505; Duncan Kennedy, 'The Structure of Blackstone's Commentaries' (1979) 28 Buff L Rev 205.

[78] Joined Cases C-368/20 and 369/20 *NW v Landespolizeidirektion Steiermark Bezirkshauptmannschaft Leibnitz* ECLI:EU:C:2022:298, para 64.

[79] Hunt (n 76) 5.

individual autonomy (self) and the community or societal interest (others).[80] Neither of these visions (individual or communitarian) can be considered dominant, with the 'correct' balance to be achieved between competing rights and interests instead depending on other factors such as prevailing social and political hierarchies.[81] CLS has also highlighted the law's entrenchment of 'existing structures of domination and illegitimate hierarchy' and bureaucratic power, for example that enjoyed by employers or management over workers, albeit that this critique has been applied largely in the context of the United States, which lacks the sophisticated—albeit itself incomplete—system for the protection of economic and social rights that has emerged within the EU.[82]

The discussion on the social function of property can be applied to the freedom to conduct a business essentially by analogy, in the absence of any detailed engagement by the CJEU with this (contested) vision of property rights. In addition, CLS scholars have engaged more explicitly in the application of the concept of 'fundamental contradiction' to at least one aspect of business freedom as a fundamental right, namely freedom of contract, albeit again outside the context of EU law. Concepts such as 'liberty of contract' and related property rights were considered so abstract that they often led to contradictory conclusions, which ultimately represented wider social divisions, for example between employers and (organized) labour.[83] This is also reflective of broader attempts at introducing 'social justice' concepts into contract law more generally, which involves 'a greater inclusion of other social values than purely market-oriented, liberal ones', but which is itself encumbered by the tension that exists between, for example, freedom and solidarity or between individualism and altruism.[84]

There can be little agreement, it is suggested, as to the precise meaning and content of concepts such as freedom of contract or business freedoms, and with such vague concepts themselves capable of being used essentially to justify almost any judicial decision.[85] Critical legal scholarship, much like the Legal Realism from which it is said to be inspired, thereby emphasizes the

[80] Robert W Gordon, 'Critical Legal Histories' (1984) 36 Stan L Rev 57, 114; Duncan Kennedy, 'Form and Substance in Private Law Adjudication' (1976) 89 Har L Rev 1685; Peter Gabel and Duncan Kennedy, 'Roll Over Beethoven' (1984) 36 Stan L Rev 1; Hunt (n 76) 25.

[81] Wacks (n 77) 358.

[82] Duncan Kennedy, 'Critical Labor Law Theory: A Comment' (1981) 4 Berkeley J Emp & Lab L 503; Peter Goodrich, 'Critical Legal Studies in England: Prospective Histories' (1992) 12 OJLS 195.

[83] Tushnet (n 77) 505; Duncan Kennedy, 'Distributive and Paternalist Motives in Contract and Tort Law' (1982) 41 Md L Rev 563; Roberto Mangabeira Unger, 'The Critical Legal Studies Movement' (1983) 96 Harv L Rev 561.

[84] Thomas Wilhelmsson, 'Varieties of Welfarism in European Contract Law' (2004) 10 ELJ 712.

[85] Tushnet (n 77) 509.

importance of power relations in the use and development of the law, which serve to undermine the law's 'predictability' in part due to the 'under determinacy' of the social function of law as well as the fundamentally contradictory concepts that are the subject of judicial reasoning.[86]

Unger, in particular, has highlighted the various 'principles' and 'counter-principles' that can operate within contract law doctrine, for example the dichotomy between freedom of contract and concepts such as fairness and community.[87] Competition between such principles increases the role of 'judicial choice', albeit that either side of fundamental contradiction(s), dichotomies, or antimonies may be emphasized by courts at any particular time, which can lead to the emergence of 'periodizations' or 'trends' in doctrinal development.[88] Unger thereby charts a path between the two poles of (1) law as essentially indeterminate, under determinate, or unpredictable; and (2) a (social) functional view of law as entrenching existing hierarchies and power structures of domination.[89]

Within the EU law context, there is also the added complexity created by the CJEU's methodological approach to the recognition of general principles from the 'common' constitutional traditions of the Member States. Inevitably, different Member State legal systems will emphasize different aspects of particular rights, such as property rights or business freedoms, which may also be animated by different values, which may themselves change over time. For example, certain Member State constitutions are more explicit in recognizing the 'social function' of property rights, thereby placing the emphasis on social or communitarian interests, while others favour individual property rights, which are thereby further shielded from legislative or regulatory intervention.[90] In a similar—and related—way, the duties required to secure the protection of a particular right may vary (as opposed necessarily to the nature of the right itself).[91]

The risk of this approach is to view the existence of potentially conflicting principles and counter-principles as a 'symptom of incoherence'.[92] Rather, it is suggested here that the freedom to conduct a business as a fundamental right contains its own internal limitations, which thereby form an inherent part of—rather than an exception to—that freedom. Article 16 CFR recognizes the

86 ibid 507; Moyn (n 40) 9.
87 Unger (n 83) 616.
88 Kennedy (n 80); Hunt (n 76) 21.
89 Moyn (n 40) 10.
90 Weiler (n 19) 1128; *Hauer* (n 15) para 20.
91 Marmor (n 69) 4.
92 Meyerson (n 73) 444.

freedom to conduct a business, but *only* to the extent to which that freedom accords with 'Union law and national laws and practices'. Of course, the latter concept also needs to be imbued with more concrete meaning, a task that has essentially been left to the CJEU in the absence of any further detail within the Explanations attached to the Charter. This absence further highlights the importance of the horizontal provisions of the Charter addressed in Chapter 1, which govern the relationship between rights, freedoms, and principles both within and beyond the Charter itself. It has also been seen that in cases concerning business freedoms as general principles, which thereby form part of 'Union law', the CJEU has articulated potential restrictions on those freedoms which may, for example, be limited in relation to their 'social function'.

A consideration of the competing interests that might lie at the heart of contractual autonomy as a component of the freedom to conduct a business is particularly important given the fact that, in cases dealing specifically with freedom of contract as a general principle, the CJEU does not refer to that freedom being limited by any social function. Rather, the case law merely states that limitations on freedom of contract—to the extent that such permissible limitations might exist—may only take the form of Union rules, setting out 'prescribed procedures' and 'imposing specific restrictions'.[93]

Freedom of contract can be said to represent the 'individualism' aspect of the fundamental contradiction, in that the concept seeks to preserve the freedom of the individual to choose the terms of any agreement without having that agreement interfered with on altruistic, protectionist, or paternalistic grounds.[94] The 'communitarian' aspect of the fundamental contradiction can be seen in the fact that the law does indeed interfere with freedom of contract, for example by seeking to protect the weaker party to contractual arrangements, thereby ensuring 'effective' consent, or to deny the enforceability of 'unfair' contracts.[95] 'Consent' or 'choice' are, of course, among the many potential values underpinning contract law generally or freedom of contract specifically, with other possible values including independence, efficiencies, promise, or collaboration.[96] The Draft Common Frame of Reference for a harmonized EU contract law, for example, espouses the 'underlying principles' of freedom, security, justice, and efficiency, which represents a narrowing down of the

[93] *Spain v Commission* (n 29) para 99; *Sukkerfabriken* (n 27) para 20.
[94] Unger (n 83) 625.
[95] ibid 632.
[96] Martijn W Hesselink, 'EU Private Law Injustices' (2022) 41 YEL 83, 108.

previously stated principles found in earlier versions and which included, for example, the principle of 'solidarity and social responsibility'.[97]

Freedom of contract can also be said to be incoherent in its own terms, in that while seeking to protect the freedom to enter into mutually beneficial contractual arrangements, that freedom simultaneously seeks to hold us to our own contractual promises even after they cease to be beneficial.[98] Of course, this view stems from a liberal conception of 'freedom' as the absence of constraint on the individual's will, and also overlooks the idea (found even within classical contract law doctrine) that voluntarily accepted restrictions on freedom of contract are legitimate.[99] As such, it is suggested that there is nothing inherently contradictory with the idea that, through the exercise of freedom of contract, the individual can freely consent to the restriction of that same freedom, for example where such restriction leads to a benefit such as continuity in the acquisition of a new business. In other words, freedom of contract can be instrumentalized to achieve economic and social goals. Restrictions and limits on freedom of contract, where accepted by everyone, can thereby be both freedom-enhancing and, as argued here, (fundamental) rights-enhancing.[100]

Understood in this way, the CLS concept of fundamental contradiction constitutes a useful framing device in rationalizing the notion that business freedoms should be limited in relation to their 'social function', ie components of the freedom to conduct a business such as freedom of contract can legitimately be restricted in the face of competing social rights or interests. The content and relative weight of the latter social rights may fluctuate over time, in part due to the indeterminacy of the concept, leading to apparent contradictions in the case law between business freedoms and its counterweights, including competing social rights concepts. These apparent contradictions are reflective of wider tensions between individual and communitarian values within Union fundamental rights, or indeed within the Union's wider legal order. In the same vein, the notion of fundamental contradiction can help to explain how the relative strength of concepts such as business freedoms have evolved over time.[101]

Of course, these changes do not operate in a legal or doctrinal vacuum, hence the necessity of assessing the scaffolding provided by the Charter and

[97] Martijn W Hesselink, 'If You Don't Like Our Principles We Have Others: On Core Values and Underlying Principles in European Private Law: A Critical Discussion of the New "Principles" Section in the Draft Common Frame of Reference' in Roger Brownsword and others (eds), *The Foundations of European Private Law* (Hart 2011) 59.

[98] Mensch (n 44) 755.

[99] Meyerson (n 73) 442.

[100] ibid 444.

[101] Niall O'Connor, 'Whose Autonomy is it Anyway? Freedom of Contract, the Right to Work and the General Principles of EU Law' (2020) 49 ILJ 285, 304.

the wider Union fundamental rights framework as addressed in Part I. The real difficulty, it is suggested, lies in establishing the relative normative weight to be attributed to broader values and concepts within the Charter such as 'solidarity', 'dignity', and 'freedom', which appear indeterminate and provide no indication as to the relationship between them. It is argued here that the legislative implementation of Charter provisions actually serves to decrease their indeterminacy, which thereby reinforces their normative value in the face of competing business freedoms, and in a way which at first glance appears inconsistent with the rights and principles distinction suggested by the Charter, but which more clearly reflects the tension between overlapping and potentially competing (conflicting) 'values' inherent in the Charter's 'indivisible' approach to the articulation of fundamental rights.[102]

There is admittedly a certain circularity here, in that the more specific provisions of the Charter, for example the right to paid annual leave found within Article 31(2) CFR, can lend normative content to the Charter's values, for example the value of 'solidarity', but which are themselves further specified within the provisions of the Charter. In a similar way, the provisions of the Charter are derived from pre-existing concepts drawn from the case law of the CJEU, notably concerning general principles, as well as Union legislation which must then itself be interpreted in light of the Charter. As such, there is the risk that fundamental rights concepts, such as the freedom to conduct a business which are articulated at a high level of abstraction, are to remain essentially devoid of precise normative content, with recourse to underlying values and the language of 'balancing' offering little assistance in this regard.[103]

It can be seen from this discussion that business freedoms—in various guises and under various labels—have a long pedigree as general principles of EU law, but as Advocate General Cruz Villalón noted in *Alemo-Herron*, 'the case-law, has not, in fact, provided a full and useful definition of this freedom. The judgments in which the Court has had occasion to rule in this area have gone no further than either referring to the right to property or simply citing the provisions of Article 16 of the Charter.'[104] It is also clear that the freedom to pursue an economic activity and freedom of contract cannot be the only components of the freedom to conduct a business. The Explanations to the Charter confirm that free competition is another element of Article 16 CFR, but it is also evident from the case law on the general principles that the right

[102] Ronald Dworkin, *Law's Empire* (Harvard University Press 1986) 268–71.
[103] Tushnet (n 77) 516.
[104] AG Opinion in Case C–426/11 *Mark Alemo-Herron v Parkwood Leisure Ltd* ECLI:EU:C:2013:82, para 49.

to work, the freedom to pursue a trade or profession, and the right to property are also relevant, albeit that those rights are now located elsewhere within the Charter.[105] It was against this confused backdrop that the freedom to conduct a business as a fundamental Charter 'right' emerged.

3.3 The Freedom to Conduct a Business as a Charter 'Right'

3.3.1 The origins of the freedom to conduct a business as a Charter right

Article 16 CFR provides that '[t]he freedom to conduct a business in accordance with Union law and national laws and practices is recognised'. Very little guidance on the *precise* purpose of this provision can be gleaned from the recently consolidated *travaux préparatoires* to the Charter, but a number of suggested amendments to the text of that provision were put forward throughout the drafting process, some of which are indicative of disagreements surrounding the reach of the freedom to conduct a business as a fundamental right.[106] The original formulation of Article 16 CFR merely provided that 'the freedom to conduct a business is recognised' without the added proviso concerning EU law, national laws and practices.[107] Some of the amendments suggested during the drafting process sought to expand the scope of the freedom to conduct a business.

One suggestion was that the term used in the French language version to describe the freedom to conduct a business, ie 'la liberté d'entreprise', should be replaced with the broader concept of 'la liberté d'entreprendre' (right of free enterprise), a suggestion that did not find its way into the final draft of the Charter.[108] Lord Goldsmith advocated the wide formulation 'freedom to conduct a business and the free movement of workers, goods, capital and services and the freedom of establishment in accordance with Community

[105] The freedom to found an educational establishment is stated in the Explanations to art 14 CFR to be 'one of the aspects of the freedom to conduct a business'.

[106] Niall Coghlan and Marc Steiert (eds), 'The Charter of Fundamental Rights of the European Union: The *travaux préparatoires* and Selected Documents' (7 January 2021); Hilary Hogan, 'The Origin and Development of Article 16 of the Charter of Fundamental Rights' (2023) 2 European Law Open 753, 758.

[107] Praesidium note: Complete Text of the Charter Proposed by the Praesidium, 28 July 2000 in Coghlan and Steiert (n 106) 3058.

[108] Observations reçues relatives au Document CHARTE 4422/00 in Coghlan and Steiert (n 106) 3387.

law shall be protected'.[109] It was observed that it would be valuable to expand on the existing formulation of Article 16 CFR to 'include the other economic freedoms which are at the heart of the Communities and are of enormous importance to many people in the Union whose jobs and livelihood depend on them'.[110]

Despite remaining inexplicit on this point, Article 16 CFR has subsequently been interpreted as being deeply intertwined with corollary economic freedoms such as the right to pursue a trade or occupation, which is now also recognized as an autonomous right in Article 15 CFR. It was also argued that the word 'recognised' sat 'unhappily' with the terms 'protected', 'guaranteed', or 'respected' used in other Charter provisions, and that '[f]reedom of enterprise is an important right which should attract similar protection'.[111] Article 51(1) CFR requires that rights be 'respected', whereas principles need only be 'observed', which suggests a reduced level of obligation on the Union and Member States in ensuring the protection of principles.

In contrast to this proposed broad formulation of the freedom to conduct a business, trade unions argued that the corporate social responsibilities ('responsabilités sociales') of companies should be recognized within the text of Article 16 CFR.[112] Another suggestion was '[t]he Union recognises and respects the entitlement to conduct a business in accordance with Community law and national law and practice', the purpose of this formulation being to ensure that Article 16 CFR was granted the status of a principle rather than a right, efforts which may ultimately have been unsuccessful given the CJEU's subsequent expansive treatment of the freedom to conduct a business, as explored in Chapter 4.[113]

Wider formulations combining the current Article 16 CFR with elements of other Charter provisions were also evident, including the right to work which is now found in Article 15 CFR. For example, the proposal from Georges Berthu MEP was formulated as '[t]he freedom to choose one's occupation, to conclude contracts and to set up a business shall be respected by Community law', with this proposal also being among the few to include explicit reference to an aspect of freedom of contract, as opposed to business freedoms more

[109] ibid 3276.
[110] ibid.
[111] ibid.
[112] Contribution de la Confédération européenne des syndicats et de la plateforme des ONGs in Coghlan and Steiert (n 106) 5631.
[113] Observations reçues relatives au Document CHARTE 4422/00 in Coghlan and Steiert (n 106) 3465.

generally, ie the right to 'conclude' a contract.[114] Other proposed amendments to the freedom to choose an occupation also included explicit reference to the freedom to 'set up in business' or the right to engage in 'business activity', which again may help explain why the freedom to conduct a business was eventually extracted to form its own Charter provision separate from—albeit intimately related to—the right to work.[115]

Despite these proposed amendments, the wording of Article 16 CFR survived relatively unchanged throughout the Convention, with the final version merely adding the reference to national laws and practices, which can also be found in other Charter provisions, and which has the cross-cutting purpose of attempting to limit the justiciability of 'principles'. The record of the Convention may be incomplete and, admittedly, only the contributions to the Convention written in French or English, but which formed the majority of contributions, were accessible to the author. Overall, however, there appears to have been minimal discussion on the inclusion of the freedom to conduct a business in the Charter, save for a reference to the potentially differing weight to be attributed to business freedoms and social rights, as well as the fact that the freedom to conduct a business was not among the rights on the list initially drawn up as a basis for discussion at the Convention.[116]

The absence of any clear rationale for the inclusion of Article 16 CFR within the catalogue of fundamental rights leads to the open question of that provision's precise purpose within the Union's fundamental rights order, including the relationship between the freedom to conduct a business and potentially competing rights and principles, notably within the Charter's Solidarity Title. The EU Fundamental Rights Agency has described the objective of Article 16 CFR as being 'to safeguard the right of each person in the EU to pursue a business without being subject to either discrimination or disproportionate restrictions'.[117] Article 16 CFR applies to both natural persons and companies who are 'conducting' a 'business'.[118] The meaning of these terms has not been addressed in any detail by the CJEU, but it has been suggested

[114] Praesidium note: amendments submitted by Members on CHARTE 4316/00 in Coghlan and Steiert (n 106) 2499.

[115] ibid 2508.

[116] 'La liberté d'entreprendre dans la Charte est absolue, mais les droits sociaux sont étroitment encadrés', Verbatim minutes from the session on 24 June 2002 in Coghlan and Steiert (n 106) 7505; Commission Communication COM(2000) 559 final on the Charter of Fundamental Rights of the EU, 13 September 2000 in Coghlan and Steiert (n 106) 3762.

[117] European Union Agency for Fundamental Rights, 'Freedom to Conduct a Business: Exploring the Dimensions of a Fundamental Right' (2015) 23.

[118] Eduardo Gill-Pedro, 'Whose Freedom is it Anyway? The Fundamental Rights of Companies in EU Law' (2022) 18 EuConst 183, 187.

that any legitimate form of profit-making activity would be covered, with the freedom to conduct a business also encompassing the entire life cycle of business activities: establishing a business, the operation of the business, as well as the closing of the business, for example in the case of insolvency.[119]

The difficulty with this broad approach to defining the scope of the freedom to conduct a business is that it overlaps significantly with other substantive (constitutional) provisions of EU law, notably those rules governing freedom of movement within the internal market, which includes the freedom of establishment.[120] The relationship between business freedoms as fundamental rights and the Union's free movement provisions therefore has the potential to reinforce the place of the freedom to conduct a business within the constitutional structure of the Union more generally. As such, the freedom to conduct a business found in Article 16 CFR risks becoming somewhat all-encompassing of rules deriving from internal market law, fundamental rights, and ordinary legislative restrictions on commercial activity, which may thereby upset existing balances, competences, and limitations placed on those rules.

Despite these ambiguities, the inclusion of Article 16 CFR within the Charter is a significant fundamental rights development, representing the first explicit expression of the freedom to conduct a business within a supranational human rights instrument.[121] Elements of the freedom to conduct a business have a long pedigree within the general principles as well as the constitutions of several Member States from which the general principles derived, but which have now been given a more prominent role by virtue of their inclusion in the Charter, and which explicitly endows those freedoms with the status of 'fundamental rights'. This is particularly true of freedom of contract, which was largely absent from the general principles case law, but which has been granted a more significant status within Article 16 of the Charter, despite its conspicuous absence from the text of that provision itself.

The most prominent element of the case law on business freedoms as general principles, namely the freedom to conduct a trade or profession, largely finds expression in the right to engage in work within Article 15 CFR rather than within the freedom to conduct a business, with the latter instead protecting the freedom to engage in 'commercial' or 'economic' activity. Earlier proposals for the drafting of the Charter combined the right of everyone 'to choose and

[119] Coghlan and Steiert (n 106) 11.
[120] Art 49 TFEU.
[121] Michelle Everson and Rui Correia Gonçalves, 'Article 16—Freedom to Conduct a Business' in Steve Peers and others (eds), *The EU Charter of Fundamental Rights: A Commentary* (2nd edn, Hart 2021) 463, 474.

to engage in [their] occupation or business'.[122] There is a strong resonance between the freedom to conduct a business in Article 16 CFR and the freedom to pursue a trade or profession in Article 15 CFR, as recognized in the earliest jurisprudence of the CJEU on the emergence of fundamental rights protection as a general principle of EU law, and with both provisions concerning the exercise of a commercial or economic activity. Broadly speaking, the difference between the two provisions lies in the fact that Article 16 CFR is intended to protect entrepreneurial activity, whereas Article 15 CFR is concerned with the participation of individuals in the labour market, although there is a continued degree of overlap between both provisions, as evident from the overlapping sources referred to in the Explanations.[123]

3.3.2 The content and status of the freedom to conduct a business

Article 16 CFR does not specify against whom the freedom to conduct a business might be enforced. It is clear that the Charter applies to the Union institutions, the Member States when they are implementing EU law, but also to private parties despite the omission of the latter from the text of Article 51 CFR. Article 16 CFR also does not specify the types of behaviour that might be caught by the provision, but it would appear to encompass an obligation to avoid the creation of disproportionate or discriminatory barriers to the conduct of businesses. Whether the freedom to conduct a business also entails positive obligations on the State to ensure a business-friendly environment remains unclear. These two aspects—namely positive and negative—are clearly linked in that taxation and regulatory policies which hinder the freedom to conduct a business may have wider economic and societal implications, including for the development of a 'stable economic environment conducive to the development of business'.[124] It is worth recalling at this stage that the Charter including Article 16 CFR is only applicable within the scope of Union law and so its reach will not extend to national policies falling outside of that scope.

The Explanations to the Charter make clear that the rights found within Article 16 CFR derive from the CJEU's earlier case law on business freedoms as general principles. The freedom to conduct a business is stated to be composed

[122] Praesidium note: Proposals for Social Rights in Coghlan and Steiert (n 106) 1355.

[123] Eleni Frantziou and Virginia Mantouvalou, 'Article 15 The Right to Work' in Steve Peers and others (eds), *The EU Charter of Fundamental Rights: A Commentary* (2nd edn, Hart 2021) 449, 451; AG Opinion in *Lidl* (n 43) para 27.

[124] European Union Agency for Fundamental Rights (n 117) 12, 37.

of three distinct elements, namely: (1) the freedom to pursue an economic or commercial activity; (2) freedom of contract; and (3) the right to free competition. The Explanations point to *Nold* and *Eridania* as sources for the first element of the freedom to conduct a business, but neither of those cases refers to the freedom to pursue an economic or commercial activity, instead referring to the right 'freely to choose and practice [a] trade or profession', which appears narrower than 'economic or commercial activity' and which finds a more explicit articulation within Article 15 CFR where it is encompassed by the more general right to 'work'.[125]

The CJEU has been inconsistent in its use of terminology in this field, referring in some cases to the 'trade or profession' formula, while in others referring to 'freedom to pursue an economic activity'.[126] In other cases, the CJEU refers to both the exercise of a trade or profession and the right to pursue a commercial or economic activity.[127] Regardless of the label chosen to describe the freedom, the cited paragraph of *Eridania*—which concerns the 'carrying on of economic activities'—also does not support the proposition that commercial freedoms of any kind are protected, with one paragraph merely referring to questions raised by the parties, which were 'based on the view that the carrying on of economic activities must be guaranteed because it forms part of the fundamental rights which Community law is also concerned to uphold', while the second cited paragraph discusses the need to reconcile competing interests.[128]

The second element of the freedom to conduct a business deriving from the general principles, namely freedom of contract, is said to originate in *Sukkerfabriken* and *Spain v Commission*, both of which have been discussed in Chapter 1 within the context of the emergence of business freedoms as general principles. Once again, the cited paragraph of *Sukkerfabriken* does not support the contention that freedom of contract is protected within the context of the freedom to conduct a business, while the relevant paragraph in *Spain v Commission* simply sates that 'the right of the parties to amend contracts concluded by them is based on the principles of contractual freedom and cannot, therefore, be limited in the absence of [Union] rules imposing specific restrictions', but without expanding on what such a freedom of contract might entail.[129]

[125] *Eridania* (n 12); *Nold* (n 4).
[126] *Alliance for Natural Health* (n 11) para 126; *Schräder* (n 10) para 15.
[127] *Swedish Match* (n 11) paras 72, 74.
[128] *Eridania* (n 12) paras 20, 31.
[129] *Spain v Commission* (n 29) para 99; *Sukkerfabriken* (n 27) para 19.

The final element of the freedom to conduct a business within Article 16 CFR is the right to free competition, which is stated to derive from Article 119(1) and (3) TFEU, and which outlines the Union's commitment to an open market economy and fiscal stability. The right to free competition is of less immediate relevance to a consideration of the relationship between the freedom to conduct a business and the Charter's economic and social rights, but it does serve to highlight some of the wider values underpinning the Union's economic constitution. For now, it can be noted that Article 16 CFR is said to have a dual character in that it is concerned both with the autonomy of the individual to conduct their business or engage in economic activity as well as a wider commitment to a 'distinct form of economic and social organisation'.[130] As Everson and Correia Gonçalves put it, the willingness of the CJEU to develop the right to an occupation and to property and 'also to extrapolate a freedom of business from them, reveals its broader aspiration to institutionalise an internationalised Economic Constitution'.[131]

In other words, the freedom to conduct a business can be viewed either as an individual fundamental right or as an overarching organizational principle underpinning the EU's economic constitution. The EU Fundamental Rights Agency suggests a more ambiguous and open-ended role for business freedoms: '[t]he essence of the freedom to conduct a business is to enable individual aspirations to flourish, and to promote entrepreneurship and innovation, which in turn is indispensable for sustainable social and economic development'.[132] No basis or source is offered for these claims, but the focus is clearly on the benefits that economic freedom grants to the individual, with the broader societal consequences merely stemming from this.

Despite the relative novelty of the inclusion of the freedom to conduct a business within an international rights instrument, Article 16 CFR appears to constitute a rather innocuous provision with the 'freedom', not the 'right', to conduct a business being merely 'recognised', not 'protected' or 'guaranteed'.[133] Indeed, the language used in Article 16 CFR has been described as 'diffident' and as standing in contrast to the more explicitly rights-oriented language used elsewhere in the Charter.[134] The wording of Article 16 CFR is reflective of its underlying purpose, which is to act as a counterweight to the social rights

[130] Everson and Correia Gonçalves (n 121) 464.
[131] ibid 468.
[132] European Union Agency for Fundamental Rights (n 117) 7.
[133] Usai (n 50) 1868.
[134] Peter Oliver, 'What Purpose does Article 16 of the Charter Serve?' in Ulf Bernitz, Xavier Groussot, and Felix Schulyok (eds), *General Principles of EU Law and European Private Law* (Kluwer 2013) 281, 285, 293.

found in the Charter's Solidarity Title (by granting both the same constitutional status), some of which are equally vaguely drafted, thereby also reserving Article 16 CFR for extreme cases.[135]

As argued in Part III, however, the fact that the CJEU has adopted an expansive approach to the freedom to conduct a business as a fundamental right has essentially led to classification of social rights as exceptions, derogations, or restrictions on that freedom, perhaps thereby reversing the intended order of precedence between the Freedoms and Solidarity Titles and despite the purported 'indivisibility' of the Charter rights, freedoms, and principles. This 'exceptions'-based approach is compounded within the collective employment rights context in that collective negotiation may itself be viewed as an exception to the principle of 'individual' contractual negotiation.[136] As will be explained, the baseline conception of freedom of contract within EU law, derived from national constitutional traditions, lends a presumptive legitimacy to pre-existing distributions, the restriction of which requires justification by the Union legislature.[137] The justification of interventionist measures then faces the additional hurdle of the CJEU's institutional gravitation towards deregulation and the facilitation of market integration.[138] This approach is now reinforced—and seemingly legitimated—by the constitutional 'value' espoused within the freedom to conduct a business as a fundamental right and which itself overlooks the constitutional value of freedom of association and the right to engage in collective bargaining as fundamental social rights, both within the Charter and within the international social rights regime.

Article 16 CFR is certainly a difficult provision to interpret, particularly given that it is framed in the language of 'freedoms', a concept not defined within the Charter and with the language used in the provision itself suggesting it is a 'principle' rather than a 'right' in the sense of the distinction contained in Article 51(1) CFR, which again stipulates 'respect' for rights but mere 'observation' of principles. Article 52(5) CFR further specifies that principles require further implementation and are confined to a more limited interpretative role in contrast to the Charter's rights, which may be relied on by litigants in and of themselves.

Of particular relevance is Article 16 CFR's reference to 'Union law and national laws and practices', which as noted in Chapter 1 may be indicative of a

[135] ibid 285, 299; AG Opinion in *Alemo-Herron* (n 104) para 52.
[136] Douglas Brodie, 'Collectivism in Labour Law: Only by Exception' (2022) 51 ILJ 464, 475.
[137] Antinori (n 53) 1842.
[138] Ian H Eliasoph, 'A "Switch in Time" for the European Community? *Lochner* Discourse and the Recalibration of Economic and Social Rights in Europe' (2007) 14 Colum J Eur L 468, 494.

principle, rather than a right. In *Sky Österreich,* however, this did not prevent the CJEU from treating freedom of contract essentially as if it were an individual 'right', with the CJEU noting that the limitation in accordance with EU law, national laws and practices meant that any grounds for justification on such limitations were wider than they would otherwise be, and encompass a 'broad range of interventions' in the general or public interest.[139] It has been suggested that, for similar reasons, the first element of the freedom to conduct a business, namely the freedom to pursue an economic activity, should also constitute a right rather than a principle.[140]

The use of the label 'freedom' also appears to blur—within the context of the freedom to conduct business—the distinction between civil and political rights on the one hand and economic and social rights on the other. It will be recalled that the very purpose of the rights and principles distinction in the Charter is to differentiate between these two broad families of rights, with positively oriented economic and social rights often considered to lack justiciability.[141] It will also be recalled that the CJEU has tended to avoid the issue of the rights and principles distinction, preferring instead to treat this as a question of whether a particular provision is capable of direct effect, ie whether the provision is sufficiently clear, precise, and unconditional to be relied on in and of itself and without further implementation.[142]

The text of Article 16 CFR self-evidently does not meet these criteria, given that the undefined 'freedom' to conduct a business is merely 'recognised' and only then to the extent provided for in Union law and national laws and practices.[143] In cases such as *Egenberger* and *Bauer*, the CJEU has confirmed that the Charter is, in principle, capable of horizontal direct effect.[144] To date, cases concerning Article 16 CFR have been confined to the interpretation rather than disapplication of EU legislation with attendant (indirect) effects on private parties, rather than true horizontal effect, ie the direct application of horizontal obligations on private parties.

The reference to 'a business' may also be indicative of an intention that Article 16 CFR *should* apply to disputes involving private parties. Given the

[139] Case C-283/11 *Sky Österreich v Österreichischer Rundfunk* ECLI:EU:C:2013:28, para 46.
[140] Oliver (n 134) 296.
[141] Lord Goldsmith QC, 'A Charter of Rights, Freedoms and Principles' (2001) 39 CMLRev 1201.
[142] eg Case C-236/09 *Association belge des Consommateurs Test-Achats v Council* ECLI:EU:C:2011:100.
[143] cf AG Opinion in Case C-261/20 *Thelen Technopark Berlin GmbH v MN* ECLI:EU:C:2021:620.
[144] Case C-414/16 *Vera Egenberger v Evangelisches Werk für Diakonie und Entwicklung eV* EU:C:2018:257; Joined Cases C-569/16 and 570/16 *Stadt Wuppertal v Maria Elisabeth Bauer and Volker Willmeroth v Martina Broßonn* ECLI:EU:C:2018:871.

correspondence between the French language versions, the term business is probably to be understood as having the same meaning as the concept of an 'undertaking' ('entreprise') within the context of the Treaty's competition law provisions, namely Articles 101 and 102 TFEU.[145] A more fundamental issue concerns the precise relationship between business freedoms as general principles and the freedom to conduct a business as a fundamental Charter right. It is argued here that a proper understanding of this relationship is necessary in order to begin to reconcile the apparent contradictions that have emerged between the various sources of business freedoms as fundamental rights.

3.4 Reconciling the Sources of Business Freedoms as Fundamental Rights

3.4.1 The relationship between overlapping general principles and the Charter

There can now be little doubt, given the terms of Article 6 TEU, that the unwritten general principles continue to play an integral methodological role alongside the written provisions of the Charter.[146] The general principles can act as an alternative tool to the Charter in the interpretation and protection of Union fundamental rights, by filling lacunae in the Charter's provisions as well as providing a basis for the development of new rights not currently found in the Charter.[147] The general principles can also act as an alternative gateway for rights deriving from the ECHR to enter the EU legal order, given the Convention's ongoing role as a source of general principles, as recognized by Article 6(3) TEU.[148]

Article 52(3) CFR requires a homogenous interpretation between the Charter and related provisions of the ECHR. The general principles require no such homogenous approach to interpretation and, as such, the rights found within the ECHR can continue to play an additional autonomous role through the general principles, which also allows for such rights to be shaped

[145] Oliver (n 134) 297.

[146] Takis Tridimas, 'The General Principles of Law: Who Needs Them?' (2016) 52 Cahiers de Droit Européen 419.

[147] Chiara Amalfitano, *General Principles of EU Law and the Protection of Fundamental Rights* (Edward Elgar 2018) 4.

[148] ibid 94.

to accommodate the needs of the Union legal order.[149] This symbiosis between codified and unwritten sources of rights is also reflected, for example, in the English common law's 'dynamic' relationship to the Human Rights Act 1998, which ensures not only that the domestication of the ECHR does not preclude the development of common law rights, but also that the Convention can inform and inspire the development of the common law itself.[150]

However, there is little consistency in the CJEU's case law concerning the relationship between the Charter and the general principles, to the extent that this relationship has been (indirectly) addressed. The CJEU continues either to refer to both the general principles and the Charter in tandem, or to one of these sources in isolation, or to neither source, despite the clear relevance of fundamental rights to the case at hand.[151] It was argued that the general principles and the Charter continue to represent *autonomous* sources of EU fundamental rights, as recognized by Article 6 TEU, ie where the relevant rights do not (entirely) coincide. A more vexed question is the extent to which the CJEU views the Charter as having subsumed those general principles that overlap or which (entirely) coincide with its provisions.

3.4.1.1 The parallel application of the Charter and the general principles

It is suggested here that there is an ongoing role for the general principles in parallel to the Charter even where the rights contained therein overlap. This is in spite of the fact that the CJEU may prefer to rely on the Charter more frequently in practice. The precise relationship between the two concepts is not, however, clearly articulated. Ostensibly, the Charter was only ever intended to codify or render more visible existing fundamental rights but does not provide any further guidance as to the relationship between these sources. The Charter and the general principles thereby essentially derive from the same sources, namely the common constitutional traditions of the Member States and the provisions of the ECHR, but with only piecemeal reference to how these sources might relate to each other.[152] For example, it can be seen from the Explanations to the Charter that there is a connection between at least some provisions of the Charter and the pre-existing general principles. Article 6 TEU also confirms that the general principles and the Charter enjoy the same constitutional status as sources of Union fundamental rights, with the CJEU

[149] ibid.
[150] Mark Elliot, 'Beyond the European Convention: Human Rights and the Common Law' (2015) CLP 1, 5.
[151] Amalfitano (n 147) 114.
[152] ibid 96.

holding that the general principles and the Charter have the same scope of application.[153] It has also been argued that the general principles, as sources of Charter rights, will continue to inform the interpretation of those rights, although the precise influence of the various sources provided for in Article 6 TEU remains elusive.[154]

Despite the limitations placed on the Charter, for example its rather restrictive scope of application as evidenced in Article 51(2) CFR, there is nothing within its provisions to suggest an intention to prevent the further development of general principles in fields not covered by the Charter, nor is it evident that the Treaty drafters wished to preclude the continued use of general principles in fields that are covered by the Charter. Some commentators have argued that the enactment of the Charter has had the effect of further deprioritizing the general principles where the two interact. It has been suggested, for example, that the Charter should replace the general principles it enshrines, leaving the general principles as a source for *new* rights, ie rights not found within the Charter.[155] However, the boundary between a 'new' right and the further development of a general principle that merely 'relates' to an existing right, but which is not necessarily 'enshrined' by that right, is difficult to determine. This approach also overlooks the fact that the general principles are to act as a guide to the interpretation of the Charter, which suggests an interdependent rather than hierarchical relationship between the two sources.

If the Charter and the general principles were interchangeable, there would be little benefit in relying on the latter as an interpretative guide. Indeed, it is often by reference to the general principles that gaps or deficiencies in the protection of a Charter provision can be identified in the first place.[156] The argument in favour of coterminous treatment between the Charter and the general principles where the two overlap does not preclude recognition of an ongoing independent role for the general principles outside of the intersection between the two sources.[157] There remains, however, the unresolved difficulty of ascertaining the precise extent of any such overlap or whether the general principles can be said to coincide with a particular Charter provision.

[153] Case C–617/10 *Åklagaren v Hans Åkerberg Fransson* ECLI:EU:C:2013:105.

[154] Tridimas (n 2); Tridimas (n 146) 424.

[155] Emily Hancox, 'The Relationship Between the Charter and General Principles: Looking Back and Looking Forward' (2020) 22 CYELS 233.

[156] Herwig CH Hofmann and Bucura C Mihaescu, 'The Relation between the Charter's Fundamental Rights and the Unwritten General Principles of EU Law: Good Administration as the Test Case' (2013) 9 EuConst 73, 78.

[157] Tridimas (n 146).

The Treaty also does not envisage any distinction between those general principles that will continue to exist alongside the Charter and those that have been replaced by it. As argued here, there are good reasons for the continued autonomous development of the general principles, including the fact that the Charter provisions themselves are often open-ended and require interpretation in light of the case law concerning the pre-existing general principles, which also continue to serve a gap-filling function within EU law more generally. Outside the context of EU law, but clearly of relevance to the maintenance of the distinction between the Charter and the general principles within UK law, is the (temporary) conversion by means of the European Union (Withdrawal) Act (EU(W)A) 2018 of references to the Charter within retained EU law to references to the corresponding general principles instead. The interpretative function of the general principles has thereby been maintained within the context of retained EU law in the UK post-Brexit and with a broad interpretation of section 5(5) EU(W)A 2018 suggesting that all Charter provisions may 'correspond' to general principles, at least for the purposes of UK law. Domestic courts in the UK have also recognized the ongoing relevance of the Charter as a source of general principles, leading to a further symbiotic role for both rights sources in the interpretation and application of provisions of the Withdrawal Agreement (WA) 'referring to Union law or to concepts or provisions thereof'.[158]

Deconstructing the relationship between the general principles and the Charter may therefore be a more difficult task than suggested by the 2018 Withdrawal Act, particularly given the ongoing uncertainty within EU law as to whether particular Charter provisions do correspond to pre-existing general principles. A notable example is the right to paid annual leave within Article 31(2) CFR, the legislative incarnation of which is to be found in Article 7 of the Working Time Directive, and which has been described as a 'particularly important principle' of Union social law, but without the CJEU addressing the status of that right as a 'general principle'.[159] The Retained EU Law (Revocation and Reform) Act 2023 now also requires the extraction of the concept of EU general principles from domestic law altogether, but again without a clear indication as to what might constitute such general principles

[158] Agreement on the withdrawal of the United Kingdom of Great Britain and Northern Ireland from the European Union and the European Atomic Energy Community [2020] OJ L29/7 (Withdrawal Agreement); *SSWP v AT* [2023] 11 WLUK 104 [87]; art 4(3) WA.

[159] Directive 2003/88/EC of the European Parliament and of the Council of 4 November 2003 concerning certain aspects of the organisation of working time [2003] OJ L299/9; Case C–214/16 *Conley King v The Sash Window Workshop Ltd ECLI:EU:C:2017:*914, para 32.

for the purposes of retained (now assimilated) EU law, and with the Act also containing the power to restate or preserve the *effects* of the general principles, but without preserving the general principle itself. Of course, both the Charter and the general principles continue to be applicable within the context of the Withdrawal Agreement given that they constitute 'Union law' for the purposes of Article 4 WA.[160]

3.4.1.2 The autonomous co-dependence of the Charter and the general principles

There are, of course, potential drawbacks to the existence of parallel systems of fundamental rights protection within the EU legal order, deriving from both the Charter and the general principles. Ladenburger, for example, notes that reliance on both the Charter and general principles as autonomous sources of rights would 'undermine the overall coherence of the Union's legal system if one attempted to develop [. . .] a separate set of horizontal rules differing from those of the Charter'.[161] The reality is that the EU fundamental rights regime has always been—and continues to be—dependent on a patchwork of pre-existing sources, including the common constitutional traditions and the ECHR, despite the purported codification of these sources within the Charter.

The argument here is also that general principles are 'autonomous' in the sense that they continue to exist as a source of rights outside the Charter. This is not to say that they should be relied on in isolation or instead of the Charter where the two overlap. Rather, there is a mutually reinforcing relationship between the two sources, which should be interpreted consistently to the extent that such an interpretation is possible. The suggestion therefore is that both sources should continue to operate in tandem, with the general principles providing interpretative guidance and substantive content to the rather sparse provisions found within the Charter. The Charter, as an express articulation of the value of some of those general principles as fundamental rights, can also act as a guide to the emergence of new general principles, but can also spur the further development and interpretation of existing general principles. In other words, while the Charter and the general principles remain autonomous sources of fundamental rights, they are also interrelated and mutually reinforcing.

Another argument that has been raised against the development of the general principles in parallel to the Charter is that the CJEU may adopt such an

[160] Art 2 WA.
[161] EU Report on 'Protection of Fundamental Rights Post-Lisbon' (FIDE Conference 2012).

approach in order to circumvent the express limitations placed on the scope and applicability of the Charter.[162] This risk is to some extent mitigated by the ongoing co-dependency between the Charter and the general principles given that the general principles form the baseline for the interpretation of many Charter rights. Of course, not all Charter rights are specified in the Explanations as deriving from pre-existing general principles case law and, even where such references exist, they are often sparse and or inaccurate, as is the case with regard to Article 16 CFR. The Charter as a declaration of existing rights is not, however, capable of independent interpretation in the sense that the CJEU must of necessity draw on pre-existing sources, including Union legislation, and general principles which are themselves derived from other national and international sources, if only to comply with the interpretative obligations imposed by Article 52(7) CFR and thereby avoid accusations of judicial activism.[163]

A further important, but largely overlooked, distinction between the general principles and the Charter is that the source of many of the latter's provisions, notably in the context of the Solidarity Title, are drawn from pre-existing legislative instruments, which can be contrasted with the general principles' grounding in national constitutional traditions as well as international *rights* instruments. The general principles therefore have a core rather than residual role in giving substantive legal and normative content to the Charter *qua* 'fundamental rights', which has the capacity to undermine the indivisibility of the Charter's provisions by endowing them with variable normative weight. A great deal of the confusion as to the relationship between the general principles and the Charter may stem from the fact that the former are logically prior to the latter, while the function of (general) principles as rationalizing rules would normally suggest that they are logically subsequent to those other norms that require rationalization.[164]

Overall, then, the interpretation of a specific Charter provision, which itself derived from a pre-existing general principle, necessitates the parallel development of that general principle, which would otherwise be denied any autonomous meaning. This would also create an artificial ceiling on the interpretation and application of fundamental rights within the Charter given that the latter depends on the general principles for further elucidation, while the development of the general principles themselves would be curtailed by the

[162] Hancox (n 155) 241–42.
[163] Takis Tridimas, 'The Court of Justice and Judicial Activism' (1996) 21 ELRev 199.
[164] Joxerramon Bengoetxea, *The Legal Reasoning of the European Court of Justice: Towards a European Jurisprudence* (OUP 1993) 73.

very enactment of the Charter. If the Charter were truly intended to hinder the development of the general principles in this way, much stronger language would be required to achieve this.

There is no doubt that divergence between the Charter and the general principles should be avoided in practice, and one approach to achieving such homogeneity might be through the application of a parallel evolutive interpretation of both sources so that the application or interpretation of one source necessarily entails a similar application or interpretation of the other. The general principles would also continue to have a genuinely independent, ie non-parallel, role in the recognition of new rights as general principles, without a corresponding influence on the interpretation or application of the Charter.[165] The Charter's provisions are themselves drafted so broadly that the CJEU may in any case be able to accommodate emerging general principles within its provisions, thereby keeping EU fundamental rights under one roof.[166]

In practice, the CJEU may also choose to avoid addressing the question of the relationship between the Charter and the general principles altogether by preferring instead to refer to the Charter in isolation, even when the relevant Charter provision is specifically stated by the Explanations to derive from pre-existing general principles. Indeed, it is understandable that the CJEU may prefer to rely on the Charter given that rules or rights can more readily guide the courts and in a more direct way by virtue of their specificity.[167] This is precisely what would happen in more recent cases where the CJEU relied on Article 16 CFR without referring to the general principles case law at all, albeit that this approach would subsequently open up space for potential inconsistency between the freedom to conduct a business as a fundamental right and the same concept as a general principle, and which overlooks the dependency of the former on the latter to provide its substantive (and normative) content.

3.4.2 The relationship between the general principles and the Charter within the context of business freedoms

Within the specific context of the freedom to conduct a business, it has been argued that even if the Charter and the general principles continued to represent different sources of business freedoms, there would be 'no point in

[165] Amalfitano (n 147) 115, 149.
[166] Tridimas (n 146) 425.
[167] Bengoetxea (n 164) 72.

maintaining in existence two overlapping but slightly different fundamental rights'.[168] Oliver, for example, suggests that 'Article 16 seamlessly replaced the pre-existing fundamental right to conduct a business which had existed as a general principle of Union law'.[169] There is quite clearly nothing within the existing general principles on business freedoms that could not be accommodated within the open-ended and vague language of Article 16 CFR.[170] The Explanations, which provide interpretative guidance in accordance with Article 52(7) CFR, also preserve an ongoing role for the general principles in the context of the freedom to conduct a business, given that they explicitly refer to pre-existing case law although this case law contains a number of inconsistencies and is not always capable of supporting the precise content of the Charter itself. The interpretative role of the general principles within the context of Article 16 CFR is emphasized by the fact that the latter does not include specific reference to freedom of contract, instead deriving that concept from the pre-existing general principles.[171]

Indeed, even though this is not apparent from the text of the provision itself, the freedom to conduct a business is clearly a 'composite' right and is dependent on each of its component parts being more definitively elucidated in the case law of the CJEU concerning the general principles.[172] Furthermore, as a freedom which must be exercised in accordance with 'national laws and practices', the freedom to conduct a business in Article 16 CFR may be conditioned by national rules, but which must themselves respect the general principles.[173] A pluralistic vision of the relationship between the Charter and general principles therefore helps to accommodate apparent contradictions between these fundamental rights sources. This is not to deny that, in practice, the CJEU may choose to begin its analysis by reference to the Charter and only then to the general principles. Such a 'lexical' approach does not necessarily imply a hierarchy of sources in the sense that one source has a superior position within the hierarchy of norms and should therefore be considered first, much in the same way as the CJEU usually begins its judgments by setting out the relevant (written) legislative provisions before then engaging with the factual background and the legal reasoning.[174]

[168] Oliver (n 134) 283.
[169] ibid.
[170] ibid.
[171] Case C-1/11 *Interseroh Scrap and Metals Trading GmbH v Sonderabfall-Management-Gesellschaft Rheinland-Pfalz mbH (SAM)* ECLI:EU:C:2012:194.
[172] Hofmann and Mihaescu (n 156) 79.
[173] Tridimas (n 146) 427.
[174] Hofmann and Mihaescu (n 156) 82–83; John Rawls, 'Justice as Fairness' (1958) 67 Phil Rev 164.

Some commentators go further in viewing the reference to the general principles case law in the Explanations to Article 16 CFR as indicative of the Charter 'taking over the mantle of the general principle'.[175] On such a view, the role of general principles codified by the Charter would be to ensure that the Charter does not fall below the pre-existing level of protection.[176] There are certainly good arguments in favour of the Charter's prioritization over the general principles given that the development of fundamental rights as general principles has always rested on a rather weak foundation, originally deriving from the common constitutional traditions of the Member States on the basis of a rather selective approach. The ongoing relevance of the common constitutional traditions—which again are sources of general principles—is confirmed by Article 52(4) CFR, which provides that '[i]n so far as this Charter recognises fundamental rights as they result from the constitutional traditions common to the Member States, those rights shall be interpreted in harmony with those traditions'. This is a weaker formulation than Article 52(3) CFR, which more explicitly ties the interpretation of the Charter to that of the ECHR. Article 52(4) CFR may not, therefore, require that the general principles and the Charter be interpreted in conformity.[177]

Nevertheless, the Charter itself is ultimately built on this relatively weak foundation, being largely dependent on pre-existing general principles, albeit that these have now had their legitimacy strengthened by the imprimatur of the Member States as masters of the treaties. Some of these general principles may themselves require further development, clarification, and elucidation, particularly given ambiguities that have emerged in existing case law on the freedom to conduct a business, for example on the relationship between the freedom to pursue economic activity and the freedom to pursue a trade or profession, as well as the role of the concept of a 'social function' as a limit on the freedom to conduct a business. The application of these pre-existing rights may well now be funnelled through Article 16 CFR, but their source continues to lie in the concept of the general principles of EU law, with both the Charter and the general principles enjoying equal constitutional status and contributing to the maximization of rights protection.[178]

It has been suggested that the courts should defer to the decision to draft a Charter provision in a specific and perhaps more restrictive way.[179] However, if

[175] Oliver (n 134) 284.
[176] Hancox (n 155) 249.
[177] ibid 237.
[178] Hofmann and Mihaescu (n 156).
[179] Sascha Prechal, 'Competence Creep and General Principles of Law' (2010) 3 Review of European Administrative Law 5, 21.

the Charter were to act as a truly autonomous, independent, and freestanding source of Union fundamental rights, its provisions would need to be drafted in much clearer terms, with specific guidance given as to its precise relationship to pre-existing rights sources. It is therefore argued that the Charter and the general principles are formally distinct but interrelated sources of fundamental rights, including with regard to the protection of the same right. Even when the Charter is used as the applicable benchmark, it is the Charter *as informed* by the general principles—or other pre-existing sources—which it purports to codify. The two sources are therefore mutually reinforcing, with this reinforcement supported by the interpretative obligations contained in Article 52(7) CFR, meaning that divergences between the two sources are likely to be avoided in practice. Indeed, one of the suggested functions of the general principle in the judicial methodology of the CJEU is to ensure consistency with established paths of argumentation, an approach which is facilitated by Article 6 TEU's continued recognition of the general principles as a source of EU fundamental rights and which thus lends a 'legitimizing force' to the general principles.[180]

The view that the Charter has subsumed the general principles when they cover the same field may have contributed to the perception that cases concerning Article 16 CFR mark a fundamental shift in the CJEU's treatment of the freedom to conduct a business.[181] A closer examination of the case law, in particular on the permissible restrictions on business freedom, reveals a more complex picture, which demonstrates the practical value of the pluralistic and more holistic approach to viewing the relationship between the Charter and the general principles. It is worth noting the language of the Explanations to Article 16 CFR, which refer to that provision being 'based on Court of Justice case-law which has recognised freedom to exercise an economic or commercial activity [...] and freedom of contract'.

The Explanations do not thereby make an explicit claim to Article 16 CFR coinciding directly with the general principles themselves, which can be contrasted with other Charter provisions such as Article 20 CFR, which is said in the Explanations to '*correspond* to a principle which is included in all European constitutions and has also been recognised by the Court of Justice as a *basic principle of Community law*'. A broader obligation of consistent interpretation

[180] Tridimas (n 146) 422.

[181] Stephen Weatherill, 'Use and Abuse of the EU's Charter of Fundamental Rights: On the Improper Veneration of "Freedom of Contract"' (2014) 10 ERCL 167; Jeremias Prassl, 'Freedom of Contract as a General Principle of EU Law? Transfers of Undertakings and the Protection of Employer Rights in EU Labour Law' (2013) 42 ILJ 434.

between the Charter and the general principles can, however, be found in the requirement of harmonious interpretation between the Charter and both the ECHR and the common constitutional traditions, both of which remain sources of general principles both within and outside the scope of the Charter.[182]

3.5 Conclusion

This chapter has explored the evolution of the freedom to conduct a business as a fundamental right as it emerged from the general principles of EU law. There is some evidence of a divergence between freedom of contract and other variations of business freedoms, for example the freedom to pursue a trade or profession, with later case law being much more concrete in its discussion of permissible limitations on business freedoms as general principles. The Charter similarly does not contain any comprehensive statement of business freedoms and again espouses a complex and—as yet unresolved—relationship between freedom of contract and business freedoms more generally. This has led to the CJEU continuing to frame the freedom to conduct a business as a weak and limited fundamental right, particularly in its relationship with competing social considerations.

It was argued that the social function of business freedoms acts as an internal or inherent restriction on those freedoms, which creates space for the consideration of social values and interests. This point is considered further in Chapter 6, where it is argued that existing understandings of the deregulatory potential of freedom of contract have largely overlooked the social dimension of economic freedoms, which constitute a potentially potent restraint on the ability of litigants to rely on the freedom to conduct a business in the face of legislative protections, notably in the employment context in which such economic freedoms may be reframed in terms of the right to (engage in) work.

Despite the CJEU's (limited) recognition of, and engagement with, the social function of business freedoms, there remain many open questions as to the precise status of the freedom to conduct a business within Article 16 CFR, though the existing case law has proceeded to treat this freedom as if it were a 'right' rather than a 'principle'.[183] It may also be the case that different elements within Article 16 CFR have differing legal and normative values, with freedom

[182] Tridimas (n 146) 425.
[183] European Union Agency for Fundamental Rights (n 117) 3.

of contract, for example, being granted the status of a 'right' even if other elements of the freedom to conduct a business might constitute mere 'principles'.[184]

This lack of clarity as to the precise status of the freedom to conduct a business has also led to a number of normative ambiguities, including in the relationship between the general principles and the Charter as well as the relative value of the freedom to conduct a business as a fundamental right in the face of competing economic and social rights within the Charter. These ambiguities ultimately derive from the uncertain foundations upon which the Charter itself was constructed, and which continue to obfuscate the Charter's precise role, its relationship to other rights sources, its material and personal scope, as well as the normative value of its provisions, with the latter emerging in particular from the continued lack of clarity surrounding the distinction between rights and principles. Despite the derivation of the freedom to conduct a business from the pre-existing general principles case law, inconsistency has been a feature of the CJEU's subsequent case law on the freedom to conduct a business as a fundamental right, which, as argued in Chapter 4, has seen the Court vacillate between restrictive and more expansive conceptions of that freedom.

[184] Case C–283/11 *Sky Österreich v Österreichischer Rundfunk* ECLI:EU:C:2013:28.

4
Competing Conceptions of the Freedom to Conduct a Business as a Fundamental Right

4.1 Introduction

This chapter builds on the re-evaluation of the evolution of the freedom to conduct a business as a fundamental right within Article 16 of the EU Charter of Fundamental Rights (CFR) by assessing the strength of that freedom in the early case law of the Court of Justice of the European Union (CJEU) following the enactment of the Charter. It is argued that competing conceptions of the freedom to conduct a business have since emerged from this case law, which have significant implications for the reach of business freedom concepts within EU law more widely. Initially, the CJEU espoused a rather weak conception of the freedom to conduct a business as a fundamental Charter right, demonstrating continuity with the case law on business freedoms as general principles (Section 4.2).

This period of relative continuity was disrupted by the seminal decision of the CJEU in the case of *Alemo-Herron*, concerning the application of collective agreements in the context of business transfers, in which a more 'expansive' conception of the freedom to conduct a business as a fundamental right—understood in terms of the strength of that concept in the face of competing social rights—emerged.[1] That case is analysed in some detail here to demonstrate its emblematic role at the intersection between the CJEU's 'restrictive' and 'expansive' conceptions of the freedom to conduct a business (Section 4.3).

Particular attention is then given to bridging a significant gap which exists within the CJEU's existing case law, namely the absence of any meaningful definition of 'freedom of contract', whether as a component of the freedom to conduct a business or as a freestanding right. The absence of a coherent Union definition of this concept is in part a result of the need to reconcile competing

[1] Case C–426/11 *Mark Alemo-Herron v Parkwood Leisure Ltd* ECLI:EU:C:2013:521.

Business Freedoms and Fundamental Rights in European Union Law. Niall O'Connor, Oxford University Press.
 DOI: 10.1093/9780191982132.003.0005

national law approaches to freedom of contract, but also results from ambiguities surrounding the regulatory role and normative underpinnings of that freedom (Section 4.4). This incoherence is exacerbated by the absence of consensus concerning the 'essence' or 'core content' of the freedom to conduct a business as a fundamental right, including in its particular incarnation in the form of freedom of contract (Section 4.5). It will be demonstrated that it is the very open-endedness of the concept of freedom of contract that makes it such a potentially radical tool within the fundamental rights context, particularly in the absence of any in-depth engagement with the potential legal counterweights to business freedoms as fundamental rights, including within the provisions of the Charter itself.

Section 4.6 concludes that the inconsistencies in the case law governing the freedom to conduct a business are merely symptoms of wider deficiencies in the CJEU's conceptualization of that freedom, but also in its approach to fundamental rights reasoning more generally. The discussion in this chapter thereby also lays the foundations for the analysis in Part III of the systemic implications of these competing conceptions for the CJEU's reasoning in the fundamental rights sphere, as well as for the Union and Member States' ability to regulate contractual relations, notably within the context of parties enjoying differing (unequal) bargaining power.

4.2 A Restrictive Conception of the Freedom to Conduct a Business

The earliest judgments in which Article 16 CFR was invoked largely followed the pattern set by the case law on business freedoms as general principles. In many cases, the CJEU simply restated the standard formula found in its earlier case law that business freedoms 'may be restricted, provided that those restrictions correspond to objectives of general interest pursued by the European Union and they do not constitute a disproportionate and intolerable interference which would affect the very substance of the right so guaranteed'.[2] Some cases referred to the 'social function' formula found in the general principles

[2] Case T-52/09 *Nycomed Danmark ApS v European Medicines Agency (EMA)* ECLI:EU:T:2011:738, para 89. See also more recent general principles case law which followed a similar restrictive pattern: Case C-280/93 *Federal Republic of Germany v Council of the European Union* ECLI:EU:C:1994:367, para 78; Case C-177/90 *Ralf-Herbert Kühn v Landwirtschaftskammer Weser-Ems* ECLI:EU:C:1992:2, para 16; Case C-5/88 *Hubert Wachauf v Bundesamt für Ernährung und Forstwirtschaft* ECLI:EU:C:1989:321, para 18; Case C-265/87 *Hermann Schräder HS Kraftfutter GmbH & Co KG v Hauptzollamt Gronau* ECLI:EU:C:1989:303, para 15.

case law.[3] Others assessed the restriction of business freedoms through the application of the proportionality principle.[4] In other cases still, the General Court relied on Article 16 CFR, but without reference to the pre-existing case law on business freedoms as general principles.[5] Indeed, the CJEU has expressed its frustration at the 'mere abstract reference to such an infringement [of business freedoms]'.[6] Perhaps demonstrative of the initial reluctance of the CJEU to engage with arguments based on the freedom to conduct a business within Article 16 CFR, there were a number of Advocate General Opinions which relied on Article 16 CFR, but which were not subsequently referred to in the judgments of the CJEU.[7]

In one such case, *Alrosa*, Advocate General Kokott addressed the distinction between business freedoms more generally, and freedom of contract specifically.[8] This case concerned a competition law commitment not to contract with a particular party, which led to the Advocate General concluding that:

> [c]ontractual freedom is one of the general principles of [Union] law. It stems from the freedom to act for persons. It is also inseparably linked to the freedom to conduct a business. In a [Union], which must observe the principle of an open market economy with free competition, contractual freedom must be guaranteed. The case law of the Court of Justice also recognises that economic operators must enjoy contractual freedom.[9]

It is clear from this statement that freedom of contract and wider business freedoms within the EU internal market are inextricably linked, which, as suggested here, has contributed to the diverging conceptions of freedom of

[3] Case C–283/11 *Sky Österreich v Österreichischer Rundfunk* ECLI:EU:C:2013:28, para 45; Case C–12/11 *Denise McDonagh v Ryanair Ltd* ECLI:EU:C:2013:43, para 60; AG Opinion in Case C–101/12 *Herbert Schaible v Land Baden-Württemberg* ECLI:EU:C:2013:334, para 30.

[4] Case C–70/10 *Scarlet Extended SA v Société belge des auteurs, compositeurs et éditeurs SCRL (SABAM)* ECLI:EU:C:2011:771.

[5] Case T–190/12 *Johannes Tomana v Council of the European Union and European Commission* ECLI:EU:T:2015:222; Case T–17/12 *Moritz Hagenmeyer and Andreas Hahn v European Commission* ECLI:EU:T:2014:234; Case T–256/11 *Ahmed Abdelaziz Ezz v Council of the European Union* ECLI:EU:T:2014:93.

[6] *Hagenmeyer* (n 5) para 122.

[7] Case C–171/11 *Fra.bo SpA v Deutsche Vereinigung des Gas- und Wasserfaches eV (DVGW)—Technisch-Wissenschaftlicher Verein* ECLI:EU:C:2012:453; Case C–59/11 *Association Kokopelli v Graines Baumaux SAS* ECLI:EU:C:2012:447; Case C–316/09 *MSD Sharp & Dohme GmbH v Merckle GmbH* ECLI:EU:C:2011:275; Joined Cases C–216/09 P and 216/09 *Commission v ArcelorMittal Luxembourg* ECLI:EU:C:2011:190; Case C–441/07 *European Commission v Alrosa Company Ltd* ECLI:EU:C:2010:377; Case C–210/00 *Käserei Champignon Hofmeister GmbH & Co KG v Hauptzollamt Hamburg-Jonas* ECLI:EU:C:2002:440.

[8] AG Opinion in Case C–441/07 *European Commission v Alrosa Company Ltd* ECLI:EU:C:2009:555.

[9] ibid para 225.

contract at Union and national level. Advocate General Kokott, despite recognizing the force of freedom of contract within EU law, nevertheless continued to apply the existing restrictive approach to the protection of that freedom, whereby contractual autonomy may be limited by simply following due legislative procedure.[10] For the Advocate General, a Commission decision to restrict potential contractual partners was not 'unfair, but a completely lawful means by which the Commission pursues the legitimate aim of effectively protecting competition against distortion' and that the risk of losing a desired contractual partner is one which 'must be borne [. . .] like any other economic operator in an open market economy. This does not impair the contractual freedom enjoyed.'[11] The overall pattern, therefore, of the earliest case law on Article 16 CFR was that arguments based on the freedom to conduct a business were usually defeated.[12]

This continuity with the general principles is well illustrated in the case of *Sky Österreich*.[13] Sky Sports held exclusive rights to the broadcast of certain football matches within Austria. The company entered into an agreement with ORF, allowing the latter to reproduce short segments of those matches for the news, in return for payment. The fees were subsequently challenged by ORF in the Austrian courts, with the company arguing that these exceeded the actual costs incurred by Sky in granting access to the footage. The Audiovisual Media Services Directives constituted the relevant EU legislation governing this field.[14] The Directives required broadcasters to provide competitor access to coverage of 'events of high interest to the public' and that compensation for access should not exceed 'the additional cost in providing services'. The CJEU was asked whether these provisions were compatible with Article 16 CFR.

The CJEU began by noting that the Directives prevented Sky Sports, as the holder of exclusive broadcasting rights, from deciding the price to charge for access and was therefore an interference with the freedom to conduct a business found in Article 16 CFR.[15] The CJEU thereby recognized the freedom to determine the price of a service as well as the choice of contractual partner

[10] AG Opinion in *Alrosa* (n 8) paras 229–30.
[11] ibid para 230.
[12] *Sky Österreich* (n 3); *Fra.bo SpA* (n 7); Case C-544/10 *Deutsches Weintor eG v Land Rheinland-Pfalz* ECLI:EU:C:2012:526; Case C-316/09 *MSD Sharp & Dohme GmbH v Merckle GmbH* ECLI:EU:C:2011:275; *Association Kokopelli* (n 7); *ArcelorMittal* (n 7); *Alrosa* (n 7); *Käserei* (n 7).
[13] *Sky Österreich* (n 3).
[14] Directive 2010/13/EU on the coordination of certain provisions laid down by law, regulation or administrative action in Member States concerning the provision of audiovisual media services (Audiovisual Media Services Directive) [2010] OJ L95/1.
[15] *Sky Österreich* (n 3) para 44.

as elements of freedom of contract within Article 16 CFR.[16] Nevertheless, the CJEU drew from the general principles case law to find that the freedom to conduct a business was not absolute, but must rather be viewed 'in light of its social function'.[17] The CJEU continued that the core content of Article 16 CFR had not been violated as the restrictions did not 'prevent a business activity from being carried out as such' and that:

> [i]n the light of the wording of Article 16 of the Charter, which differs from the wording of the other fundamental freedoms laid down in Title II thereof, yet is similar to that of certain provisions of Title IV of the Charter, the freedom to conduct a business may be subject to a broad range of interventions on the part of public authorities which may limit the exercise of economic activity in the public interest.[18]

The parallels drawn between the freedom to conduct a business and the Solidarity Title are important and reflect the drafters' intention to grant these sources at least formal equal footing within the Charter.[19] The CJEU then placed particular emphasis on the words 'in accordance with Union law and national laws and practices' found in Article 16 CFR. This formula was seen as giving greater freedom to public authorities to restrict the freedom to conduct a business in the public interest. As Oliver comments, the CJEU 'considers this language to have been inserted into Article 16 so as to reflect its own case law which has always been ambiguous towards the freedom to conduct a business'.[20] The CJEU concluded that the legislature had 'ensured that the extent of the interference with the freedom to conduct a business [. . .] [is] confined within precise limits'.[21] Again, this is reflective of the earlier case law in which the CJEU held that business freedoms as general principles could be restricted provided that there was clear legal authority to do so.

This is the only judgment preceding *Alemo-Herron* relating to Article 16 CFR to deal specifically with freedom of contract as an element of the freedom

[16] ibid para 43, referring to Joined Cases C–90/90 and 91/90 *Jean Neu v Secrétaire d'État à l'Agriculture and à la Viticulture* ECLI:EU:C:1991:303; Case C–437/04 *Commission of the European Communities v Kingdom of Belgium* ECLI:EU:C:2007:178; Case C–213/10 *F-Tex SIA v Lietuvos-Anglijos UAB 'Jadecloud-Vilma'* ECLI:EU:C:2012:215.

[17] *Sky Österreich* (n 3) para 45.

[18] ibid paras 49, 46.

[19] Peter Oliver, 'What Purpose Does Article 16 of the Charter Serve?' in Ulf Bernitz, Xavier Groussot, and Felix Schulyok (eds), *General Principles of EU Law and European Private Law* (Kluwer 2013) 281, 293.

[20] ibid 292–93.

[21] *Sky Österreich* (n 3) para 61.

to conduct a business; however, no reference is made to the case law on freedom of contract as a general principle.[22] In any case, the judgment shows the CJEU's continued willingness to accept restrictions on the freedom to conduct a business in the face of competing (economic and social) interests, which is suggested here as a characteristic of a 'restrictive' as opposed to an 'expansive' conception of the freedom to conduct a business.

Given the close connection highlighted in the Explanations between Article 16 CFR and the general principles, it was by and large expected that this pattern would continue and that limitations traditionally imposed by the CJEU on the freedom to conduct a business would continue to apply, despite its codification as a fundamental right.[23] The fact that Charter provisions continue to be subject to restrictions is made clear in Article 52 CFR, which governs permissible limitations on Charter rights and which provides that:

> [a]ny limitation on the exercise of the rights and freedoms recognised by this Charter must be provided for by law and respect the essence of those rights and freedoms. Subject to the principle of proportionality, limitations may be made only if they are necessary and genuinely meet objectives of general interest recognised by the Union or the need to protect the rights and freedoms of others.

This provision is largely reflective of the formula followed by the CJEU in its case law on the restriction of business freedoms as general principles, as evaluated in Chapter 3 when deconstructing the 'social function' of business freedoms as general principles.

The only case pre-dating *Alemo-Herron* in which arguments based on the freedom to conduct a business were 'successful' was *Scarlet Extended*.[24] In that case, SABAM, a Belgian copyright organization, sued Scarlet Extended, an Internet Service Provider for allegedly permitting the sharing of files by its users. The court of first instance mandated that Scarlet Extended monitor its services at its own expense, and to block any unauthorized sharing. The CJEU was tasked with determining whether this injunction was compatible with Directive 2000/31 read in light of Article 16 CFR.[25] The Court stressed the

[22] ibid para 49.
[23] Michelle Everson and Rui Correia Gonçalves, 'Article 16—Freedom to Conduct a Business' in Steve Peers and others (eds), *The EU Charter of Fundamental Rights: A Commentary* (2nd edn, Hart 2021) 463, 484.
[24] *Scarlet Extended* (n 4).
[25] Directive 2000/31/EU of the European Parliament and of the Council of 8 June 2000 on certain legal aspects of information society services, in particular electronic commerce, in the Internal Market [2000] OJ L278/1.

need to strike a 'fair balance' between the competing interests of the freedom to conduct a business and the protection of intellectual property. In the present case, the injunction failed to strike such a balance as it 'has no limitation in time, is directed at all future infringements and is intended to protect not only existing works, but also future works that have not yet been created at the time when the system is introduced'.[26]

Perhaps in recognition of the relative weakness of the rights protected under Article 16 CFR, the CJEU reinforced its arguments by reference to additional Charter rights such as Articles 8 and 11 CFR on the protection of personal data and the right to receive and impart information, respectively.[27] Despite the introduction of a new 'balancing' approach to cases dealing with Article 16 CFR, the CJEU still raised that provision with trepidation and only found an infringement in conjunction with EU legislation and additional fundamental rights.[28] Interestingly, this is also the first judgment within the context of business freedoms more generally—as opposed to freedom of contract, specifically—not to make any reference to the limitation of that freedom in relation to its 'social function', and may therefore represent an early indication of the CJEU's willingness to depart from its pre-existing restrictive approach to the protection of business freedoms as general principles, which continued in its early case law concerning the freedom to conduct a business within Article 16 of the Charter.

In its more recent jurisprudence, the CJEU has shown a commitment to a much stronger notion of the freedom to conduct a business as a fundamental right, particularly in its treatment of freedom of contract specifically. This more radical approach to Article 16 CFR has its origins in a series of controversial decisions handed down in the employment context, beginning with the seminal case of *Alemo-Herron*, which involved the interpretation of the EU Directive on the transfer of undertakings, and which has also arisen in subsequent cases concerning the freedom to conduct a business as a fundamental right.[29] The purpose of this legislation is to ensure that that employment conditions are not negatively impacted as a result of the transfer of a business from one employer to another. The dispute in *Alemo-Herron* also arose within the context

[26] *Scarlet Extended* (n 4) para 47.

[27] ibid para 50.

[28] Confirmed in Case C–314/12 *UPC Telekabel Wien GmbH v Constantin Film Verleih GmbH and Wega Filmproduktionsgesellschaft mbH* ECLI:EU:C:2014:192 and Case C–360/10 *Belgische Vereniging van Auteurs, Componisten en Uitgevers CVBA (SABAM) v Netlog NV* ECLI:EU:C:2012:85.

[29] Directive 2001/23/EC on the approximation of the laws of the Member States relating to the safeguarding of employees' rights in the event of transfers of undertakings, businesses or parts of undertakings or businesses [2001] OJ L82/16.

of UK law and thus provides a useful illustration of the potential future status of protective Union legislation, including the influence of the Charter within the UK legal order in the wake of Brexit. The following section considers the background to that case before turning to the CJEU's subsequent reliance on Article 16 CFR in Chapter 5, with Part III also more broadly assessing the implications (for legislative employment protections) of the CJEU's treatment of the freedom to conduct a business as a fundamental right.

4.3 An Expansive Conception of the Freedom to Conduct a Business

4.3.1 The tentative application of the freedom to conduct a business

The first significant judgment in the *Alemo-Herron* 'line' of cases is *Werhof*, a case in which the CJEU was asked to interpret Article 3(1) of the Transfer of Undertakings Directive (TUD), which provides that '[t]he transferor's rights and obligations arising from a contract of employment or from an employment relationship existing on the date of a transfer shall, by reason of such transfer, be transferred to the transferee'.[30] In other words, the employee's existing terms and conditions are transferred to the new employer. Werhof had been an employee of the company DUEWAG. According to the employment contract, the relationship was to be governed by the framework collective agreement, and by the wage agreement in force for the Nord Rhine-Westphalia (NRW) iron and steel, metal, and electrical industries. This collective agreement had been concluded between the NRW metal and Electrical Industry Federation (AGV)—of which Werhof was a member—and the trade union for the metal industry (IG Metall).

The company was subsequently converted into Siemens DUEWAG and was later transferred to Freeway, the defendant company. Freeway was not a member of any employers' association and so was not involved in the negotiation of any collective agreements. After the transfer, Werhof agreed via a works agreement to waive all individual rights to wage increases pursuant to collective agreements entered into prior to that agreement. This was followed by a supplemental provision to the employment contract setting out basic pay and performance bonuses. IG Metall and AGV later concluded a new collective

[30] Case C–499/04 *Hans Werhof v Freeway Traffic Systems GmbH & Co KG* ECLI:EU:C:2006:168.

agreement, providing for wage increases. Werhof sought to claim these additional wages from Freeway, but the German appeal court found that Werhof had no claim based on the domestic implementing legislation. However, doubts were raised as to the compatibility of domestic law with the Transfer of Undertakings Directive, which has the purpose of protecting employment conditions in the event of a change in employer. The CJEU was, therefore, asked to determine whether Article 3(1) TUD should be interpreted dynamically or statically. According to the 'static' approach, new employers should be bound only by collectively agreed terms in force at the time of the transfer. The 'dynamic' approach would bind the new employer to collectively agreed terms negotiated after the transfer.

Werhof argued in favour of a dynamic interpretation of the clause incorporating a collective agreement into an employment contract. This would allow for the continuation of the collective agreement, despite the fact that the new employer was not involved in the negotiation of that agreement. It was argued that this approach follows from the spirit and purpose of the Directive, namely the protection of employees in the event of a change of owner of the undertaking and, in particular, the safeguarding of their rights.[31] Freeway, on the other hand, argued that only the collective agreement in force at the time of the transfer should be applicable. To hold otherwise, they suggested, would be to impose an obligation on the new employer that would hinder their freedom of association and their freedom to contract.[32]

Advocate General Ruiz-Jarabo Colomer found in favour of Freeway, noting that the 'right of the person acquiring an undertaking must prevail over any other of lesser importance, such as the right of the employee to the financial advantages arising from the development of the collective agreements signed by the transferor of the company'.[33] Nowhere in the Directive is it suggested that any such right of an acquiring undertaking exists, let alone prevails over the competing rights of employees. Nonetheless, the CJEU agreed, noting that an essential characteristic of any contract is the freedom of the parties to arrange their own affairs and that 'in a situation such as the one in the main proceedings where the defendant is not a member of any employers' association and is not bound by any collective agreement, the rights and obligations arising from such an agreement do not therefore apply to it, as a rule'.[34] The Court did note once again that freedom of contract was not absolute. To hold otherwise would

[31] ibid para 17.
[32] ibid para 19.
[33] AG Opinion in Case C-499/04 *Hans Werhof v Freeway Traffic Systems GmbH & Co KG* ECLI:EU:C:2005:686, para 51.
[34] *Werhof* (n 30) para 23.

be to erode the rights of employees, which would defeat the very purpose of the legislation, which was to protect such employees from the absolute application of the principle of freedom of contract.[35] This was not, however, the only interest to be protected and 'the interests [...] of the transferee, who must be in a position to make the adjustments and changes necessary to carry on his operations, cannot be disregarded'.[36] The CJEU went on to find that:

> Article 3(1) of the Directive must be interpreted as *not precluding*, in a situation where the contract of employment refers to a collective agreement binding the transferor, that the transferee, who is not party to such an agreement, is not bound by collective agreements subsequent to the one which was in force at the time of the transfer of the business.[37]

In other words, the Transfer of Undertakings Directive does not require the dynamic interpretation of clauses incorporating collective agreements. The CJEU reinforced this position with reference to the freedom of association, which is itself a (Union) fundamental right.[38] To require a dynamic approach would mean that 'future collective agreements apply to a transferee who is not party to a collective agreement and that his fundamental right not to join an association could be affected'.[39] That is to say that the freedom of association implies a freedom to dissociate.[40] An employer who was not a member of an association and therefore was not involved in negotiating the collective agreement could not be bound by it.[41] To hold otherwise would infringe the principle that contracts cannot impose obligations on third parties. A further effect might be to impose more obligations 'on an employer who had not been a party to an agreement than on the person who had been, leaving the former in uncertainty and exposed to the risk that conditions might be introduced behind his back'.[42] The CJEU was, therefore, willing to *permit* the static approach, but did not require it. This position would change following the decision in *Alemo-Herron*, which demonstrates the potential deregulatory effects within the employment context of the freedom to conduct a business as a fundamental right.

[35] ibid para 24.
[36] ibid para 31.
[37] ibid para 37.
[38] Case C-415/93 *Union royale belge des sociétés de football association ASBL v Jean-Marc Bosman, Royal club liégeois SA v Jean-Marc Bosman and Union des associations européennes de football (UEFA) v Jean-Marc Bosman* ECLI:EU:C:1995:463.
[39] *Werhof* (n 30) para 34.
[40] *Young, James and Webster v UK* (1983) 5 EHRR CD519.
[41] *Werhof* (n 30) para 23.
[42] ibid para 58.

4.3.2 The radical application of the freedom to conduct a business

The claimant in *Alemo-Herron* was a former employee of Lewisham Borough Council working under an employment contract which expressly incorporated the terms of collective agreements—including pay—'as negotiated from time to time' by the National Joint Council (NJC), which is an external negotiating body for local authority employees. The local authority sold its leisure activities to a private undertaking, which subsequently transferred the business to Parkwood Leisure. The NJC agreement in question had expired before the transfer to Parkwood had taken place. Parkwood in reliance on *Werhof* refused to recognize the outcome of the subsequent negotiations in which it had not been involved.

The transferred employees brought a claim before the Employment Tribunal, which was dismissed, for the reason that the CJEU's decision in *Werhof* had ruled out the possibility of any transfer of dynamic clauses referring to collective agreements in the context of the transfer of an undertaking. The Employment Appeal Tribunal (EAT) set this decision aside and found for the employees, noting that *Werhof* did not apply to circumstances such as those covered by UK law. The EAT remarked in particular that '[i]t is not uncommon for an employer to agree with employees or a trade union that it will abide by wages set in a different forum by a third party, here a local authority bargaining structure'.[43] The EAT continued that 'TUPE [the domestic implementing regulations] and the Directive are both measures aimed at protection, or safeguarding, of employees' rights, and it would to be odd if those rights which are accepted to be part of the canon in domestic labour law could be taken away by a subsequent interpretation of the Directive, as to which Member States have a margin'.[44]

The Court of Appeal disagreed, noting that '[b]ut for the decision in *Werhof*, [it] would regard the claimants' case as unanswerable. The inclusion in their contracts of a term providing (inter alia) for their pay from time to time to be fixed by a third-party body was a conventional contractual provision'.[45] The CJEU's decision in *Werhof*, which the Court of Appeal considered indistinguishable from the present case, was decisive. Finally, the employees brought an appeal to the UK Supreme Court (UKSC). Again, it was remarked that 'had

[43] *Alemo-Herron v Parkwood Leisure* [2009] ICR 703 [14].
[44] ibid [49].
[45] *Parkwood Leisure Ltd v Alemo-Herron* [2010] ICR 793 [46]; Charles Wynn-Evans, 'TUPE, Collective Agreements and the Static-Dynamic Debate' (2010) 39 ILJ 275.

this issue been solely one of domestic law, the question would have been open only to one answer'.[46] Lord Hope noted that the dynamic approach was:

> [e]ntirely consistent with the common law principle of freedom of contract [. . .] There can be no objection in principle to parties including a term in their contract that the employee's pay is to be determined from time to time by a third party such as the NJC of which the employer is not a member or on which it is not represented. It all depends on what the parties have agreed to, as revealed by the words they have used in their contract.[47]

In other words, the domestic approach combining common law and legislative provisions was entirely adequate to protect the interests of employees. Given the doubts surrounding the interpretation of *Werhof*, the UKSC made a preliminary reference to the CJEU, asking whether the dynamic approach adopted within English law was compatible with Article 3 TUD read alongside the CJEU's judgment in *Werhof*.

Advocate General Cruz Villalón started by noting that *Werhof* ruled out any requirement to provide for a dynamic interpretation of the Directive.[48] However, the CJEU's remaining reasoning in that case was largely confined to the facts, which 'were appreciably different from those of the case now before the Supreme Court'.[49] Parkwood, unlike Freeway, had acquired an undertaking that was originally in the public sector. Consequently, Parkwood could neither take part in nor indirectly influence the collective bargaining process that occurs within the NJC, which is exclusively a body for local government collective bargaining.[50] The Advocate General concluded that 'in the context of the transfer of an undertaking, there is no obstacle to Member States allowing a transfer of dynamic clauses referring to future collective agreements'.[51] He noted that although the principal aim of the Directive was to protect workers in the event of a change of employer, there were also several employer-protective elements that could be discerned.[52]

The Advocate General thought that *Werhof* should not be read as laying down any general principle that it was 'incompatible with the Directive to

[46] *Parkwood Leisure Ltd v Alemo-Herron* [2011] 4 All ER 800 [7].
[47] ibid [9].
[48] AG Opinion in Case C-426/11 *Mark Alemo-Herron v Parkwood Leisure Ltd* ECLI:EU:C:2013:82.
[49] ibid para 19.
[50] ibid.
[51] ibid para 20.
[52] ibid paras 21–22.

preserve the effects of dynamic clauses referring to future collective agreements'.[53] Rather, *Werhof* should be confined to the specific circumstances in that case which dealt with certain peculiarities of German contract law. Furthermore, the expectations created by this clause for the employees of the transferred undertaking were markedly different from those generated by the relevant clause found in *Werhof*. In that case, the contractual clause was explicitly static and there was no real question that it could be interpreted dynamically. In *Alemo-Herron* by contrast, the entitlements relied on were 'more in the nature of certainties, as the clauses have been freely and expressly agreed between the parties, in accordance with the law in force at the time and are recorded in the contract of employment'.[54]

The Transfer of Undertakings Directive was therefore no 'impediment to the United Kingdom allowing parties to use dynamic clauses referring to future collective agreements and accepting that such clauses are transferable as a consequence of the transfer of an undertaking'.[55] This part of the Advocate General's Opinion is no more than a confirmation of the accepted view that the Directive, far from constituting a ceiling on Member State action, would allow for the continuation of the long-standing English law approach to dynamic clauses referring to future agreements. It is further worth noting that, at that time, the UK had chosen not to benefit from the limitation period on the continuation of collective agreements which is contained in Article 3(3) TUD, and which provides that 'Member States may limit the period for observing such terms and conditions with the proviso that it shall not be less than one year'.

The next stage of the Opinion is more problematic. The Advocate General rather tersely dealt with the argument raised in *Werhof* that the freedom of association, which is guaranteed by both Article 12 CFR and Article 11 of the European Convention on Human Rights (ECHR) was being infringed. According to the Advocate General, the issue in *Alemo-Herron* was not that the new employer would be compelled to join an organization in order to influence the contractual terms, but rather that it had no means of being so represented, as the NJC was a public body.[56] The real issue was instead the employer's 'fundamental right to conduct a business'.[57] Despite highlighting the importance of the freedom to conduct a business in Article 16 CFR, the Advocate General went on to hold that a dynamic interpretation would not run contrary to that

[53] ibid para 31.
[54] ibid para 38.
[55] ibid para 39.
[56] ibid para 44.
[57] ibid para 46.

provision so long as it was not unconditional or irreversible.[58] It was noted that although freedom of contract was indeed a component of the freedom to conduct a business, the absence of extended rulings on the matter and the lack of binding force of collective agreements in the UK meant that Article 16 CFR had not been violated in the present case.[59]

In its judgment, the CJEU, ostensibly relying on *Werhof*, preferred to adopt the German static approach, holding that where a transferee does not have the opportunity to participate in negotiations that are concluded after the date of transfer, the outcome of the negotiations should not be binding. The Directive must therefore be interpreted as *precluding* dynamic clauses referring to collective agreements negotiated after the date of transfer being enforceable against the transferee.[60] Like the Advocate General, the CJEU held that a fair balance must be sought between the competing interests of employers and employees, with due weight being given to the employer's freedom of contract found in Article 16 of the Charter:

> It is apparent that, by reason of the freedom to conduct a business, the transferee must be able to assert its interests effectively in a contractual process to which it is party and to negotiate the aspects determining changes in the working conditions of its employees with a view to its future economic activity.[61]

To hold otherwise would be to reduce employer freedom 'to the point that such a limitation is liable to adversely affect the very essence of its freedom to conduct a business'.[62] This was despite the fact that Article 8 TUD permits the Member States to provide for greater employee protection, ie this case arose within the context of a minimum harmonization directive.[63]

The CJEU went on to note that a dynamic interpretation would limit the employer's room for manoeuvre to make adjustments and changes, particularly as 'the transfer is of an undertaking from the public sector to the private sector, the continuation of the transferee's operations will require significant adjustments and changes, given the inevitable differences in working conditions

[58] *Alemo-Herron* (n 1) para 58.
[59] ibid para 54.
[60] ibid para 37.
[61] ibid para 33.
[62] ibid para 35.
[63] Marija Bartl and Candida Leone, 'Minimum Harmonisation after *Alemo-Herron*: The Janus Face of EU Fundamental Rights Review' (2015) 11 EuConst 140.

that exist between those two sectors'.[64] Due to the employer's need for room to manoeuvre, the dynamic interpretation would be 'liable to undermine the fair balance between the interests of the transferee in its capacity as employer, on the one hand, and those of the employees, on the other'.[65] Indeed, in previous case law concerning the Transfer of Undertakings Directive the CJEU has recognized that the purpose of legislative intervention in this field was twofold, namely to safeguard the rights of employees, but also to harmonize the costs of these protective rules for undertakings.[66] Despite this language of 'balance' and the (itself dubious) recognition that the Directive protects competing interests, the CJEU gave precedence to an employer's freedom of contract over the rights of employees as expressed in the Directive, which itself makes no reference to the necessity of such a balancing exercise at all, referring instead at Recital 3 to 'the protection of employees in the event of a change of employer, in particular to ensure that their rights are safeguarded'.

The CJEU also adopted a subtle yet fundamental change in approach between the present case and its earlier jurisprudence dealing with the freedom to conduct a business. In *Scarlet Extended*, for example, the CJEU noted that a 'fair balance' needed to be achieved between Article 16 CFR and competing fundamental rights.[67] In *Alemo-Herron*, on the other hand, the CJEU reinforced the move towards the test of the 'core content'. Under the *Scarlet Extended* test, litigants merely had to show that the outcome represented a fair compromise between two competing fundamental rights of equal value. The *Alemo-Herron* approach—despite also referring to the need to balance rights—requires that the irreducible core of one right has not been affected, ie there is actually no need to balance. Once the core content of freedom of contract has been eroded, it is irrelevant that a competing—and perhaps stronger—social right has been invoked. *Alemo-Herron* is not the first case to refer to the core content of the freedom to conduct a business, but in earlier cases such as *Sky Österreich* the CJEU defined this concept restrictively, noting that the limitation in question did not 'prevent a business activity from being carried out as such'.[68] Nevertheless, the concept of the essence of a fundamental right remains elusive and difficult to discern.[69]

[64] *Alemo-Herron* (n 1) para 27.
[65] ibid para 29.
[66] Case C-382/92 *Commission of the European Communities v United Kingdom of Great Britain and Northern Ireland* ECLI:EU:C:1994:233, para 15.
[67] *Scarlet Extended* (n 4) para 45.
[68] *Sky Österreich* (n 3) para 49.
[69] Maja Brkan, 'The Concept of Essence of Fundamental Rights in the EU Legal Order: Peeling the Onion to its Core' (2018) 14 EuConst 332, 333.

Another, and related, difficulty with the CJEU's approach to preserving the core or essence of the freedom to conduct a business is that it overlooks the oft-cited importance of that freedom being read in relation to its social function, as already discussed in Chapter 3. One of the major criticisms of the liberal conception of property is the instinct to align the 'core' of property rights with the autonomy of the individual and thereby to insulate that same core from any limitations, save in the face of the most important of societal interests.[70] As explored further in Part III, it is possible to reimagine the 'core' of economic rights and freedoms to reflect the plurality of values that such rights are capable of serving in society, including respect for fundamental economic and social rights as limitations on individualistic conceptions of property rights, or, as argued here, business freedoms.[71] Before engaging with the meaning of freedom of contract within EU law, and ascertaining the rights that lie at the core of that freedom, it is worth considering whether it might be possible on a more immediate, and doctrinal, level to rationalize the obvious tensions that exist between the dynamic and static approaches to the interpretation of the Transfer of Undertakings Directive, and which have led to radically different levels of protection being granted to employee interests.

4.3.3 Rationalizing the divergence between the dynamic and static approaches

The case of *Vittoria Graf* offers a potential insight into the seemingly contrasting approaches adopted by the CJEU in relation to Article 16 CFR in both *Werhof* and *Alemo-Herron*. In order to rationalize the tensions between the two cases it is necessary to examine the purpose of the Transfer of Undertakings Directive holistically and having regard to the underlying rationale for the existence of dynamic clauses, with that rationale also potentially diverging depending on the Member State legal system in question.[72] Under German law, for example, the rationale for the existence of such dynamic clauses is to allow for the application by employers of collective agreements to employees who are not members of a trade union as well as to allow employers who are

[70] Sheila R Foster and Daniel Bonilla, 'Symposium on the Social Function of Property: A Comparative Law Perspective' (2011) 80 Fordham L Rev 101, 109; Duncan Kennedy, 'Form and Substance in Private Law Adjudication' (1976) 89 Harv L Rev 1685, 1737.

[71] Gregory S Alexander, 'Reply: The Complex Core of Property' (2009) 94 Cornell L Rev 1063.

[72] AG Opinion in Joined Cases C–680/15 and 681/15 *Asklepios Kliniken Langen-Seligenstadt GmbH v Ivan Felja and Asklepios Dienstleistungsgesellschaft mbH v Vittoria Graf* ECLI:EU:C:2017:30.

not—or cannot—be involved in the relevant collective bargaining machinery nevertheless to apply collective agreements to their workforce. This is precisely what occurred in *Vittoria Graf*, but subsequent to the transfer of the business the transferee employer refused to honour future changes to the relevant collective agreement in the same way as in *Alemo-Herron*. According to Advocate General Bot, the Transfer of Undertakings Directive precludes the transferee from being obliged to apply the terms arising from future changes to collective agreements.[73]

The Advocate General noted that in *Werhof*, the CJEU had started from the position that the transfer of dynamic clauses—as with the transfer of any contractually agreed term or condition of employment—fell within the scope of the Directive. The effect was that the dynamic clause transferred regardless of whether or not the transferee employer was a party to that collective agreement. The next step in the CJEU's reasoning was to ask whether the Directive must be interpreted as transferring only those terms and conditions that existed on the date of the transfer, or whether the term incorporating the collective agreement should be construed dynamically. Article 3(1) TUD would suggest that the term should be transferred, but that provision also had to be read alongside Article 3(3) TUD, which provides that a collective agreement is 'to continue to be observed only until the date of its termination or expiry, or the entry into force or application of another collective agreement'. That same provision allows Member States to limit the obligation to respect collective agreements, as long as this period is not less than one year (an option not initially exercised by the UK). The final stage in *Werhof* was for the CJEU to assess the dynamic approach to the interpretation of the contractual clause in light of the employer's freedom of association.

The reasoning process in *Alemo-Herron* was different in that the CJEU initially recalled that, following *Werhof*, the Transfer of Undertakings Directive should not be interpreted as *requiring* a dynamic interpretation. The Court then observed that Article 8 TUD permitted Member States to increase the level of protection granted to employees, ie once again the Directive is a minimum harmonization measure. The CJEU, having concluded that the dynamic approach was indeed more protective of employees, went on to assess the precise extent of Member State discretion to go beyond the minimum levels of protection granted by the Directive. For the CJEU, the aims of the Directive were to ensure a fair balance between the interests of employees and the employer, the latter of which must be in a position to make the necessary changes

[73] ibid para 12.

to its operations, particularly in the context of a transfer from a public to a private undertaking.[74] The CJEU then considered whether the dynamic approach was compatible with the freedom to conduct a business found in Article 16 of the Charter, concluding that although the Member States enjoy some discretion, that discretion could not be exercised in a manner such as to undermine the very essence of the employer's freedom to conduct a business.

As to the relationship between Article 3 TUD and Article 8 TUD, Advocate General Bot noted that the starting point as in *Werhof* was that a contractual clause referring to a future collective agreement does fall within the scope of Article 3(1) TUD and is automatically transferred. The second stage is to read Article 3(1) TUD in light of Article 3(3) TUD, which 'provides a compromise intended to reconcile the interests of the transferee and those of the employees'.[75] The overall conclusion in *Vittoria Graf*, which more closely aligned with *Werhof* than with *Alemo-Herron*, was that

> the dynamic reference clause ceases to have effect [. . .] where [the collective agreement] expires, terminates or is replaced and, if the Member State has so provided, where at least one year has passed since the undertaking was transferred. Those clauses do not therefore apply to collective agreements concluded after the date of transfer, unless the new employer expresses a different wish.[76]

It made no difference whether or not the German implementing legislation allowed for both consensual and unilateral changes to be made by the transferor for the reason that, although Article 8 TUD did allow for greater protection, this could not be allowed entirely to circumvent the rules in Article 3 TUD. This conclusion was reached following the approach adopted in *Werhof* without the need to invoke the freedom to conduct a business within Article 16 of the Charter at all, the conclusion being that 'by refraining from imposing on the transferee in an unlimited and uncertain fashion obligations arising from future collective agreements over which it has no influence', concerns relating to the transferee's freedom to conduct a business were already adequately addressed.[77]

[74] A balance already considered within the legislation itself: Marija Bartl and Candida Leone, 'Minimum Harmonisation and Article 16 of the CFREU: Difficult Times Ahead for Social Legislation?' in Hugh Collins (ed), *European Contract Law and the Charter of Fundamental Rights* (Intersentia 2017) 113, 114.

[75] AG Opinion in *Vittoria Graf* (n 72) para 77.

[76] ibid para 81.

[77] ibid para 113.

With regard to the UK context, which had arisen in *Alemo-Herron*, it should first be noted that this case represents a clear illustration of the Charter's applicability to the UK during that country's membership of the EU, despite the supposed opt-out. Not only was the Charter applicable there, but it was used to overturn a long-standing line of domestic case law, albeit one that the UK government was more than willing to see overturned. The government had advocated that the Court adopt an interpretation of the Directive that would require, rather than merely permit, the static approach.[78] The immediate consequence for the UK of the CJEU's judgment in *Alemo-Herron* was the insertion of Regulation 4A of the Transfer of Undertakings (Protection of Employment) Regulations 2006 (TUPE) to reflect the static approach.[79] It is clear that up until the decision in *Werhof*, the UK courts had been interpreting both the Directive and the domestic regulations in a dynamic way. *Alemo-Herron* therefore represented an overturning of the long-standing domestic law approach whereby contractual terms containing explicit references to future collective agreements were binding on the new employer.[80]

The parties to the dispute in *Alemo-Herron* both agreed that this was a common contractual practice, particularly in the public sector.[81] This is reflective of the UK's 'flexible' approach to collective bargaining, whereby collective agreements are denied legal effect and must instead be incorporated by reference into the contract of employment through a bridging term giving effect to the collective agreement, a term which can itself be renegotiated.[82] Of course, this approach to the interpretation of dynamic clauses was derived from the underlying EU legislation which overturned the pre-existing common law position whereby the transfer of the business had the effect of terminating the employment contract.

At the end of the post-Brexit transition period, domestic legislation implementing EU directives was granted the status of 'retained EU law' in accordance with section 2 of the European Union (Withdrawal) Act 2018 (EU(W)A 2018), while underlying EU directives were not granted such status save to the extent that any directly effective rights are preserved under section 4 EU(W)A 2018. At the same time, the CJEU continued to act as a guide to

[78] Jeremias Prassl, 'Freedom of Contract as a General Principle of EU Law? Transfers of Undertakings and the Protection of Employer Rights in EU Labour Law' (2013) 42 ILJ 434, 444.

[79] SI 2006/246.

[80] *Whent v T Cartledge* [1997] IRLR 153; *BET Catering Services Ltd v Ball* EAT/637/96; *Glendale Grounds Management v Bradley* EAT/485/97.

[81] AG Opinion in *Alemo-Herron* (n 48) para 6.

[82] *Ford Motor Co Ltd v Amalgamated Union of Engineering and Foundry Workers* [1969] 2 QB 303; Case C–324/86 *Foreningen af Arbejdsledere i Danmark v Daddy's Dance Hall A/S* ECLI:EU:C:1988:72.

the interpretation of retained EU law in the guise of retained EU case law in compliance with section 6 EU(W)A 2018, thereby preserving the interpretative influence of cases such as *Alemo-Herron*. However, section 5(5) EU(W) A 2018 makes it clear that any references to the Charter should now be read as referring to corresponding general principles instead, emphasizing the importance of the latter as a distinct source of Union and now domestic fundamental rights. Although the CJEU does not refer to the general principles in *Alemo-Herron*, business freedoms generally, and the freedom of contract specifically, have long constituted general principles, with those principles thereby meeting the requirement of being 'recognised' before the end of the transition period.

As noted in Chapter 2, from 31 December 2023 retained EU law has been relabelled 'assimilated EU law', in accordance with section 5 of the Retained EU Law (Revocation and Reform) Act (REULA) 2023. Crucially, however, section 4 REULA 2023 removes the general principles of EU law from domestic law altogether, thereby further eroding their formal interpretative value. The 2023 Act also contains powers enabling ministers to reproduce the 'effects' of concepts such as the general principles without reproducing the general principles themselves.[83] Of course, freedom of contract has also long existed as a (foundational) common law principle with the relationship between the domestic and Union-derived conceptions of freedom of contract also showing evidence of divergence even prior to Brexit, as addressed in the assessment of the CJEU's decision in *Alemo-Herron*.

Assimilated EU case law also remains essentially unmodified by the Act but with section 6 REULA 2023 seeking to facilitate—if not necessarily encourage—lower courts to depart from assimilated EU case law by means of the newly introduced reference mechanism. Section 6(3) REULA 2023 provides a list of factors to which ('among other things') the domestic courts should 'have regard' when considering a departure from retained EU law. These factors include the fact that decisions of 'foreign' courts are not usually considered binding, with the Act further encouraging domestic courts to consider any changes in circumstances and, importantly, the extent to which retained EU case law restricts the 'proper development' of domestic law.

[83] REULA 2023, s 12.

The CJEU's application of the freedom to conduct a business in *Alemo-Herron* disrupted the long-standing and permissive common law approach to the dynamic incorporation of the terms of collective agreements. The extent to which this approach can be said to have restricted or interrupted the proper development of domestic law must however be doubted, particularly given the UK government's support for the static approach to the interpretation of the Transfer of Undertakings Directive. After Brexit, the UK therefore has the opportunity to depart from the expansive approach to the freedom to conduct a business and the consequent restrictions on the protection of economic and rights although such a departure is highly unlikely in practice, with erosion of underlying transfer rights, ie substantive employment rights, constituting a more likely longer-term risk despite the added (limited) 'embedment' of Union social rights, as provided for in both the Withdrawal Agreement and the Trade and Cooperation Agreement.

Overall, the changes introduced under the REULA 2023 have no immediate effect on the domestic status of the TUPE Regulations which, as implementing legislation, were already embedded into domestic law. For the same reason, ie it is essentially entirely a creature of domestic law, the legislation remains vulnerable to repeal in the same way as other provisions of retained and assimilated EU law, given the now further entrenched absence of a supremacy principle governing the relationship between domestic and Union-derived norms, save to the extent that the hierarchy between legislative sources is modified in accordance with the terms of the REULA 2023.

To date, only relatively minor changes to TUPE have been proposed, notably the removal of the obligation to consult with employee representatives in the case of the transfer of fewer than 10 employees in businesses of fewer than 50 employees.[84] Of course, former EU legislation now operates within a very different legislative and normative context, including the application of domestic contractual autonomy concepts, which may or may not be informed by pre-existing Union law concepts. A glaring omission from the CJEU's existing case law on the freedom to conduct a business is the absence of any engagement regarding the actual meaning of freedom of contract, whether as a component of the freedom to conduct a business or within the wider EU law context.

[84] UK Government, 'Smarter Regulation to Grow the Economy', 10 May 2023, para 4.2.

4.4 The Meaning of Freedom of Contract in European Union Law

4.4.1 Freedom of contract as a regulatory technique

A major difficulty in ascertaining the meaning of freedom of contract within EU law is that this freedom is highly dependent on the underlying social, political, and economic 'framework' applicable to particular communities (jurisdictions) leading to divergences in national conceptions of freedom of contract across the various Member States, beyond perhaps the basic requirement of the existence of a *market* economy.[85] As Bartl and Leone note, 'freedom of contract is tightly linked to the interpretation of the scope of the market in a particular community. Its content follows narrowly the community's understanding of the relation between market and society.'[86] As argued here, the manner in which this relationship is conceived can also change over time, leading to apparent inconsistencies or contradictions in judicial treatment of concepts such as freedom of contract, particularly in the fundamental rights field which is itself characterized by potentially competing or conflicting values.

The absence of a comprehensive legislative harmonization of Union-level contract law thereby renders difficult the ascertainment of the basic level of protection to be granted to freedom of contract within EU law, whether as a component of the fundamental freedom to conduct a business or more generally. The Draft Common Frame of Reference (DCFR) for a harmonized EU contract law, compiled by academic experts, describes contractual autonomy as no more than a 'starting point'.[87] Article II-1:102(1) provides that '[p]arties are free to make a contract or other juridical act and to determine its contents, subject to any applicable mandatory rules.' Similarly, Article 0:101 of the Principes Directeurs provides that '[e]ach party is free to contract and to choose who will be the other party. The parties are free to determine the content of the contract and the rules of form which apply to it. Freedom of contract operates subject to compliance with mandatory rules.' From this, it can be said that the principle of contractual autonomy embraces the freedom to enter a

[85] Bartl and Leone (n 63) 149.
[86] ibid.
[87] Christian von Bar and others (eds), 'Principles, Definitions and Model Rules of European Private Law Draft Common Frame of Reference (DCFR)' Outline Edition 65.

contract, the freedom to select a contractual partner, and the freedom of classification and content.[88]

In addition, the DCFR itself recognizes a number of permissible limitations on the contractual autonomy principle. First, third-party contracting is not permitted. Secondly, contracts which are harmful to third persons and society in general may be invalidated, for example if it is illegal or contrary to public policy. Thirdly, it may be unjust to enforce a contract when one of the parties is in a comparatively weak bargaining position or where consent is defective, for example in cases of mistake or fraud. This ensures that 'contractual freedom is genuine freedom'.[89] Fourthly, the freedom to choose a contractual partner is curtailed where this freedom would lead to discrimination. Fifthly, parties will not always be permitted to withhold information at the pre-contractual stage. Sixthly, there is a need to ensure party information as to the terms of the contract, for example where the terms are not individually negotiated or accessible to one party. Finally, the DCFR recognizes that 'take it or leave it contracts' are increasingly prevalent, and that the law must therefore address inequality of bargaining power.[90] Having said all this, the DCFR concludes that 'the interference with freedom of contract should be the minimum that will solve the problem [...] it must be asked whether it is necessary to make a particular term mandatory or whether a flexible test such as "fairness" would suffice to protect the weaker party'.[91] Overall, the emphasis in the DCFR is on the restrictive, rather than expansive or pervasive, nature of freedom of contract in EU law, which is also reflective of the early case law on freedom of contract as a general principle which was largely permissive of restrictions on that principle.

Three broad models for such restriction of freedom of contract within the EU context have been suggested, namely the paternalistic, the social, and the perfectionist models. Under the paternalistic approach, the State is entitled to interfere with freedom of contract as long as this intervention is authorized by the law and is subject to strict limits.[92] This model is reflected in the case law of the CJEU on freedom of contract as a general principle. The idea underlying this model is that individuals are unable, in certain circumstances, to identify their own preferences. The State therefore intervenes to give effect to the *true*

[88] Carsten Herresthal, 'Constitutionalisation of the Freedom of Contract in European Union Law' in Katja S Ziegler and Peter M Huber (eds), *Current Problems in the Protection of Human Rights* (Hart 2013) 89, 96.

[89] DCFR (n 87) 65.

[90] ibid 67.

[91] ibid.

[92] Maria Marella, 'The Old and the New Limits to Freedom of Contract in Europe' (2006) 2 ERCL 257, 261.

desires of the parties. Within the employment context, this paternalism is illustrated through the concept of 'non-waivability', ie essentially in recognition of the employee's weaker bargaining position, legislative employment rights generally cannot be waived.[93] The second model is the social model. This model seeks to control the formation of contracts where weak parties face strong parties. Under this approach, freedom of contract is seen as a source of social injustice.[94] Therefore, parties are considered *unable* to identify their own preferences. Finally, the perfectionist model is a more stringent form of paternalism, which views the parties as having the *wrong* set of preferences.[95]

Connecting these three potential models for restricting freedom of contract is the idea of 'choice', which ties into broader discussions concerning the behavioural regulation of contractual relations, and which is aimed at encouraging 'minimalist forms of government action that preserve freedom of choice'.[96] The employment contract necessarily requires at least one human party, and so it is almost inevitable that employment legislation will touch upon aspects of human 'behaviour'. It can be said that such a behavioural element exists where the purpose of the legislation is to change human behaviour or where behavioural responses might hinder the purpose of legislation.[97] In particular, 'nudges' as a subset of behavioural regulation seek to overcome human inaction by making choices easier and as such must be 'choice-preserving'.[98] Nudges are essentially interventions by the State or private actors that steer people in (predictable) welfare-enhancing directions, as judged by the individual themselves but without forbidding any options or involving the use of 'incentives'.[99] Nudges are often presented as a cheaper and more efficient alternative to legislation, but which can also be used in combination with traditional regulatory techniques, so the two are not necessarily mutually exclusive.[100]

Despite the emphasis on freedom of choice, nudges also have to be 'chosen', which creates a potential tension (or indeed contradiction) between paternalist (welfare-enhancing) intervention and unfettered (due to possible opt-out)

[93] Guy Davidov, 'Non-waivability in Labour Law' (2020) 40 OJLS 482, 483.

[94] Marella (n 92) 269.

[95] ibid.

[96] Ryan Bubb and Richard H Pildes, 'How Behavioral Economics Trims its Sails and Why' (2014) 127 Harv L Rev 1593, 1595.

[97] Fabiana Di Porto and Nicoletta Rangone, 'Behavioural Sciences in Practice: Lessons for EU Rule Makers' in Alberto Alemanno and Anne-Lise Sibony (eds), *Nudging and the Law* (Hart 2015) 29, 31.

[98] Alberto Alemanno and Anne-Lise Sibony, 'The Emergence of Behavioural Policy-Making: A European Perspective' in Alberto Alemanno and Anne-Lise Sibony (eds), *Nudging and the Law* (Hart 2015) 1, 3.

[99] Cass R Sunstein, 'The Ethics of Nudging' in Alberto Alemanno and Anne-Lise Sibony (eds), *Nudging and the Law* (Hart 2015) v.

[100] Alemanno and Sibony (n 98) 2.

freedom of choice, which has led some commentators to describe nudging as 'libertarian paternalism'.[101] As Bubb and Pildes put it, 'it would be surprising if the main policy implication of the mounting evidence documenting the failure of individual choice was a turn towards regulatory instruments that preserve individual choice'.[102] As such, individual autonomy is at once being presented as the cause and the cure of regulatory failings. The concept of libertarian paternalism may therefore appear to be an oxymoron, with the paternalistic elements of nudge theory undercutting the 'key libertarian assumption that individuals are the best judges and protectors of their own welfare'.[103] However, not all forms of nudge face the same objections from an autonomy-protection point of view. Rather, a distinction can be made between various 'degrees' of nudging.

First-degree nudges are the most respectful of autonomy in that they merely enhance individual reflection, for example through the provision of information or reminders.[104] Second-degree nudges exploit human behavioural limitations so as to 'bias' a decision in the direction chosen by the regulator. Such nudges are identifiable if the chooser reflects on the matter, ie the chooser will know that they have been nudged.[105] Finally, third-degree nudges are highly intrusive, consisting of the manipulation of human behaviour, for example through framing devices (the manner in which information is presented). The chooser does not know and cannot know that he has been nudged.[106] The degree of 'interference' with autonomy principles is also a different question to that of the 'type' of nudge to select.[107] Of particular relevance both to the employment context, but also to the balancing of autonomy and regulatory intervention is the use of 'defaults'.

Defaults, as with other (behavioural) regulatory tools, are intimately linked with the notions of 'choice' and 'consent'. A default rule 'specifies the outcome in a given situation if people make no choice at all'.[108] Defaults interact with behavioural insights in three ways. First, defaults can be used to exploit human inertia, ie our unwillingness to choose. In this sense, defaults can be used to

[101] Cass R Sunstein and Richard H Thaler, 'Libertarian Paternalism is not an Oxymoron' (2003) 70 U Chi L Rev 1159, 1161–62.

[102] Bubb and Pildes (n 96) 1595.

[103] Gregory Mitchell, 'Libertarian Paternalism is an Oxymoron' (2005) 99 Northwest U L Rev 1245, 1249.

[104] Robert Baldwin, 'From Regulation to Behaviour Change: Giving Nudge the Third Degree' (2014) 77 MLR 831, 835.

[105] ibid 835–36.

[106] ibid 836.

[107] ibid 835.

[108] Di Porto and Rangone (n 97) 37.

achieve a regulatory aim, although in order to be a 'nudge' defaults would have to increase welfare as judged by the individual being nudged. Secondly, defaults can be considered as creating an implicit endorsement over the choice set out therein. In other words, choosers consider that the default has been chosen by the legislator (or the employer) for a (good) reason. Finally, there is the 'endowment effect', ie choosers prefer not to have something taken away from them, even if there is a chance that what they might receive instead would be more valuable to them, and with the acceptance of the default also costing nothing in time or effort.[109]

Default rules are also less 'covert' than other forms of nudging, which resonates with the CJEU's emphasis on 'participation' as a crucial element of contractual consent in cases such as *Alemo-Herron*, which involved the *exclusion* of the transferee employer from the collective bargaining process.

In order to comply with autonomy principles, it must always be possible to opt out of a default rule, ie the rule is 'derogable', which can undermine the rationale underpinning the default in that 'those who opt-out are not consistently the ones who are better off outside of the default'.[110] Moreover, defaults can be liberty—rather than welfare—enhancing.[111] In this respect, it is necessary to consider the values underpinning the relevant default rule if such rules are not to be 'arbitrary' in the absence of the parties' freedom to deviate from those defaults.[112] The use of defaults is not alien to the employment law context, which is reflective of the distinction between *ius dispositivum*, ie norms that may be varied by the parties to the employment contract, and *ius cogens*, ie mandatory norms that are not subject to contractual (re)negotiation, that is to say they are 'non-waivable'.[113]

While this distinction is largely a product of the civil law tradition, within the UK context (most) legislative protections can also be conceived as *ius cogens*, largely due to the recognition of the inequality of bargaining power as between the parties to the employment relationship, with the purpose underpinning protective legislation being undermined if 'contracting out' were to be permissible.[114] Having said this, the traditional regulatory role of collective

[109] ibid 38.
[110] ibid 51.
[111] Mitchell (n 103) 1260.
[112] Roger Brownsword, 'The Theoretical Foundation of European Private Law: A Time to Stand and Stare' in Roger Brownsword and others (eds), *The Foundations of European Private Law* (Hart 2011) 159, 170.
[113] Mark Freedland, 'Ius Cogens, Ius Dispositivum, and the Law of Personal Work Contracts' in Peter Birks and Arianna Pretto (eds), *Themes in Comparative Law: In Honour of Bernard Rudden* (OUP 2002) 165; Bernard Rudden, 'Ius Cogens, Ius Dispositivum' (1980) 11 Cambrian Law Review 87.
[114] Alan Bogg, 'Default Norms in Labour Law: Form Private Right to Public Law' in Birke Hacker and Johannes Ungerer (eds), *Default Rules in Private Law* (forthcoming, Hart); Lord Wedderburn,

agreements within the UK serves to emphasize the ongoing relevance of *ius dispositivum* in the regulation of contractual (employment) relationships, save to the extent that the basic features of an (employment) contract cannot be waived, as otherwise the agreement would not constitute an (employment) 'contract' at all.[115] In other words, there is likely to be a limit to the extent of the parties' ability—whether individually or collectively—to avoid basic employee-protective terms through the exercise of their freedom of contract—whether those terms are derived from legislation or implied at common law—while still holding a contract of *employment*.

Within the EU labour law context, one of the clearest examples of a default rule being employed is the opt-out to the 48-hour working week found within Article 6 of the Working Time Directive (WTD).[116] Article 22(1) WTD allows Member States to derogate from the protections granted by Article 6 WTD subject to certain conditions, ie the legislation itself permits contracting out. Article 18 WTD also allows for collective derogation from other specified provisions of the Directive. The default rule is that workers enjoy the right to a working week of no more than 48 hours' duration, calculated over an appropriate reference period. This particular default rule is unusual in a number of respects. First, the Member State in question must have provided for the default in its implementing legislation. Secondly, one of the conditions for the application of the opt-out from the 48-hour working week is obtaining the consent of the employee. In *Pfeiffer*, the CJEU held that:

> [i]f a worker [. . .] is encouraged to relinquish a social right which has been directly conferred on him by the directive, he must do so freely and with full knowledge of the facts. Those requirements are all the more important given that the worker must be regarded as the weaker party to the employment contract and it is therefore necessary to prevent the employer being in a position to disregard the intentions of the [worker] to impose [. . .] a restriction of his rights without him having expressly given his consent.[117]

'Inderogability, Collective Agreements, and Community Law' (1992) 21 ILJ 245; *Uber BV v Aslam* [2021] 4 All ER 209.

[115] *Photo Production Ltd v Securicor Transport Ltd* [1980] AC 827, 848, 849 (Lord Diplock).

[116] Directive 2003/88/EC of the European Parliament and of the Council of 4 November 2003 concerning certain aspects of the organisation of working time [2003] OJ L299/9.

[117] Joined Cases C-397/01–403/01 *Bernhard Pfeiffer v Deutsches Rotes Kreuz, Kreisverband Waldshut eV* ECLI:EU:C:2004:584, para 82.

Thirdly, the opt-out from the Directive is easily exercised and has been used widely in practice.[118] Usually, however, defaults will not be so easily opted out of. This is largely because the exercise of this option both 'assumes a level of competence, rationality and volitional control that contradicts the underpinning assumptions of behavioural economics' and 'understates the extent to which opt-outs discriminate against parties who are less able to exercise them'.[119] Moreover, default rules are predicated on an approach based on the 'defence of normative individualism', which emphasizes a formal notion of freedom as being 'freedom of *choice*' rather than individual—to say nothing of collective—'autonomy'.[120] Seeking to steer choosers in a particular direction is not the only function of the default rule. Rather, their more traditional function has been to fill gaps in incomplete contracts. In other words, 'they govern unless the parties contract around them' and to that extent they differ from immutable rules which 'govern even if the parties attempt to contract around them'.[121] Within the employment context, this function is usually performed by implied terms, which may or may not constitute default rules depending on whether they are capable of giving way to the manifested assent of the parties.[122]

Barnett suggests that the gap-filling function of default rules seems to undermine the neat distinction between terms that have been assented to and those that are imposed by law. Rather, a more appropriate trichotomy can be put forward, namely: (1) terms that have been assented to by the parties; (2) terms imposed by law; and (3) a new category of terms that are supplied by law, but nonetheless reflect the consent of the parties.[123] In other words, by entering a contract in the first place the parties are assenting to be bound by the background rules that the courts and legislature have imposed on the contracting process. In addition, far from interfering with the autonomy of the parties, such an approach views gap-filling defaults as completing lacunae left in the manifested consent of the parties. In order to maintain its status as a default rule (as opposed to an immutable rule), two conditions would have to be met. First,

[118] Catherine Barnard, Simon Deakin, and Richard Hobbs, 'Opting Out of the 48-Hour Week: Employer Necessity or Individual Choice? An Empirical Study of the Operation of Article 18(1)(b) of the Working Time Directive in the UK' (2003) 32 ILJ 223.

[119] Baldwin (n 104) 847.

[120] Alberto Alemanno and Anne-Lise Sibony, 'The Legitimacy and Practicability of EU Behavioural Policy-Making' in Alberto Alemanno and Anne-Lise Sibony (eds), *Nudging and the Law* (Hart 2015) 325, 325–26; Karen Yeung, 'Nudge as Fudge' (2012) 75 MLR 122.

[121] Ian Ayres and Robert Gertner, 'Filling Gaps in Incomplete Contracts: An Economic Theory of Default Rules' (1989) 99 Yale L J 87.

[122] Randy E Barnett, 'The Sound of Silence: Default Rules and Contractual Consent' (1992) 78 Va L Rev 821, 825.

[123] ibid 826.

indirect consent to a particular default cannot stem from the overall agreement to be bound by a contract if the parties have no reason to be aware of the default. Secondly, consent cannot be inferred if contracting around the rule is too costly.[124]

The discussion on the use of default rules demonstrates that the existing potential models for restricting freedom of contract are incomplete and overlook other legitimate reasons for seeking to impede the (absolute) application of freedom of contract, for example the removal of market distortions and externalities (such as those dealt with in the DCFR); cases of coercion or incapacity; or indeed, as argued here, to encourage respect for (competing) fundamental rights.[125] Furthermore, these difficulties may impede the (autonomous) harmonization of contract law, and thereby freedom of contract, within the Union context. Any such attempt will likely necessitate the adoption of both a common core and minimum common factor approach, leading to reductionism and thereby to 'an extremely narrow notion of freedom of contract' at Union level.[126]

4.4.2 Autonomous conceptions of freedom of contract

In the absence of formal harmonization of the concept of freedom of contract at Union level, the CJEU has had to derive an autonomous vision of that concept from the medley of existing common constitutional traditions of the Member States. Any legislative efforts at codifying a Union-wide definition of freedom of contract would also need to comply with fundamental rights concepts, including the business freedoms found within both the Charter and the general principles. It should be noted that only one Member State, Cyprus, grants a specific constitutional protection to the notion of contractual autonomy as opposed to the wider commitments to business freedoms that can be found in other Member States.[127]

German law has been particularly influential in the construction of business freedoms and property rights in the EU law context, with many of the earliest cases concerning the freedom to pursue a trade or occupation, as well as the right to property, originating in Germany. The idea that property

[124] ibid 866.
[125] Michael J Trebilcock, *The Limits of Freedom of Contract* (Harvard 1993).
[126] Marella (n 92) 260.
[127] European Agency for Fundamental Rights, 'Freedom to Conduct a Business: Exploring the Dimensions of a Fundamental Right' (2015) 28.

rights and business freedoms might enjoy a 'social function' has strong roots in the German *Sozialstaat* principle, with German law thereby adopting a strong commitment to 'social' paternalism.[128] English contract law by way of contrast, is underpinned by a more explicitly 'liberal' conception of contractual autonomy, with the law being used as a tool to promote free commerce. Under this model, freedom of contract 'means first and foremost the economic freedom to voluntarily engage in economic transactions without any risk of statutory interferences'.[129] Such interference is only permitted to the extent that it 'pragmatically' solves concrete concerns.[130] The latter conception of freedom of contract would seem to diverge from Union (fundamental rights) law conceptions of the same right, given that in cases such as *Alemo-Herron* a restriction that would have been compatible with the application of domestic English law was nevertheless found to violate freedom of contract as a component of the freedom to conduct a business as a fundamental right in Article 16 of the Charter.

It will be recalled that Lord Hope in the UKSC remarked that 'had this issue been solely one of domestic law, the question would have been open only to one answer'.[131] In the Employment Appeal Tribunal, Judge Hicks said that 'there is simply no reason why parties should not, if they choose, agree that matters such as remuneration be fixed by processes in which they do not themselves participate'.[132] In other words, being bound by dynamic clauses was no more than an ordinary application of the principle of freedom of contract. Everything turns on the interpretation of the words used in the contract itself, ie on the intention of the parties as expressed in the contract.

Of course, the Transfer of Undertakings Directive is a somewhat unusual example in that, at common law, the transfer of an employment contract actually had the effect of terminating the contract. Here, we see the common law concept of freedom of contract in its *interaction* with protective employment legislation. As Rimer LJ put it in the Court of Appeal, decisions such as *Whent* amount to no more than a conventional application of ordinary principles of contract law to the statutory consequences apparently created by Regulation 5 of TUPE.[133] This is a clear articulation of the fact that contractual autonomy as a common law principle is subject to legislative intervention. What we can

[128] Hans W Micklitz, 'On the Intellectual History of Freedom of Contract and Regulation' (2015) 4 Penn State Journal of Law & International Affairs 1.
[129] ibid 23.
[130] ibid 16.
[131] *Parkwood Leisure Ltd v Alemo-Herron* [2011] 4 All ER 800 [7].
[132] *Alemo-Herron v Parkwood Leisure* [2009] ICR 703 [16].
[133] *Parkwood Leisure Ltd v Alemo-Herron* [2010] ICR 793 [46]; *Whent v T Cartledge* [1997] IRLR 153.

see, then, is that at common law it is precisely freedom of contract that allows for the dynamic approach, whereas as a Union fundamental right it is that very freedom that prevents a dynamic interpretation. Nonetheless, it is important to emphasize the role that the legislation plays in steering the common law in an employee-protective direction. Outside the scope of legislative protections, the common law has continued to demonstrate a relatively strong commitment to contractual autonomy, despite the absence of a principled definition of that concept.[134]

This lack of a coherent legal definition of freedom of contract in English law stems largely from the fact that this principle was not originally a 'legal' concept as such but rather 'an economic and even political ideal, which probably had its roots in the personal, religious and intellectual freedoms which had their origins in the Reformation.'[135] It was only in the nineteenth century that freedom of contract as a *legal* rather than a political or philosophical principle began to emerge. At that stage, the ideal of freedom of contract was simply that 'persons of full capacity should in general be allowed to make what contracts they liked.'[136] The classic statement of contractual autonomy was made by Sir George Jessel when he said:

> [i]f there is one thing which more than another public policy requires it is that men of full age and competent understanding shall have the utmost liberty of contracting and that their contracts when entered into freely and voluntarily shall be held sacred and shall be enforced by Courts of Justice. Therefore, you have this paramount public policy to consider—that you are not lightly to interfere with this freedom of contract.[137]

Two more precise concepts are embedded within freedom of contract. First, there is the freedom of a party to choose to enter a contract and on whatever terms, thereby placing contractual obligations firmly within the will of the parties.[138] Secondly, there is a negative aspect of freedom of contract. This is the idea that there can be no liability without consent.[139] Although these elements remain the core of freedom of contract at common law, it is now widely recognized that they must give way in the face of competing legislative intervention.

[134] eg *Arnold v Britton* [2015] AC 1619.

[135] Patrick S Atiyah, *Essays on Contract* (OUP 1986) 355.

[136] Jack Beatson, Andrew Burrows, and John Cartwright (eds), *Anson's Law of Contract* (30th edn, OUP 2016) 3.

[137] *Printing & Numerical Registry Co v Sampson* (1875) LR 19 Eq 462, 465.

[138] Beatson, Burrows, and Cartwright (n 136) 4.

[139] ibid.

Four overarching restrictions on contractual autonomy at common law have been suggested. These are (1) public policy; (2) the parties' ability to exclude liability for fraud; (3) personal capacity; and, the most important for present purposes, (4) statutory regulation.[140] In the modern context, therefore, freedom of contract is still recognized but it is 'generally regarded as a reasonable social ideal only to the extent that equality of bargaining power between contracting parties can be assumed, and no injury is done to the economic interests of the community at large'.[141] Indeed, the English common law also exhibits additional values such as fairness or cooperation, and which can reinforce the protection of weaker parties to contractual arrangements.[142]

For example, the implied term of mutual trust and confidence exists as a 'necessary incident' of the employment contract, ie it is a (default) term implied in law regardless of the intention of the parties, which acts as a constraint on the behaviour of both employers and employees. In *Malik*, the implied term of mutual trust and confidence, which originated in the context of legislative protections against unfair dismissal, was formulated as requiring that the employer should not 'without reasonable and proper cause, conduct itself in a manner calculated and likely to destroy or seriously damage the relationship of confidence and trust between employer and employee', which is reflective of the 'relational'—as opposed to 'transactional'—nature of the employment contract.[143]

As Collins suggests, the requirement of mutual and trust and confidence may circumvent the general absence of 'good faith' requirements in English contract law and with the implied terms thereby constituting a tool for avoiding '[t]he philosophy of robust individualism that underlies the classical common law of contract'.[144] Moreover, the implied term of mutual trust and confidence is a prime candidate for recognition as a non-derogable or mandatory term, at least to the extent to which the absence of such a term means that the relevant contract will not be one of 'employment' at all.[145] Moreover, employment rights straddle the divide between the public and the private, notably due to the regulatory function of collective agreements which can contribute

[140] Neil Andrews, *Contract Law* (CUP 2015).
[141] ibid.
[142] Hugh Collins, *The Law of Contract* (4th edn, CUP 2003) 10–29.
[143] *Malik v Bank of Credit and Commerce International SA* [1998] AC 20; *Johnstone v Bloomsbury Health Authority* [1992] QB 333; Gabrielle Golding, *Shaping Contracts for Work* (OUP 2023); Hugh Collins, 'Employment as a Relational Contract' (2021) 137 LQR 426, 442.
[144] Collins (n 143).
[145] Hugh Collins, 'Implied Terms in the Contract of Employment' in Mark Freedland and others (eds), *The Contract of Employment* (OUP 2016) 471.

to the 'decommodification' of labour, in part by de-emphasizing its individual dimensions.[146]

Indeed, employment legislation has encroached extensively into the principle of freedom of contract, at times going so far as to impose terms on the individual contract of employment.[147] At the same time, a more substantive view of freedom of contract also envisages legislative intervention to ensure that the weaker party to the contract may enjoy real contractual autonomy in substance.[148] To achieve this, it will be necessary to end the conception of legislative intervention as an 'exception' or limitation to contractual autonomy.[149] Within the consumer law context, for example, Union legislation has adopted the position that consumers as a 'category' warrant particular protection as the weaker party, regardless of whether an actual power imbalance exists in a particular case, ie the focus is on 'structural' imbalance.[150] In the same way, employment legislation can still be envisaged as protecting the 'weaker' party to the employment relationship even within the context of collective agreements which have the purpose of counteracting the imbalance of bargaining power between employers and employees.[151]

It is certainly true that the domestic legal systems of the EU Member States have largely developed a concept of the employment contract which has a certain degree of autonomy from general private law principles, being 'treated as a special kind of contract that is analysed and regulated in a different way from other types of market contracts'.[152] At an EU level, it is interesting to note that the architects of the DCFR regarded the employment contract as being excluded from their remit.[153] This has been described as 'an operation of isolating [. . .] employment law into its own enclave in which it is accepted that "general private law" does not rule, and in which a general notion of freedom of contract is specially subordinated'.[154]

[146] Vladimir Bogoeski, 'Nonwaivability of Labour Rights, Individual Waivers and the Emancipatory Function of Labour Law' (2023) 52 ILJ 179, 183.
[147] Equality Act 2010, ss 64–70; Golding (n 143) 119.
[148] Aurelia Colombi Ciacchi, 'Party Autonomy as a Fundamental Right in the European Union' (2010) 6 ERCL 303.
[149] ibid 303–04.
[150] Martijn W Hesselink, 'EU Private Law Injustices' (2022) 41 YEL 83, 106.
[151] Thomas Wilhelmsson, 'Varieties of Welfarism in European Contract Law' (2004) 10 ELJ 711, 720.
[152] Hugh Collins, 'Social Dumping, Multi-level Governance and Private Law in Employment Relationships' in Dorota Leczykiewicz and Stephen Weatherill (eds), *The Involvement of EU Law in Private Law Relationships* (Hart 2013) 223, 224.
[153] Mark Freedland, 'The Involvement of EU Law in Personal Work Relations: A Defining Issue for European Private Law?' in Dorota Leczykiewicz and Stephen Weatherill (eds), *The Involvement of EU Law in Private Law Relationships* (Hart 2013) 279, 284.
[154] ibid.

As a result of this separation, 'the law of and about the contract of employment is thus located in a special place, as if it were in private law but not of private law'.[155] Nevertheless, the 'equilibrium' between general private law principles and employment law remains distinctly 'fragile' in that the employment relationship is essentially a private contractual relationship.[156] As such, freedom of contract as well as other principles of general contract law continue to provide the background rules against which employee-protective legislation must operate, with the *contract* of employment constituting the gateway to accessing the most significant of these legislative protections.[157]

Overall, English law can be characterized by the absence of an overarching commitment to a principled conception of freedom of contract, the operation of which must therefore be demonstrated through the examination of concrete cases. As Atiyah put in in his seminal treatise on freedom of contract at common law, '[o]ne of its principal characteristics was its abstractness, its lack of particularity, and its attempt to treat all contracts as being of the same general character'.[158] By way of contrast, civilian legal systems, unlike their common law counterparts, have long recognized that there are different categories of contract underpinned by a more or less pervasive vision of contractual autonomy. This is considered anathema to the common law of *contract*, ie there is only one contract law as opposed to the law of *contracts*.[159] In practice, however, the distinction has never been that strong.

First, the common law courts have refused to enforce certain types of agreement, for example on the basis of moral or social reasons, the characteristics of the contracting parties, changes in circumstances, and even the 'basic fairness' of contractual terms.[160] Secondly, and most importantly, the legislature itself has intervened to limit freedom of contract. In the first instance, the contracting process has been modified when weak parties (eg employees or consumers) face stronger parties, for example through the requirement that certain basic employment terms and conditions be provided in written form.[161] Another technique has been the regulation of the *content* of certain contracts, for example the imposition of a minimum wage.[162] The latter technique has been

155 Douglas Brodie, 'The Autonomy of the Common Law of the Contract of Employment from the General Law of Contract' in Mark Freedland and others (eds), *The Contract of Employment* (OUP 2016) 124.

156 Freedland (n 153) 284.

157 Employment Rights Act 1996, s 230.

158 Patrick S Atiyah, *The Rise and Fall of Freedom of Contract* (OUP 1979) 402–05.

159 Stephen A Smith, *Atiyah's Introduction to the Law of Contract* (6th edn, OUP 2006).

160 ibid 6.

161 Employment Rights Act 1996, s 1. See also *Autoclenz Ltd v Belcher* [2011] 4 All ER 745 [35] on the value to be placed on the written agreement.

162 National Minimum Wage Act 1998.

particularly prevalent in the employment field, to the extent that the genuinely 'contractual' nature of that relationship can be questioned.[163]

Of course, as with the CJEU's approach to the discovery of general principles, it is not possible to reduce the EU law conceptualization of contractual autonomy to a sum of the component Member State approaches. Rather, contractual autonomy in EU law is 'bound to trans-border business and European economic integration', ie it is functional and instrumental to the creation of the internal market.[164] In this way, the EU also lacks a 'general' competence to act in the field of private law, with the Union instead constitutionalizing the 'market-instrumentality' of its private law.[165] In a similar way, Gill-Pedro has contrasted the 'freedom' value espoused by the Treaties, which he argues relates to the 'intrinsic' freedom of the individual, rather than the 'instrumental' freedom of companies.[166] In this sense, the granting of protections to the freedom of companies is merely a result of protections granted to individual humans rather than an end in itself.

As has been suggested here, however, the emerging connection between the freedom to conduct a business and the fundamental freedoms of the internal market has had the consequence that business freedoms as fundamental rights have themselves become 'instrumentalized', whether as a means of facilitating privatization (as in *Alemo-Herron*) or economic restructuring (as in *AGET Iraklis*). Viewed in this way, the freedom to conduct a business as a fundamental right disrupts existing approaches to the interpretation of the (protective) 'purpose' of underlying legislative protections. Conversely, the freedom to conduct a business serves as a mechanism for the reconceptualization of the internal market freedoms as 'fundamental rights'. All four freedoms (persons, services, goods, and capital) are referenced in the preamble to the Charter, but only the free movement of persons has been granted the status of a Charter right in Article 45 CFR.

EU law certainly poses a profound challenge for the traditional division between the public and private spheres, notably through its conceptualization of private law in a manner that diverges from the national legal orders of the Member States, with the (regulatory) relationship between private parties being viewed essentially through the lens of the internal market.[167] As such,

163 Golding (n 143).

164 Micklitz (n 128) 1; Rufat Babayev, 'Duality of Economic Freedom Protection in the Interplay of Article 16 CFR and Article 102 TFEU' (2020) 45 ELRev 694, 699.

165 Hesselink (n 150) 103.

166 Eduardo Gill-Pedro, 'Whose Freedom Is it Anyway? The Fundamental Rights of Companies in EU Law' (2022) 18 EuConst 183, 184.

167 Olha O Cherednychenko, 'Rediscovering the Public/Private Divide in EU Private Law' (2020) 26 ELJ 27, 32; Herresthal (n 88) 89, 90.

freedom of contract can be viewed as 'one of the most important structural issues in a liberal market order'.[168] It is certainly difficult to envisage a continental internal market without some level of commitment to contractual and business freedom. The link between Article 16 CFR and the fundamental internal market freedoms should not therefore be surprising. The European Fundamental Rights Agency has suggested, for example, that Article 16 CFR merely 'adds' to the Treaty freedoms by 'providing for an "enhanced" protection for business to conduct their affairs', enhanced in the sense of going beyond the need for a cross-border scenario which remains the trigger for the application of the internal market freedoms.[169] This is not to suggest, however, that freedom of contract is somehow a fundamental value underpinning that internal market, nor does EU internal market law embody a right to engage in the unhindered pursuit of commerce.[170] In other words, it cannot be concluded from the Treaty that the fundamental freedoms somehow *guarantee* freedom of contract.[171]

The Treaty freedoms have one essential aim and that is to open up national markets, with obstacles to the creation of that open market being set aside unless justified.[172] In this regard, the CJEU has also demonstrated a willingness both to recognize, but also to ensure the protection of social rights and interests in the face of the Treaty's economic freedoms, which, for example, includes recognition of a specific 'worker protection' derogation.[173] The CJEU has long recognized worker protection as a legitimate derogation allowing Member States to justify national laws providing substantive protection to the weaker party, so long as the derogation respected the limits of EU law and did not render the economic freedom illusory.[174] In a similar way to the suggestion here that freedom of contract itself exhibits a 'social' dimension, it can be said that the right to freedom of movement, guaranteeing as it does the right of workers to benefit from employment opportunities anywhere in the

168 Jürgen Basedow, 'Freedom of Contract in the European Union' (2008) 6 ERPL 901, 902.

169 European Agency for Fundamental Rights (n 127) 12.

170 Gareth Davies, 'Freedom of Movement, Horizontal Effect, and Freedom of Contract' (2012) 3 ERPL 805; AG Opinion in Case C-292/92 *Ruth Hünermund v Landesapothekerkammer Baden-Württemberg* ECLI:EU:C:1993:863.

171 Jacobien W Rutgers, 'The European Economic Constitution, Freedom of Contract and the DCFR' (2009) 5 ERCL 95, 102.

172 ibid 103.

173 Catherine Barnard, 'The Worker Protection Justification: Lessons from Consumer Law' in Panos Koutrakos, Niamh Nic Shuibhne, and Phil Syrpis (eds), *Exceptions from EU Free Movement Law* (Hart 2016) 108.

174 ibid 113.

Union, constitutes a 'social right' in itself.[175] This argument is reinforced by the mutual interdependence between freedom of movement and the right to work within and beyond EU law.[176] There is however a risk here in conflating worker welfare (the enjoyment of the opportunities offered by the market) and worker protection (derived from legislation). As the jurisprudence of the CJEU demonstrates, social dimensions of freedom of movement may become subject—if not subordinate—to the economic rationale inherent in the Treaty provisions.[177] Any such economic rationale does not necessarily lead to the conclusion that free movement law somehow embodies a principle of contractual autonomy.

Beyond considerations relating to the internal market, Union legislation also exhibits concern for the quality of consent of contracting parties in particular circumstances.[178] In other words, freedom of contract can be viewed either as an overarching economic principle underpinning all markets, the 'market vision', or it can be seen as a moral principle, based on the will of individuals, the 'voluntarist' vision of contractual autonomy.[179] Both visions can be found in EU law, with the fundamental freedoms representing the market vision but with EU legislation—notably in the consumer context—being concerned with the consent of the contracting parties.[180] In most instances, the outcome in an individual case will not depend on which of these visions prevails. Sometimes, however, focusing on the quality of consent or the will of the individual may lead to private transactions being impeded rather than facilitated.[181] In cases such as *Alemo-Herron*, it seems that the CJEU was concerned not to impede or discourage the acquiring of undertakings—particularly in the context of privatization. This is perhaps unsurprising when we consider that the very rationale for the adoption of the Transfer of Undertakings Directive was to facilitate mergers and acquisitions, although this should not be equated with the 'protection' of the employer.

[175] Dorota Leczykiewicz, 'Conceptualising Conflict between the Economic and the Social in EU Law after *Viking* and *Laval*' in Mark Freedland and Jeremias Prassl (eds), *Viking, Laval and Beyond* (Hart 2016) 307, 308.

[176] Niall O'Connor and Darren Harvey, 'Freedom of Movement and the Normative Value of the Right to Work in the United Kingdom Post-Brexit' (2024) CYELS Online First.

[177] Case C-341/05 *Laval un Partneri Ltd v Svenska Byggnadsarbetareförbundet, Svenska Byggnadsarbetareförbundets avdelning 1, Byggettan and Svenska Elektrikerförbundet* ECLI:EU:C:2007:809; Case C-438/05 *International Transport Workers' Federation and Finnish Seamen's Union v Viking Line ABP and OÜ Viking Line Eesti* ECLI:EU:C:2007:772.

[178] Simon Whittaker, 'The Optional Instrument of European Contract Law and Freedom of Contract' (2011) 3 ERCL 372, 373–74.

[179] ibid.

[180] ibid 375–76.

[181] ibid 374.

The case law concerning the CJEU's interpretation of the freedom to conduct a business as a fundamental right is thereby illustrative of wider potential distortions in the interpretation of the purpose of protective legislation. At the same time, (protective) legislation plays a crucial role in altering the baseline provided by general principles of contract law including freedom of contract, which is thereby reflective of competing social rights and values as explored further when addressing the deregulatory potential of the freedom to conduct a business as a fundamental right. The problem with conceptualizing freedom of contract as a fundamental right—as has occurred in the Union law context—is that the diversity of national law perspectives from which that freedom originated is essentially lost with freedom of contract becoming a fulcrum, a uniform 'value' to be promoted and protected. Freedom of contract itself is potentially composed of 'competing' social values in the form of that freedom's 'social function', which also has the potential to mould the essence or core content of the freedom to conduct a business as a Union fundamental right.

4.5 Unravelling the Essence of the Freedom to Conduct a Business

4.5.1 Determining the essence of fundamental rights

It is only rarely that Union legislation has been found to infringe the essence of fundamental rights, with this concept thereby constituting a potential barrier to reliance on business freedoms 'in the face of' social legislation.[182] Ultimately, the 'essence' of Union fundamental rights derives from Article 52(1) CFR governing permissible limitations on Charter rights, which itself draws on a long line of previous case law—including within the context of business freedoms as fundamental rights—providing that the 'very substance' of fundamental rights must be protected.[183] Article 52(1) CFR provides that 'any limitation on the exercise of the rights and freedoms recognised by this Charter must be provided for by law and *respect the essence* of those rights and freedoms [emphasis added]', with any limitations also being '[s]ubject to the principle

[182] Jeremias Prassl, 'Business Freedoms and Employment Rights in the European Union' (2015) 17 CYELS 189, 197.

[183] Joined Cases C-184/02 and 233/02 *Kingdom of Spain and Republic of Finland v European Parliament and Council of the European Union* ECLI:EU:C:2004:497, para 60; *Wachauf* (n 2) para 18; Case C-44/79 *Liselotte Hauer v Land Rheinland-Pfalz* ECLI:EU:C:1979:290, para 23; Brkan (n 69) 345.

of proportionality'.[184] On a conceptual level, the notion of a right's 'essence' is rather nebulous and further exacerbates the complexities associated with defining the nature of fundamental rights (and principles) themselves.[185]

A further difficulty with the essence approach is that it removes the need to balance competing interests, and instead identifies a core content of the relevant right where no justification or permissible restrictions can be relied upon.[186] In cases such as *Alemo-Herron*, what appeared to be no more than a fairly innocuous application of the long-standing dynamic approach to the application of the Transfer of Undertakings Directive was nevertheless found to penetrate the very core of the freedom to conduct a business as a fundamental right, but without delineating the precise extent of that core. There is also an unclear relationship between the concept of the very essence of a right and the proportionality principle. A measure undermining the essence of a Charter right will necessarily be disproportionate, while it is not necessarily the case that a measure respecting the core of a right will be proportionate.[187] In this way, EU law adopts an 'absolute' rather than a 'relative' approach to the relationship between the essence of a right and the proportionality principle whereby the core or essence of a right is not capable of limitation, meaning that there are no potential justifications for such a limitation and the proportionality principle does not apply at all.[188]

The absolute approach can be criticized on both doctrinal and normative grounds in that (1) the 'essence' or substance of a right is difficult to determine, while also adding little to a proportionality analysis, as would be applicable to the periphery of the relevant right; and (2) it undermines the 'culture of justification', whereby public bodies are to account for the reasons underlying their decisions.[189] As to the latter point, it is not the case that a finding by the CJEU that the essence of particular right has been infringed precludes the advancement of justifications on the part of the relevant actor, which would necessarily have taken place at an earlier stage of the proceedings, and may well have been dealt with by the Advocate General. Of course, this does not guarantee the (quality of the) CJEU's engagement with those justifications in its final judgment. It is also suggested that the real risk of the essence approach

[184] Art 19(2) of the German Basic Law recognizes the concept of an essential component of rights.

[185] Orlando Scarcello, 'Preserving the "Essence" of Fundamental Rights under Article 52(1) of the Charter: A Sisyphean Task? (2020) 16 EuConst 647, 654.

[186] Koen Lenaerts, 'Limits on Limitations: The Essence of Fundamental Rights in the EU' (2019) Ger Law J 779, 784.

[187] ibid 781.

[188] Brkan (n 69) 336; Scarcello (n 185) 648.

[189] Darren Harvey, 'The Essence of EU Fundamental Rights—Reflections in Light of the UK Experience' (2023) 5 EHRLR 438.

as far as justifications on potential restrictions of fundamental rights are concerned, lies rather in the CJEU's failure adequately to elucidate and justify its own findings.

As to the first point concerning the indeterminate nature of a right's 'essence' including in its relationship to the proportionality principle, it is useful to start by noting that in the case law on business freedoms as general principles, despite also recognizing the concept of the essence, or very substance of such freedoms, measures which appeared to intrude further into the freedom to conduct a business of the relevant undertakings were nevertheless compatible with the general principle. In subsequent case law, the CJEU has defined respect for the essence of a right to mean that the right 'is not called into question as such', suggesting a rather high barrier to a finding that the core content of the right has been infringed, with the CJEU essentially requiring that the relevant right be 'entirely extinguished', which may suggest a stricter approach when compared with cases using the related 'very substance' formula.[190] Furthermore, an absolute approach to the concept of the essence of fundamental rights overlooks the necessary 'balancing' that takes place at an earlier stage, ie prior to any conflict with potentially competing rights.[191] The freedom to conduct a business is 'internally' limited in relation to its social function, which allows for the (re) conceptualization of business freedoms around social concerns and which involves a form of balancing that avoids the (full) application of the proportionality principle.[192]

In certain cases concerning Article 16 CFR, notably *AGET Iraklis*, the CJEU also examined the essence of the freedom to conduct a business within the broader context of 'proportionality', thereby demonstrating the potential overlap between the two tests. In that case, the CJEU found that the 'very essence' of the freedom to conduct a business had not been violated by the national legislative regime governing the authorization of collective redundancies because the right was not excluded entirely, but that the regime's implementation, notably the assessment criteria, did not meet the relevant tests for permissible restrictions on fundamental rights and freedoms, ie a legitimate aim; that the measure was appropriate to achieve that aim; and that

[190] Case C–524/15 *Criminal proceedings against Luca Menci* ECLI:EU: C:2018:197; Steve Peers and Sacha Prechal, 'Article 52—Scope and Interpretation of Rights and Principles' in Steve Peers and others (eds), *The EU Charter of Fundamental Rights: A Commentary* (2nd edn, Hart 2020) 1611, 1634.

[191] Andrei Marmor, 'On the Limits of Rights' (1997) 16 Law & Phil 1.

[192] Scarcello (n 185) 661.

the measure did not go beyond what was necessary to achieve that aim.[193] In *Alemo-Herron*, there was no reference to Article 52(1) of the Charter, nor did the CJEU explicitly state that the essence of the freedom to conduct a business had been infringed. Rather, the Court noted that the dynamic approach was '*liable* to adversely affect the very essence of its freedom to conduct a business'.[194] The French language version of the judgment uses the term '*susceptible*', which similarly suggests doubt as to whether the restrictions found within that case *actually* interfered with the very essence of the freedom to conduct a business.

The finding in *Alemo-Herron* might better be explained by the distinction between objective and subjective interference with the essence of a fundamental right, with the former concerning the infringement of the right of all potential rights-holders rather than the particular individual party to the litigation, and with such limitations more likely to derive from the legislature.[195] It is not entirely evident whether the CJEU considered the restriction in that case to amount to an objective or subjective limitation on the freedom to conduct a business. The reason being that the CJEU stipulated that it was both the exclusion of the private employer from the public sector negotiating procedures and the more employee-protective approach to the incorporation of collective agreements that amounted to the restriction on the essence of the freedom to conduct a business.[196] Indeed, it has been suggested that 'privatization advocates promiscuously invoke the language of freedom, property rights, autonomy and dignity, albeit often in ways that are entirely alien to agreed international human rights standards'.[197]

It can be argued that it was the former and therefore subjective limitation that was at issue in *Alemo-Herron*, as further evidenced by subsequent case law in which no particular undertaking had been excluded, leading to a finding that the essence of the freedom to conduct a business had not been infringed.[198] Another reading of *Alemo-Herron* is possible however, in that the CJEU considered the domestic UK approach to the incorporation of collective agreements so *inherently* incompatible with the core content of the freedom to conduct a business that it eschewed the need for more detailed analysis of the precise extent and nature of the restriction in that case. The dynamic approach

193 Case C-201/15 *Anonymi Geniki Etairia Tsimenton Iraklis (AGET Iraklis)* ECLI:EU: C:2016:972, paras 84, 102.

194 *Alemo-Herron* (n 1) paras 35, 36.

195 Brkan (n 69) 351.

196 *Alemo-Herron* (n 1) paras 34–36.

197 Philip Alston, 'Report of the Special Rapporteur on Extreme Poverty and Human Rights' 73 UN Doc A/HRC/34/51, 18 January 2017, 22.

198 Brkan (n 69) 364; *AGET Iraklis* (n 193) paras 84–88.

did not *necessarily* exclude the transferee employer from the negotiating process, rather it was the fact that private parties could not be represented before the National Joint Council that led to the exclusion.

A further consequence of the CJEU's approach is that the meaning and content of the core or essence of the freedom to conduct a business is not explicitly addressed.[199] There are broader difficulties associated with the interpretation of the essence of a right given that such an interpretation requires application to concrete cases, making it difficult to extrapolate general criteria for defining the essence of a right.[200] Further confusion is caused in *Alemo-Herron* by the CJEU's reference both to the need to achieve a 'fair balance' between competing interests, but also the need to respect the essence of the freedom to conduct a business. The absolute approach to the protection of the essence of a fundamental right suggests that there is no need to conduct a balancing exercise of any sort as the proportionality principle does not apply to restrictions on the substance of a fundamental right. The reality may be that despite the CJEU's suggestion that essence and proportionality are separate concepts, there is overlap between the two in practice.[201]

As such, the 'bifurcation' that has been identified in relation to Article 51(2) CFR between the 'essence' test and the proportionality principle may not be as stark as it first appears. In addition, particular judgments that have been held out as evidencing a clear delineation between the two tests do not necessarily offer strong support for the distinction. In *ZZ*, for example, the CJEU noted that 'any limitation must in particular respect the essence of the fundamental right in question and requires, *in addition*, that subject to the principle of proportionality, the limitation must be necessary and genuinely meet objectives of general interest recognised by the European Union [emphasis added]'.[202] This statement is broadly reflective of the wording of Article 52(1) CFR itself, with the CJEU also not explicitly addressing whether the mentioned proportionality principle was applicable to the core content of the relevant right, as opposed merely to its periphery.

The proportionality principle nevertheless remains important in determining the 'extent' of the interference with the essence of a right, with the

[199] Lehavi suggests instead that property rights have no 'inherent essence', but merely structural and institutional 'traits': Amnon Lehavi, *The Construction of Property: Norms, Institutions, Challenges* (2013 CUP) 2.

[200] Takis Tridimas and Giulia Gentile, 'The Essence of Rights: An Unreliable Boundary?' (2019) Ger Law J 794, 804.

[201] ibid 811.

[202] Case C–300/11 *ZZ v Secretary of State for the Home Department* ECLI:EU:C:2013:363, para 51; Harvey (n 189) 441, 442.

'determining factors' being the severity and scope of the limitation of the relevant right.[203] 'Pragmatic' (as opposed to 'radical') variations on the absolute approach to a right's essence do indeed recognize the connection between the principle of proportionality and the concept of the essence of a fundamental right, whereby any interference with a right's core will be found to be disproportionate, thereby also distinguishing pragmatic absolutism from the relative approach to the essence of rights.[204]

It is suggested that the added value of relying on the essence of a right is that it acts as a powerful *ex-ante* signal to the legislature as to the potential permissible extent of restrictions on the right in question. The rather indeterminate nature of Union fundamental rights, deriving as they do from other diverse and dispersed rights sources, also requires the CJEU to elucidate the precise meaning and content of fundamental rights as they pertain to Union law, the core content of which may differ from similar rights found at Member State level. Moreover, it is not inconceivable that the 'essence', 'very substance', or 'core content' of a right might evolve over time, with the proportionality principle having a potential role to play in modulating the precise boundaries of this core at a given point. In other words, behaviour that was not considered an interference with the essence of a right in the past may become so due to changes in the CJEU's understanding of the content of that right.

An obvious avenue for such a possibility is the obligation contained in Article 52(3) CFR, which ensures interpretative consistency between the Charter and the ECHR. The latter has long been characterized by the ECtHR as a 'living instrument', capable of adapting to changes in social conditions.[205] Such a change in approach can for example be seen in the ECtHR's finding—contrary to its earlier decisions on the matter—that the right to bargain collectively had '*become* one of the essential elements [emphasis added]' of the right to form and to join a trade union under Article 11 ECHR, as opposed to its previous finding in *Wilson and Palmer* that collective bargaining was not an 'inherent element' of Article 11 ECHR, nor was it 'indispensable' to the effective enjoyment of trade union freedom, a conclusion the Court reached 'having regard to the developments in labour law, both international and national, and to the practice of Contracting States in such matters'.[206]

[203] Harvey (n 189) 443.

[204] Sébastien Van Drooghenbroeck and Cecilia Rizcallah, 'The ECHR and the Essence of Fundamental Rights: Searching for Sugar in Hot Milk' (2019) 20 Ger Law J 904, 911.

[205] *Tyrer v UK* (1979–80) 2 EHRR 1; Daniel Moeckli and Nigel D White, 'Treaties as "Living Instruments"' in Dino Kritsiotis and Michael Bowman (eds), *Conceptual and Contextual Perspectives on the Modern Law of Treaties* (CUP 2018) 136.

[206] *Demir and Baykara v Turkey* (2009) 48 EHRR 54, para 154; *Wilson and Palmer v UK* (2002) 35 EHRR 20, para 44.

The reviewed international sources included the Charter, which at Article 28 CFR provides for 'the right to negotiate and conclude collective agreements', with the Charter thereby containing specific collective bargaining rights in addition to the more general freedom of association in Article 12 CFR, which also contains specific reference to trade union matters. The right to bargain collectively has since explicitly been recognized by the CJEU as constituting a fundamental *right*.[207] The right of collective bargaining is yet another iteration of the circularity that is argued to characterize the Charter's provisions. The Explanations to Article 28 CFR cite Article 11 ECHR (among other social rights instruments) as a source for the applicable trade union rights, while at the same time the European Court of Human Rights (ECtHR) in *Demir*, relied on Article 28 CFR (again, alongside other social rights instruments) as an aid in the determination of the essential content of the trade union rights found within Article 11 ECHR, ie that they extended to a right to bargain collectively.

Of course, the 'very substance' or 'essence' test is not one that the ECtHR itself usually adopts.[208] The concept of a right's essence also has a rather ambiguous role within the context of the ECHR, notably due to its absence from the text of the Convention.[209] Nevertheless, the concept has played an important role in acting as a 'limit on limits' in the sense of providing a benchmark against which to scrutinize restrictions on Convention rights, a function that finds its origins in Article 19(2) of the German Basic Law which provides that basic rights may not be infringed upon in their essential content ('in no case may the essence of a basic right be affected').[210] Finally, the concept of the core, substance, or essence of a right has a potential role to play in establishing a priority between potentially competing rights. For example, courts, in resolving conflicts between rights, can assess whether the infringement into the core of one right is particularly extensive when compared with the relevant competing right.[211] In addition, the fact that a particular right does not require further legislative specification might indicate that its essence is horizontally applicable to private disputes.[212]

The ease with which the essence of the freedom to conduct a business has been found to be violated comes close to declaring that freedom to be *absolute* in nature, which contradicts the CJEU's earlier—albeit rather

[207] Case C-699/17 *Allianz Vorsorgekasse AG* ECLI:EU:C:2019:290, para 56.
[208] Peers and Prechal (n 190) 1621.
[209] Van Drooghenbroeck and Rizcallah (n 204) 904.
[210] ibid 906.
[211] ibid 918.
[212] Mark Dawson, Orla Lynskey, and Elise Muir, 'What is the Added Value of the Concept of the "Essence" of EU Fundamental Rights?' (2019) 20 Ger Law J 767.

tenuous—recognition that economic freedoms may be restricted in relation to their social function, ie the meaning of the concept of social function was left undefined. The precise content of Article 16 CFR's essence or substance itself remains ill-defined, as does the scope of the right itself, with this confusion both contributing to—and deriving from—the tensions in the case law concerning the reach of the freedom to conduct a business as a fundamental right.

In a similar way, the core content of a particular right must also be conditioned in accordance with competing rights and principles. In other words, particular provisions must be viewed within the context of the totality of the relevant framework, for example the Charter or the Union's fundamental rights ecosystem more broadly. The broader competing 'values' espoused by the Solidary and Freedoms Titles of the Charter, as well as the interrelationship between them, are addressed in Chapter 6 when considering the normative counterweights to the freedom to conduct a business as a fundamental right, but for now our attention will be directed at the more immediate provisions governing the contours of the freedom to conduct a business as a fundamental right, and which contribute to the delineation of that freedom's essence or core content.

4.5.2 Limitations on the essence of the freedom to conduct a business

It is argued throughout this book that *within* the freedom to conduct a business, there exist competing conceptions of that same freedom (and related property rights) in addition to competing conceptions within subcomponents of that freedom including freedom of contract, notably as mediated through the concept of a 'social function'. These limitations on the scope and content of freedom of contract can be conceived as an inherent aspect of that freedom, rather than a 'restriction' as such. In other words, freedom of contract contains the seeds for its own limitation, which reflects the broader reality that such a freedom remains 'an ill-defined standard, a general rule riddled with exceptions' and 'a single basic right with many facets', both individual and communitarian.[213] Article 16 CFR as a provision is itself further contoured by 'internal' limitations notably the textual limits contained in that provision. In particular, Article 16 CFR exhibits the textual features of a 'principle' rather than a 'right',

[213] David N Mayer, 'Substantive Due Process Rediscovered: The Rise and Fall of Liberty of Contract' (2009) 60 Mercer Law Review 563, 572, 628.

including the condition that the freedom to conduct a business be exercised in accordance with Union law, national laws and practices. It has been suggested here that these conditions have essentially been misconstrued by the CJEU in reliance on an overly broad interpretation of freedom of contract, and one that is supported neither by the Charter nor by the pre-existing general principles.

The next source of potential limitations on the freedom to conduct a business, are those related provisions found within the Freedoms Title of the Charter (Title II), and which, as argued here, may be relied on to condition the scope and content of the freedom to conduct a business, namely the right to property (Article 17 CFR) and crucially, the (social) right to work (Article 15 CFR). In other words, these provisions transcend the narrow context of the freedom to conduct a business but at the same time are deeply intertwined with it, while also being framed within the overarching normative context of the value of 'freedom', ie these limitations derive from the same 'cluster' of rights. Article 15 CFR on the right to engage in work has particular resonance with the freedom to conduct a business in Article 16 CFR given their shared origins in the freedom to pursue a trade or occupation as a general principle. As argued further in Chapter 6, the right to work provides a potential mechanism for reconceiving freedom of contract in 'socialized' terms, and in a manner that is also reflective of the social function of business freedoms.

In other words, there is an overlap between Article 16 CFR's internal limitations (social function) and the competing rights (right to work) found elsewhere within the Freedoms Title. These competing rights are also reinforced by other provisions of the Charter, notably within the Solidarity Title, that might resist the deregulatory pull of the freedom to conduct a business. These provisions found elsewhere within the Charter are also subject to the same constraints applicable to the Freedoms Title. At the same time, these provisions have the potential to emerge as genuine counter-principles to the freedom to conduct a business given both their detachment from the latter, but also in their symbiotic relationship to sources 'external' to the Charter, including other international rights instruments as well as Union legislation, which serve to reinforce the normative value of those provisions despite the Charter's purported distinction between 'rights' and 'principles', with the latter requiring further legislative intervention in order to ensure their justiciability or enforcement.

The CJEU has itself noted that the wording of Article 16 CFR differs from the other fundamental freedoms laid down in the Freedoms Title, yet is similar to that of certain provisions of the Solidarity Title, with this leading to the conclusion that 'the freedom to conduct a business may be subject to a broad range of interventions on the part of public authorities which may limit the exercise of economic activity in the public interest'.[214] The freedom to conduct a business appears to be particularly powerful in the face of *collectively* agreed terms. It has also just been noted that the freedom of association (as it relates to trade unions), and the right to engage in collective bargaining, both constitute rights within Article 12 CFR and Article 28 CFR respectively, and yet neither has (so far) had any resonance as a counterweight to the freedom to conduct a business in Article 16 CFR.

Article 28 CFR, in particular, includes the specific 'right to negotiate and conclude collective agreements at the appropriate levels', with the CJEU also confirming that the right to bargain collectively constitutes a 'fundamental right' albeit one that is subject to 'Union laws, national laws and practices', which may be indicative of a 'principle' in accordance with Article 52 CFR.[215] The Explanations to Article 28 CFR clarify that this right is 'based on' Article 6 of the European Social Charter, with the right of 'collective action' stipulated as being 'recognised' as forming part of the freedom of association found within Article 11 ECHR. Indeed, the ECtHR has recognized collective bargaining as forming an 'essential element' of the freedom of association, which lends normative weight to the right to bargain collectively as a fundamental right.[216]

Article 6 of the European Social Charter, for its part, requires States 'to *promote*, where necessary and appropriate, machinery for voluntary negotiations between employers or employers' organisations, with a view to the regulation of terms and conditions of employment by means of collective agreements [emphasis added]', and which thereby constitutes a vision for 'collective autonomy', albeit one that has yet to be interpreted as 'prevailing' over 'individual autonomy'.[217] Moreover, the very subject matter of the collective bargaining process is inherently related to negotiations concerning terms and conditions of employment, and is thereby connected to broader employment rights concepts such as fair and just working conditions, which themselves constitute fundamental social rights.[218] The right to bargain collectively as a fundamental right thereby exhibits features of a 'hybrid' civil, political, *and* social right, a characteristic which, as argued here, also applies to the freedom to conduct a business. In particular, collective bargaining is connected to notions of

[214] *Sky Österreich* (n 3) para 46.
[215] Case C-271/08 *Commission v Germany* ECLI:EU:C:2010:426, para 38.
[216] *Demir and Baykara v Turkey* (2009) 48 EHRR 54.
[217] Filip Dorssemont, 'The Right to Bargain Collectively' in Niklas Bruun and others (eds), *The European Social Charter and the Employment Relation* (Hart 2017) 249, 259.
[218] Arts 6 and 7 International Covenant on Economic, Social and Cultural Rights; art 31 CFR; arts 2–4 European Social Charter.

worker 'solidarity' and the counteracting of the stronger bargaining position of employers.[219]

A final point of note in regard to the essence of Article 16 CFR is that in the cases dealing with the freedom to conduct a business as a fundamental right, the CJEU seeks to ensure that the 'essence' or substance of that right is not undermined by EU or national measures. This can be contrasted with the CJEU's reliance on the concept of the essence of a right in the context of Article 31(2) CFR which provides for fair and just working conditions, with that concept being used not to insulate the core of that right from external interference, but rather to shape its potential horizontal application.[220] The latter approach was achieved, albeit indirectly, by distinguishing between the *existence* of the right to paid annual leave and non-essential elements of that right, such as the duration and frequency of that leave, which are subject to legislative implementation and which are characterized as 'modalities'.[221] In other words, it is *only* where the very existence (essence) of the right to paid annual leave is threatened that Article 31(2) CFR will be applied (found to be violated) in disputes between private parties. The 'essence' approach has also been relied on to affirm the 'rights' status of Article 31(2) CFR. For example in *King*, Advocate General Tanchev noted that '[t]he dominance in the case-law of disagreements concerning the conditions for the exercise of paid annual leave, rather than its existence, might well be reflective of the status of that right'.[222]

Article 16 CFR appears to have a rather expansive—albeit undefined—core content, and one that is used to resist legislative interference, whereas Article 31(2) CFR has a much more restrictive essence or core content, which may thereby hinder the invocability of that provision.[223] In other words, the 'essence' test is rights 'enhancing' when applied to Article 16 CFR but rights 'restrictive' in relation to Article 31(2) CFR, in the sense of narrowing the scope of that provision's (horizontal) applicability. More broadly, the concept of an 'essence' or 'minimum core' of obligations within the context of international

[219] Antoine Jacobs, 'Article 11: The Right to Bargain Collectively' in Filip Dorssemont, Klaus Lörcher, and Isabelle Schömann (eds), *The European Convention on Human Rights and the Employment Relation* (Hart 2013) 309, 312.

[220] Joined Cases C–569/16 and 570/16 *Stadt Wuppertal v Maria Elisabeth Bauer and Volker Willmeroth v Martina Broßonn* ECLI:EU:C:2018:871.

[221] Koen Lenaerts, 'The Role of the EU Charter in the Member States' in Michal Bobek and Jeremias Adams-Prassl (eds), *The EU Charter of Fundamental Rights in the Member States* (Hart 2020) 19, 33.

[222] AG Opinion in Case C–214/16 *Conley King v The Sash Window Workshop Ltd and Richard Dollar* ECLI:EU:C:2017:439, para 29.

[223] In *AGET Iraklis* (n 193) para 88, the CJEU did refer to the imposition of a 'framework on that ability' as opposed to 'entirely excluding' it, but without directly applying the same distinction to the freedom to conduct a business in art 16 CFR. The CJEU noted, at para 84, that the mechanism was not 'such as to affect the essence of the freedom to conduct a business'.

economic and social rights is rather nebulous, leading to uncertainty in the precise delineation of particular rights. The purpose of the minimum core is 'to ensure the satisfaction of, at the very least, minimum essential levels of each of the rights is incumbent upon every State party'.[224]

An 'absolute' or 'essential' approach to this minimum core which involves the identification of a right's essential content represents an explicitly normative exercise, but which can thereby lead to the right's further abstraction potentially preventing its enforcement in positive law or by asserting an unwarranted level of determinacy.[225] In particular, the minimum core concept may be incapable of (1) providing predetermined content to the underlying right; (2) determining the relative weight of that right in relation to other rights provisions; or (3) providing clear criteria for permissible restrictions on that right.[226] The essence approach further fails to acknowledge that the core or essence of a particular right can evolve over time in the same way as the general right itself, which can exacerbate the perceived indeterminacy of rights, as explored further in Chapter 5. Furthermore, doubts that surround the concept of a right's 'essence' within the context of international economic and social rights can be contrasted not only with the CJEU's rather expansive and absolutist interpretation of the core content of the freedom to conduct a business, but also with that Court's much more ambiguous and amorphous approach to the essence of the Charter's social rights, notably the right to fair and just working conditions in Article 31(2) CFR.

Comparing the CJEU's treatment of the essence of both Article 16 CFR and Article 31(2) CFR thereby demonstrates potential divergence between the freedom to conduct a business and the right to paid annual leave, with that divergence also serving as an indication of the relative normative value of each provision. It is the very divergence in the 'values' encompassed by potentially competing Charter provisions—or indeed within EU law more generally—that impedes the use of the values concept in articulating the core content or essence of Union fundamental rights, whether those values are derived from Article 2 TEU or from the Charter itself. This is despite the Charter's emphasis on the 'inviolable' right to 'human dignity' as the foundation or 'real basis' of *all* rights, which risks a collapse towards Charter rights—including the freedom

[224] United Nations Committee on Economic, Social, and Cultural Rights, 'General Comment No 3: The Nature of States Parties' Obligations' E/199/23, 14 December 1990, para 10.

[225] Katherine G Young, 'The Minimum Core of Economic and Social Rights: A Concept in Search of Content' (2008) 33 Yale J Int'l Law 113, 116, 117.

[226] ibid 116.

to conduct a business—acting as irrefutable 'trumps'.[227] Despite this, the Charter's competing underpinning values do have a role in determining the relative legal and normative weight of the Charter's provisions, including in the relationship between them, despite not offering much assistance in determining a right's core content.

The CJEU's reluctance to adopt an expansive approach to protecting the essence of the Charter's social rights, including the right to fair and just working conditions, might partially be explained by the distinct approaches adopted in international law to the 'essence' of civil and political rights on the one hand, and the 'minimum core' of economic and social rights on the other.[228] In particular, the essence of civil and political rights has been linked to the concepts of non-derogability or non-restrictability, while the minimum core of economic and social rights instead focuses principally—though not exclusively—on the obligations imposed on States in guaranteeing an essential level of protection, regardless of resource implications.[229] 'Non-derogability' refers to the State's inability to derogate from essential rights, ie the entire right is essential, while 'non-restrictability' refers to the existence of a periphery and a core or essence, only the former of which can be restricted. Finally, the obligations approach re-emphasizes the issue of 'justiciability', which is used to distinguish further (positive) economic and social rights from (negative) civil and political rights, as well as to distinguish Charter rights from Charter principles.[230]

An illustration of this approach to economic and social rights can be seen in the treatment of the right to work as a fundamental right, which is a corollary of the freedom to conduct a business. The right to work is found in a number of international rights instruments, which have a crucial connection to the right to work in Article 15 CFR, as made clear by the Charter's Explanations.[231] The right to work is also conceptually interesting in that it transcends the traditional boundary between civil and political rights, and economic and social rights. Features of the right to work, which cut across each of the relevant instruments, albeit with varying degrees of emphasis include (1) the freedom to

[227] Francesco de Cecco, 'The Trouble with Trumps: On How (and Why) Not to Define the Core of Fundamental Rights' (2023) 60 CMLRev 1551; Ronald Dworkin, 'Rights as Trumps' in Jeremy Waldron (ed), *Theories of Rights* (OUP 1984) 153.

[228] Advocate General Bot has used the term 'hard core minimum' within the context of art 31(2) CFR: AG Opinion in Joined Cases C-609/17 and 610/17 *Terveys- ja sosiaalialan neuvottelujärjestö (TSN) ry v Hyvinvointialan liitto ry, other party Fimlab Laboratoriot Oy and Auto- ja Kuljetusalan Työntekijäliitto AKT ry v Satamaoperaattorit ry, other party Kemi Shipping Oy* ECLI:EU:C:2019:459, para 69.

[229] Pierre Thielberger, 'The "Essence" of International Human Rights' (2019) 20 Ger Law J 924, 926.

[230] ibid 936.

[231] art 1 European Social Charter (ESC); art 6 International Covenant on Economic Social and Cultural Rights (ICESCR).

enter and pursue a freely chosen occupation; (2) the freedom to seek, accept offers of, and perform employment; and (3) protections against work-based discrimination.

The 'negative' dimension of the right to work includes the right of non-discriminatory access to employment, while the 'positive' dimension relates to the State's obligation to create the economic conditions necessary to avoid unemployment, ie the right to a 'job'.[232] This positive dimension may also extend to the right to 'decent' work, which demonstrates the relevance of the substantive employment rights found both within the Charter as well as other rights instruments such as the right to fair and just working conditions, although notably the concept of fair remuneration is absent from the Charter.[233] As O'Cinneide notes, the 'conceptual core' of the right to work is relatively easy to delineate in that it 'protects and gives expression to the human interest in engaging in productive labour'.[234]

At the same time, the precise content of that right remains ambiguous, notably due to the relative absence of judicial engagement with the right to work as a fundamental right, including in its relationship with substantive employment rights. As such, the 'essence(s)' of this composite or 'aggregate' right remain difficult to establish, which may explain the continued emphasis on state obligations, whether negative or positive, in the context of the right to work, notably but non-exhaustively (1) full employment; (2) non-discriminatory access to employment; and (3) free choice of employment.[235] More broadly, the concept of 'core' labour standards as adjudged by the International Labour Organization Conventions are suggestive of minimum or 'basic' protections, such as freedom from forced or child labour, which provide a consensus-based framework, and which are centred largely on the most egregious forms of labour rights violations.[236]

This approach can notably be contrasted with the CJEU's more maximalist approach to the 'discovery' of business freedoms as general principles, and the subsequent expansive interpretation of freedom of contract as a core

[232] Hugh Collins, 'Progress Towards the Right to Work in the United Kingdom' in Virginia Mantouvalou (ed), *The Right to Work: Legal and Philosophical Perspectives* (Hart 2017) 229.

[233] Art 31(2) CFR; art 7 ICESCR; arts 2–4 ESC.

[234] Colm O'Cinneide, 'The Right to Work in International Human Rights Law' in Virginia Mantouvalou (ed), *The Right to Work: Legal and Philosophical Perspectives* (Hart 2017) 99, 100.

[235] Richard Lewis Siegel, 'The Right to Work: Core Minimum Obligations' in Audrey R Chapman and Sage Russell (eds), *Introduction to Core Obligations: Building a Framework for Economic, Social and Cultural Rights* (Intersentia 2002) 21, 28; United Nations Committee on Economic, Social and Cultural Rights, 'General Comment No 18 on the Right to Work concerning art 6 ICESCR' E/C.12/GC/18, 6 February 2006.

[236] General Comment No 18 (n 235) 31.

component of the freedom to conduct a business as a fundamental right. In delineating the core content of freedom of contract, the CJEU treats the entire scope of that freedom as its 'essence', leading to the inescapable conclusion that in unravelling the freedom to conduct a business's essence, its essence essentially unravels, with the CJEU failing to specify precisely what the 'very essence' of either the freedom to conduct a business, or freedom of contract, might be. Furthermore, the nebulous nature of freedom of contract itself impedes its potential construction as forming part of the essence of wider business freedoms. This is also reflective of wider deficiencies in defining freedom of contract for the purposes of Union law, including ongoing doubts as to the potential limitations on the concept.

It is evident that the exercise of articulating the core content of Charter rights remains both normatively difficult and also fraught with practical barriers to its realization, particularly in the absence of any clear criteria as to how the essence of a right is to be identified. Moreover, and as is clear from the case law concerning the freedom to conduct a business within Article 16 CFR, the language of 'essence' may lead to the conflation of the core content of a particular right with the broader notion of an 'absolute' right, and in a way that is reflective of constitutional discourse in the United States concerning the use of rights as absolute barriers to the attainment of competing public interest goals.[237]

4.6 Conclusion

This chapter has demonstrated that freedom of contract is an essentially contested and ambiguous concept both as a Union fundamental right, and also within the broader context of EU and domestic law, which goes some way to explaining the apparent inconsistencies in the CJEU's treatment of the freedom to conduct a business as a fundamental right. In its initial case law concerning the freedom to conduct a business within Article 16 of the Charter, the CJEU demonstrated a degree of continuity with its long-held restrictive approach to business freedoms as general principles, a continuity that was disrupted by the CJEU's landmark judgment in *Alemo-Herron*. The CJEU's judgment in that case bears similarities to the CJEU's treatment of (social) restrictions on the fundamental economic freedoms, which demonstrates that decision's 'emblematic' role in emphasizing wider structural imbalances between economic

[237] de Cecco (n 227) 1561.

and social interests in the legal reasoning of the CJEU. The Charter as interpreted in that case has had the effect of disrupting the CJEU's existing balanced approach to the recognition of business freedom as both a general principle and in its early case law on the freedom to conduct a business as a fundamental right.

Also problematic is the elevation of freedom of contract to a more fundamental position within Article 16 CFR, a position that is not evident from a reading of the text itself.[238] Perhaps more significant is the apparent divergence that *Alemo-Herron* signifies with the CJEU's existing jurisprudence on business freedoms as both general principles and fundamental Charter rights. Clearly, the judgment is not consistent with *Werhof*, which it purports to apply. The CJEU in that case interpreted the Directive as *not precluding* the fact that the transferee was *not bound* by subsequent collective agreements.[239] The CJEU's treatment of the Charter in *Alemo-Herron* also appears to mark a rupture with the Court's case law on business freedom as a general principle as well as the CJEU's early treatment of Article 16 as a fundamental Charter right.[240]

The case law on Article 16 CFR and business freedoms as a general principle diverges in the language used to describe the permissible limitations on those freedoms, but such divergence could also be found within the case law on business freedoms as a general principle itself, with the Court adopting different language to describe freedom of contract and broader notions such as the freedom to pursue a trade or occupation. As will also be examined in Chapter 5, the CJEU in its more recent case law has been equally inconsistent. In some cases Article 16 CFR is relied on explicitly, while in others it is overlooked entirely.

Undoubtedly, there are wider problems with the *Alemo-Herron* judgment beyond the fact that it does not explicitly engage in any meaningful way with pre-existing case law, and which are indicative of the potential disruptive force of the freedom of contract as a fundamental right. The starting point of the CJEU's analysis was reversed, with the Court no longer accepting that restrictions on business freedoms are prima facie lawful. The CJEU also placed greater emphasis on the effects of the restrictions on individual traders, while the distinction between the *exercise* and the *substance* of business freedom has become blurred. In some respects, the legislative context was key to the decision in that case, with the legislation governing the transfer of undertakings

238 Prassl (n 78) 441.
239 *Werhof* (n 30) para 37.
240 Prassl (n 78).

being inherently concerned with limitations on the business freedoms of the transferee employer.

More fundamentally, the jurisprudence of the CJEU concerning freedom of contract lacks any meaningful engagement with the meaning or normative value of that freedom. Despite the CJEU's recognition of the need to respect the 'essence' or 'core content' of the freedom to conduct a business, no guidance is forthcoming in identifying this content, nor is it clear whether or not freedom of contract represents part of the 'core' of the wider freedom to conduct a business. It is the ambiguous and open-ended nature of the freedom to conduct a business that facilitates its use as a disruptive tool within the fundamental rights context by, for example, overturning the balance between economic and social rights, or by distorting traditional understandings of the relationship (or distinction) between rights, freedoms, and principles.

Beyond the immediate effects of the decision in *Alemo-Herron* itself, that judgment also gave an insight into potential *systemic* issues stemming from the freedom to conduct a business as a fundamental right. First, the CJEU made use of the freedom to conduct a business to disrupt existing approaches to the interpretation and application not only of the Transfer of Undertakings Directive, but potentially also of minimum harmonization measures more generally. Secondly, the CJEU failed to place the freedom to conduct a business within the wider framework of EU constitutional and free movement law, where such a principle has always been (indirectly) recognized but has been subject to restrictions. Finally, the Court gave no particular weight to the public interest, nor did it consider any potential counterweights to the freedom to conduct a business as a fundamental right.

Given these wider considerations, it will also be necessary to assess the precedential value of cases such as *Alemo-Herron* to examine the extent to which the expansive notion of the freedom to conduct a business as a fundamental right has now been embedded within the subsequent jurisprudence of the CJEU. Indeed, there is something particularly problematic with fundamental rights instruments being used in such a way as to defeat competing rights and interests which are themselves underpinned by fundamental (economic and social) rights. It is the wider implications of the potential entrenchment of such an approach to business freedoms, for the legal reasoning of the CJEU but also for the capacity of Member States to introduce protective measures going beyond the floor provided by EU law, as well as the ability of the EU itself to regulate contractual relations notably in the presence of a weaker party, which will now be addressed in Part III.

PART III

THE ENTRENCHMENT OF THE FREEDOM TO CONDUCT A BUSINESS AS A FUNDAMENTAL RIGHT

5

The Jurisprudential Significance of the Freedom to Conduct a Business as a Fundamental Right

5.1 Introduction

This chapter explores the extent of the influence of the (expansive conception of the) freedom to conduct a business on the judicial reasoning of the Court of Justice of the European Union (CJEU). It begins by assessing the (material) jurisprudential value of the CJEU's case law on the freedom to conduct a business as a fundamental right (Section 5.2). It is shown that the Court continues to oscillate between reinforcing and retreating from the expansive conception of the freedom to conduct a business. It will be recalled that this 'strong' or expansive conception of the freedom to conduct a business is defined not necessarily in relation to cases in which business freedom arguments were *successfully* raised as such, but rather in the use of those arguments to undermine the effectiveness of 'protective' legislation, whether through its regressive interpretation or through an assessment of that legislation's compatibility with the freedom to conduct a business as a fundamental right.

It is suggested here that the Court's apparent inconsistency is merely a reflection of that institution's broader approach to the interpretation and application of EU law, including the absence of a formal or 'doctrinal' concept of precedent within the EU legal order. At the same time, it is argued that the normative (constitutional) value of the freedom to conduct a business is reinforced through its connection to the fundamental freedoms of the Union's internal market, which thereby risks the importation of deregulatory values in the absence of genuine consideration of competing social rights and interests. Moreover, the enactment of the Charter—and the inclusion of the freedom to conduct a business therein—reinforces the 'fundamental rights' nature of those very same internal market freedoms leading to the mutual reinforcement of deregulatory concepts.

Business Freedoms and Fundamental Rights in European Union Law. Niall O'Connor, Oxford University Press.
 DOI: 10.1093/9780191982132.003.0006

Finally, it is argued that coherence in the CJEU's approach to the interpretation of the freedom to conduct a business in Article 16 of the EU Charter of Fundamental Rights (CFR) is undermined by the absence of a clear normative vision of that freedom, which thereby impedes consistency in the Court's fundamental rights reasoning (Section 5.3). Section 5.4 concludes that the CJEU's legal reasoning in relation to the freedom to conduct a business has hitherto been divorced from wider fundamental (social) rights concepts found both within and outside the Charter, thereby undermining the purported indivisibility of the social and economic rights and principles found amongst its provisions, and which compounds the CJEU's reluctance to *engage* with the social limitations that inhere within business freedom concepts, ie their 'social function'.

5.2 The Materiality of the Freedom to Conduct a Business in Judicial Reasoning

An exploration of the CJEU's more recent case law shows continued evidence of inconsistency in the Court's treatment of the freedom to conduct a business as a fundamental right. In some cases, the CJEU has maintained its commitment to a strong or expansive conception of the freedom to conduct a business, while in others it has shown evidence of a retrenchment from that same freedom. Indeed, there has been a proliferation of cases before the CJEU 'referring' to the freedom to conduct a business in Article 16 CFR. In many of these cases the Charter is only raised in passing, while in others both Advocates General and the CJEU continue merely to repeat the wording of Article 16 CFR, rather than adding any clarification to the content or normative value of that provision.[1] Some cases are at least more specific with regard to the articulation of the protected elements within Article 16 CFR, referring, for example, to the freedom with whom to do business; the freedom to determine the price of a service; and the right freely to use available resources of an economic, financial, and technical nature and which may assist in filling the lacunae in the assessment of the essential elements of freedom of contract.[2]

The purpose here is to analyse the case law to demonstrate the emerging patterns in the CJEU's treatment of the freedom to conduct a business as a

[1] AG Opinion in Case C–101/12 *Herbert Schaible v Land Baden-Württemberg* ECLI:EU:C:2013:334, para 25.

[2] AG Opinion in Case C–134/15 *Lidl GmbH & Co KG v Freistaat Sachsen* ECLI:EU:C:2016:169, para 26.

fundamental right. Particularly important cases will also be discussed in more detail, notably where they illustrate an ongoing commitment to an expansive conception of business freedoms or where they clearly diverge from the CJEU's approach to freedom of contract in earlier cases. It is argued here that language matters, and that what appear to be subtle changes or omissions may actually represent a wider change in the CJEU's treatment of the freedom to conduct a business as a fundamental right. The use of repetitive 'building blocks'—derived in part from the fact that French is the working language of the Court without being the first or even second language of many of the judges—may obfuscate evolutions in the law or signal that, when the CJEU's language does change, this was a deliberate choice to enact a meaningful evolution in the law, whether intended or not.[3]

The examination of the case law in this chapter will also allow for a broader legal, practical, and normative view to be taken in Chapter 6 of the implications and consequences of the freedom to conduct a business as a fundamental right, both for the regulatory and legislative autonomy of the Union and its Member States, and also for the CJEU's ability to assess the relative weight of economic freedoms and social rights concepts. These problems are now compounded by the ambiguities surrounding the Charter, including the unclear distinction between rights and principles as well as the relative weight of economic freedoms and fundamental social rights.

The overarching pattern from the case law, to the extent that one can be discerned, continues to be that the freedom to conduct a business is not absolute but may 'be subject to a broad range of intervention on the part of the public authorities which may limit the exercise of economic activity in the public interest'.[4] The CJEU also uses the more general formulation derived ultimately from Article 52(1) CFR that its provisions 'may be subject to certain limitations, as long as they are provided for by law, respect the essence of those rights and freedoms, are necessary and genuinely meet objectives of general interest recognised by the European Union'.[5] The CJEU usually finds that although the measure in question represents a limitation or restriction on the freedom to conduct a business, that limitation or restriction is nevertheless justified and

[3] Marc Jacob, *Precedents and Case-based Reasoning in the European Court of Justice* (CUP 2014) 97.

[4] AG Opinion in Case C–547/14 *Philip Morris Brands SARL v Secretary of State for Health* ECLI:EU:C:2015:853, para 148; Case C–348/12 P *Council of the European Union v Manufacturing Support & Procurement Kala Naft Co., Tehran* ECLI:EU:C:2013:776, para 123; AG Opinion in *Herbert Schaible* (n 1) para 28.

[5] Case C–422/14 *Bayer CropScience SA-NV and Stichting De Bijenstichting v College voor de toelating van gewasbeschermingsmiddelen en biociden* ECLI:EU:C:2016:890, para 98.

proportionate.[6] Of the cases dealing with freedom of contract specifically, it has usually been found that there was no infringement of Article 16 CFR.[7]

In particular, the CJEU has recognized the importance of competing substantive rights and interests, for example consumer protection, freedom of information, and Intellectual Property rights, although often in passing, and without always referring to the relevant Charter provision providing protection for those same rights.[8] In certain cases, the CJEU also continues to refer to the 'social function' of the freedom to conduct a business, its 'function in society', 'societal function', 'social purpose', or to the 'social interests of the community', thereby connecting the case law on Article 16 CFR to the case law on business freedoms as general principles, as well as the early case law on the freedom to conduct a business as a fundamental Charter right.[9] In other cases, the Court finds that the 'very essence' of the freedom to conduct a business has been preserved.[10]

[6] Case T–155/15 *Khaled Kaddour v Council of the European Union* ECLI:EU:T:2016:628, para 120; Case T–154/15 *Aiman Jaber v Council of the European Union* ECLI:EU:T:2016:629, para 122; Case T–153/15 *Mohamad Hamcho and Hamcho International v Council of the European Union* ECLI:EU:T:2016:630, para 123; AG Opinion in Case C–314/12 *UPC Telekabel Wien GmbH v Constantin Film Verleih GmbH and Wega Filmproduktionsgesellschaft mbH* ECLI:EU:C:2013:781; AG Opinion in *Herbert Schaible* (n 1) para 75.

[7] Case C–356/21 *JK v TP S.A.* ECLI:EU:C:2023:9, para 76; Case C–223/19 *YS v NK* ECLI:EU:C:2020:753, para 89; Joined Cases C–798/18 and 799/18 *Federazione nazionale delle imprese elettrotecniche ed elettroniche (Anie) and Athesia Energy Srl v Ministero dello Sviluppo Economico and Gestore dei servizi energetici (GSE) SpA* ECLI:EU:C:2021:280, para 61; AG Opinion in Case C–188/15 *Asma Bougnaoui and Association de défense des droits de l'homme (ADDH) v Micropole SA* ECLI:EU:C:2016:553, para 100.

[8] Case C–28/20 *Airhelp Ltd v Scandinavian Airlines System Denmark—Norway—Sweden* ECLI:EU:C:2021:226; Case C–570/19 *Irish Ferries Ltd v National Transport Authority* ECLI:EU:C:2021:664; AG Opinion in Case C–430/17 *Walbusch Walter Busch GmbH & Co KG v Zentrale zur Bekämpfung unlauteren Wettbewerbs Frankfurt am Main eV* ECLI:EU:C:2018:759, para 58; AG Opinion in *Lidl* (n 2) para 47; AG Opinion in Case C–484/14 *Tobias Mc Fadden v Sony Music Entertainment Germany GmbH* ECLI:EU:C:2016:170, paras 111, 112; AG Opinion in Case C–390/12 *Robert Pfleger* ECLI:EU:C:2013:747, para 71; Case C–314/12 *UPC Telekabel Wien GmbH v Constantin Film Verleih GmbH and Wega Filmproduktionsgesellschaft mbH* ECLI:EU:C:2014:192, para 47.

[9] *Irish Ferries* (n 8) para 170; AG Opinion in Joined Cases C–724/18 and 727/18 *Cali Apartments SCI and HX v Procureur général près la cour d'appel de Paris, Ville de Paris* ECLI:EU:C:2020:251, para 95; Case C–190/16 *Werner Fries v Lufthansa CityLine GmbH* ECLI:EU:C:2017:513, para 73; AG Opinion *Bougnaoui* (n 7) para 100; Case C–134/15 *Lidl GmbH & Co KG v Freistaat Sachsen* ECLI:EU:C:2016:498, para 34; AG Opinion in Case C–477/14 *Pillbox 38 (UK) Limited v The Secretary of State for Health* ECLI:EU:C:2015:854, para 185; Case C–422/14 *Bayer CropScience* (n 5) para 168; Case C–397/14 *Polkomtel sp. z o.o v Prezes Urzędu Komunikacji Elektronicznej* ECLI:EU:C:2016:256, para 60; Case C–157/14 *Société Neptune Distribution v Ministre de l'Économie et des Finances* ECLI:EU:C:2015:823, para 66; Joined Cases T–429/13 and 451/13 *Bayer CropScience AG and Syngenta Crop Protection AG v European Commission* ECLI:EU:T:2018:280, para 586; AG Opinion in *Robert Pfleger* (n 8) para 68; AG Opinion in *UPC* (n 6).

[10] Case C–540/16 *UAB 'Spika' v Žuvininkystės tarnyba prie Lietuvos Respublikos žemės ūkio ministerijos* ECLI:EU:C:2018:565, para 38; Case T–251/18 *International Forum for Sustainable Underwater Activities (IFSUA) v Council of the European Union* ECLI:EU:T:2020:89, para 154; AG Opinion in Case C–157/14 *Société Neptune Distribution v Ministre de l'Économie et des Finances* ECLI:EU:C:2015:460, para 44.

The CJEU often avoids explicit discussion on the freedom to conduct a business found within Article 16 CFR by instead assessing the contested measure through the lens of the fundamental internal market freedoms.[11] The case law also continues to evidence the intimate entwinement of the freedom to conduct a business in Article 16 CFR, the right to work in Article 15 CFR, and the right to property in Article 17 CFR.[12] Similarly, the CJEU has noted the overlap between Article 16 CFR and the provisions found within the Solidarity Title, with Article 16 CFR differing 'from the wording of the other fundamental freedoms laid down in Title II thereof [Freedoms], [while being] similar to that of certain provisions of Title IV of the Charter [Solidarity]'.[13] There are only very few cases in which the contested measure, whether in whole or in part, has been found to constitute an unjustified or disproportionate breach of Article 16 CFR.[14] Indeed, in some cases the CJEU goes further and retreats to the pre-existing restrictive conception of the freedom to conduct a business, which views that freedom as being limited in the face of competing economic and social interests.

5.2.1 Congruence with the restrictive conception of the freedom to conduct a business

Cases immediately following *Alemo-Herron*, and dealing with broadly similar subject areas, demonstrate remarkably little engagement with the expansive conception of the freedom to conduct a business as a fundamental right. In *Österreicher Gewerksschaftsbund* which concerned the interpretation of Article 3 of the Transfer of Undertakings Directive (TUD), the CJEU followed the approach adopted in *Alemo-Herron* but *without* any reference to Article 16 of the Charter.[15] This case involved the potential continuation post-transfer of

[11] Case C-465/18 *AV and BU v Comune di Bernareggio* ECLI:EU:C:2019:812, para 35; AG Opinion in Case C-235/17 *European Commission v Hungary* ECLI:EU:C:2018:971, paras 114–16; Case C-322/16 *Global Starnet Ltd v Ministero dell'Economia e delle Finanze and Amministrazione Autonoma Monopoli di Stato* ECLI:EU:C:2017:985, para 50; Case C-390/12 *Robert Pfleger* ECLI:EU:C:2014:281, para 57; AG Opinion in *Robert Pfleger* (n 8) para 70; Case C-367/12 *Susanne Sokoll-Seebacher* ECLI:EU:C:2014:68, para 23.

[12] *Airhelp* (n 8); AG Opinion in Case C-223/19 *YS v NK* ECLI:EU:C:2020:356; AG Opinion in *Lidl* (n 2) para 20; AG Opinion in *Robert Pfleger* (n 8); *UPC* (n 8).

[13] Case C-124/20 *Bank Melli Iran v Telekom Deutschland GmbH* ECLI:EU:C:2021:1035, para 81; AG Opinion in Case C-686/18 *OC e.a. v Banca d'Italia* ECLI:EU:C:2020:90, para 84; AG Opinion in Case C-566/17 *Związek Gmin Zagłębia Miedziowego w Polkowicach v Szef Krajowej Administracji Skarbowej* ECLI:EU:C:2018:995, para 103.

[14] Case C-484/14 *Tobias Mc Fadden v Sony Music Entertainment Germany GmbH* ECLI:EU:C:2016:689, para 82; AG Opinion in *Robert Pfleger* (n 8) para 90.

[15] Case C-328/13 *Österreichischer Gewerkschaftsbund v Wirtschaftskammer Österreich—Fachverband Autobus-, Luftfahrt- und Schifffahrtsunternehmungen* ECLI:EU:C:2014:2197.

the terms of a collective agreement that had been rescinded. The Austrian legislation at issue provided for the continuation of the legal effects of collective agreements until a new agreement—whether collective or individual—had taken effect.[16] The national court, in its preliminary reference, further clarified that under the relevant Austrian law collective agreements do not become part of the employment contract, but rather have the same effect as legislation on the contract of employment. The Chamber of Commerce, for its part, argued that the expired collective agreement that had been applicable to the parent company could not logically be imposed on the transferee as such an agreement could not 'continue' to apply given that it had already been rescinded.[17]

The Austrian Supreme Court, in its preliminary reference, sought clarification from the CJEU as to whether Article 3(3) TUD, which provides for the continuation of collective agreements post-transfer, should be interpreted as also applying to terms of a collective agreement having indefinite continuing effect in accordance with national law despite the fact that the initial agreement had been terminated. The CJEU was also asked whether the term 'application of another collective agreement' found in the national legislation should be interpreted as including the continuing effect of the terminated agreement. The CJEU began by reiterating that the Directive is only a partial harmonization measure and so was not intended to create uniform protection for the continuation of collective agreements across the Union.[18] The Court then noted that the purpose of Article 3(3) TUD was not to preserve the continuing effects of collective agreements as such, but rather to ensure continuity of all terms and conditions of employment regardless of their source of origin.[19]

Terms and conditions of employment therefore come within the scope of the Directive 'irrespective of the method used to make those terms [. . .] applicable to the persons concerned', for example through legislative measures maintaining the effects of collectively agreed terms post-transfer.[20] The CJEU recalled that the purpose of the Directive is to prevent a sudden rupture in the terms and conditions of employment and that the adopted interpretation of the Directive conforms to its—as is argued here, *contested*—objectives of ensuring a fair balance between the interests of employees and the transferee employer. The CJEU relied on *Alemo-Herron* to find that the new employer must

[16] Arbeitsverfassungsgesetz, BGB1. 22/1974, para 13.
[17] *Österreichischer Gewerkschaftsbund* (n 15) para 12.
[18] ibid para 22.
[19] ibid paras 23–24.
[20] ibid para 25.

'be in a position to make the adjustments and changes necessary to carry on its operations'.[21] This led to the CJEU holding that:

> [t]he rule maintaining the effects of a collective agreement [. . .] has limited effects, since it maintains only the legal effects of a collective agreement on the employment relationships directly subject to it before its recission [. . .] In those circumstances, it does not appear that such a rule hinders the transferee's ability to make adjustments and changes necessary to carry on its operations.[22]

There is a clear contrast, in both tone and substance, between this judgment and the decision of the CJEU in *Alemo-Herron*. In the former, the Court had no difficulty in concluding that the continuation of the collectively agreed terms did not amount to an interference with the employer's room for manoeuvre, while in the latter, a similar provision was found to represent an intolerable interference with the transferee employer's freedom to conduct a business. The dissonance between the two judgments is also apparent from the Opinion of Advocate General Cruz Villalón, who had also delivered the Opinion in *Alemo-Herron*. It will be recalled that in *Alemo-Herron*, Advocate General Cruz Villalón found that the dynamic approach to the incorporation of collectively agreed terms was not incompatible with the employer's freedom to conduct a business. In *Österreicher Gewerksschaftsbund*, the Advocate General similarly found that:

> [t]he primary objective of the continuing effect is that of a guarantee; it simply maintains the status quo in the interests of legal certainty. In such cases, the rights and obligations arising from a collective agreement with continuing effect, a mere extension of the pre-existing situations, are 'the terms and conditions agreed'.[23]

The continuing effect of the collective agreement in question was both a weaker and a temporary extension of the effects of the pre-existing agreement. The effects were weaker in the sense that the provisions of the agreement could always be waived by the parties at any time. The effects were also temporary in

[21] ibid para 29.
[22] ibid para 30.
[23] AG Opinion in Case C–328/13 *Österreichischer Gewerkschaftsbund v Wirtschaftskammer Österreich—Fachverband Autobus-, Luftfahrt- und Schifffahrtsunternehmungen* ECLI:EU:C:2014:909, para 49.

that they would cease to apply upon the conclusion of any new collective agreement. As the Advocate General put it:

> [a] collective agreement is not converted into an agreement with continuing effect as a result of a decision of one or both parties to the employment relationship [but rather] because the legislature has expressly provided that, in exhaustively listed circumstances and with a view to maintaining legal certainty in the employment relationship, the agreement will continue to be observed on a weaker, temporary basis.[24]

This interpretation was wholly consistent with *Werhof*, in which the continuing effect of a dynamic clause was rejected on the grounds that the Transfer of Undertakings Directive was not intended to protect 'mere expectations':

> In other words, Directive 2001/23 is not intended to perpetuate a contractual situation, particularly where the situation perpetuated encompasses future rather than current rights. That is the kind of continuation of effects which upsets the balance of the contractual relationship between employer and employee, something which is prohibited by Directive 2001/23 and the case-law.[25]

The present case, by way of contrast, concerned an express legislative provision in force at the time the contract was concluded, which provided for the continuation of collectively agreed terms, albeit on a weaker and more temporary basis. This situation was therefore 'far from being a "mere expectation" or a "hypothetical advantage flowing from future changes to collective agreements"'.[26]

Once again, there appear to be differing rationales underpinning the approach taken by the CJEU in its application of the freedom to conduct a business as a fundamental right. The contrasting approaches adopted by the CJEU in both *Alemo-Herron* and *Österreichischer Gewerkschaftsbund* would suggest that it was the absence of negotiation in the former that led to the finding of incompatibility with the freedom to conduct a business as a fundamental right. In other words, the transferee employer in *Alemo-Herron* had been excluded from the collective agreement machinery from the outset given that it was a

[24] ibid para 46.
[25] ibid para 50.
[26] ibid para 51.

private sector employer and could not therefore engage with the National Joint Council. Another reading of these cases would suggest that it was the source of the continuation of the collectively agreed terms that proved to be problematic, despite the Advocate General's insistence to the contrary in *Österreichischer Gewerkschaftsbund*. In that case, the continuing effects of the collective agreements were provided for in national legislation, whereas in *Alemo-Herron* the continuation derived from the bridging term in the employment contract which allowed for the collective agreement to be dynamically incorporated, although ultimately it had been thought that such an approach was permitted by the underlying domestic legislation implementing the Directive.

There is a tension between the holding in *Österreichischer Gewerkschaftsbund* that legislatively imposed terms were acceptable from the perspective of the freedom to conduct a business while in *Alemo-Herron*, an agreed contractual term providing for the dynamic approach was found to be incompatible with the same freedom. The CJEU in *Österreichischer Gewerkschaftsbund* emphasized the temporary nature of the continuation, but of course in *Alemo-Herron* the effect of the collective agreement was also temporary, in the sense that it could always be renegotiated by the parties in exercise of their freedom of contract.

Mensch, discussing the enforcement of covenants in restraint of trade (ie agreements restricting potential competition), argues that interference with freedom of contract in order to 'save it', is 'suspiciously paradoxical' and that 'a contract that is no longer value-enhancing to one party can be impeached by the claim that free traders would no longer agree to the exchange'.[27] In other words, the enforcement of restrictive covenants could not be justified on the basis of freedom of contract, but only on competing principles such as security of expectation. As Mensch puts it, '[f]reedom logic requires a new formation process whenever performance is no longer in accord with the will of the parties', as otherwise this would lead to a situation whereby '[t]he complaining party is either free to renegotiate or unfreely bound by the prior bargain'.[28] On this view, the logic of freedom of contract offers no solution to the seemingly intractable conflict between contractual certainty or security, and the (present) will of the parties.

It has already been suggested that there is nothing inherently contradictory in a recognition that voluntarily accepted restrictions on freedom of contract

[27] Betty Mensch, 'Freedom of Contract as Ideology' (1981) 33 Stan L Rev 759; Patrick S Atiyah, *The Rise and Fall of Freedom of Contract* (1985 OUP) 697–703.

[28] Mensch (n 27) 759, 760.

may represent a legitimate exercise of that same freedom. Within the context of the dynamic application of collectively agreed terms upon the transfer of a business, the argument that the will of (one of) the parties has changed also cannot be sustained in light of the fact the transferee employer voluntarily assumes the existing terms and conditions of employment in full knowledge of the applicability of the relevant collective agreements. In addition, legislation governing the transfer of undertakings merely provides that the transfer itself—or a reason connected with the transfer—cannot lead to contractual variations. This does not preclude the future renegotiation of the employment contract for reasons unrelated to the transfer.

In *Anie*, Advocate General Saugmandsgaard Øe similarly noted, in relation to legislative changes to an incentive scheme in the energy sector, that it is no part of the purpose of the freedom to conduct a business within Article 16 CFR 'to create rights for those parties which go beyond those already provided for in their contract, or to enable them to demand terms other than those already contained in that contract'.[29] In that case, the relevant party had 'simply been bound by the contractual terms which they freely accepted when they entered into the agreements' and so there was no infringement of their freedom of contract.[30] The CJEU also held that 'where the contract is a standard form contract drawn up by one of the contracting parties, the freedom of contract of the other party consists, essentially, in deciding whether or not to accept the terms of such a contract'.[31]

Further evidence of a retrenchment from the CJEU's approach to the freedom to conduct a business can be seen in the case of *Vittoria Graf*, which once again concerned the interpretation of Article 3 TUD.[32] The Opinion of Advocate General Bot has been suggested as a potential source for reconciling the CJEU's contrasting approaches to the interpretation and application of the freedom to conduct a business as a fundamental right, at least in the context of business transfers. The CJEU, choosing not to follow the opinion of the Advocate General, found that the relevant German legislation was actually *compatible* with the Directive, holding that:

[29] AG Opinion in Joined Cases C-798/18 and 799/18 *Federazione nazionale delle imprese elettrotecniche ed elettroniche (Anie) and Athesia Energy Srl v Ministero dello Sviluppo Economico* ECLI:EU:C:2020:876, para 70.

[30] ibid paras 73, 74.

[31] *Anie* (n 7) para 60.

[32] Joined Cases C-680/15 and 681/15 *Asklepios Kliniken Langen-Seligenstadt GmbH v Ivan Felja and Asklepios Dienstleistungsgesellschaft mbH v Vittoria Graf* ECLI:EU:C:2017:317.

> it is clear from the decision to refer and, in particular, from the wording of the questions referred [. . .] that the national legislation at issue [. . .] provides for the possibility, after the transfer, for the transferee to adjust the working conditions existing at the date of the transfer, either consensually or unilaterally.[33]

The transferee's allegation that changes were unlikely to occur in practice was found to be an issue for the national court to determine and therefore the legislation at issue was compatible with the conditions set out in *Alemo-Herron*, ie 'the transferee must be able to assert its interest effectively in a contractual process to which it is party and to negotiate aspects determining changes in the working conditions of its employees with a view to its future economic activity'.[34] Finally, and thereby avoiding engagement in any meaningful way with the freedom to conduct a business as a fundamental right, the CJEU concluded that given that *Alemo-Herron* already 'takes into consideration Article 16 [. . .] there is no longer any need to examine further the compatibility of the national legislation at issue [. . .] with that provision'.[35] In this way, the CJEU subsumed discussion on Article 16 CFR into its application of earlier case law without explicitly addressing the implications of that provision, an approach with potentially negative implications for transparency of the CJEU's application of the Charter, an instrument which was explicitly intended to render rights more 'visible'.

As examined in Part I, the source of a particular right, whether that be within the general principles, the Charter, or Union legislation, has an important bearing on the legal and normative weight to be attributed to that right. The difficulty lies in unravelling the relationship between overlapping sources that result from the complex fundamental rights architecture that has emerged within EU law, and which itself has the capacity to obscure the origin of rights concepts. These ambiguities are further compounded by the diffidence often evident in the CJEU's rights-based reasoning. This reticence opens up the possibility for inconsistency in the Court's application and interpretation of fundamental rights concepts. Despite the apparently restrictive nature of some of the decisions immediately following *Alemo-Herron*, other cases do demonstrate a continuing parallel commitment to a strong or expansive conception of the freedom to conduct a business.

[33] ibid para 24.
[34] ibid para 23.
[35] ibid para 26.

5.2.2 Parallel continuity with the expansive conception of the freedom to conduct a business

Despite the elements of continuity with the CJEU's earlier approach to the treatment of the freedom to conduct a business, there are other cases which emphasize the consonance of the freedom to conduct a business as a fundamental right with the wider constitutional and institutional context of EU law, while at the same time marking a departure from how those constitutional concepts are traditionally understood, thereby demonstrating further convergence and contestation within the freedom to conduct a business as a fundamental right.

Perhaps the most important pronouncement evidencing a strong conception of the freedom to conduct a business can be seen in the Opinion of Advocate General Szpunar in *Thelen Technopark Berlin*, a case concerning German minimum pricing rules for architectural and engineering services which had themselves already been found to be incompatible with Article 15 of the Services Directive 2006/123, precluding discriminatory or disproportionate ceilings or floors on tariffs for service providers.[36] The Opinion, which was referred to in the opening paragraph of this book, is particularly notable for its relatively extensive treatment of freedom of *contract* as a component of the freedom to conduct a business. The Advocate General remarked that:

> [t]he internal market and a highly competitive social market economy, as referred to in Article 3(3) TEU, as well as the adoption of an economic policy which is conducted in accordance with the principle of an open market economy with free competition, as referred to in Article 119 TFEU, would be inconceivable without [freedom of contract]. Yet, it remains hidden behind the entire system of other EU principles and laws.[37]

It was then noted that freedom of contract is a distinct part of the freedom to conduct a business, and which may be subject to considerations that are not necessarily applicable to the other elements found within Article 16 of the Charter:

[36] AG Opinion in Case C-261/20 *Thelen Technopark Berlin GmbH v MN* ECLI:EU:C:2021:620; Case C-377/17 *Commission v Germany* ECLI:EU:C:2019:562; Verordnung über die Honorare für Architekten- und Ingenieurleistungen, para 7; Directive 2006/123/EC of the European Parliament and of the Council of 12 December 2006 on services in the internal market [2006] OJ L376/36.

[37] AG Opinion in *Thelen Technopark* (n 36) para 76.

> A given provision of the Charter may guarantee various rights and freedoms and lay down various principles, some of which can provide rationales for rulings in national proceedings, and some not. The fact that Article 16 of the Charter deals, inter alia, with freedom of contract does not mean that the conditions for relying on it before national courts will also apply to the other rights or freedoms guaranteed in that article.[38]

The 'assumed' content of freedom of contract was said to include 'at least' the freedom to conclude or amend a contract; to choose the counterparty; and to determine the content and form of the contract, as well as the contractual relationship, with the latter also including the right to determine freely the amount of mutual benefits, including price or remuneration.[39] In particular, any State-imposed obligation to enter a contract 'constitutes a significant interference with freedom of contract'.[40] Other restrictions on freedom of contract would include any interference with the autonomy of the parties' will, for example through the imposition of specific terms or the prescription of the conclusion or termination of a contract.[41]

This is not to say that there is no recognition of the potential justified limitations that can be imposed on the freedom to conduct a business including freedom of contract, such as the fact that the freedom may be restricted in relation to its social function. Indeed, the reference to 'Union law and national laws and practices' within Article 16 CFR serves to emphasize the greater permissibility of state interference with that freedom than with other rights not subject to the same formula. There is no indication, however, that Article 16 CFR is subject to a reduction in the level of protection granted to the rights contained therein nor that the freedom to conduct a business merely has the 'status of a principle or of a "second-class" right'.[42]

In that respect, Article 16 CFR differs from certain provisions in the Solidarity Title, for example Article 27 CFR, in that the Explanations do further specify the rights contained therein and so the provision is not dependent on further elucidation in the manner required of Article 27 CFR.[43] Article 16 CFR is therefore a 'self-executing' (directly effective) provision, with the right of the parties to set the price being 'so obvious, clear and unambiguous that it

[38] ibid para 79.
[39] ibid paras 82, 83.
[40] ibid para 83.
[41] ibid para 84.
[42] ibid para 89.
[43] ibid para 86.

does not need to be given specific expression in EU law or national law in order for its content to be determined'.[44]

It is not at all obvious that Article 16 CFR should be considered a directly effective provision whether in whole or in relation to its component parts with that provision therefore remaining of ambiguous legal and normal value. Nevertheless, the Advocate General noted that this was not a typical dispute between individuals, which would usually concern subjective individual rights, giving rise to obligations on the other party to the dispute. In the present case, concerning the right to set the price of a service, what is at stake is the right of the individual to be free 'from interference in the autonomy of the will of the parties', a right that is not easily quantifiable.[45]

In addition, the source of the restriction on that right derives not from the other party to the contract, but from the State and is thus not a case of horizontal direct effect in the classical sense 'where a provision is addressed to an individual and thus imposes [. . .] an obligation to act in a certain way'.[46] Freedom of contract thereby protects *both* parties to the contract from external interference rather than protecting the contractual parties from each other, ie the right to set the price of the contract is a *joint* right.[47] The freedom to conduct a business is instead being used as the standard against which the lawfulness of the national provision is assessed.[48]

Of particular interest is the suggested approach whereby national law will be found to violate Article 16 CFR if there is an interference with freedom of contract and that interference violates a legislative instrument, under which the balance of competing interests and a proportionality assessment has already been conducted.[49] Such an approach would, however, necessitate a determination of whether a particular legislative provision was implementing or rendering more concrete a fundamental right (or principle) such as freedom of contract. The case law on Article 16 CFR demonstrates that this provision can be easily invoked and that the CJEU frequently finds that there has been a restriction or limitation on the freedom to conduct a business, albeit usually finding that such restrictions are justified and proportionate. In addition, almost any legislative provision granting rights to parties to contractual relationships could be said to represent an expression or specification of freedom of

[44] ibid paras 92, 93.
[45] ibid para 98.
[46] ibid para 104.
[47] ibid para 100.
[48] ibid para 104.
[49] ibid, para 110; Justin Lindeboom, '*Thelen Technopark* and the Legal Effects of the Services Directive in Purely Internal and Horizontal Disputes' (2022) 7 European Papers 305, 323.

contract and the freedom to conduct a business more generally. Ultimately, the Advocate General found the national provision to be unlawful on the ground that 'the fundamental right to freedom of contract must be respected as regards the parties' right to set the price'.[50] In practice, however, this may have differing effects on both parties, leading either to additional rights or additional obligations.[51]

Essentially, the Advocate General found that the Directive was indeed horizontally applicable either as a concrete expression of the freedom of establishment in Article 49 of the Treaty on the Functioning of the European Union (TFEU) which is itself horizontally directly effective, or as a legislative harmonization of the proportionality of an interference with the freedom to conduct a business.[52] In rejecting this position, the CJEU avoided the extension within the context of the internal market freedoms of the *Mangold* line of reasoning, whereby a directive merely gives expression to a general principle.[53] The CJEU did not engage with either freedom of contract or the freedom to conduct a business as fundamental rights, focusing instead of the lack of horizontal direct effect of the relevant directive and the consequent lack of obligation on the part of the national court to disapply conflicting national legislation on the basis of EU law in a dispute between two private parties.[54] The situation was also wholly internal and so the Treaty freedoms could not apply.[55]

The CJEU thereby opted to avoid discussion on the freedom to conduct a business, perhaps part of a wider desire to avoid engagement with the horizontal direct effect of directives and again demonstrating how the freedom to conduct a business, and indeed fundamental rights more generally, have become entwined with fundamental constitutional concepts within the EU legal order. This case does however provide an indication of the essential role played by Union legislation in elucidating the content and normative value of a Charter provision. In the opinion of the Advocate General, the very absence of legislative implementation was relied on as an indication that the freedom to conduct a business was directly effective, ie essentially a 'right', whereas the same status is denied to certain provisions of the Solidarity Title for the very reason that they are dependent on further implementation in Union or national legislation.

[50] AG Opinion in *Thelen Technopark* (n 36) para 113.
[51] ibid para 102.
[52] Lindeboom (n 49) 305.
[53] ibid.
[54] Case C-261/20 *Thelen Technopark Berlin GmbH v MN* ECLI:EU:C:2022:33, para 48.
[55] ibid para 52.

A particularly important case which demonstrates the continued (albeit more nuanced) strength of the freedom to conduct a business as a fundamental right is *AGET Iraklis*.[56] That case concerned a Greek prior authorization procedure that had to be complied with before an undertaking could proceed with collective redundancies. The national law in question required employers to notify the relevant public authorities of any planned collective redundancies. If the parties could not agree, the prefect or the relevant minister had the power to authorize the projected redundancies by way of a reasoned decision but only after taking account of the relevant documents, assessing the conditions in the labour market, the situation of the undertaking, and the interests of the national economy.

In that case, a cement company submitted a request for the approval of collective redundancies to the Ministry of Labour as required by the national legislation. The Ministry subsequently prepared a report relating to the conditions of the market, the situation of the undertaking, and the interests of the wider economy, and refused to authorize the requested collective redundancies. The company therefore sought to challenge the compatibility of the national legislation which implemented the EU Collective Redundancies Directive with that directive read in light of Union fundamental rights concepts, including the freedom of establishment found in Article 49 TFEU and the freedom to conduct a business in Article 16 of the Charter.[57] The national referring court noted that although the Collective Redundancies Directive does not provide for any authorization period, Article 5 of the Directive nevertheless permits Member States to increase the level of protection granted to employees, ie it is a minimum harmonization measure in the same way as the Transfer of Undertakings Directive, the legislation which had been at issue in *Alemo-Herron*.

Advocate General Wahl began by noting that the purpose of the Directive was to protect workers, but also to harmonize the costs of collective redundancies for employers.[58] The Advocate General held that the prior authorization procedure did amount to a restriction on the freedom of establishment found in Article 49 TFEU and that 'the provisions of EU law must be interpreted in accordance with the fundamental rights as set out in the Charter.

[56] Case C-201/15 *Anonymi Geniki Etairia Tsimenton Iraklis (AGET Iraklis) v Ypourgos Ergasias, Koinonikis Asfalisis kai Koinonikis Allilengyis* ECLI:EU:C:2016:972.

[57] Council Directive 98/59/EC of 20 July 1998 on the approximation of the laws of the Member States relating to collective redundancies [1998] OJ L225/16.

[58] AG Opinion in Case C-201/15 *Anonymi Geniki Etairia Tsimenton Iraklis (AGET Iraklis) v Ypourgos Ergasias, Koinonikis Asfalisis kai Koinonikis Allilengyis* ECLI:EU:C:2016:429.

Hence Article 49 TFEU must be interpreted in accordance with Article 16.'[59] Accordingly, the restriction on the freedom of establishment 'also amounts to a restriction on the exercise of the freedom to conduct a business. Moreover, it restricts the freedom of contract of employers, inasmuch as they are required to seek prior authorisation.'[60] The Advocate General concluded that '[t]he rule at issue applies in a non-discriminatory way. Therefore, it is necessary to consider whether the remaining criteria [. . .] are met, given that this exercise, in my view, is basically one and the same under Article 49 [. . .] and Article 16.'[61] The Directive was therefore said to represent a compromise between worker protection and consideration of the interests of employers. Unilaterally to impose additional obligations on the employer risked 'upsetting the equilibrium from the point of view of Article 49 [and] Article 16.'[62]

The CJEU adopted a somewhat different approach in its judgment, recalling that the Directive was a minimum harmonization measure but that 'the fact remains that the limited character of such harmonization cannot have the consequence of depriving the provisions of that directive of practical effect.'[63] Such would be the case should an authorization procedure actually prevent collective redundancies from ever taking place in practice. As the Court put it, the Directive is based 'on the premise that collective redundancies must—once the procedures established by those provisions have been exhausted [. . .] at least remain conceivable.'[64] Concerning freedom of establishment, the CJEU held that the decision to engage in collective redundancies is a fundamental decision in the life of an undertaking and, as such, the national legislation was likely to hinder or make less attractive that freedom, given the need to obtain authorization. As a result, the national rules also hindered or limited the exercise of the freedom to conduct a business but could potentially be justified on the grounds of worker protection.[65]

The case therefore came down to the question of whether the restrictions on the freedom to conduct a business were proportionate. The CJEU started from the proposition that the authorization procedure was not capable in and of itself of undermining the essence of the freedom to conduct a business under Article 16 CFR. There was therefore nothing in principle preventing national authorities from instituting a prior authorization procedure to enhance the

[59] ibid para 49.
[60] ibid para 50.
[61] ibid para 53.
[62] ibid para 63.
[63] *AGET Iraklis* (n 56) para 36.
[64] ibid para 40.
[65] ibid para 73.

protection of workers. However, the CJEU went on to find that the Greek regime was not compatible with either Article 16 CFR or Article 49 TFEU in that the national rules provided no details as to how the power contained in the authorization procedure was to be exercised and which thereby prevented effective judicial review of any decision not to authorize collective redundancies.[66]

In particular, the CJEU was concerned that some of the criteria, notably those relating to the situation of the undertaking and the national labour market, were formulated in very general terms.[67] It can been questioned whether Article 16 of the Charter added any value to the outcome of this case over and above the decision that would have been reached had the CJEU relied exclusively on Article 49 TFEU.[68] It is nevertheless argued here that Article 16 CFR imbues the freedom of establishment with the—albeit somewhat indeterminate—normative content of a fundamental right, while Article 49 TFEU simultaneously infiltrates this fundamental rights provision with the logic of the internal market.

The very fact that the national measure in *AGET Iraklis* failed to comply with both Article 49 TFEU and Article 16 CFR '[o]n identical grounds' thereby enhances rather than undermines the deregulatory potential of the Charter, notably by relating it to the market access principle and thereby impeding the effective balance of that provision against the other fundamental economic and social rights found elsewhere in the Charter, and indeed competing rights and interests within domestic and EU law more generally. In other words, the interaction between the freedom of establishment and the freedom to conduct a business within the Charter signifies that cases such as *AGET Iraklis* represent more than an ordinary application of the CJEU's standard approach to the justification of restrictions on economic freedoms, despite the softening in 'tone' when compared with previous highly deregulatory judgments prioritizing market freedoms over competing social rights, including the (perfunctory) recognition of competing social rights in the form of protection from unjustified dismissal in Article 30 CFR.[69] At the same time, the CJEU underplays the potential differences in the meaning of 'autonomy' within the context of Article 16 CFR and Article 49 TFEU, for example the extent to which the

[66] ibid para 49.
[67] ibid para 103.
[68] Menelaos Markakis, 'Can Governments Control Mass Layoffs by Employers? Economic Freedoms vs Labour Rights in Case C–201/15 *AGET Iraklis*' (2017) 13 EuConst 724, 739.
[69] ibid 743; Case C–230/18 *PI v Landespolizeidirektion Tirol* ECLI:EU:C:2019:383. art 16 CFR and the Treaty's free movement provisions are also connected by virtue of art 52(2) CFR.

freedom to conduct a business as a fundamental right might be invoked to limit the horizontal application of free movement rules, ie their applicability to private parties.[70] This divergence is also reflective of the 'functional' approach to freedom of contract within the context of EU (internal market) law, ie freedom of contract within EU law serves the function of ensuring access to the market, rather than protecting individual autonomy as an intrinsic end in itself.[71]

Overall, the case law demonstrates that even when the freedom to conduct a business is raised, and arguments based on that freedom are successful, there is nevertheless a consideration of competing rights and values, at least implicitly through the recognition that the freedom to conduct a business is not absolute but may be limited. Even cases such as *AGET Iraklis*, which appear highly deregulatory, may have resulted not as a consequence of the application of the freedom to conduct a business itself but rather through the connection drawn between that freedom and the fundamental freedoms of the EU internal market. Indeed, aspects of the reasoning found in *AGET Iraklis* are reflected in a long line of CJEU case law concerning restrictions on market access.[72]

To the extent that a pattern in the CJEU's reasoning can be ascertained, it appears that contractual or legislative terms involving 'collective' negotiation or terms that have been imposed with no negotiation at all are particularly likely to be caught by the freedom to conduct a business, or freedom of contract in particular. This renders legislation governing the employment relationship especially vulnerable to challenge given that this is a field in which there is a 'weaker' party to the contractual arrangements, which rely—to a greater or lesser extent on collectively agreed, mandatory, or standard form terms, depending on the legal system in question—and which are susceptible to the invocation of the freedom to conduct a business as a fundamental right. Of course, whether those terms may be found compatible with the freedom to conduct a business is largely dependent on the CJEU's approach to the interpretation and application of Article 16 of the Charter.

The freedom to conduct a business as a fundamental right is also beginning to show its strength in other substantive areas of EU law including in the equality context, which may have been thought particularly worthy of being shielded from business freedoms and contractual autonomy principles. The potential reach of the freedom to conduct a business—even where arguments based on that freedom are unsuccessful—is perhaps most evident in the case

[70] Rufut Babayev, 'Private Autonomy at Union Level: On Article 16 CFREU and Free Movement Rights' (2016) 53 CMLRev 979, 982.
[71] ibid 981.
[72] Markakis (n 68) 734.

law concerning employer prohibitions on the wearing of religious symbols in the workplace. In *Achbita*, the CJEU was required to determine whether the Framework Equality Directive 2000/78 should be interpreted so as to permit a private employer to prohibit female Muslim employees from wearing a headscarf in the workplace and consequently whether that employer was permitted to dismiss an employee for failure to comply with that prohibition.[73] For Advocate General Kokott:

> [i]n a Union which regards itself as being committed to a social market economy [. . .] and seeks to achieve this in accordance with the requirements of an open market economy with free competition [. . .] the importance that attaches to the freedom to conduct a business is not to be underestimated.[74]

Therefore, the Directive may well permit such a derogation from the principle of equality, but it is one which must be interpreted strictly and with the freedom to conduct a business itself being subject to a 'broad range of restrictions'.[75] The CJEU agreed that the employer's desire to safeguard its image of neutrality in its relationship with customers did engage the freedom to conduct a business.[76] That is to say that businesses enjoy 'expressive' fundamental rights going beyond mere 'profit-maximization' interests.[77] Therefore, reliance on the freedom to conduct a business supported the finding that the neutrality rule amounted to a legitimate aim, even though it was left to the national court to determine if the rule was justified in the circumstances.[78]

By way of contrast, in *Bougnaoui* Advocate General Sharpston accepted that the freedom to conduct a business represents a legitimate aim, particularly given its status as a general principle now enshrined in Article 16 of the Charter, but that the freedom was not absolute and so had to be considered in relation to its social function.[79] In other words, business or commercial interests did not come within the concept of a 'genuine and determining occupational

[73] Case C-157/15 *Samira Achbita and Centrum voor gelijkheid van kansen en voor racismebestrijding v G4S Secure Solutions NV* ECLI:EU:C:2017:203; Council Directive 2000/78/EC of 27 November 2000 establishing a general framework for equal treatment in employment and occupation [2000] OJ L303/16.

[74] AG Opinion in Case C-157/15 *Samira Achbita and Centrum voor gelijkheid van kansen en voor racismebestrijding v G4S Secure Solutions* ECLI:EU:C:2016:382, para 134.

[75] ibid para 136.

[76] *Achbita* (n 73) para 38.

[77] Elke Cloots, 'Safe Harbour or Open Sea for Corporate Headscarf Bans? *Achbita and Bougnaoui*' (2018) 55 CMLRev 589, 614; Peter Oliver, 'Companies and their Fundamental Rights: A Comparative Perspective' (2015) 64 ICLQ 661.

[78] Sarah Fraser Butlin, 'The CJEU Confused Over Religion' (2017) 76 CLJ 246, 248.

[79] AG Opinion in *Bougnaoui* (n 7), para 115.

requirement'. The CJEU, on the other hand, did not address the freedom to conduct a business point, which is perhaps suggestive of a reticence on the part of the Court to engage more fully with the consequences of its expansive conception of the freedom to conduct a business espoused in earlier cases, unless strictly necessary to address the question at issue in a particular case.

Nevertheless, the CJEU has subsequently continued to engage with the freedom to conduct a business in cases concerning religious dress in the workplace. In *LF*, the CJEU recognized the potential prioritization of religion or belief over the freedom to conduct a business when the national court conducts its balancing exercise at the justification stage of an indirect discrimination claim, while in *IX*, the CJEU confirmed the need to strike a fair balance between the freedom to conduct a business and other fundamental rights, such as the principle of non-discrimination and freedom of thought, conscience, and religion.[80] Interestingly, in *OP*, Advocate General Collins noted that in the case of the prohibition of religious or political symbols by a *public* employer, it was not possible to rely on the freedom to conduct a business in Article 16 CFR.[81]

Overall, arguments based on Article 16 CFR remain successful in only very few cases outside of the social or employment field, but even then, the freedom to conduct a business is just one of a number of provisions invoked before the Court and so it is difficult to ascertain the precise influence of that provision. It seems from the case law that collectively agreed or imposed terms, particularly when reached without negotiation or where those terms endure for a considerable period, are likely to constitute infringements of the freedom to conduct a business. In some cases, however, the freedom to conduct a business in Article 16 of the Charter is referenced only very briefly but without any engagement with the substance of that provision, while in other cases the CJEU attempts to limit the application of expansive decisions such as *Alemo-Herron* to the facts of that case.

What is notable, however, is that many cases in which arguments based on the freedom to conduct a business succeed actually involve freedom *of contract* specifically rather than other elements of Article 16 CFR, such as the freedom

[80] Case C–344/20 *L.F. v SCRL* ECLI:EU:C:2022:774, para 52; Joined Cases C–804/18 and 341/19 *IX v WABE eV and MH Müller Handels GmbH v MJ* ECLI:EU:C:2021:594, para 84; Erica Howard, '*LF v SCRL* and the CJEU's Failure to Engage with the Reality of Muslim Women in the Labour Market' (2023) 52 ILJ 997.

[81] AG Opinion in Case C–148/22 *OP v Commune d'Ans* EU:C:2023:378, para 64. Freedom of contract as a fundamental right has also been successfully invoked outside of the employment sphere: AG Opinion in Case C–132/19 P *Groupe Canal + v European Commission* ECLI:EU:C:2020:35, paras 119, 125; Case C–132/19 P *Groupe Canal + v European Commission* ECLI:EU:C:2020:1007, para 107; Case C–534/16 *Finančné riaditeľstvo Slovenskej republiky v BB construct s. r. o* ECLI:EU:C:2017:820, para 41.

to pursue a trade or occupation. One of the criticisms of the CJEU's judgment in *Alemo-Herron* was that the Court's approach to the freedom to conduct a business was not consistent with its earlier case law on business freedoms as general principles.[82] Indeed, one of the suggested functions of the general principles in the judicial methodology of the CJEU is to ensure consistency with established paths of argumentation, an approach which is facilitated by Article 6 of the Treaty on European Union's (TEU) continued recognition of the general principles as a source of EU fundamental rights, which thus lends a 'legitimizing force' to the general principles.[83] There is also some evidence of inconsistency in the subsequent case law on the freedom to conduct a business as a fundamental right in Article 16 CFR, with the CJEU veering between an expansive and a restrictive conception of that right. This opens up broader questions as to the value placed on consistency in the legal reasoning of the CJEU, particularly in the context of rather nebulous fundamental rights concepts such as the freedom to conduct a business and particularly freedom of contract, the strength of which may also fluctuate depending on the underlying political, economic, and social context.

5.3 Coherence Within the Freedom to Conduct a Business as a Fundamental Right

As has been seen, the freedom to conduct a business within Article 16 of the Charter, as well as the same concept found within the general principles, can act as a guide to the interpretation of both EU law as well as national law that falls within the scope of EU law. It was shown that the freedom to conduct a business as a fundamental right has been used to undermine the purpose of protective legislation, notably in the employment context. This section instead addresses the potential causes of the CJEU's inconsistent interpretation and application of the freedom to conduct a business, including the manner in which the CJEU's approach to that freedom fits in with its broader interpretative methodology. It has been argued, drawing from the Critical Legal Studies concept of 'fundamental contradiction', that consistency should not necessarily

[82] Stephen Weatherill, 'Use and Abuse of the EU's Charter of Fundamental Rights: On the Improper Veneration of 'Freedom of Contract' (2014) 10 ERCL 167; Jeremias Prassl, 'Freedom of Contract as a General Principle of EU Law? Transfers of Undertakings and the Protection of Employer Rights in EU Labour Law' (2013) 42 ILJ 434, 444.

[83] Takis Tridimas, 'The General Principles of Law: Who Needs Them?' (2016) 52 Cahiers de Droit Européen 419, 422.

be expected in the context of the interpretation of concepts as value-laden and nebulous as 'contractual autonomy' or 'business freedoms'. These contradictions are compounded by the CJEU's approach to legal reasoning, including the absence of a clear doctrine of precedent, as well as the method by which it identifies or discovers general principles. While the CJEU has drawn from the common constitutional traditions in its construction of the freedom to conduct a business as a general principle and subsequently a Charter right, it does so without any proper engagement with the national context in which those rights emerged.

This is perhaps understandable given the need to ensure the malleability of national law concepts to the EU context, as indeed has been recognized by the CJEU itself in its development of fundamental rights as general principles. However, the CJEU fails to then explain precisely how concepts such as the freedom to pursue a trade or occupation and freedom of contract *are* adapted to the EU law context. As such, the existing case law on the freedom to conduct a business as a fundamental right, particularly with regards to freedom of contract, is divorced from the wider normative context of how those concepts are viewed within national law and indeed within the wider EU law context as evidenced by earlier discussions analysing the meaning of freedom of contract within both EU law and domestic law. These ambiguities are also compounded by the CJEU's methods of legal reasoning, characterized by its 'Cartesian style [...] its pretense of logical reasoning and inevitability of results'.[84]

The absence of a clear normative underpinning for the concept of freedom to conduct a business is all the more striking given the use to which that concept has been put in the interpretation of legislation in order to disrupt existing purposive interpretative methods, leading to the erosion of worker-protective legislative concepts. The purpose of the present section is to demonstrate the manner in which the absence of a clear doctrine of precedent within EU law, coupled with the CJEU's perfunctory elucidation of its interpretative methods in the fundamental rights context, serve to undermine the consistency and coherence of the freedom to conduct a business as a fundamental right. As has been noted elsewhere, 'consistency' requires no more than that subsequent interpretation of norms does not contradict earlier interpretations, while 'coherence' serves to rationalize a set of rules.[85] Both concepts have been notably absent from the CJEU's discourse concerning the freedom to conduct a

[84] Joseph HH Weiler, 'Epilogue: The Judicial Après Nice' in Gráinne de Búrca and Joseph HH Weiler (eds), *The European Court of Justice* (OUP 2001) 215, 224.

[85] Joxerramon Bengoetxea, *The Legal Reasoning of the European Court of Justice: Towards a European Jurisprudence* (OUP 1993) 224.

business as a fundamental right. Of course, it is possible for a court to be consistently and coherently incorrect in its interpretation or application of legal concepts, but coherence serves as a useful shorthand or 'surrogate' for 'correct' decisions in the sense that the application of a precedent is apposite to the case at hand, leading to predictability and increased legal certainty in accordance with the exigencies of 'the system'.[86]

5.3.1 The value of precedent in European Union law

Evaluation of the CJEU's legal reasoning has tended to focus on whether the Court's rulings display sufficient consistency, whether outcomes are well founded, whether the CJEU defers to the EU and Member State legislatures where appropriate, and crucially for present purposes, whether the results in a particular judgment were 'reasonably predictable'.[87] One of the major criticisms that can be levelled at the CJEU's case law on business freedoms as general principles and the freedom to conduct a business as a Charter right is that there are inconsistencies within and between those judgments. The difficulty remains that EU law lacks a clear doctrine of precedent, whereby the CJEU would be bound by its previous decisions.

It is suggested here that problems of (in)consistency and (un)predictability are exacerbated in the context of fundamental rights adjudication which operates in a realm of open-textured and interrelated sources, with the CJEU having the task of interpreting and balancing these sources in cases of conflict. This is particularly true of *contested* concepts, such as the freedom to conduct a business or freedom of contract, which despite having been raised by the CJEU in its earliest case law on the protection of fundamental rights as general principles nevertheless continue to lack a clear normative grounding in the wider framework of EU law and can thereby appear as somewhat of an outlier in the fundamental rights field, particularly given the usual absence of business freedoms from international human rights instruments. Having said this, the CJEU's judgments do tend to become embedded and difficult to dislodge, as demonstrated by the longevity of some of its most 'activist' judgments, particularly those concerning (contested) foundational constitutional principles of the Union legal order such as direct effect and primacy, which

[86] Jacob (n 3) 145, 148, 150.

[87] Maurice Adams and others, 'Introduction: Judging Europe's Judges' in Maurice Adams and others (eds), *Judging Europe's Judges: The Legitimacy of the Case Law of the European Court of Justice* (Hart 2013) 1, 8.

are now considered crucial underpinnings of EU law but which lacked a clear textual (or indeed normative) basis in the founding Treaties.

Of course, the possibility always remains open to the political institutions—or the Member States with regard to Treaty provisions—to amend legislation to reflect their own preferences after the CJEU has offered its view on the interpretation of the relevant legislative provisions.[88] However, it is only in a select few cases that the Treaty drafters have explicitly provided for the 'political reversal' of a decision of the CJEU, although in the absence of explicit exclusion the CJEU itself continues to maintain oversight and interpretative control over all Treaty provisions, including those provisions which purport to overturn its previous rulings.[89] Decisions of the CJEU in response to preliminary references are always 'binding' on the national referring court. In practice, interpretative rulings by the CJEU also have a bearing on other courts.[90]

The nature of the preliminary reference procedure allows the national courts to continue to refer questions to the CJEU on issues that have been addressed previously, although the Court may decide to issue a reasoned order rather than a full judgment.[91] In a similar way, a judgment upholding the validity of a particular provision of EU law does not preclude a future challenge to the validity of that provision.[92] National courts are not under an obligation to refer a question to the CJEU when the question raised has already been addressed in the case law of the CJEU (*acte éclairé*) or where the correct application of EU law is so obvious as to leave no room for doubt (*acte clair*).[93] Finally, the most difficult question relates to the effect of a CJEU judgment ruling on the *interpretation* of an EU measure. While there remains no binding doctrine of precedent in EU law, the interpretation granted to a particular provision by the CJEU is likely to enjoy at least de facto precedential effect, given the exclusive competence granted to the CJEU over the interpretation of EU law and the duty imposed on national courts to interpret national law in conformity with EU law insofar as possible.[94]

[88] Anthony Arnull, 'Me and My Shadow: The European Court of Justice and the Disintegration of European Union Law' (2007) 31 Fordham Int'l L J 1174, 1187.

[89] ibid 1174; Thomas Horsley, *The Court of Justice of the European Union as an Institutional Actor* (CUP 2018) 29.

[90] AG Opinion in Case C–112/76 *Renato Manzoni v Fonds national de retraite des ouvriers mineurs* ECLI:EU:C:1977:133.

[91] Art 267 TFEU; art 99 Rules of Procedure of the Court of Justice [2012] OJ L265/1.

[92] Case C–8/78 *Milac GmbH, Groß- und Außenhandel v Hauptzollamt Freiburg* ECLI:EU:C:1978:157.

[93] Case C–283/81 *Srl CILFIT and Lanificio di Gavardo SpA v Ministry of Health*. ECLI:EU:C:1982:335; Case C–561/19 *Consorzio Italian Management e Catania Multiservizi and Catania Multiservizi* ECLI:EU:C:2021:799.

[94] Case C–14/83 *Sabine von Colson and Elisabeth Kamann v Land Nordrhein-Westfalen* ECLI:EU:C:1984:153; Case C–453/00 *Kühne & Heitz NV v Produktschap voor Pluimvee en Eieren* ECLI:EU:C:2004:17.

The doctrine of precedent in its strong sense, namely the requirement that a judge or court follow a decision handed down in a previous case, is a particular feature of the English common law and thereby has a 'profound effect' on how judgments are reasoned.[95] In contrast, the CJEU is not formally bound by its own previous decisions, although in practice it is rare for the Court explicitly to depart from them, particularly in such a way as to retreat from previously held positions.[96] As Davies put it, '[e]xamples where the change in doctrine is towards a more restrictive reading of the law, rather than a more expansive one, are exceptionally scarce'.[97] A corollary of the absence of a doctrine of binding precedent is that the entirety of a particular CJEU judgment may be regarded as operative and there is therefore no distinction between the *ratio decidendi* of a judgment and *obiter dicta*.[98] Furthermore, Member State courts may contest the binding nature of CJEU judgments.[99] For example, the German Constitutional Court has demonstrated 'conditional' acceptance of CJEU case law concerning the application of Union fundamental rights, thereby reserving the right to exercise its own fundamental rights review where the level of protection falls below that guaranteed by the German Basic Law.[100]

It should also be recalled that the CJEU is a court of last instance and, even within the context of common law legal systems, it is possible for higher courts to depart from their own precedents. The UK Supreme Court (UKSC), for example, may depart from its own earlier rulings if it considers it 'right to do so'.[101] This was also the test applied by the UKSC when deciding whether or not to depart from retained EU case law, ie decisions of the CJEU relating to retained EU law and which were handed down prior to the end of the transition period on 31 December 2020. Domestic courts were also invited to have 'regard' to CJEU decisions handed down after this time.[102] The same courts are also required to have 'due regard' to relevant case law of the CJEU in the interpretation and application of the Withdrawal Agreement between the EU

[95] Anthony Arnull, 'Owning up to Fallibility: Precedent and the Court of Justice' (1993) 30 CMLRev 247.
[96] ibid 248.
[97] Gareth Davies, 'How the Court's Path Dependence Affects is Role as a Relational Actor' (2023) 2 European Law Open 271.
[98] Arnull (n 95) 249.
[99] Bundesverfassungsgericht Case No 2 BvR 859/15 (5 May 2020) (PSPP judgment), para 234; Case C-493/17 *Proceedings brought by Heinrich Weiss* ECLI:EU:C:2018:1000; Tomi Tuominen, 'Reconceptualizing the Primacy-Supremacy Debate in EU Law' (2020) 47 LIEI 245, 256.
[100] *Solange II* [1987] 3 CMLR 225.
[101] Practice Statement (HL: Judicial Precedent) [1966] 3 All ER 77 (26 July 1966) and UK Supreme Court Practice Direction 3.1.3; Rupert Cross and JW Harris, *Precedent in English Law* (4th edn, Clarendon Press 1991).
[102] European Union (Withdrawal) Act (EU(W)A) 2018, s 6.

and UK and which may therefore have an indirect impact on the conceptualization of domesticated EU law concepts, for example the general principles, supremacy, and direct effect.

In addition, the Retained EU Law (Revocation and Reform) Act (REULA) 2023 facilitates the modification of these concepts within the context of the UK's desire to detach its legal order further from that which prevailed during its membership of the Union.[103] UK courts have similarly been given more explicit instructions as to the (non-exhaustive) factors to consider when deciding whether or not to depart from what is now known as 'assimilated' EU case law, including the fact that the CJEU is a 'foreign' court.[104] This guidance supersedes the earlier extension of the power to depart from retained EU case law from the UKSC to other higher courts such as the Court of Appeal in England and Wales, which had already further undermined legal certainty.[105]

It is as yet unclear whether the UKSC will be as circumspect in departing from retained or assimilated EU case law as it usually is in deciding whether to depart from its own previous case law. The UKSC's Practice Statement—unchanged in this respect since 1966—urges particular caution in overruling cases which might retrospectively disturb the basis on which contractual or commercial transactions have been entered into, given the need for legal and commercial certainty.[106] The UK courts remain bound by decisions of the CJEU handed down prior to the end of the transition in relation to questions of the interpretation of concepts of EU law found within the UK-EU Withdrawal Agreement, with the possibility of continued references to the CJEU on the interpretation of concepts of EU law found within the Agreement.[107]

Of course, the absence of an explicit doctrine of precedent within EU law is not a licence for inconsistency in the jurisprudence of the CJEU. Indeed, that court—like any court—should strive to make decisions in accordance with established pronouncements in order to ensure that the legitimate expectations of litigants are met, but also to bolster the legitimacy of the Court itself by having its decisions fit smoothly within the wider legal framework.[108] The difficulty really lies in the Court's reticence when dealing with its previous

[103] Agreement on the withdrawal of the United Kingdom of Great Britain and Northern Ireland from the European Union and the European Atomic Energy Community [2020] OJ L29/7 (Withdrawal Agreement), art 4.

[104] REULA 2023, s 6(3) and (4).

[105] EU(W)A 2018, s 6; European Union (Withdrawal) Act 2018 (Relevant Court) (Retained EU Case Law) Regulations 2020 (SI 2020/1525).

[106] Lord Reed of Allermuir, 'Departing from Precedent: The Experience of the UK Supreme Court' (International Conference on Implementation of the Rule of Law, 20 January 2023) 4.

[107] Arts 4 and 174; European Union (Withdrawal Agreement) Act 2020, s 5; EU(W)A 2018, s 7A.

[108] Jacob (n 3) 13 and 14.

judgments, at times repeating passages from earlier case law verbatim but without acknowledging the source, while in other cases departing from a previous outcome but without explanation.[109] In certain judgments, the CJEU may also overturn existing orthodoxy but without necessitating an overruling of previous case law.[110]

The CJEU is however increasingly referencing its previous case law, at times even distinguishing or overruling such decisions, a symptom perhaps of a growing recognition of its jurisprudence as a 'source' of law.[111] The CJEU also frequently uses the term 'settled case law' (*jurisprudence constante de la Cour*) in its decisions, thereby connecting its judgments to earlier rulings, although without always engaging in any meaningful way with that pre-existing case law. The lack of in-depth engagement with existing judgments—at times referring to only tangentially relevant case law—may also have more to do with the Court's syllogistic style of reasoning, constrained as it is by the collegiate nature of its deliberations and the fact that it must issue a single judgment, with the role of potential dissenter left to the Advocate General when an Opinion is delivered.[112] The overall difficulty, then, lies in uncovering the rationale for an earlier decision, with precedents containing different pieces of 'legal information' that can be adduced according to the situation, which can then be claimed as the relevant rationale underpinning the decision, and which can therefore vary over time according to the issue.[113]

Overall, it can be said that despite the absence of strict rules of precedent the CJEU nevertheless tends to follow its existing case law, but usually through general references and without any engagement with the reasons underpinning those earlier pronouncements. The CJEU explicitly departs from earlier case law only rarely and will more often seek to *distinguish* a case from its earlier jurisprudence. The CJEU often refers to the fact that it is not 'formally, 'legally', or 'technically' bound by earlier case law, which suggests that precedents nevertheless impose an argumentative burden on the Court.[114] This approach also amounts to a (tentative) recognition of the normative value of the CJEU's jurisprudence even in the absence of strict 'bindingness'. Indeed, judicial decision making can be constrained outside of the two extremes of 'binding' or

[109] Arnull (n 95) 252, 253.
[110] Davies (n 97) 276.
[111] Jacob (n 3) 43.
[112] eg in *Alemo-Herron* the CJEU referred to Case C–544/10 *Deutsches Weintor eG v Land Rheinland-Pfalz* ECLI:EU:C:2012:526, in which legislative restrictions on business freedoms were found to be justified.
[113] Jacob (n 3) 71.
[114] ibid 244.

'not binding', with the CJEU continuing to apply its earlier jurisprudence out of a desire to preserve the coherence of the 'system', meaning that alternative approaches need to be argued for by those seeking a divergent solution.[115]

Within the particular context of the freedom to conduct a business as a fundamental right, the CJEU has referred to the—as argued here, 'landmark'—case of *Alemo-Herron* only relatively infrequently even where Article 16 of the Charter is relevant to the case at hand. It is important, however, not to place too much emphasis on the citation or absence thereof of previous cases, regardless of their relative importance, given what has been said about the CJEU's approach to precedent. As also noted by Jacob, the perception of a case's importance (as precedent) often owes much to the subsequent 'talking up' of a decision.[116] This is not to say that cases dealing with the freedom to conduct a business a fundamental right will not have a significant wider impact, but rather to acknowledge that the CJEU has thus far provided only a rather superficial sketching of the content and meaning of the freedom to conduct a business as well as even ostensibly more *specific* concepts such as freedom of contract. The absence of explicit reasoning in cases such as *Alemo-Herron* makes it difficult to argue for a departure from—or distinction of—such cases.

The CJEU is loath to admit that previous decisions were 'wrong' and in any case, the generality of its reasoning makes such a determination difficult to maintain in practice. However, the CJEU does more frequently have recourse to distinction as a method of 'avoiding' the consequences of a previous ruling, for example by holding that the relevant precedent did not actually establish what is now being argued for or by increasing the specificity of the earlier judgment.[117] There have been efforts to distinguish *Alemo-Herron* or at the very least confine that case to the particular circumstances that arose therein. In *AGET Iraklis*, for example, the Court noted that '[i]t is true that the Court has *previously held*, in respect of national legislation by virtue of which certain undertakings were unable to participate in the collective bargaining body [. . .] and therefore could not assert their interests effectively [. . .] that in such a case the contractual freedom of those undertakings is seriously reduced'.[118] The CJEU then held '*[h]owever*, [the present regime] does not have, in any way, the consequence of entirely excluding, by its very nature, the ability of undertakings to effect collective redundancies [. . .] Therefore, such a regime cannot be considered to affect the essence of the freedom to conduct a

115 ibid 253 and 219.
116 ibid 198.
117 ibid 129.
118 *AGET Iraklis* (n 56) para 87.

business' [emphasis added].[119] In the same vein, the CJEU in *Alemo-Herron* had distinguished the earlier case of *Werhof*, noting that the facts of the situation in the latter case were 'appreciably different'.[120]

The concept of a right's 'very essence' or 'core content' is notoriously difficult to define and thereby grants the CJEU a wide margin of discretion in determining a measure's compatibility with the freedom to conduct a business as a fundamental right. The difficulty is that the inherent vagueness of the language used to describe that right and its limitations means that the influence of Article 16 CFR continues to be pervasive even if its very generality might undermine its value as 'precedent'. Vagueness can thereby enhance a norm's stability, while at the same time leaving the Court unconstrained by narrow or prescriptive interpretations of a particular concept.[121]

The Court's treatment of the freedom to conduct a business as a fundamental right falls somewhere in between the two extremes of being: (1) overly prescriptive; or (2) excessively vague as a precedent in that, while not entirely devoid of content and clearly related (however indirectly) back to concepts within the case law on general principles, it has nevertheless been interpreted in such a way as to encompass multiple facets of commercial and business activity within its scope. This leads to variations in the use of language when describing various aspects of the freedom to conduct a business and its limitations, thereby leading to the perception of inconsistency in the CJEU's interpretation of that concept as a fundamental right.

5.3.2 Interpretative consistency and the freedom to conduct a business

The doctrine of precedent, to the extent that such a doctrine exists within EU law, can be said to represent a 'steadying' or 'limiting' factor on the CJEU's approach to interpretation by creating a strong normative presumption that relatively similar cases should be decided consistently, albeit that judge-made rules are generally less 'stable' than written rules.[122] It has been suggested that the CJEU, when exercising its interpretative functions, should be required to demonstrate a much closer engagement with the Treaty framework as

[119] ibid para 88.
[120] AG Opinion in Case C-426/11 *Mark Alemo-Herron v Parkwood Leisure Ltd* ECLI:EU:C:2013:82, para 19.
[121] Gunnar Beck, *The Legal Reasoning of the Court of Justice of the EU* (Hart 2013) 269.
[122] ibid 339, 340.

'constitutional touchstone'.[123] It is argued here that this touchstone should now be interpreted as including the Charter, which enjoys the same status as the Treaties and indeed has been incorporated by reference within Article 6 TEU. Absent from the Court's current interpretation of the freedom to conduct a business as a fundamental right is any semblance of real engagement with the underlying normative content and value to be attributed to the freedom to conduct a business, as argued in Chapter 4.

It should also be noted that the CJEU is well known for pronouncing on important constitutional concepts at a particularly high level of generality. As Horsley suggests, '[d]ecisions of immense constitutional, political and socio-economic importance are routinely delivered as short, sparsely reasoned proclamations'.[124] It is, therefore, possible to bring almost any subsequent case within the concepts found in earlier judgments of the CJEU. In other words, rather than focusing on the similarity of particular cases, it is necessary instead to explore the CJEU's application of broader 'concepts'.[125] Therefore, the problem with the existing case law on freedom of contract is not so much its inconsistency with the general principles, but rather the absence of any engagement with the normative content of that concept, which was itself already a feature of the case law on business freedoms as general principles.

The CJEU, when dealing with open-textured provisions of the Treaty or secondary legislation, tends to adopt a systemic or purposive approach to the interpretation of those provisions, or as the CJEU itself has put it, '[a]ccording to the Court's settled case-law, for the purpose of interpreting a provision of EU law, it is necessary to consider not only its wording but also the context in which it occurs and the objectives pursued by the rules of which it is part'.[126] The classic formulation of the CJEU's approach to the interpretation of the Treaty is that it should consider the 'sprit, the general scheme [and only then] the wording of these provisions'.[127] In practice, the CJEU is likely to start by examining the wording of the relevant provision but is also well known for eschewing a literal interpretative approach, preferring instead to adopt arguments based on the 'general scheme or context of application'.[128] Literal approaches to interpretation are of limited assistance to the Court due to the fact

[123] Horsley (n 89) 17, 24.
[124] ibid 254.
[125] Gerard Conway, *The Limits of Legal Reasoning and the European Court of Justice* (CUP 2012) 245.
[126] Case C-19/15 *Verband Sozialer Wettbewerb eV v Innova Vital GmbH* ECLI:EU:C:2016:563, para 23.
[127] Case C-26/62 *NV Algemene Transport- en Expeditie Onderneming van Gend & Loos v Netherlands Inland Revenue Administration* ECLI:EU:C:1963:1, 12.
[128] Bengoetxea (n 85) 233.

that all language versions of a particular provision are equally authoritative, thereby necessitating autonomous EU law meanings derived from the wider context.[129]

Three broad criteria have been identified to explain the CJEU's approach to interpretation beyond linguistic or 'semiotic' approaches, namely contextual, systemic, and dynamic criteria. Contextual criteria are used to examine a textual provision in a spatial context, for example interpreting a legislative provision within the context of the legislation as a whole.[130] Systemic criteria involve the drawing of inferences from interrelated norms within the system, while dynamic criteria look to the dynamic context in which norms operate and interrelate with each other.[131] The latter category can further be divided into functional, teleological, and consequentialist arguments (interpretation in a broad sense). Functional arguments look to the 'effectiveness' or '*effet utile*' of a particular interpretation; teleological approaches examine a provision from the perspective of the objectives the norm seeks to achieve; while consequentialist arguments look to the consequences of a proposed interpretation, whether in the sense of 'repercussions' of the decision or its 'juridical implications'.[132] For example, the Court may point to the undesirable outcome of a particular approach, such as the fact that it goes against the objectives of the provision in question.[133]

In *Alemo-Herron*, the CJEU noted that the dynamic approach to collectively agreed terms was 'liable adversely to affect the very essence of the transferee's freedom to conduct a business'.[134] It should also be recalled that the decisions in cases such as *Alemo-Herron* and *AGET Iraklis* were also handed down in the immediate wake of the financial and eurozone crises and with the Troika of the European Commission, International Monetary Fund, and the European Central Bank imposing highly deregulatory economic adjustment programmes on particular Member States. In *AGET Iraklis*, there was explicit recognition of the context of 'acute economic crisis', but that this context did not affect the answers provided by the CJEU.[135] The CJEU in that case was also led by the questions referred by the national court, which had explicitly asked whether the economic context made any difference to the legal reasoning.

[129] Elina Paunio, *Legal Certainty in Multilingual EU Law* (Ashgate 2013).
[130] Suvi Sankari, *European Court of Justice Legal Reasoning in Context* (Europa Law Publishing 2013).
[131] Bengoetxea (n 85) 251.
[132] ibid 233, 256, 257.
[133] ibid 253.
[134] Case C-426/11 *Mark Alemo-Herron v Parkwood Leisure Ltd* ECLI:EU:C:2013:521, para 36.
[135] *AGET Iraklis* (n 56) para 108.

In *Alemo-Herron*, the CJEU also examined the purpose or objectives of the relevant legislation, noting that its 'aim' was not 'solely to safeguard the interests of employees in the event of transfer of an undertaking, but seeks to ensure a fair balance between the interests of those employees, on the one hand, and those of the transferee, on the other'.[136] A literal approach to interpretation would not be particularly helpful if applied to Article 16 CFR, which provides that '[t]he freedom to conduct a business in accordance with Union law and national laws and practices is recognised'. This provision is quite clearly open-ended and inherently vague, and the supporting references to the earlier case law through the Explanations add very little by way of explaining that freedom's normative content. There is also a failure properly to consider the freedom to conduct a business in the wider context of a Charter that is replete with competing social and economic rights, albeit of varying degrees of enforceability or justiciability. As such, the CJEU has failed in most cases properly to engage with the interpretation of the freedom to conduct a business even on its own terms, as also evidenced by the Court's use of Article 16 CFR as an interpretative tool in undermining the protective force of social legislation.

At a more basic level, the CJEU has not offered any adequate justification for its interpretation of the freedom to conduct a business in cases such as *Alemo-Herron*, regardless of whether or not that case has explicitly been followed in later decisions. Bengoetxea has suggested a distinction between 'formal' and 'material' legal justification, defined as providing 'legally good' reasons in support of a decision.[137] Formal justification only looks at the legal validity of the inference from the premise to the final decision, regardless of the actual content of that premise. Material justification on the other hand assesses whether the underlying premises are themselves justified. Premises include the individuation, interpretation, and formulation of the applicable norm.[138] The CJEU, in its case law on the freedom to conduct a business as a fundamental right, makes very little effort to elucidate any justification for its strong interpretation of that freedom, merely explaining why the existence of the freedom to conduct a business leads to the relevant consequences (ie a formal rather than a material approach).

It is also worth remembering that it was Advocate General Cruz Villalón who had invoked Article 16 CFR without that provision being raised by the parties, thereby making a choice as to the applicable norm, but without any explicit

[136] ibid para 25.
[137] Bengoetxea (n 85) 141.
[138] ibid 172.

justification other than the fact that this provision was more relevant than the freedom of association found within Article 11 of the European Convention on Human Rights (also found in Article 12 of the Charter) and which had been raised by the referring court.[139] As also suggested here, we should perhaps not expect consistency of interpretation (from any court) when engaging with fundamental rights concepts, which tend to be rather open-ended and nebulous. This is all the more so when it comes to the interpretation of contested, ill-defined, and indeed politically or ideologically charged concepts such as the freedom to conduct a business and freedom of contract.

5.4 Conclusion

The purpose of this chapter has been to explore the wider influence of the (expansive conception of the) freedom to conduct a business on the judicial reasoning of the CJEU, primarily by assessing the jurisprudential implications of that freedom, including in relation to the (absence of a) doctrine of precedent in EU law. The Court continues to move between an expansive and a restrictive interpretation and application of the freedom to conduct a business depending on the context and on the particular element of Article 16 CFR at issue. The term 'strong' or 'expansive' conception of freedom to conduct a business was used to account for those cases in which the freedom to conduct a business has been used to disrupt the protective value of legislation, notably legislation involving (weaker) parties to contractual relations in the employment context.

There are a number of inconsistencies in the CJEU's approach to the interpretation and application of the freedom to conduct a business as a fundamental right, both between the general principles and Article 16 of the Charter, and within the freedom to conduct a business itself. These inconsistencies were tied into broader questions about the CJEU's approach to fundamental rights reasoning. In particular, it was argued that the real problem with the CJEU's case law on the freedom to conduct a business is the lack of engagement with the normative content of that right, including in its relationship with competing social rights. It is now further argued in Chapter 6 that the freedom to conduct a business as a fundamental right, but notably freedom of contract, is composed of potentially competing but also mutually reinforcing values, necessitating a reconceptualization of business freedoms in relation to their

[139] AG Opinion in *Alemo-Herron* (n 120) para 46.

social dimension. This reconceptualization also provides the backdrop for an assessment of the wider 'systemic' (de)regulatory implications of the freedom to conduct a business as a fundamental right within the legal reasoning of the CJEU, including in that court's interpretation and application of protective legislation.

6
The Systemic Implications of the Freedom to Conduct a Business as a Fundamental Right

6.1 Introduction

This chapter assesses the wider or systemic (deregulatory) implications of constitutional legal reasoning based on the freedom to conduct a business as a fundamental right. It is suggested that the case law on Article 16 of the European Union Charter of Fundamental Rights (CFR) should be viewed within the broader context of existing deregulatory jurisprudence prioritizing economic rights and freedoms over competing social rights considerations. Parallels are drawn with the infamous *Lochner* jurisprudence of the United States Supreme Court (USSC), in order to assess the extent to which business freedom concepts can become jurisprudentially 'embedded', leading to the conceptualization of competing social rights as limitations or a 'cost' on businesses, which can become difficult to justify due to the jurisprudential tilt in favour of business freedoms over (other) economic and social rights.[1] This approach can be seen in the Court of Justice of the European Union's (CJEU) expansive interpretation of freedom of contract as a component of Article 16 CFR, but the question to be addressed here is just how systemic this prioritization of business freedom concepts within the CJEU's legal reasoning might be, with this question essentially being addressed through an analysis of the (competing) economic and social values implicated by the freedom to conduct a business as a fundamental right.

In furtherance of the argument advanced throughout this book that the freedom to conduct a business can only be properly understood in relation to its social dimensions, it is suggested that there are inbuilt safeguards within the Union's legislative acquis as well as the Charter, which can—where properly conceived and applied—act as limitations on the CJEU's expansive approach

[1] *Lochner v New York* 198 US 45 (1905).

Business Freedoms and Fundamental Rights in European Union Law. Niall O'Connor, Oxford University Press.
 DOI: 10.1093/9780191982132.003.0007

to the freedom to conduct a business as a fundamental right, and thereby its deregulatory potential (Section 6.2). The purpose is therefore to conduct a broader assessment of the consequences of prioritizing business freedoms over competing social rights within the case law of the CJEU, including for the effectiveness of protective (social) legislation. This assessment reinforces the argument that the freedom to conduct a business as conceived around its 'social function', consists of potentially competing economic and social values but which inhere to the freedom itself. Nevertheless, there remains the risk that deregulatory concepts such as freedom of contract or the freedom to conduct a business can become (unintentionally) embedded within constitutional judicial reasoning (Section 6.3).

The overall conclusion in Section 6.4 is that when assessed holistically the precise reach of the freedom to conduct a business, but particularly freedom of contract as a fundamental right, is more opaque than perhaps envisaged even by the drafters of the Charter, with that freedom enjoying a particularly complex relationship with the Charter's social rights, a complexity that is (only just) beginning to be recognized in the case law of the CJEU and which further complicates any assessment of the relationship between the economic freedoms and social rights found among the Charter's provisions. Moreover, the proposed (re)conceptualization of freedom of contract around social values reinforces the argument advanced in Chapter 1 that the formal 'hierarchy of norms' within Union (fundamental rights) law obfuscates the true normative value of the Charter's provisions, cloaked as they are in the language of—potentially conflicting—'rights', 'freedoms', and 'principles' with ostensibly differing legal values, and which thereby risks an overly formalist interpretation of those provisions and the relationship between them.

6.2 The Deregulatory Potential of the Freedom to Conduct a Business

The early twentieth century—indeed, the contemporary—USSC and the CJEU quite clearly operate in fundamentally different economic, social, and political contexts, but with the focus here on the use of business freedom concepts in *legal reasoning*, it is argued that the constitutionalization of freedom of contract expressed in the USSC decision in *Lochner*, as well as the manner in which this expansive approach was eventually overcome, may provide a potential avenue of legal reasoning allowing for resistance to business freedom concepts within the EU context. It had long been thought that the EU had very little to learn from *Lochner*. As one commentator, writing before the Charter had been granted legal effect, put it '[i]n the perspective of a typical European jurist, *Lochner* would likely be dismissed as old news, bad news, and news that does not belong on the old Continent'.[2] It has also been noted that the USSC's 'formalist protection of individual economic freedom may appear impossibly distant from the "social" core of current European constitutionalism, and therefore ultimately uninteresting'.[3] It is well known, however, that the European Social Constitution is far from complete, with essential aspects of the modern 'welfare state' remaining firmly ensconced within the national sphere of competence despite the inroads made by the free movement of persons and the concept of Union citizenship, which have led to increased coordination across the social sphere.[4] These freedoms are also increasingly assessed strictly by the CJEU, which adheres to the formal Treaty criteria for access to citizenship and free movement rights despite their 'fundamental' status.[5]

It would quite clearly be an exaggeration to suggest that the EU is likely to witness a *Lochner*-like era of widespread judicially led deregulation any time soon, or at least one that would not lead to a legislative or Treaty-based counterreaction.[6] The United Kingdom (UK), on the other hand, now finds itself outside these legislative and constitutional protections, thereby increasing the risk of greater divergence from existing EU social standards, or at least to the extent permitted by the withdrawal and future trading arrangements between the Union and the UK. Within the EU context, novel legal instruments such as the nascent Pillar of Social Rights (the Pillar) also demonstrate a wider commitment to the protection of (fundamental) social rights, albeit through non-binding soft law measures given the relative lack of Union legislative activity in the social field, though this is also beginning to change, notably in response to changing patterns of work and the emergence of new technologies.[7]

[2] Daniela Caruso, '*Lochner* in Europe: A Comment on Keith Whittington's "Congress Before the *Lochner* Court"' (2005) 85 BULRev 867, 869.

[3] ibid 871.

[4] Catherine Barnard, 'EU "Social" Policy: From Employment Law to Labour Market Reform' in Paul Craig and Gráinne de Búrca (eds), *The Evolution of EU Law* (3rd edn, OUP 2021) 678; Thomas Wilhelmsson, *Varieties of Welfarism in European Contract Law* (2004) 10 ELJ 712.

[5] Case C-333/13 *Elisabeta Dano and Florin Dano v Jobcenter Leipzig* ECLI:EU:C:2014:2358; Niamh Nic Shuibhne, 'The Resilience of EU Market Citizenship' (2010) 47 CMLRev 1597.

[6] Stefano Giubboni, 'Freedom to Conduct a Business and EU Labour Law' (2018) 14 EuConst 172, 184.

[7] Proposal for a Directive of the European Parliament and of the Council on improving working conditions in platform work COM/2021/762 final; Directive 2022/2381 of the European Parliament and of the Council of 23 November 2022 on improving gender balance among directors of listed companies and related measures [2022] OJ L315/44; Directive 2022/2041 of the European Parliament and of the Council of 19 October 2022 on adequate minimum wages in the European Union [2022] OJ L275/33; Directive 2019/1158 of the European Parliament and of the Council of 20 June 2019 on work-life balance for parents and carers and repealing Council Directive 2010/18/EU [2019] OJ L188/79.

The enshrinement of shared fundamental social rights within the Charter represents, at least to some extent, a reaction to the imbalance between the Union's competences over economic and social matters.[8] It is further suggested that the Pillar has the potential to reinfuse legal reasoning with social rights considerations. Although the precise relationship between the Pillar and the Charter, particularly the Solidarity Title, remains largely undetermined, the former has the potential to act as an entryway for the latter in the determination and measurement of targets relating to the 'decent work' agenda as part of the European Semester concerning the economic governance of the Member States, thereby facilitating the mainstreaming of (human) social rights within the Union's broader policymaking processes.[9] Indeed, the Pillar has the potential to reinforce the protections provided by the Solidarity Title, which by itself proved to be a particularly weak instrument in resisting deregulatory measures imposed by the Union institutions following the financial and eurozone crises.[10]

Despite these more recent social rights developments it is argued that there is a great deal to be learned from *Lochner*, including in its consequences for the protection of economic and social (legislative) rights. In particular, lessons can be drawn from how business freedoms were prioritized in (constitutional) legal reasoning, including the manner in which the embeddedness of constitutionalized business freedom concepts was later overcome. The latter aspect, in particular, has been overlooked in the literature particularly in the European context, with academic attention there focusing mainly on the potential negative consequences of *Lochner*-like reasoning.[11] As is argued throughout this chapter, *Lochner* and its progeny have potential resonance not only for understanding how unenumerated—or at least partially enumerated—business freedom concepts come to be constitutionally embedded, but also in understanding the (constitutional) limitations that can emerge to counteract such concepts.

[8] Ian H Eliasoph, 'A "Switch in Time" For the European Community? *Lochner* Discourse and the Recalibration of Economic and Social Rights in Europe' (2007) 14 Colum J Eur L 468, 494.

[9] Simon Deakin, 'In Search of the EU's Social Constitution: Using the Charter to Recalibrate Social and Economic Rights' in Filip Dorssemont and others (eds), *The Charter of Fundamental Rights of the European Union and the Employment Relation* (Hart 2019) 52.

[10] Claire Kilpatrick, 'The Human Rights Puzzle of the Euro-Crisis: Why Massive Breaches of Human Rights but None of the EU Charter of Fundamental Rights?' in Maribel González Pascual and Aida Torres Pérez (eds), *Social Rights and the European Monetary Union: Challenges Ahead* (Edward Elgar 2022) 121.

[11] David E Bernstein, 'The History of "Substantive" Due Process: It's Complicated' (2016) 95 Tex L Rev 1, 6.

6.2.1 The prioritization of the freedom to conduct a business in constitutional reasoning

In the *Lochner* case, the USSC in a close 5-4 decision declared that a New York state law limiting working hours for bakers was incompatible with the United States Constitution, notably the substantive due process clause contained in the Fourteenth Amendment, understood as protecting 'liberty' in the sense of shielding contract and property rights from unreasonable or arbitrary interference.[12] Lochner, the owner of a bakery who had permitted his workers to work beyond the statutory 60-hour weekly limit provided for in the 1895 Bakeshop Act, argued that the Fourteenth Amendment contains freedom of contract among the rights encompassed by the (seemingly oxymoronic) concept of 'substantive' (economic) due 'process'.[13] In *Lochner*, the USSC was said to have 'developed a medley of juridical doctrines that effectively insulated the marketplace from a broad swath of governmental regulations and from collective action by laborers'.[14]

The majority, led by Justice Peckham, accepted that the State retained certain 'police powers' which enabled it to legislate in areas such as health and safety and which might also include the ability to prevent individuals from entering certain types of contract.[15] At the same time, the Fourteenth Amendment prohibited the deprivation by the State of life, liberty, or property without due process of law. Justice Peckham saw this clause as protecting freedom of contract.[16] This freedom has subsequently been defined broadly within the US context to mean that 'the freedom of individuals capable of entering into a contract and giving consent to its terms could not be curtailed by government except for "reasonable" legislation narrowly tailored to protect the public health, safety, or morals'.[17] This imposition of substantive restrictions on the exercise of the police power by the State thereby leads to the essential question of 'whether there had been a fair, reasonable and appropriate exercise of the police power, as opposed to an unreasonable, unnecessary and arbitrary interference with the individual's right to personal or contractual liberty'.[18] *Lochner* was not the first case in which liberty of contract was recognized as forming part of the

[12] ibid 1.
[13] *Lochner* (n 1).
[14] Eliasoph (n 8) 468.
[15] *Lochner* (n 1) 54; Daniel Nicol, 'Europe's *Lochner* Moment' (2011) 2 PL 308.
[16] *Lochner* (n 1) 61.
[17] David N Mayer, 'Substantive Due Process Rediscovered: The Rise and Fall of Liberty of Contract' (2009) 60 Mercer Law Review 563, fn 1.
[18] Nicol (n 15) 309.

police power but in most earlier cases, the contested measures were found to be a valid exercise of that same power.[19]

The concept of the states' 'police power' and its potential limitation echoes the idea that there exists a 'fundamental contradiction' between communitarian and individual 'liberty' values. In other words, the idea that it is possible to restrict individual freedom just enough so that overall freedom is enhanced but that the balance to be achieved between individual and collective freedom will vary over time and place, leading to inconsistencies and potential contradictions.[20] In fact, the decision in *Lochner* would go on to inspire the emergence of the field of Legal Realism in the US, which advocated legal reasoning based on 'social facts' as opposed to first principles, and which would eventually become influential in the development of Critical Legal Studies, though the latter then went further in espousing the idea that conflicting ideological approaches manifest through particular judicial policy preferences.[21] The application of critical approaches to explaining the decision in *Lochner* further contributed to the shift away from a critique of the *Lochner* court's 'activism', towards a critique based on the ideological underpinning of that court's articulation of—and normative commitment to—freedom of contract as a fundamental right protected within the concept of substantive due process and in such a way as to entrench wealth and power distributions.[22]

The majority in *Lochner* found that the State should not have the power to protect individuals from their own poor decisions and that baking was not an inherently dangerous activity, meaning that the State measure in question was essentially a disguised labour law rather than a health measure. Justice Peckham accepted that both parties to the employment relationship enjoyed freedom of contract, noting that:

> [o]f course the liberty of contract relating to labor includes both parties to it. The one has as much right to purchase as the other to sell labor [. . .] The question of whether this act is valid as a labor law, pure and simple, may be dismissed in a few words. There is no reasonable ground for interfering with

[19] David E Bernstein, '*Lochner v New York*: A Centennial Retrospective' (2005) 83 Wash U L Q 1469, 1494; Frederick N Judson, 'Liberty of Contract under the Police Power' (1891) 25 Am L Rev 871.

[20] Duncan Kennedy, 'Form and Substance in Private Law Adjudication' (1976) 89 Har L Rev 1685.

[21] Bernstein (n 19) 1504; Mark Tushnet, 'Critical Legal Studies and Constitutional Law: An Essay in Deconstruction' (1984) 36 Stan L Rev 623.

[22] Sujit Choudhry, 'The *Lochner* Era and Comparative Constitutionalism' (2004) 2 ICON 1, 11, 12; Claudio J Katz, 'Protective Labour Legislation in the Courts: Substantive Due Process and Fairness in the Progressive Era' (2013) 31 Law & Hist Rev 275.

> the liberty of person or the right of free contract, by determining the hours of labor, in the occupation of a baker.[23]

This vision of 'liberty of contract' was viewed through the lens of the distinction between 'general' and 'partial' legislation. The former is applicable to all classes of person and has been described as constitutionally required 'neutrality' (inaction) whereas the latter singles out a particular category for additional protections.[24] In *Lochner*, the majority was able to characterize the relevant working time legislation as a disguised labour law rather than a health measure as the protected class (in the majority's view) had no particular vulnerabilities, which led to that legislation being conceived as protecting partial interests, rather than as furthering public or general interests.[25] The USSC's interpretation of 'neutrality' in that case failed to acknowledge the derivation of rights to property and freedom of contract from state action, ie it is only through legislative and constitutional provisions that such rights can be (effectively) protected.[26]

The Court further overlooked that the workers were in a weaker bargaining position, which itself necessitates legislative intervention in order to ensure the genuine consent of the weaker party. Indeed, state legislatures at the time were wise to avoid any suggestion of an intent to address such disparities in order to avoid being struck down as infringing the strictures of due process, with particularly 'aggressive' judicial scrutiny being reserved for cases concerning the restoration of workers' relative bargaining power.[27] This is despite the fact that arguments based on bargaining disparities had been accepted elsewhere by the Supreme Court, partly as a rebuttal to the 'free labor' principle elucidated below, and also in recognition of the fact that inequality of bargaining power constitutes a market failure, making 'self-interest', ie unfettered contractual autonomy, an 'unsafe guide'.[28]

Particularly egregious for the majority in *Lochner* was that the statute did not *permit* employees to work above the threshold (as opposed to merely prohibiting compulsion). It was a mandatory provision with no account taken of

[23] *Lochner* (n 1) 56, 57.
[24] G Edward White, 'Revisiting Substantive Due Process and Holmes's *Lochner* Dissent' (1997) 63 Brook L Rev 87, 97.
[25] ibid 98; Cass R Sunstein, '*Lochner's* Legacy' (1987) 87 Colum L Rev 873, 874; *Holden v Hardy* 169 US 366 (1898); Case C-84/94 *United Kingdom of Great Britain and Northern Ireland v Council of the European Union* ECLI:EU:C:1996:431.
[26] Choudhry (n 22) 13; Sunstein (n 25).
[27] Katz (n 22) 278; Matthew J Lindsay, 'In Search of "Laissez-Faire Constitutionalism"' (2010) 123 Harv L Rev 56, 75.
[28] Katz (n 22) 297–99; Justice Brown in *Holden* (n 25) 397.

potential emergency situations or possible derogations. The use of mandatory provisions can be contrasted with the notion of 'defaults' within the employment law context in an assessment of their relative compliance with contractual autonomy principles. Indeed, the European Commission when outlining the potential structure of a contract law Common Frame of Reference suggested that 'mandatory rules' were the 'exception' to the principle of contractual freedom but that such exceptions would be 'applicable in limited circumstance, in particular where a contract is concluded with a weaker party'.[29] The USSC in *Lochner* was instead of the view that contractual autonomy could not be interfered with through legislative measures except to the extent that the beneficiaries were *incapable* of active market participation.[30] This approach evidences the view that workers have a proprietary interest in their labour 'power' which they are able to 'sell' in exercise of their freedom of contract. This concept has a long pedigree, with James Madison, for example, arguing that 'as a man is said to have a right to his property, he may be equally said to have a property in his rights', while also decrying arbitrary restrictions on the individual's free choice of occupation, 'which not only constitute their property in the general sense of the word but are the means of acquiring property strictly so called'.[31]

The upshot of this approach, at least as articulated in *Lochner*, is both to overlook the fact that the worker is the weaker party to the contractual relationship and, perhaps more significantly, to ignore the more recent, but by now long held ideal that labour is not (just) a 'commodity' or at least not an 'ordinary' or 'mere' commodity.[32] Indeed, the more general concept of 'job property' or 'ownership of jobs' within the context of employment security is rather limited given the unlikelihood in practice of employees being empowered to sell or 'alienate' their job right—as opposed to their own labour—to another person, with the more usual approach involving *ex post* compensation for the termination of an employment relationship.[33] Moreover, the structural inequality of bargaining power that pertains between capital and labour leads to formal freedom of contract masking the fact that labour has little influence over the terms of the 'bid'—ie employment conditions—itself, hence the

[29] Communication from the Commission to the European Parliament and the Council, 'European Contract Law and the Revision of the Acquis: The Way Forward' COM (2004) 651, Annex I, 15.
[30] Eliasoph (n 8) 472.
[31] James Madison, 'Property' *National Gazette* (27 March 1792).
[32] Stein Evju, 'Labour is Not a Commodity: Reappraising the Origins of the Maxim' (2013) 4 ELLJ 222; Paul O'Higgins, '"Labour is not a Commodity"—an Irish Contribution to International Labour Law' (1997) 26 ILJ 225.
[33] Zoe Adams and others (eds), *Deakin and Morris' Labour Law* (7th edn, Hart 2021) 380.

importance of developing collective 'agency' both within and beyond the confines of the employment contract.[34]

In reaching their conclusion, the majority in *Lochner* also relied on earlier case law concerning the concept of the freedom to carry out a trade or profession, which constitutes a core aspect of the freedom to conduct a business in EU law. In *Allgeyer*—the first case in which the USSC explicitly endorsed the protection of freedom of contract—Justice Peckham had held that the notion of 'liberty' within the Fourteenth Amendment:

> is deemed to embrace the right of the citizen to be free in the enjoyment of all his faculties, to be free to use them in all lawful ways, to live and work where he will, to earn his livelihood by any lawful calling, to pursue any livelihood or avocation, and for that purpose to enter into all contracts which may be proper, necessary, and essential to his carrying out to a successful conclusion the purposes above mentioned.[35]

While not concerned with the 'commodification' of labour as such, there is evidence here of the equation of business freedom concepts—including freedom of contract—with the (itself non-absolute) right to pursue a livelihood. Elements of such an approach can also be seen in the context of business freedoms as general principles within EU law. A core element of business freedoms as general principles is the freedom to pursue a freely chosen trade or profession, or to engage in commercial or business activity. While this aspect of business freedoms can be found within the concept of the freedom to conduct a business as a fundamental right, as made clear by the Explanations to Article 16 of the Charter, it actually has greater resonance with Article 15 CFR concerning the right to work.

This leads to a somewhat uncertain relationship between the freedom to conduct a business in Article 16 CFR and the right to work in Article 15 CFR, despite the inclusion of both provisions within the Freedoms Title of the Charter. Aspects of this interrelationship have been considered in discussion concerning the intertwinement of corollary economic freedoms within the Charter, including the fact that both the freedom to conduct a business and the freedom to choose an occupation derive from the CJEU's earlier case law on the development of fundamental rights as general principles.[36] As such,

[34] Vladimir Bogoeski, 'Nonwaivability of Labour Rights, Individual Waivers and the Emancipatory Function of Labour Law' (2023) 52 ILJ 179, 186, 187.

[35] *Allgeyer v Louisiana* 165 US 578, 589 (1897).

[36] Case C–4/73 *J. Nold, Kohlen- und Baustoffgroßhandlung v Commission of the European Communities* ECLI:EU:C:1974:51; Eleni Frantziou and Virginia Mantouvalou, 'Article 15 The Right

the right to work in its incarnation as the right to choose freely and to practise a profession emerged from the wider context of the exercise of business freedoms. The parallel evolution of the freedom to conduct a business and the right to work within the Charter may thereby provide a potential avenue for the 'socialization' of business freedom concepts, ie their infusion with social—as opposed to merely economic or contractual—rights values.

6.2.2 The socialization of the freedom to conduct a business in constitutional reasoning

Article 15(1) CFR provides that '*[e]veryone* has the right to engage in work and to pursue a freely chosen or accepted occupation' [emphasis added], which is thereby framed as a universal right, and which utilizes much more robust and rights-oriented language than that found in Article 16 CFR, or indeed within the provisions of the Charter's Solidarity Title. This is not to say that reliance on Article 15 CFR always leads to a worker-protective outcome given that this provision is subject to the same limitations imposed on other Charter provisions. In *Fries*, for example, the applicant pilot was dismissed when he reached the age of 65 as required by EU law.[37] This was despite the fact that his existing contract would not expire for a further two months as the statutory pension age was reached at 65 years and two months. Due to the restrictive scope of the age limitation, it could not be said to adversely affect the very essence of the right to pursue a freely chosen occupation. Rather, according to Advocate General Bobek, '[i]t affects the possibility to pursue a professional career in a certain sector with regard to a particular activity, at a limited stage: it operates in the later years of a professional career, which are close to, even if they do not coincide with, retirement'.[38]

In another case, the same Advocate General accepted that there was a connection between Article 15 CFR and Article 16 CFR but added that 'the fact that the Charter today contains two separate provisions suggests that there ought to be some differentiation'.[39] In particular, it was noted that Article 16 CFR, unlike Article 15 CFR, is subject to Union law, and national laws and

to Work' in Steve Peers and others (eds), *The EU Charter of Fundamental Rights: A Commentary* (2nd edn, Hart 2021) 449.

[37] AG Opinion in Case C-190/16 *Werner Fries v Lufthansa CityLine GmbH* ECLI:EU:C:2017:225.
[38] ibid para 69.
[39] AG Opinion in Case C-134/15 *Lidl GmbH & Co KG v Freistaat Sachsen* ECLI:EU:C:2016:169, para 22.

practices, which meant that 'Article 16 allows for a broader margin of appreciation when it comes to regulation that might interfere with the freedom to conduct a business'.[40] From the case law on the general principles, it was also clear that the freedom to conduct a business may be subject to a broad range of interventions on the part of public authorities which may limit the exercise of economic activity in the public interest.[41] This led to the conclusion that there is no doubt that in terms of permissible limitations, 'Article 16 [CFR] [. . .] allows for a greater degree of State intervention than Article 15 [CFR]'.[42]

This amounts to a clear recognition that the freedom to conduct a business is subject to competing rights and interests. However, the difficulty in ascertaining the normative value of the right to work as a fundamental Union right—particularly as it relates to this freedom to conduct a business—is that there remains a general lack of consensus as to the nature and meaning of the right to work. For some, the right to work is just that—a right, and one which is destined to provide for human self-realization.[43] For others, the right to work is best conceptualized not as a right at all, but rather as a series of duties placed on the State (or employers) which may in fact run in parallel with the *right* to work.[44] This particular view is also apt to be confused with the idea of a correlative *duty* to work.[45] Beyond the nature of the right, there is also scant agreement as to its precise content given that it is a composite right made up of 'multiple layers and more particular rights that are intertwined and inseparable'.[46] More concrete iterations of the rights falling within the overall sphere of the 'right to work' include the right to be engaged in employment, the right to be given work once engaged, and the right to be reinstated after unjustified dismissal.[47]

The difficulty remains that the right to work within the context of the Charter is essentially encapsulated in the freedom to choose an 'economic activity' which is also reflected in other international rights sources such as Article 1(2) of the European Social Charter, and which can be considered the 'least objectionable' aspect of the right to work in that, were a constitution to

[40] ibid para 23.
[41] ibid.
[42] ibid para 25.
[43] Hugh Collins, 'Is There a Human Right to Work?' in Virginia Mantouvalou (ed), *The Right to Work: Legal and Philosophical Perspectives* (Hart 2017) 17, 29.
[44] Alan Bogg, 'Only Fools and Horses: Some Sceptical Reflections on the Right to Work' in Virginia Mantouvalou (ed), *The Right to Work: Legal and Philosophical Perspectives* (Hart 2017) 149, 150.
[45] Guy Mundlak, 'The Right to Work, the Value of Work' in Daphne Barak-Erez and Aeyal Gross (eds), *Exploring Social Rights: Between Theory and Practice* (Hart 2007) 341, 343.
[46] Guy Mundlak, 'The Right to Work: Linking Human Rights and Employment Policy' (2007) 146 Int'l Lab Rev 189, 192.
[47] Bob Hepple, 'A Right to Work' (1981) 10 ILJ 65, 73.

'stop here in defining the dimensions of this right, it is actually rejecting recognition of the right to work in its broader sense'.[48] As such, the right to work, despite its clear social rights connotations, may well represent no more than a bare right to non-discriminatory labour market access, with all of its 'social' elements stripped away.[49]

Such a reading of the right to 'engage in' work within Article 15(1) CFR is perhaps reinforced by the reference in Article 15(2) CFR to the freedom of Union citizens 'to seek employment' and 'to work' 'in any Member State'. In other words, the freedom to pursue an occupation is intimately connected to wider fundamental freedoms within the internal market, which echoes the interrelationship between the freedom to conduct a business as a fundamental right and the Treaty-based freedom of establishment.[50] A further difficulty lies in the continued (relative) underdevelopment of the Union's social constitution which leaves significant legislative gaps in the protection of social (employment) rights at Union level, thereby reducing the potential scope of the Charter's applicability.[51]

The right to work is therefore of uncertain normative value, which is perhaps reflective of the fact that the right to work as a fundamental right also contains both positive and negative elements. The 'positive' dimension of the right to work includes the right to have work, with a corresponding obligation (duty) on the State to provide work (but not necessarily a particular job). This element of the right to work has a potential connection to the provisions of the Charter's Solidarity Title, particularly those provisions governing employment conditions, which allow the right to work to be (re)conceived as a (socialized) right to *decent* work or, as argued here, a conception of the right to work that recognizes and respects wider fundamental employment rights, and which also accords with wider international trends recognizing a potential 'common interpretative approach' between various rights instruments governing the right to work.[52]

The freedom to pursue an occupation has strong resonance with the idea that freedom of contract may exercise a 'social function'. There can perhaps be no clearer social function of that freedom than a right to earn a living from

[48] Mundlak (n 46) 193.

[49] Simon Deakin, 'Article 15' in Filip Dorssemont and others (eds), *The Charter of Fundamental Rights of the European Union and the Employment Relation* (Hart 2019) 331, 333.

[50] Case C–201/15 *Anonymi Geniki Etairia Tsimenton Iraklis (AGET Iraklis) v Ypourgos Ergasias, Koinonikis Asfalisis kai Koinonikis Allilengyis* ECLI:EU:C:2016:972.

[51] Deakin (n 49) 334; Deakin (n 9).

[52] Collins (n 43) 299; Colm O'Cinneide, 'The Right to Work in International Human Rights Law' in Virginia Mantouvalou (ed), *The Right to Work: Legal and Philosophical Perspectives* (Hart 2017) 99, 115; Bob Hepple, 'The EU Charter of Fundamental Rights' (2001) 30 ILJ 225, 226.

an occupation freely chosen, with the normative value of that freedom also being reinforced by its connection to 'liberty' concepts. The 'negative' aspect of the right to work involves the ability of the individual to access employment without unjustified or discriminatory restrictions and thereby enjoys a stronger resonance with the first limb of the freedom to conduct a business as a fundamental right, ie the freedom to pursue a commercial activity, as also expressed in the form of the freedom to pursue an occupation within the general principles case law. The latter is a somewhat unusual right in that it exhibits features of a traditional civil liberty right, while at the same time being located within the broader context of an economic and social right, with the right to work thereby spanning the traditional (if contested) dichotomy between economic and social rights on the one hand, and civil and political rights on the other, in much the same way as other 'hybrid' employment rights such as the freedom of association and right to strike found within Article 12 CFR and Article 28 CFR.[53]

As such, it is argued here that the freedom to pursue a freely chosen occupation may be useful in bridging the normative gap between business freedoms and the economic and social rights found in the Charter's Solidarity Title. This is achieved essentially by reconceiving that freedom as a right for workers to enter contractual relations to their benefit. At the same, this freedom is also imbued with respect for underlying economic and social rights found elsewhere within both the Charter and Union legislative instruments, particularly given the recognition that 'personal autonomy', 'human dignity', and 'self-realization' lie at the foundation of the rights found in Article 15 CFR.[54] As such, it is argued that the negative aspect of the right to work also requires legislative intervention to ensure that non-discriminatory access to employment is achieved in practice. It is further argued that this distinct normative underpinning allows for that provision to be vitally distanced from the freedom to conduct a business as a fundamental right in Article 16 CFR despite the common origins of both provisions within the earliest CJEU case law establishing fundamental rights as general principles of EU law.

Given the link between the freedom to conduct a business and the freedom to pursue an occupation, it may therefore be possible to conceive of the right to work as essentially an emanation of a form of socialized freedom of contract of workers, reinforced through the value of 'solidarity' as given expression through the concrete provisions of the Charter's Solidarity Title. This

[53] Sandra Fredman, *Comparative Human Rights Law* (OUP 2018) 59.
[54] AG Opinion in *Fries* (n 37) para 66.

approach is also supported by normative arguments advanced in favour of the recognition of freedom of contract itself; namely that freedom of contract is autonomy-enhancing, with the assumption being that agreements resulting from the exercise of that freedom are reflective of choices beneficial to the parties.[55] Indeed, freedom of contract in its more modern incarnation goes well beyond the eighteenth-century conception of that freedom as being essentially about the enforcement of promises.[56] Only later did freedom of contract come to be viewed as an essential underpinning of laissez-faire doctrines advocating limited state interference, but even then the chief function of the doctrine was to 'enforce by law the obligations created by contract'.[57]

The traditional normative underpinnings of freedom of contract are evidently undermined when contractual arrangements do not reflect the genuine wishes of the parties, for example where one party is in a weaker bargaining position or where there are information or resource asymmetries. There are also evident risks in reframing the right to work as a 'worker friendly' conception of freedom of contract, including the fact that the right to work itself has historically been used to allow individual workers to resist the collective action of 'powerful' trade unions, ie to undermine collective organization and action.[58] The right to work also implies a right not to be (forced to) work but the necessary corollary of such a right is the ability of the employer to dismiss (or refuse to employ) the worker for whatever reason, which represents the English common law position in the absence of employee-protective legislation.[59]

Indeed, the right to work has been said to be 'synonymous with unfettered freedom of contract, namely freedom from the sort of state interference which empowers trade unions to regulate terms and conditions jointly with employers'.[60] Such an approach may also view employment regulation and protective legislation as inherently restrictive of freedom of contract and the right to work in the sense of freedom to obtain employment where it leads to employers becoming more reluctant to recruit workers.[61] The point here, though, is that the right to work within EU law can now be said to embody—if not entirely underpin—the edifice of the social rights in the Charter, particularly within the Solidarity Title, given that without access to employment, labour

[55] Michael J Trebilcock, *The Limits of Freedom of Contract* (Harvard 1993) ch 1.
[56] Roscoe Pound, 'Liberty of Contract' (1909) 18 Yale L J 454, 456.
[57] ibid.
[58] Hepple (n 47) 79.
[59] *Malloch v Aberdeen Corporation* [1971] 1 WLR 1578, 1581.
[60] Diamond Ashiagbor, 'The Right to Work' in Gráinne de Búrca and Bruno de Witte (eds), *Social Rights in Europe* (OUP 2005) 241, 258.
[61] David A Strauss, 'Why Was *Lochner* Wrong?' (2003) 70 U Chi L Rev 373, 385.

rights such as fair and just working conditions (Article 31 CFR), or protections from unjustified dismissal (Article 30 CFR) become essentially meaningless. The right to work within EU law thereby encapsulates the circularity that has been argued here to characterize the relationship between sources of fundamental rights in the Union legal order.

It can be said that the right to work provides a potential (although inexplicit) normative underpinning for the employment rights protected in the Solidarity Title, while at the same time the right to work derives its normative strength from the fact that it can act as a gateway to accessing these employment rights in the first place, which thereby risks denuding the right to work of its 'independent' value as a fundamental right. A similar risk also arises from the right to work's status as an 'instrumental' right, ie a right used to access other, more 'substantive' rights, including broader economic and social rights, such as the right to food, housing, or healthcare.[62]

Despite these potential ambiguities, the right to work in the guise of the freedom to pursue a freely chosen occupation can provide an entryway for legal reasoning based on a 'social' conception of freedom of contract and one that is reflective of the CJEU's earlier jurisprudence recognizing the 'social function' of business freedoms. In other words, workers have a social interest in exercising their freedom of contract in order to obtain—or continue in—employment, and in a manner that recognizes the necessity of counteracting the strength of the competing bargaining power of employers. In this way, the right to work viewed as the legitimate exercise of workers' contractual autonomy is capable of offering a strong counterweight to employer assertions of their own freedom of contract as encapsulated in the freedom to conduct a business in Article 16 CFR, with the freedom to pursue a freely chosen occupation acting as a conduit between the freedom to conduct a business and the employment rights found in the Solidarity Title. In this way, it is possible both for (employee) freedom of contract *within* Article 15 CFR to be reframed in social terms, including through reliance on the fundamental social rights found in the Charter, but also for employees to rely on the right to work encapsulated in Article 15 CFR to *resist* the exercise of freedom of contract by employers in such a way as to inhibit access to work, or to erode terms and conditions of employment.

The freedom of the employee to 'sell' their labour, as recognized by the USSC in *Lochner*, falls well short of this suggested 'social' conception of the right to work, which is unsurprising given the historical and constitutional context.

[62] Collins (n 43) 24; Bogg (n 44) 151.

Indeed, devoid of any social rights connotations *Lochner* may well have been decided similarly on grounds of the employee's right to work in the same way that the right to work within the English common law has historically been used to undermine (collective) trade union rights.[63] This approach is also partially reflected in the emergence of the 'free labor' principle in the US, which originates in the antislavery movement, whereby workers are free to sell their services on whatever terms they so choose and which inspired the Fourteenth Amendment.[64] Indeed, the 'free labor' concept provided a crucial 'precedent for the constitutionalization of liberty', notably through its infusion with the principle, propounded by Adam Smith, that '[t]he property which every man has in his own labour, as it is the original foundation of all other property, so it is the most sacred and inviolable'.[65] This approach is clearly articulated in the dissent of Justice Field in the *Slaughter-House Cases*, where he held that:

> [t]his equality of right [. . .] in the lawful pursuits of life [. . .] is the distinguished privilege of citizens of the United States. To them, everywhere all pursuits, all professions, all avocations are open without other restrictions than such as are imposed equally upon all others [. . .] The patrimony of the poor man lies in the strength and dexterity of his own hands; and to hinder him from employing his strength and dexterity in what manner he thinks proper, without injury to his neighbor, is a plain violation of this most sacred property.[66]

The 'free labor' principle was thereby released from its traditional confines within the context of the self-employed to also embrace 'wage laborers'.[67] At the same time, the principle has always been somewhat illusory given the existence (and frequent judicial acceptance) of legislative as well as socio-economic constraints on the provision of services by workers, albeit that the essence of the underlying principle may be preserved through the presence of derogable as opposed to mandatory terms.[68] Nevertheless, the free labor principle—combined with faith in the distributive function of the competitive market—was influential in shaping judicial reluctance to uphold legislative intrusions

[63] Jeff King, *Judging Social Rights* (CUP 2012) 109.
[64] Victoria F Nourse, 'A Tale of Two Lochners: The Untold Story of Substantive Due Process and the Idea of Fundamental Rights' (2009) 97 CLR 751, 777.
[65] Lindsay (n 27) 71; Adam Smith, *An Inquiry into the Nature and Causes of the Wealth of Nations* (Liberty Classics 1981) 138.
[66] *Slaughter-House Cases* 83 US 36, 110 (1873).
[67] Lindsay (n 27) 70.
[68] White (n 24) 100.

into the employment relationship.[69] This narrow vision of the free labor principle, as espoused by some—but certainly not all—courts, at both state and federal level, failed to recognize the importance of legislative and regulatory intervention in preserving freedom of contract and indeed overlooked those decisions in which courts were willing to uphold 'non-market' standards governing core aspects of the employment contract.[70]

In this way, it is possible to conceptualize *Lochner* not as striking down protections granted to a particular class, ie bakers or even workers, but rather as ensuring that members of that class were not denied 'fundamental private rights, as embedded in the baseline entitlement of "liberty of contract"'.[71] The 'contractual' vision of workers' rights espoused in *Lochner* is also reflected in the English case law on the transfer of undertakings, predating the CJEU's decision in *Alemo-Herron*, albeit that the contractual approach happened to be exercised in a 'rights-enhancing' manner. In *Whent*, for example, Judge Hicks held that:

> there is simply no reason why parties should not, if they choose, agree that matters such as remuneration be fixed by processes in which they do not themselves participate. The tribunal [. . .] accepts that that is true of some employers who are not local authorities. It must, on the agreed facts set out near the beginning of this judgment, equally be true of non-union employees.[72]

In other words, both parties, exercising their freedom of contract, agreed that remuneration would be set externally. In denying the rights of workers who in good faith agreed to be so bound, the CJEU in cases such as *Alemo-Herron* was interfering with their freedom of contract and thereby their right to work viewed as an expression of worker autonomy. The interventionist nature of the CJEU's approach can be seen from the fact that in UK law, collective agreements are presumed not to be legally enforceable, with the parties being required to take the additional positive step of 'incorporating' the provisions of a collective agreement into the contract of employment through the medium of a 'bridging term', which thereby represents a clear signal of the parties' intention to be bound.[73] Moreover, the very absence of binding effect of collective

[69] Katz (n 22) 276 and 277.
[70] ibid 280 and 295.
[71] White (n 24) 98, fn 28.
[72] *Whent v T Cartledge* [1997] IRLR 153 [16].
[73] Trade Union and Labour Relations (Consolidation) Act 1992, s 179; *Ford Motor Co Ltd v Amalgamated Union of Engineering and Foundry Workers* [1969] 2 QB 303.

agreements, coupled with broader deficiencies in the 'mandatory' nature of the domestic collective bargaining system, raises significant doubts as to the compatibility of the UK regime with international human rights law governing the right to bargain collectively.[74]

It was the dynamic nature of the bridging term in *Alemo-Herron* which incorporated collectively agreed terms as 'negotiated from time to time' that negated the transferee employer's freedom of contract. In this way, it can be argued that the English dynamic approach is more respectful of party autonomy *as a whole* than that adopted by the CJEU in its interpretation and application of freedom of contract as a component of the freedom to conduct a business as a fundamental right in Article 16 CFR. Of course, the dynamic approach to the incorporation of collectively agreed terms was itself facilitated by the underlying EU-derived protective legislation, namely the Transfer of Undertakings Directive, as implemented domestically via the Transfer of Undertakings and Protection of Employment Regulations 2006, thereby demonstrating the importance of legislative intervention in supporting both the normative content and practical implementation of fundamental Charter rights.

The very purpose of the Transfer of Undertakings Directive is to ensure that, upon the transfer of a business from one employer to another, the entire workforce is transferred with minimal exceptions, leading to what has been described as 'a quasi labour aristocracy as far as the protection of the courts is concerned'.[75] At common law, by way of contrast, workers enjoy no continued entitlement to employment, nor any right to hold the new employer to previously agreed contractual terms.[76] The protections offered by the subsequently developed English law dynamic approach to collectively agreed terms thereby demonstrates the importance of the underlying legislatively enshrined protections in ensuring respect for worker autonomy in the sense that, were employment conditions potentially to deteriorate post-transfer, workers would be less likely to consent to the transfer in exercise of their own freedom of contract.

Within the CJEU's expansive interpretation of the freedom to conduct a business as a fundamental right, this 'autonomy-enhancing' legislation was itself found to be incompatible with the freedom of contract of employers, thereby negating the 'genuine' consent of employees, while also eroding legislative efforts at protecting the employee as the weaker party to the employment contract in much the same way as the USSC had done in *Lochner*, albeit that

[74] Keith Ewing and John Hendy, 'New Perspectives on Collective Labour Law: Trade Union Recognition and Collective Bargaining' (2017) 46 ILJ 23.

[75] John McMullen, 'Takeovers, Transfers and Business Re-organisations' (1992) 21 ILJ 15.

[76] Charles Wynn-Evans, *The Law of TUPE Transfers* (2nd edn, OUP 2016) 4.

the CJEU *did* have a rich backcloth of both legislative and Treaty-based social rights from which to draw. These potential counterweights include the provisions of the Charter's Solidarity Title which are themselves reflective of the fundamental values underpinning the Charter as a whole, and without which the prioritization of liberal or economic conceptions of business freedoms risks becoming constitutionally 'embedded' in judicial reasoning.

6.3 The Constitutional Embedment of the Freedom to Conduct a Business

Lochner is considered one of the most important and controversial decisions ever handed down by the USSC and would eventually lend its name to the *Lochner* 'era', a period of jurisprudence-led deregulation ranging from the late 1890s until 1937 in which the Supreme Court developed and applied doctrines insulating market-based rights from legislatively (or collectively) imposed constraints, including legislation governing worker but also consumer protections.[77] The decision has attracted much consternation, probably having received 'more clearly unanimous criticism than any other [decision] of the twentieth century'.[78] The decision continues to be controversial and has been cited—often with disapproval—by the USSC in its legal reasoning well into the twenty-first century.[79]

From a comparative constitutionalism perspective, *Lochner* has also been held up as an 'anti-model' or 'anti-precedent', ie a lesson for other legal systems and courts in what *not* to do in the judicial review of (social) legislation.[80] The outcome in *Lochner* has been described as sounding the 'Court's call to batter against social and economic regulatory legislation'.[81] At the same time, *Lochner* is reflective of a particular ideological proclivity shared by the USSC (as then constituted) and wider conservative political thought at the time, which was aimed at realizing 'a common vision of limited government with a decentralized federal system'.[82] There was therefore nothing 'inevitable' about the USSC's decision in *Lochner*, with the United States Constitution and now also the EU legal order both encompassing competing values of at least ostensibly

[77] Eliasoph (n 8) 47.
[78] Robert G McCloskey, *The Modern Supreme Court* (Harvard University Press 1972) 279.
[79] Bernstein (n 19) 1469.
[80] Choudhry (n 22) 3; Strauss (n 61) 373.
[81] D Grier Stephenson, 'The Supreme Court and Constitutional Change: *Lochner v New York* Revisited' (1976) 21 Vill L Rev 217–18.
[82] Keith E Whittington, 'Congress Before the *Lochner* Court' (2005) 85 BULRev 821, 823.

equivalent—if not more compelling—normative weight than freedom of contract, or indeed wider business freedom concepts. Within the decision of the majority in *Lochner* itself, there was also recognition of the potential constitutional validity of worker-protective statutes, with legislation governing the time and manner of wage payment, as well as working time in hazardous industries having already been upheld by the USSC as falling within the proper scope of the police power.[83]

The 'embedment' of *Lochner*-like freedom of contract-based reasoning can nevertheless be seen in later USSC cases such as *Adkins*.[84] The legislation at issue in that case governed the minimum wage of women, who were singled out for particular protection due to their (as then perceived) reduced bargaining power. Justice Sutherland held that 'the right to contract about one's affairs is part of the liberty of the individual [as has been] settled by the decisions of this Court and is no longer open to question', and further remarked that '[t]here is, of course, no such thing as absolute freedom of contract. It is subject to a great variety of restraints. But freedom of contract is, nevertheless, the general rule and restraint the exception.'[85]

The legislation in question was found to be 'partial' in protecting a confined class, ie adult women, and was thereby unconstitutional.[86] The majority in that case has been said to have adopted a conception of freedom of contract that 'functioned as a surrogate for the presumption that government could not interfere with private economic transactions to the betterment or detriment of one party to the transaction.'[87] This approach also echoes the burden of proof established by the majority in *Lochner*, which required the legislature to demonstrate that the relevant legislation has a 'direct relation, as a means to an end', with that end also being 'appropriate and legitimate.'[88] In contrast, Justice Harlan had argued in favour of a presumption of constitutionality that the employer was required to rebut.[89]

Within the EU context the freedom to conduct a business has similarly—albeit more implicitly—been framed as the 'right' to be preserved from erosion from competing economic and social interests, which are themselves framed as derogations or restrictions on that right. Both the USSC and the CJEU relied

[83] *Holden* (n 25) 366; *Knoxville Iron Co v Harbison* 183 US 13 (1901).
[84] *Adkins v Children's Hospital* 261 US 525 (1923), overruled in *West Coast Hotel Co v Parrish* 300 US 379 (1937).
[85] *Adkins* (n 84) 545, 546.
[86] ibid 554–58.
[87] White (n 24) 119.
[88] *Lochner* (n 1) 57–58.
[89] ibid 68.

on the language of 'balancing' to undermine the State's regulatory authority but without making explicit the rationale behind this balancing exercise. This is also despite the fact that both courts recognized that neither the employer's freedom of contract nor the competing interests of employees were 'absolute'.

Despite contemplating the existence of potential restrictions or limitations on business freedoms, those same freedoms derive a quality of quasi-absoluteness from the sequence in which competing rights are considered, with freedom of contract representing the starting point, thereby placing competing interests (if even raised) on the backfoot from the outset. The potential consequences of the (counter-majoritarian) entrenchment of the prioritization of business freedoms over legislative intervention seeking to preserve competing rights was recognized in *Lochner* in the dissent of Justice Holmes, who held that 'a constitution is not intended to embody a particular economic theory, whether of paternalism [...] or of laissez faire'.[90] Justice Holmes thereby advocated an approach based on deference to the legislative will in contrast to the dissent of Justice Harlan, who had held that the measure represented a legitimate exercise of the police power.[91]

Similar language to that found in *Lochner* has subsequently found its way into the jurisprudence of the national courts of the EU's Member States. Notably, the German Constitutional Court has held that the freedom to conduct economic activity was not absolute, where it also noted that 'the "constituent power" has not adopted a specific economic system [...] Although the present economic and social order is [...] congruent with the Basic Law, it is by no means the only one possible.'[92] While the CJEU does not draw on any particular legal system when devising the general principles, the earliest case law on the emergence of economic freedoms—indeed fundamental rights—as general principles centred around the occupational freedoms and property rights found in Articles 12 and 14 of the German Basic Law, and at a time when the CJEU had fewer Member State legal (common constitutional) traditions from which to draw inspiration.[93]

Article 12 of the German Basic Law recognizes the right to choose an occupation or profession the practice of which 'may be regulated by or pursuant to law', while the right to property in Article 14 of the German Basic Law

[90] ibid 75.
[91] ibid 69.
[92] BVerfGE 7 (1954).
[93] Case C-234/85 *Staatsanwaltschaft Freiburg v Franz Keller* ECLI:EU:C:1986:377; Case C-44/79 *Liselotte Hauer v Land Rheinland-Pfalz* ECLI:EU:C:1979:290; Case C-4/73 *J. Nold, Kohlen- und Baustoffgroßhandlung v Commission of the European Communities* ECLI:EU:C:1974:51.

'guarantees' such rights insofar as their 'content and limits shall be defined by the *law*'.[94] Furthermore—and reflective of the 'social function' of property rights and business freedoms—Article 14 of the German Basic Law provides that '[p]roperty entails obligations. Its use shall also serve the public good', with this explicit constitutional commitment to 'the social obligations of property' also being held to permit extensive regulation.[95] Within German constitutional law, 'property' thereby serves 'dual'—and seemingly incompatible—functions, underpinned by two equally important constitutional values, namely: (1) an individual function, based on individual autonomy; and (2) a social function which is animated by the common good.[96]

In a similar way to the same concepts developed within EU law, property rights and the freedom to pursue an occupation are closely connected in German law in that both relate essentially to concepts of personal freedom or individual autonomy, which are themselves seen as essential for accessing other freedoms.[97] At the same time, both the EU and German conception of property rights, in contrast to their US counterparts, are explicit not only in articulating a 'positive' fundamental right to private property but also in considering the individual's place in the wider 'social order', ie the social function of property rights as has similarly been ascribed to the freedom to conduct a business in the EU context.[98] It is further clear from the German position that the social function or purpose of property changes over time in response to economic and social conditions.[99] Moreover, German law recognizes that certain types of property, for example the 'home', may serve a '*distinctively* social function', which can lead to the prioritization of public regulation over individual property rights.[100]

The non-absolute nature of property rights in German constitutional law is also reflective of a wider commitment to the principle of Sozialstaat (social state) in Articles 20(1) and 28(1) of the German Basic Law, which calls for active

[94] The text of the German Basic Law uses the term 'Gesetz', which has also been translated as 'statute': David P Currie, *The Constitution of the Federal Republic of Germany* (University of Chicago Press 1994) 290.

[95] Currie (n 94) 291; Basic Law for the Federal Republic of Germany in the revised version published in the Federal Law Gazette Part III, classification 100-1, as last amended by the Act of 28 June 2022 (Federal Law Gazette I p. 968). The term 'public good' has also been translated as 'public weal' or 'public interest': Currie (n 94) 290; AJ Van Der Walt, *Constitutional Property Clauses: A Comparative Analysis* (Juta 1999) 121.

[96] Michael R Antinori, 'Does *Lochner* Live in Luxembourg? An Analysis of the Property Rights Jurisprudence of the European Court of Justice' (1995) 18 Fordham Int'l L J 1778, 1793.

[97] 24 BVerfGE 367 (1968).

[98] Rebecca Lubens, 'The Social Obligation of Property Ownership: A Comparison of German and U.S. Law' (2007) 24 Ariz J Int'l & Comp L 389.

[99] ibid 427.

[100] Antinori (n 96) 1795, 1796.

state involvement in market and social orders with the aim of counteracting inequalities, but which is essentially reflective of the essential *absence* of basic social rights in that constitution.[101] According to the German Constitutional Court, '[w]hile freedom and individual dignity are fundamentally guaranteed, it cannot be overlooked that the image of man in the [Constitution] is not that of an individual in arbitrary isolation but of a person in the community, to which the person is obligated in many ways'.[102] In other words, Article 14 of the German Basic Law constitutes a 'union of rights and restraints' within which the social and economic objectives of the Sozialstaat can be achieved while at the same time respecting the (property) rights of the individual.[103]

However, there is also evidence within the German case law of the emergence of *Lochner*-type substantive limits on the regulation of property rights.[104] In particular, property rights may be limited in accordance with social obligations but *only* to the extent that such limitation furthers the public interest. In addition, the essential core of property rights must be shielded from regulatory intervention, with that core content varying depending on the individual property owner's circumstances.[105] These potentially contradictory principles within Article 14 of the German Basic Law are reflective of wider conceptual tensions between justification of, and limitations on, the regulation of property rights, with that provision permitting the legislative conceptualization of property as an exercise of the 'social restriction' while simultaneously limiting this power through the protection of the essential core of property rights.[106]

In *Lochner* itself, despite recognizing the potential limitation of liberty of contract the USSC nevertheless passed over the first opportunity 'for constitutional confirmation of the modern regulatory state'.[107] It also remains the case that courts in resolving disputes are required 'to choose from a plethora of societal values those which will guide its policy foundation'.[108] The CJEU certainly has a more wide-ranging array of social and economic values from which to draw than the USSC had, or continues to have. Indeed, at the time of the USSC's decision in *Lochner*, it was a widely held view that 'government regulation of private affairs was deemed a grave offence against citizens', and

[101] Currie (n 94) 294, 299; Christian Bommarius, '*Lecture*—Germany's *Sozialstaat* Principles and the Founding Period' (2011) 12 GLJ 1880, 1884; Antinori (n 96) 1790.
[102] BVerfGE 7 (1954); Lubens (n 98) 402.
[103] Antinori (n 96) 1793.
[104] Currie (n 94) 296.
[105] Lubens (n 98) 448.
[106] ibid 438.
[107] Stephenson (n 81) 221.
[108] ibid 222.

thereby incapable of justification in the public interest.[109] In this way, it is possible to view *Lochner* and its progeny as essentially a product of the assumptions of the era and therefore 'correctly' decided at the time.[110]

Despite the passage of time and indeed their differing constitutional contexts, there are similarities between the constitutional foundations of the US and EU legal orders, notably in the potential erosion by their respective 'supreme' courts, of (Member) state-level regimes of social protection.[111] Perhaps the most significant difference between the Charter and the US Constitution for the present analysis is that the Fourteenth Amendment to the US Constitution has a much wider application beyond the economic or business context, ie it is protective of broader fundamental civil liberties such as freedom of expression or privacy-based rights.[112] Nevertheless, echoes of the *Lochner* court's laissez-faire individualism can be found within EU law, which undermines efforts at enhancing the legislative protection of weaker parties to contractual arrangements, particularly as has been argued here, within the employment context.

Lochner-like qualities have been ascribed to various aspects of the EU's internal market jurisprudence outside of the context of the Union's fundamental rights regime. Caruso, for example, finds elements of *Lochner* in cases such as *Franzén*, in which the CJEU overruled a Swedish monopoly on alcohol distribution despite its intended public protection and human health purposes.[113] According to Caruso, '[t]his story bears a number of analogies with *Lochner*. State legislation enacted with the aim of protecting citizens [. . .] was weakened by a supreme court' although not, in this case, 'in the name of freedom of contract, but due to an equally basic faith in the Common Market'.[114] Other commentators have expressed similar sentiments that the EU's free movement rules represent Europe's own (nascent) version of economic due process. Eliasoph in particular remarks that '[w]hile the [CJEU] did not intervene with social legislation in a manner approaching the extent of the activism exhibited by the Supreme Court [. . .] the [CJEU] had "placed itself in a pivotal position to influence the pace and direction of legislative integration on matters of economic and social regulation"', with this jurisprudence resembling 'liberty to contract and substantive due process'.[115]

[109] ibid.
[110] Jack M Balkin, '"Wrong the Day it Was Decided": *Lochner* and Constitutional Historicism' (2005) 85 BULRev 677, 679.
[111] Eliasoph (n 8) 471.
[112] Bernstein (n 19) 1509.
[113] Case C–189/95 *Criminal Proceedings against Harry Franzén* ECLI:EU:C:1997:504.
[114] Caruso (n 2) 872–73.
[115] Eliasoph (n 8) 485, quoting Catherine Barnard and Simon Deakin, '"Negative" and "Positive" Harmonization of Labour Law in the European Union' 8 (2002) Colum J Eur L 389, 391.

The quasi-symbiotic relationship between the Union's internal market freedoms and the freedom to conduct a business is notably evident in the case of *AGET Iraklis* in which the freedom of establishment in Article 49 of the Treaty on the Functioning of the European Union (TFEU) and the freedom to conduct a business in Article 16 CFR were treated as essentially synonymous.[116] It will be recalled that the CJEU found that the Greek legislation requiring prior authorization for collective redundancies constituted 'a significant interference in certain freedoms which economic operators generally enjoy'.[117] The ability to effect collective redundancies was to be considered 'a fundamental decision in the life of an undertaking'.[118]

The CJEU, by adopting a standard freedom of establishment approach, found that this legislation constituted a restriction on Article 49 TFEU in that it was likely 'to render access to the Greek market less attractive and, following access to that market, to reduce considerably—or even eliminate—the ability of economic operators from other Member States who have chosen to set up in a new market to adjust subsequently'.[119] Advocate General Wahl was more explicit in making a direct connection between Article 16 CFR and the Treaty, finding that 'the restriction on the freedom of establishment [. . .] *also* [. . .] amounts to a restriction on the exercise of freedom to conduct a business'.[120]

Article 49 TFEU provides that 'restrictions on the freedom of establishment of nationals of a Member State in the territory of another Member State shall be prohibited [. . .] Freedom of establishment shall include the right to take up and pursue activities as self-employed persons.' This freedom enables persons to set up a primary or secondary establishment in another Member State. Although the principle of non-discrimination on the grounds of nationality forms the core of this freedom, more recently the CJEU has moved towards a market access or 'restrictions' approach which more closely aligns with the limitation or restriction-based approach found within the context of the freedom to conduct a business. The effect of the restrictions approach has frequently been to undermine the protections offered by social rights considerations in the face of

[116] *AGET Iraklis* (n 50). Similarly, Advocate General Wahl has noted that 'an examination of the restrictive effects of national legislation [. . .] from the point of view of, for example, Article 56 TFEU [on the freedom to provide services] covers also possible limitations on the exercise of the rights and freedoms provided in Articles 15 to 17 of the Charter': AG Opinion in Case C–322/16 *Global Starnet Ltd v Ministero dell'Economia e delle Finanze and Amministrazione Autonoma Monopoli di Stato* ECLI:EU:C:2017:442, para 61.

[117] *AGET Iraklis* (n 50) para 55.

[118] ibid para 54.

[119] ibid para 56.

[120] AG Opinion in Case C–201/15 *Anonymi Geniki Etairia Tsimenton Iraklis (AGET Iraklis) v Ypourgos Ergasias, Koinonikis Asfalisis kai Koinonikis Allilengyis* ECLI:EU:C:2016:429, para 50.

economic (free movement) interests, principally as a result of the broad range of state measures that are capable of infringing access to the market of another Member State.[121]

In *Gebhard*, for example, the CJEU noted that the concept of 'national measures liable to hinder or make less attractive the exercise of fundamental freedoms' is very broad and extends the freedom beyond directly or indirectly discriminatory measures.[122] Both Article 16 CFR and Article 49 TFEU are thereby easily engaged but with the free movement provisions also being subject to derogations and justifiable limitations. Indeed, it is the issue of permissible derogations that most closely connects the CJEU's case law on Article 49 TFEU and the freedom to conduct a business in Article 16 CFR. In *AGET Iraklis*, for example, the CJEU, in drawing the connection between traditional Treaty derogations and Article 16 CFR, noted that any justification for restricting freedom of establishment must *also* comply with the Charter.[123] The case law demonstrating the interlacing of the freedom to conduct a business and the economic freedoms found within EU internal market law is thereby illustrative of wider systemic deficiencies embedded within the Union's constitutional order when it comes to the protection of social rights in relation to business freedoms. In particular, the CJEU's expansive approach to the freedom to conduct a business as a fundamental right resonates strongly with that court's now infamous decisions in *Viking* and *Laval*, which are themselves redolent of the systemic deregulatory thrust embodied by *Lochner*.

In *Viking*, the CJEU found that a company could invoke the freedom of establishment contained in Article 49 TFEU against a trade union involved in industrial action. The CJEU in that case explicitly acknowledged for the first time that the right to take collective action, including the right to strike, was a fundamental right forming part of the general principles of EU law and which is also reflected in Article 28 CFR.[124] The litigants were nevertheless required to show that their restriction of the company's freedom of establishment was in pursuance of a legitimate aim compatible with the Treaty, and that it was proportionate. In other words, industrial action had to be taken as a last resort, and only where the aim was to protect jobs.[125]

[121] Catherine Barnard, *The Substantive Law of the European Union: The Four Freedoms* (7th edn, OUP, 2022) 25–31.
[122] Case C–55/94 *Reinhard Gebhard v Consiglio dell'Ordine degli Avvocati e Procuratori di Milano* ECLI:EU:C:1995:411, para 37.
[123] *AGET Iraklis* (n 50) para 94.
[124] Case C–438/05 *International Transport Workers' Federation and Finnish Seamen's Union v Viking Line ABP and OÜ Viking Line Eesti* ECLI:EU:C:2007:772, para 44.
[125] ibid para 81.

In *Laval*, the CJEU had to determine whether the relevant industrial action was compatible with Article 56 TFEU on the freedom to provide services read in conjunction with the Posted Workers Directive.[126] In that case, the CJEU once again accepted the right to strike as a fundamental right but repeated its long held approach to the limitation of fundamental Treaty freedoms, in that restrictions on those freedoms must pursue legitimate objectives compatible with the Treaty, be proportionate, be suitable to attain the objective, and be justified by overriding reasons of public interest for the reason that 'the freedom to provide services is one of the fundamental principles of the [Union]'.[127]

The outcome in both *Viking* and *Laval* thereby coincided with the CJEU's efforts at opening up the internal market, which also complemented the Union's wider (legislative) liberalization agenda.[128] In particular, it can be seen that the CJEU took the employer's freedom of movement as the basis for its analysis rather than the (fundamental) right to take collective (industrial) action. In this respect, the CJEU views such collective action as an obstacle to freedom of movement 'instead of accepting that the status of collective action as a fundamental right compels a less strict approach'.[129] This is similar to the approach adopted by the USSC in *Lochner*, whereby freedom of contract was viewed as the entrenched economic right in light of which competing legislative rights had to be justified. At the same time, the CJEU has not yet espoused 'pure' economic due process as an overarching guiding principle and continues to recognize the significance of competing (coexisting) social interests, including the protection of workers' rights as a legitimate objective.[130]

It is suggested, therefore, that at least insofar as the *Lochner* doctrine has a chilling effect on the regulation of the employment relationship, it is *Alemo-Herron* rather than *Viking* and *Laval* which bears the closest resemblance to the USSC's approach. This is perhaps most evident in discussion as to what exactly was 'wrong' with *Lochner* although even that is open to interpretation depending on precisely which aspect of the decision is under examination.[131] Of course, the focus of the present discussion is on the USSC's embrace of a 'strong' (albeit unenumerated) conception of property rights and contractual

[126] Case C-341/05 *Laval un Partneri Ltd v Svenska Byggnadsarbetareförbundet, Svenska Byggnadsarbetareförbundets avdelning 1, Byggettan and Svenska Elektrikerförbundet* ECLI:EU:C:2007:809; Directive 96/71/EC of the European Parliament and of the Council of 16 December 1996 concerning the posting of workers in the framework of the provision of services [1997] OJ L18/1.

[127] *Laval* (n 126) para 101.

[128] Nicol (n 15) 312–13.

[129] ibid 321.

[130] Caruso (n 2) 871.

[131] Nourse (n 64) 758, 759; Mayer (n 17).

freedoms rather than on wider concerns about that court's judicial activism or indeed the 'discovery' of unenumerated rights. As Strauss puts it:

> The *Lochner*-era Court acted defensibly in recognizing freedom of contract but indefensibly in exalting it. Freedom of contract, judged by the standards that developed in the last half of the twentieth century, is a plausible constitutional right. It might merit careful, case-by-case enforcement, undertaken with sensitivity to the limitations of the right as well as its value. The *Lochner*-era Court went far beyond that. It treated freedom of contract as a cornerstone of the constitutional order and systematically undervalued reasons for limiting or overriding the right.[132]

Alemo-Herron more closely aligns with *Lochner*'s contest between constitutionally protected economic freedoms and ordinary legislative protections, albeit that the former concerned the interpretation of protective Union legislation as implemented domestically, whereas the latter constituted part of a longer held judicial commitment to ensuring the protection of federal constitutional rights in the face of competition from the various states. In that way, *Lochner* did not constitute any profound constitutional or jurisprudential novation.[133] *Alemo-Herron*, on the other hand, is very different in the sense that it marked a departure from existing case law on business freedoms as a fundamental right in which the concept of freedom of contract was barely addressed, thereby leading to the development of constitutionally (judicially) imposed restrictions on the powers of the regulatory state.

Both *Alemo-Herron* and *Lochner* can therefore be criticized for the use of (dubious) fundamental rights concepts, notably freedom of contract, in order to undermine legislatively recognized economic and social interests. The CJEU has in fact already been faced with a remarkably similar case to *Lochner* which demonstrates the Court's subsequent departure from its hitherto muted engagement with business freedom concepts. In *Oebel*—as in *Lochner*—a bakery owner was prosecuted for failing to comply with a regulation banning night-time work in bakeries. In that case, the CJEU held that:

> [i]t cannot be disputed that the prohibition in the bread and confectionary industry on working before 4 a.m. in itself constitutes a legitimate element of

[132] Strauss (n 61) 375.
[133] Nicol (n 15) 321.

> economic and social policy, consistent with the objectives of public interest pursued by the Treaty.[134]

Lochner, *Alemo-Herron*, and their progeny also evidence profound consequences for wider fundamental rights constitutionalism within both legal systems. In particular, both cases raise significant questions as to the 'deepest values' underlying their respective constitutional orders and whether freedom of contract or wider business freedom concepts can be said to constitute such a value.[135] The 'appeal to tradition' can be seen in the (positivist) dissent of Justice Holmes in *Lochner*, where he held:

> I think the word liberty in the Fourteenth Amendment is perverted when it is held to prevent the natural outcome of a dominant opinion, unless it can be said that a rational and fair man necessarily would admit that the statute proposed would infringe *fundamental principles* [or fundamental rights] *as they have been understood by the traditions of our people and our law*. [emphasis added][136]

The question then becomes one of which rights are to be recognized as 'fundamental' or 'deeply rooted' within the relevant constitutional order or indeed which rights are fundamental to the maintenance of the private sphere of (ordered) liberty.[137] The CJEU's treatment of the freedom to conduct a business as a fundamental right evolved alongside—and resulted from—the development of the very structure of the Union's legal and constitutional order. Indeed, the emergence of fundamental rights as general principles, drawing on the common constitutional traditions of the Member States, is an appeal to tradition par excellence in that the CJEU is essentially involved in the assessment of the roots of a particular right in national legal traditions, with the aim of determining whether those rights merit (constitutional) recognition at Union level. This methodology places social rights at a disadvantage, in that such rights—as economic and social rights—tend to be granted *legislative* rather than *constitutional* protection at national level.

While there have been disagreements as to the precise origins of freedom of contract as a (constitutional) doctrine in US law, it is clear that this freedom

[134] Case C-155/80 *Summary proceedings against Sergius Oebel* ECLI:EU:C:1981:177.
[135] Joshua D Hawley, 'The Intellectual Origins of (Modern) Substantive Due Process' (2014) 93 Tex L Rev 275; Lindsay (n 27).
[136] *Lochner* (n 1) 76.
[137] *Palko v Connecticut* 302 US 319 (1937).

existed at common law long before the enactment of the US—or indeed the states'—constitutions, a point also applicable to the protection of freedom of contract as a 'right' in the UK within the context of Brexit.[138] Despite the existence of a common law baseline, the importance of the constitutionalization of business freedom concepts should not be underestimated in the determination of the value of such rights and their weight relative to potentially competing legislative protections. As Yackle notes, 'the very formalism we associate with *Lochner* and rightly condemn [is] a refusal to acknowledge that the occasion calls for serious policy judgment and an attempt to hide the value choices that are actually being made behind the façade of labels'.[139] Indeed, despite attempts at downplaying the significance of the rights-based arguments in *Lochner*, the USSC's selective constitutionalization of aspects of economic liberty concepts may be illustrative of the judicial priority granted to such concepts, thereby triggering the constitutional scrutiny of legislative restrictions.[140]

Therefore, the question in cases like *Lochner* was not necessarily whether freedom from arbitrary or unreasonable regulation of contractual relations existed as plausible principles or doctrines, but rather the extent to which judges had the authority to recognize and enforce such principles as constitutional *rights*.[141] At the same time, the meaning of such concepts, even when deeply embedded as constitutional concepts, can change over time. Hawley, for example, has noted the evolution of the (ambiguous) concept of 'liberty' within the context of substantive due process from one based on (natural or pre-political) visions of freedom of contract and property rights (as in *Lochner*), to one based on wider concepts of autonomy, self-development, and personal moral choice, ie going beyond the context of contract and property, but in a manner that is redolent of the normative underpinnings of the right to work, itself a facet of the freedom to conduct a business in EU law.[142] In other words, more recent fundamental rights jurisprudence within the context of substantive due process may represent more than an 'updated' version or revitalization of concepts derived from *Lochner*, and rather constitute entirely distinct concepts.[143]

138 Steven G Calabresi and Sarah E Agudo, 'Individual Rights Under State Constitutions When the Fourteenth Amendment Was Ratified in 1868: What Rights Are Deeply Rooted in American History or Tradition?' (2008) 87 Tex L Rev 7; Pound (n 56); Mayer (n 17).

139 Larry Yackle, '*Lochner*: Another Time, Another Place' (2005) 85 BULRev 765, 771.

140 Lindsay (n 27) 75.

141 Bernstein (n 19) 1488.

142 Hawley (n 135) 278; Collins (n 43).

143 Hawley (n 135) 279.

For example in *West Coast Hotel*, the case which signalled the end of the (de-regulatory) *Lochner* era, Chief Justice Hughes noted that '[l]iberty in each of its phases has its history and connotation'.[144] That case was also decided in the shadow of a proposal from President Franklin Roosevelt to 'pack' the Court with additional pro-New Deal justices, although the extent to which this threat influenced the USSC's change of approach remains uncertain. In *West Coast Hotel*, the Court upheld state minimum wage legislation, thereby abandoning the notion that the Fourteenth Amendment protects (expansive conceptions of) freedom of contract, albeit without *Lochner* itself formally being over-ruled.[145] As Chief Justice Hughes remarked:

> What is this freedom? The Constitution does not speak of freedom of contract. It speaks of liberty and prohibits the deprivation of liberty without due process of law. In prohibiting that deprivation, the Constitution does not recognize an absolute and uncontrollable liberty [. . .] freedom of contract is a qualified, not an absolute right. There is no absolute freedom to do as one wills or to contract as one chooses [. . .] Liberty implies the absence of arbitrary restraint, not immunity from reasonable regulations and prohibitions imposed in the interests of the community.[146]

In particular, it was held that freedom of contract could be restricted where such restrictions were aimed at protecting 'vulnerable groups' (among others). Finally, the Court noted that the workers in that case were in 'an unequal position with respect to bargaining power [which] casts a direct burden for their support upon the community'.[147] This represents a significant change from the earlier formalist approach adopted by the USSC, whereby both parties to the employment relationship were seen as 'equal'.[148] For Chief Justice Hughes, the existing case law had established that due process liberties were subject to 'reasonable regulations and prohibitions imposed in the interests of the community'.[149] Once again, there is evidence here of a recognition of the essential mutability of concepts such as 'freedom of contract' or 'liberty', which are thereby malleable in the face of competing values or interests and which may themselves vary over time.[150]

[144] *West Coast Hotel* (n 84) 391.
[145] Stephenson (n 81) 391–92.
[146] *West Coast Hotel* (n 84) 379.
[147] ibid 399.
[148] Pound (n 56) 454.
[149] White (n 24) 120.
[150] ibid 123.

In other words, the majority accepted the continued reviewability of economic legislation to prevent arbitrary infringements of freedom of contract but with proper consideration of the competing legislative interests at stake.[151] This case followed on from an earlier judgment in which the USSC found that freedom of contract was not a constitutionally protected right.[152] In that case, Justice Owen Roberts, in an apparent departure from his earlier opinions concerning similar New Deal legislation governing minimum wages, remarked that 'neither property rights nor contract rights are absolute'.[153] *West Coast Hotel* also overturned *Adkins*, in which earlier cases suggesting a potential retrenchment from *Lochner* had also been distinguished on the basis that they concerned maximum hours as opposed to a minimum wage.[154]

More recent USSC jurisprudence, while falling outside of the commercial context, has nevertheless demonstrated a revitalized judicial interest in 'individual liberty' concepts, which may suggest an indirect renewal of *Lochner*-based reasoning without wholeheartedly reviving *Lochner* itself.[155] *Lochner* continues to cast a long shadow over the case law of the USSC even if only to illustrate the negative consequences of a return to the prioritization of freedom of contract as a constitutional right over regulatory intervention to secure competing economic and social rights and interests.[156] The fundamental problem with *Lochner*, which has striking echoes in European cases such as *Alemo-Herron*, is that the USSC instead chose as the baseline of its analysis 'the status quo, as reflected in market ordering under the common law system'.[157] The idea here is that the USSC defined constitutionally protected private rights by reference to the protection the claimant would have received under the common law of property and contract without properly granting due weight to competing (social) considerations.[158]

This is all the more surprising in the EU context given that the CJEU has long recognized potential social restrictions on the Treaty's free movement provisions and has even gone as far as to insulate particular categories of social intervention, namely collective agreements, from the logic of Union competition

[151] Bernstein (n 19) 1510.
[152] *Nebbia v New York* 291 US 503 (1934).
[153] *Morehead v New York ex rel Tipaldo* 298 US 587 (1936).
[154] *Adkins* (n 84) 525; *Muller v Oregon* 208 US 412 (1908); *Bunting v Oregon* 243 US 426 (1917).
[155] James B Stewart, 'Did the Supreme Court Open the Door to Reviving One of its Worst Decisions?', *New York Times* (2 July 2022), discussing *Dobbs v Jackson Women's Health Organization* 1392 US 597 (2022).
[156] Justice Breyer dissenting in *William H Sorrell, Attorney General of Vermont et al v IMS Health Inc et al* 10-779 US 564 (2011).
[157] Sunstein (n 25) 903.
[158] Antinori (n 96) 1819.

law rules. In *Albany*, for example, the CJEU recognized that the 'social function' of the contested compulsory pension scheme would be undermined through the application of those competition provisions prohibiting anticompetitive agreements and concerted practices.[159] In that case, the relevant social function was the effective management of the public social security service, a function that had also been recognized elsewhere in Union law.[160] This case is thereby much more explicit in its articulation of the relevant social function than those cases concerning business freedoms as general principles, with the CJEU's judgment being reminiscent of the latter's 'purposive' approach to the interpretation of protective legislation. *Albany* has also been held out as evidence of the CJEU's recognition of the 'perceived disequilibrium' between the Treaty's economic and social policies.[161]

The overall effect of the CJEU's finding in *Albany* was essentially to protect collective agreements from the application of EU competition law where: (1) the collective agreement is reached between management and labour (or their representatives); and (2) the agreement aims to improve terms and conditions of employment.[162] More broadly, the CJEU has taken the view that entities with a 'solidarity function' do not fall within the definition of an 'undertaking' for the purposes of the Treaty's competition law provisions.[163] Solidarity in this context is defined in redistributive terms as the 'uncommercial act' of 'involuntary subsidisation', for example in relation to pension schemes.[164]

The right to bargain collectively is recognized as a fundamental right in Article 28 CFR, which also draws on Article 11 ECHR in accordance with the Charter's Explanations. This recognition lends normative weight to the 'social'—if not the 'solidarity'—function of collective bargaining, the aim of which is principally to secure and further worker interests.[165] In *Albany*, Advocate General Jacobs concluded that a trade union—in the exercise of its collective bargaining function—is not engaged in 'economic activity', with unions merely acting as agents for the employees.[166] Bradshaw argues that when engaged in collective bargaining, workers are actually acting outside of the employment

[159] Case C-67/96 *Albany International BV v Stichting Bedrijfspensioenfonds Textielindustrie* ECLI:EU:C:1999:430.
[160] ibid paras 105–06.
[161] Eliasoph (n 8) 500.
[162] *Albany* (n 159) paras 59, 60.
[163] Shaun Bradshaw, 'Is a Trade Union an Undertaking under EU Competition Law?' (2016) 12 ECJ 320, 334.
[164] ibid; AG Opinion in Case C-70/95 *Sodemare SA, Anni Azzurri Holding SpA and Anni Azzurri Rezzato Srl v Regione Lombardia* ECLI:EU:C:1997:55, para 29.
[165] *Demir and Baykara v Turkey* (2009) 48 EHRR 54; Bradshaw (n 163) 336, 337.
[166] AG Opinion in Case C-67/96 *Albany International BV v Stichting Bedrijfspensioenfonds Textielindustrie* ECLI:EU:C:1999:28, paras 227, 228.

relationship in that unions are negotiating with the employer to 'sell' the (continued) services of their membership, but under new terms and conditions.[167] This view may be plausible to the extent that in the UK collective agreements do not enjoy contractual value in and of themselves, but it overlooks the potential existence of a bridging clause which may form an inherent part of the employment contract.

More broadly, cases such as *Albany* represent judicial recognition of the wider economic and social values which infiltrate the constitutional edifice of the Union's legal order, including its fundamental rights regime. Article 3(3) of the Treaty on European Union (TEU), for example, stipulates that the Union shall promote 'a highly competitive social market economy, aiming at full employment and social progress', while Article 9 TFEU commits the Union to take account of the need to promote a high level of employment, to guarantee adequate social protection and to combat social exclusion. This is coupled with the commitment in Article 153 TFEU to facilitating 'dialogue between the social partners'. Finally, and perhaps most significantly, Article 28 CFR recognizes the fundamental right of collective bargaining and action. Outside of this protective social (rights and policy) framework, competing interests within the Union's economic constitution are of more forceful application, with the competition rules, for example, being applicable to the genuinely self-employed who—in contrast to workers—do fall within the scope of the concept of an 'undertaking'.[168]

Ultimately, it was the USSC's failure both to recognize and to accommodate disparate constitutional values that led to the decline in *Lochner*-era jurisprudence and that Court's strong commitment to freedom of contract.[169] As this book has argued, the freedom to conduct a business, in a similar way to more 'traditional' property rights, enjoys both individual and collective or 'social' dimensions, but with the CJEU in its Article 16 CFR jurisprudence essentially prioritizing the economic liberty aspect of that freedom at the expense of social conceptions of autonomy. More broadly, the CJEU has overlooked the social function of the freedom to conduct a business—including freedom of contract—that both inheres in the social dimensions of those freedoms, but which also finds reflection in the competing social rights, freedoms, and principles found within the Charter, notably its Solidarity Title.

[167] Bradshaw (n 163) 327, 328, 336.

[168] Communication from the Commission Guidelines on the application of Union competition law to collective agreements regarding the working conditions of solo self-employed persons [2022] OJ C374/2.

[169] Antinori (n 96) 1779.

6.4 Conclusion

This chapter has demonstrated that the deregulatory potential of the freedom to conduct a business can be curtailed through a proper understanding of the 'limits' that inhere in that freedom as well as through a proper understanding of the relationship between Article 16 CFR and 'competing' social rights within the Charter, notably the right to engage in work which—as incarnated in the 'freedom to pursue a trade or profession'—remains quasi-internal to the freedom to conduct a business itself. In other words, social rights—including as articulated within the right to work, as well as within Union employment legislation—can be autonomy *enhancing* rather than merely being 'restrictive'. Understood in this way, the freedom to conduct a business can be reconceptualized as a genuine bridge between the Charter's professed values of freedom and solidarity, and thereby the additional value of 'equality' through the recognition of their equivalent normative weight, ie their constitutional 'fundamentality'. Respect for these core values is as significant as ensuring respect for the core content or essence of individual Charter provisions, and yet the CJEU's engagement with these value concepts within the context of the Charter has been minimal. Viewing the freedom to conduct a business as a composite of competing aims and values, far from engendering inconsistency or uncertainty would allow for the rationalization of that freedom in its relations with other Charter provisions as well as with the bounded contextual framework provided by Union (employment) legislation, albeit that the precise constellation of these competing rights, principles, and values may vary over time.

Viewed in this way, the proposed contextual reconceptualization of freedom of contract as a component of the freedom to conduct a business advanced here goes some way to addressing the criticisms levelled at 'activist' judicial pronouncements, such as those delivered by the *Lochner* court, that eschewed an approach based on 'workable' doctrines essential due to the absence of 'an understanding of freedom of contract that might have enabled it to develop a plausible legal regime'.[170] *Lochner* was relied on not merely to demonstrate the potential deregulatory effects of judicial adherence to expansive conceptions of freedom of contract, ie in the sense of invalidating social legislation, but rather to demonstrate the ease with which business freedom concepts can become embedded in jurisprudence, thereby proving difficult to dislodge. In the EU context, the expansive conception of the freedom to conduct a business

[170] Strauss (n 61) 383, 386.

within Article 16 CFR can therefore be viewed as forming part of the broader context of the CJEU's approach to balancing competing economic and social rights considerations within the Union integration process (or disintegration process as discussed in relation to the emerging relationship between the EU and UK legal orders), including in its contribution to the ever-evolving—and interrelated—European economic and social constitutions. The *Lochner* era, despite its obvious contextual and institutional divergence from the modern EU, provides ongoing and profound lessons as to the manner in which social conceptions of freedom of contract can infiltrate autonomy arguments in order to overcome strict liberty conceptions of that same freedom.

Conclusion

The purpose of this book has been to provide an understanding of the freedom to conduct a business as a fundamental right within European Union (EU) law, notably in the form of its most contested and contestable element, namely freedom of contract. In particular, new light was shed on the constitutional and social (rights) function(s) played by the freedom to conduct a business as a fundamental right by bridging the gap between that freedom and potentially competing social rights found within the Solidarity Title of the European Union Charter of Fundamental Rights (CFR). It was argued that a proper consideration of the legal and normative value of business freedoms as fundamental rights necessitates the re-evaluation of such concepts in relation to their constitutional and social dimensions, which includes an openness to drawing on legal concepts external to the Union legal order strictly speaking. Part I explored the 'constitutional contours' of both the freedom to conduct a business and competing social rights concepts, which facilitated an assessment of the 'reconstitution' of business freedoms as constitutionalized 'rights' in Part II. Finally, Part III evaluated the potential 'entrenchment' of the freedom to conduct a business as an expansive fundamental right, including the systemic implications of such entrenchment for the protection of social rights.

Understanding the relative weight of the (potentially competing) rights, principles, and freedoms found within the Charter was vital to (re)conceptualizing the interrelationship between business freedoms and wider sources of economic and social rights within the Union's legal system. Fundamental social rights concepts have long struggled to overcome the internal market logic so prevalent within EU law. The endowment of the freedom to conduct a business with fundamental rights status has made the perception of this relationship all the more difficult, with the jurisprudence of the Court of Justice of the European Union (CJEU) also demonstrating that reliance on fundamental rights concepts can lead to the diminishment—as much as the advancement—of the protection of social rights, interests, and values. This need not be the case, and it was shown that business freedoms enjoy a social dimension, which can be used to conceive such freedoms in a way that is not *inherently* deregulatory,

Business Freedoms and Fundamental Rights in European Union Law. Niall O'Connor, Oxford University Press.
 DOI: 10.1093/9780191982132.003.0008

and which also allows for legislative interventions to be conceived as pursuing rather than necessarily restricting business rights and economic freedoms.

Business freedoms, fundamental rights, general principles, and legislative protections are deeply intertwined and mutually reinforcing concepts within the Union's fundamental rights order. In particular, it was argued that the general principles have an ongoing constitutional function as a source of fundamental rights despite the enactment of the Charter, a role which adds to the complexity of the Union's fundamental rights regime while simultaneously filling the gaps in protection derived from written sources of rights. The general principles which lie at the intersection of the various interrelated sources of Union fundamental rights remain crucial to understanding the origins, nature, and value of the freedom to conduct a business as a constitutional 'right'. Conversely, the development of business freedom concepts illustrates the important constitutional (interpretative and evaluative) functions performed by the general principles.

The emphasis of the book was on the legal reasoning of the CJEU, largely in recognition of the crucial role that the Court exercises within the fundamental rights field. However, the (legislative) 'balancing' of competing economic and social rights also lies in the arena of democratic processes, with business freedoms themselves playing a potential role in ensuring a 'robust democracy' in the sense of empowering individuals, albeit that disputes concerning the interpretation and application of competing economic and social rights concepts will remain dependent on the CJEU.[1] In particular, the CJEU in its expansive conception of the freedom to conduct a business as a fundamental right has adopted a quasi-legislative role, which is perhaps reflective of a wider jurisprudential tilt in favour of economic over social considerations. Critical approaches, including the notion of 'fundamental contradiction', were relied on to explain the apparent inconsistencies that have emerged in the Court's treatment of the freedom to conduct a business. The CJEU, despite more recent case law confirming the horizontality of particular social rights, has also been reluctant to invoke the Charter in such a way as to extend the influence of fundamental social rights as a 'counterweight' to the economic freedoms of the internal market.

The United Kingdom's withdrawal from the Union provided an additional case study through which to explore the regulatory and constitutional consequences of a Member State's departure from the Charter's protective sphere,

[1] Sacha Garben, 'Balancing Social and Economic Fundamental Rights in the EU Legal Order' (2020) 11 ELLJ 364, 386, 389.

leaving EU-derived legislation to be interpreted in light of domestic constitutional and contract law concepts. The dispute in *Alemo-Herron* also allowed for a consideration of the competing conceptions of freedom of contract within both Union law and the English common law. The discussion concerning the compatibility of mandatory (ie non-default) terms with freedom of contract may also be applicable beyond the English legal system. An outstanding question is whether Brexit will lead to a retrenchment from the CJEU's expansive approach to freedom of contract or whether the wider deregulatory thrust provided by Brexit will eventually lead to an increased emphasis on contractual autonomy concepts within domestic employment law, particularly at the expense of protective legislation which is already more vulnerable to repeal outside of the Union law context.

The Union's reaction to Brexit also suggests a potential recalibration of the relative (legislative) emphasis on economic and social protections within EU law more generally. This approach can be seen not only in the provisions of the Withdrawal Agreement and Trade and Cooperation Agreement, providing for the ongoing protection of EU-derived (social) rights concepts but also in the emergence of the Pillar of Social Rights, which—while not a *consequence* of Brexit, as such—has provoked a recent increase in Union legislative activity in the employment sphere.[2] The Pillar, though also not a source of 'rights', is intimately linked to the Charter's social rights in the sense that: (1) the Pillar can serve as a road map encouraging Member States to increase the level of social rights protection whether or not the Union enjoys competence over the relevant legal field; and (2) because the Charter is one of the sources of inspiration of the Pillar, meaning that the former can lead to a more expansive reading of the latter where the two instruments overlap, as is the case for example with the right to fair working conditions which is found in both Article 31 CFR and Principle 5 of the Pillar.

The Pillar also goes beyond the Charter, for example in providing for 'the right to fair wages', which is found in Principle 6 of the Pillar. The Pillar thereby has the potential to bolster a protective interpretation of the Charter's social rights within the legal reasoning of the CJEU and may one day become a source of rights in itself in the same way that the Charter was transformed from a non-binding to a legally enforceable source of rights, and which may thereby lead to further legislative divergence between the EU and the UK despite the non-derogation and rebalancing provisions of the Trade and Cooperation Agreement. The emerging discourse between the Charter and the Pillar will be

[2] Interinstitutional Proclamation on the European Pillar of Social Rights [2017] OJ C428/10; Sacha Garben, 'The European Pillar of Social Rights: An Assessment of its Meaning and Significance' (2019) 21 CYELS 101.

influential in determining the direction of future legislative proposals in the social sphere. To date, however, little consideration has been given to the precise relationship between the Pillar and the Charter, notably in those areas where the two overlap. The implications of Article 16 CFR have also yet to be considered fully, including its clear potential to hamper legislative efforts aimed at increasing social rights protections.

Brexit, as well as the drawing of lessons from the decision of the United States Supreme Court (USSC) in *Lochner*, also allowed for wider consideration of business freedoms within different constitutional settings, which complemented the discussion concerning the (diverging) value of freedom of contract within the (internal EU) context of the general principles, and the now codified freedom to conduct a business as a fundamental Charter right. It was argued that there is value in drawing on the United States constitutional context in exploring the manner in which constitutional courts come to read a strong or expansive conception of freedom of contract and wider business freedoms into a constitutional text that does not necessarily support such a reading. More significantly, cases subsequent to *Lochner* were relied on to support a reconceptualization of freedom of contract as a 'socialized' constitutional right through its connection with competing social rights concepts, with the USSC's eventual abandonment of *Lochner* also providing potential lessons for the CJEU in this regard, particularly given that the USSC remains the CJEU's 'closest peer', despite the obvious institutional and constitutional divergences between the EU and US legal systems.[3]

There are however limitations to the reconceptualization of business freedoms in relation to both its social and constitutional dimensions, at least as proposed here. First, the freedom to conduct a business is prioritized as the lens through which to examine the relative weight of the Charter's economic freedoms and social rights, thereby emulating the (criticized) approach of the CJEU. The reason for adopting this approach is that Article 16 CFR is a 'disruptive' provision, which has been shown to 'distort' existing constitutional fundamental rights concepts, with the freedom to conduct a business thereby requiring recalibration, with that freedom's constitutional and social dimensions being chosen as the medium through which to achieve this reconceptualization. Secondly, reliance on the social right 'to work' and the application of employment rights as fundamental rights is not (directly) transferable to other regulatory fields in which the freedom to conduct a business as a fundamental right may be implicated.

[3] Gareth Davies, 'How the Courts' Path Dependence Affects its Role as a Relational Actor' (2023) 3 European Law Open 271.

In discussing the development of the CJEU's case law on the freedom to conduct a business within Article 16 CFR as well as business freedoms as general principles, consumer protections were found to constitute a potential counterweight to that freedom, including in recognition of the latter's 'social function'. Union consumer protection legislation is by now extensive, but with such legislation also playing a crucial role in facilitating consumer participation in the 'internal market'.[4] The freedom to conduct a business as a fundamental right evidently has the potential to undermine existing legislative balances between consumer protection and market access, for example through a questioning of the 'genuineness' of the contractual 'agreement' between the parties with regard to freedom of contract. There is also a potential overlap between the collective negotiation of terms within the employment context and the use of standard terms in consumer law, which raises further questions concerning the relationship between individual and collective autonomy. At the same time, the CJEU's existing case law demonstrates a willingness to accept potential infringements of Article 16 CFR in the consumer law context as justified and proportionate, in contrast to its case law on workers' rights.[5] Another question worthy of further study is the extent to which Union law conceptions of the 'social function' of fundamental rights, including business freedoms, are reflective of the same functions found within domestic law, including their potential use in resisting private property rights in various legislative or regulatory contexts.[6]

The Charter also has clear implications for Union governance mechanisms such as the European Monetary Union and the European Semester. In particular, it has been suggested that the Charter's Solidarity Title can play a key role in redressing the imbalance between social and economic aspects of the Union's constitution.[7] More widely, business freedom concepts have clear relevance for the changes that are taking place in the world of work, such as the emerging 'gig' economy, which is provoking the emergence of new forms of contractual relationship that are often explicitly designed to avoid the

[4] Olha O Cherednychenko, 'Fundamental Freedoms, Fundamental Rights, and the Many Faces of Freedom of Contract in the EU' in Mads Andenas, Tarjei Bekkedal, and Luca Pantaleo (eds), *The Reach of Free Movement* (Asser 2017) 273, 279.

[5] Hilary Hogan, 'The Origin and Development of Article 16 of the Charter of Fundamental Rights' (2023) 2 European Law Open 753, 768, 775, also noting the CJEU's reliance on consumer protection rather than the right to strike in Case C–28/20 *Airhelp Ltd v Scandinavian Airlines System Denmark—Norway—Sweden* ECLI:EU:C:2021:226.

[6] Colm O'Cinneide, 'The Present Limits and Future Potential of European Social Constitutionalism' in Katherine G Young (ed), *The Future of Economic and Social Rights* (CUP 2019) 324, 332.

[7] Simon Deakin, 'Social Policy, Economic Governance and EMU: An Alternative to Austerity' in Niklas Bruun and others (eds), *The Economic and Financial Crisis and Collective Labour Law in Europe* (Hart 2014).

protections granted in employment legislation (including employment rights derived from EU law). It is not difficult to see how the freedom to conduct a business as a fundamental right—or at least its domestic law equivalents—could be raised to bolster such efforts in the name of contractual autonomy.

Thirdly and perhaps more fundamentally, it can be countered that reconceiving freedom of contract in relation to social rights concepts is merely to infuse the latter with liberty or autonomy-based values, which is also reflective of the 'duality' of the right to work as both a civil liberty and a social right. This also relates to the wider argument that social rights are necessary to ensure 'economic autonomy' at a constitutional level, in that social regulation contributes to the creation of the necessary conditions for the operation of the (internal) market, thereby facilitating the exercise of business freedoms.[8] Of course, there are also other ways of reconceiving the notion of freedom of contract whether in relation to broader (social justice) approaches to protecting the weaker party to contractual arrangements, or through potentially narrower concepts such as 'good faith' or 'fairness', with these alternative approaches also possibly implicating fundamental (social) rights concepts.[9] In addition, concepts such as 'solidarity' may themselves require reconceptualization to accommodate the diverse—in both constitutional and regulatory terms—range of interests protected by the 'Solidarity' Title of the Charter, with that concept also having a connection to broader constitutional concepts such as 'social citizenship'.[10]

The opening paragraphs of this book invoked the concerns raised by Advocate General Szpunar in the case of *Thelen Technopark* that freedom of contract—as a component of wider business freedoms— 'has not yet found its rightful place in the system of EU law'.[11] The legal and normative gaps in our understanding of freedom of contract as a fundamental right were essentially addressed first by exploring the *emergence* and origins of business freedoms within the EU's legal order. The second step was to consider the *institutional* aspects of freedom of contract, including the CJEU's adoption of an expansive approach to that freedom. The third step was to examine the related issue of the *replication* of freedom of contract as a fundamental right, including the extent to which this notion is reflected in domestic (constitutional) law, as well as the subsequent jurisprudence of the CJEU dealing with that concept as both a

[8] Jeremias Prassl, 'Business Freedoms and Employment Rights in the European Union' (2015) 17 CYELS 189, 193.

[9] Cherednychenko (n 4) 275.

[10] Guy Davidov, *A Purposive Approach to Labour Law* (OUP 2016) 63.

[11] AG Opinion in Case C-261/20 *Thelen Technopark Berlin GmbH v MN* ECLI:EU:C:2021:620, para 76.

general principle and a fundamental right as part of the wider freedom to conduct a business. The fourth step was to evaluate the systemic regulatory *implications* of freedom of contract, with a particular focus on the employment context.

Overall, the book can be said to represent a *reaction* to this most contested of fundamental rights concepts, albeit one that results from its own partialities, including the choice of regulatory sphere against which to conduct the assessment, or indeed in the adoption of a relatively restrictive conception of 'social rights' as well as broader normative inclinations towards the favouring of (social) legislative interventions.[12] The fourth limitation of the adopted approach is that freedom of contract and the wider freedom to conduct a business will remain malleable and open-ended concepts, and which will necessitate their constant re-evaluation in light of new constitutional and regulatory challenges.[13] There can be no doubting that the concept of the freedom to conduct a business as a fundamental right—and notably as encapsulated in freedom of contract—will continue to play a prominent role in future legal and political debates as to the regulatory reach of Union law in both the employment context and beyond, with these freedoms thereby escaping definitive definition.

This book has shown that deregulatory (economic or liberty) values do not necessarily (or exclusively) inhere within the freedom to conduct a business, with that freedom equally capable of being conceived around its social or 'solidarity' dimensions, which perhaps necessitates a more 'inclusive' conceptualization of the fundamental values underpinning European private law more generally.[14] Inevitably, this will involve the CJEU in the assessment of value judgements in its interpretation and application of fundamental rights, freedoms, and principles. What this book has sought to do is to ensure that the competing economic and social dimensions of the freedom to conduct a business as a fundamental right are positively articulated, thereby reducing the potential for the judicial 'smuggling' of ideological preferences in the guise of constitutional disputes.[15]

[12] Social rights can, for example, be defined more broadly as all rights with a non-economic objective: Vanessa Mak, *Legal Pluralism in European Contract Law* (OUP 2020) 76. Norbert Reich, *General Principles of EU Civil Law* (Intersentia 2014) 40 suggests a general principle of protection for the weaker party.

[13] Oliver Gerstenberg, 'Fundamental Rights and Democratic Sovereignty in the EU: The Role of the Charter of Fundamental Rights of the EU (CFREU) in Regulating the European Social Market Economy' (2020) 39 YEL 199, 227.

[14] Martijn W Hesselink, 'If You Don't Like Our Principles We Have Others: On Core Values and Underlying Principles in European Private Law: A Critical Discussion of the New "Principles" Section in the Draft Common Frame of Reference"' in Roger Brownsword and others (eds), *The Foundations of European Private Law* (Hart 2011) 59, 66.

[15] O'Cinneide (n 6) 344.

Bibliography

1. ACADEMIC LITERATURE

i. Books

Adams Z and others, *Deakin and Morris' Labour Law* (7th edn, Hart 2021)
Alexy R, *A Theory of Constitutional Rights* (OUP 2004)
Amalfitano C, *General Principles of EU Law and the Protection of Fundamental Rights* (Edward Elgar 2018)
Andrews N, *Contract Law* (CUP 2015)
Atiyah PS, *The Rise and Fall of Freedom of Contract* (OUP 1979)
—— *Essays on Contract* (OUP 1986)
Barnard C, *EU Employment Law* (4th edn, OUP 2012)
—— *The Substantive Law of the European Union: The Four Freedoms* (7th edn, OUP 2022)
Beatson J, Burrows A, and Cartwright J (eds), *Anson's Law of Contract* (30th edn, OUP 2016)
Beck G, *The Legal Reasoning of the Court of Justice of the EU* (Hart 2013)
Bengoetxea J, *The Legal Reasoning of the European Court of Justice: Towards a European Jurisprudence* (OUP 1993)
Bogg A and others (eds), *The Autonomy of Labour Law* (Hart 2015)
Bojarski L, Hofbauer JA, and Mileszyk N (eds), The European Charter of Fundamental Rights as a Living Instrument: Guidelines for Civil Society (Facultas 2014)
Collins H, *The Law of Contract* (4th edn, CUP 2003)
Collins P, *Putting Human Rights to Work: Labour Law, The ECHR, and the Employment Relation* (OUP 2022)
Conway G, *The Limits of Legal Reasoning and the European Court of Justice* (CUP 2012)
Craig P, *The Lisbon Treaty: Law, Politics and Treaty Reform* (OUP 2010)
Cross R and Harris JW, *Precedent in English Law* (4th edn, Clarendon Press 1991)
Currie DP, *The Constitution of the Federal Republic of Germany* (University of Chicago Press 1994)
Davidov G, *A Purposive Approach to Labour Law* (OUP 2016)
Dawson M, *The Governance of EU Fundamental Rights* (CUP 2017)
de Vries S, Bernitz U, and Weatherill S (eds), *The Protection of Fundamental Rights in the EU After Lisbon* (Hart 2013)
Duguit L, *Las transformaciónes del derecho público y privado* (Buenos Aires: Editorial Heliasta, 1975)
Dworkin R, *Taking Rights Seriously* (Duckworth 1977)
—— *Law's Empire* (Harvard University Press 1986)
Fabbrini F, *Fundamental Rights in Europe* (OUP 2014)
Frantziou E, *The Horizontal Effect of Fundamental Rights in the European Union: A Constitutional Analysis* (OUP 2019)
Fredman S, *Comparative Human Rights Law* (OUP 2018)

Gearty C and Mantouvalou V, *Debating Social Rights* (Hart 2011)
Golding G, *Shaping Contracts for Work* (OUP 2023)
Groussot X, *General Principles of Community Law* (European Law Publishing 2006)
Horsley T, *The Court of Justice of the European Union as an Institutional Actor* (CUP 2018)
Imamović Š, *The Architecture of Fundamental Rights in the European Union* (Hart 2022)
Jacob M, *Precedents and Case-based Reasoning in the European Court of Justice* (CUP 2014)
King J, *Judging Social Rights* (CUP 2012)
Leczykiewicz D and Weatherill S (eds), *The Involvement of EU Law in Private Law Relationships* (Hart 2013)
Lehavi A, *The Construction of Property: Norms, Institutions, Challenges* (CUP 2013)
Mak V, *Legal Pluralism in European Contract Law* (OUP 2020)
McCloskey RG, *The Modern Supreme Court* (Harvard University Press 1972)
Paunio E, *Legal Certainty in Multilingual EU Law* (Ashgate 2013)
Reich N, *General Principles of EU Civil Law* (Intersentia 2014)
Sankari S, *European Court of Justice Legal Reasoning in Context* (Europa Law Publishing 2013)
Smith A, *An Inquiry into the Nature and Causes of the Wealth of Nations* (Liberty Classics 1981)
Smith SA, *Atiyah's Introduction to the Law of Contract* (6th edn, OUP 2006)
Trebilcock MJ, *The Limits of Freedom of Contract* (Harvard 1993)
Tridimas T, *The General Principles of EU Law* (2nd edn, OUP 2006)
Van Der Walt AJ, *Constitutional Property Clauses: A Comparative Analysis* (Juta 1999)
Violini L and Baraggia A (eds), *The Fragmented Landscape of Fundamental Rights Protection in Europe: The Role of Judicial and Non-Judicial Actors* (Edward Elgar 2018)
Vogenauer S and Weatherill S (eds), *General Principles of Law: European and Comparative Perspectives* (Hart 2017)
Wacks R, *Understanding Jurisprudence: An Introduction to Legal Theory* (6th edn, OUP 2020)
Waldron J, *The Right to Private Property* (OUP 1990)
Wynn-Evans C, *The Law of TUPE Transfers* (2nd edn, OUP 2016)

ii. Journal articles, research reports, and working papers

Ahmed T and de Jesús Butler I, 'The EU and Human Rights: An International Law Perspective' (2006) 17 EJIL 771
Alexander GS, 'Reply: The Complex Core of Property' (2009) 94 Cornell L Rev 1063
Antinori MR, 'Does *Lochner* Live in Luxembourg? An Analysis of the Property Rights Jurisprudence of the European Court of Justice' (1995) 18 Fordham Int'l L J 1778
Antonaki I, 'Collective Redundancies in Greece: *AGET* Iraklis' (2017) 54 CMLRev 1513
Arnull A, 'Owning up to Fallibility: Precedent and the Court of Justice' (1993) 30 CMLRev 247
—— 'Me and My Shadow: The European Court of Justice and the Disintegration of European Union Law' (2007) 31 Fordham Int'l L J 1174
Ayres I and Gertner R, 'Filling Gaps in Incomplete Contracts: An Economic Theory of Default Rules' (1989) 99 Yale L J 87
Babayev R, 'Private Autonomy at Union Level: On Article 16 CFREU and Free Movement Rights' (2016) 53 CMLRev 979
—— 'Duality of Economic Freedom Protection in the Interplay of Article 16 CFR and Article 102 TFEU' (2020) 45 ELRev 694

Baldwin R, 'From Regulation to Behaviour Change: Giving Nudge the Third Degree' (2014) 77 MLR 831
Balkin JM, '"Wrong the Day it was Decided": *Lochner* and Constitutional Historicism' (2005) 85 BULRev 677
Barnard C and Deakin S, '"Negative" and "Positive" Harmonization of Labour Law in the European Union' 8 (2002) Colum J Eur L 389
Barnard C, 'Social Dumping or Dumping Socialism' (2008) 67 CLJ 262
—— 'So Long, Farewell, Auf Wiedersehen, Adieu: Brexit and the Charter of Fundamental Rights' (2019) 82 MLR 350
—— Deakin S and Hobbs R, 'Opting Out of the 48-Hour Week: Employer Necessity or Individual Choice? An Empirical Study of the Operation of Article 18(1)(b) of the Working Time Directive in the UK' (2003) 32 ILJ 223
Barnett RE, 'The Sound of Silence: Default Rules and Contractual Consent' (1992) 78 Va L Rev 821
Bartl M and Leone C, 'Minimum Harmonisation after *Alemo-Herron*: The Janus Face of EU Fundamental Rights Review' (2015) 11 EuConst 140
Basedow J, 'Freedom of Contract in the European Union' (2008) 6 ERPL 901
Belling V, 'Supranational Fundamental Rights or Primacy of Sovereignty? Legal Effects of the So-Called Opt-Out from the EU Charter of Fundamental Rights' (2012) 18 ELJ 251
Bering Liisberg J, 'Does the EU Charter of Fundamental Rights Threaten the Supremacy of Community Law?' (2001) 38 CMLRev 1171
Bernstein DE, '*Lochner v New York*: A Centennial Retrospective' (2005) 83 Wash U L Q 1469
—— 'The History of "Substantive" Due Process: It's Complicated' (2016) 95 Tex L Rev 1
Besselink LFM, 'Entrapped by the Maximum Standard: On Fundamental Rights, Pluralism and Subsidiarity in the European Union' (1998) 35 CMLRev 629
Betten L, 'The EU Charter of Fundamental Rights: A Trojan Horse or a Mouse?' (2001) 17 Int J Comp LLIR 151
Bogoeski V, 'Nonwaivability of Labour Rights, Individual Waivers and the Emancipatory Function of Labour Law' (2023) 52 ILJ 179
Bojarski L, Hofbauer JA, and Mileszyk N (eds), 'The European Charter of Fundamental Rights as a Living Instrument: Guidelines for Civil Society' (2014) 9
Bommarius C, '*Lecture*—Germany's *Sozialstaat* Principles and the Founding Period' (2011) 12 Ger Law J 1880
Boyle K and Busby N, 'Subnational Incorporation of Economic, Social and Cultural Rights – Can Devolution become a Vehicle for Progressive Human Rights Reform?' (2023) 74 NILQ 63
Bradshaw S, 'Is a Trade Union an Undertaking under EU Competition Law?' (2016) 12 ECJ 320
Brkan M, 'The Concept of Essence of Fundamental Rights in the EU Legal Order: Peeling the Onion to its Core' (2018) 14 EuConst 332
Brodie D, 'Collectivism in Labour Law: Only by Exception' (2022) 51 ILJ 464
Bubb R and Pildes RH, 'How Behavioral Economics Trims its Sails and Why' (2014) 127 Harv L Rev 1593
Burchardt D, 'The Relationship between the Law of the European Union and the Law of its Member States—A Norm-based Conceptual Framework' (2019) 15 EuConst 73
Cabral P and Neves R, 'General Principles of EU Law and Horizontal Direct Effect' (2011) 17 EPL 437

Calabresi SG and Agudo SE, 'Individual Rights Under State Constitutions When the Fourteenth Amendment Was Ratified in 1868: What Rights Are Deeply Rooted in American History or Tradition?' (2008) 87 Tex L Rev 7

Caruso D, '*Lochner* in Europe: A Comment on Keith Whittington's "Congress Before the *Lochner* Court"' (2005) 85 BULRev 867

Casla K, 'The Right to Property Taking Economic, Social, and Cultural Rights Seriously' (2023) 45 Hum Rts Q 171

Cherednychenko OO, 'Fundamental Rights and Private Law: A Relationship of Subordination or Complementarity?' (2007) 3 Utrecht Law Review 1

—— 'Rediscovering the Public/Private Divide in EU Private Law' (2020) 26 ELJ 27

Choudhry S, 'The *Lochner* Era and Comparative Constitutionalism' (2004) 2 ICON 1

Clayton R, 'The Empire Strikes Back: Common Law Rights and the Human Rights Act' (2015) PL 3

—— and Murphy CC, 'The Emergence of the EU Charter of Fundamental Rights in UK Law' (2014) 5 EHRLR 469

Cloots E, 'Safe Harbour or Open Sea for Corporate Headscarf Bans? *Achbita* and *Bougnaoui*' (2018) 55 CMLRev 589

Coghlan N and Steiert M (eds), 'The Charter of Fundamental Rights of the European Union: The travaux préparatoires and selected documents', 7 January 2021

Collins H, 'Employment as a Relational Contract' (2021) 137 LQR 426

Colombi Ciacchi A, 'Party Autonomy as a Fundamental Right in the European Union' (2010) 6 ERCL 303

—— 'The Direct Horizontal Effect of EU Fundamental Rights' (2019) 15 EuConst 294

Crawford C, 'The Social Function of Property and the Human Capacity to Flourish' (2011) 80 Fordham L Rev 1089

Davidov G, 'Non-waivability in Labour Law' (2020) 40 OJLS 482

Davies A, 'Has the Court of Justice Changed its Management and Approach towards the Social Acquis?' (2018) 14 EuConst 154

Davies G, 'Freedom of Movement, Horizontal Effect, and Freedom of Contract' (2012) 3 ERPL 805

—— 'How the Court's Path Dependence Affects its Role as a Relational Actor' (2023) 2 European Law Open 271

Dawson M, 'Fundamental Rights in European Union Policy-Making: The Effects and Advantages of Institutional Diversity' (2020) 20 HRLRev 50

—— Lynskey O, and Muir E, 'What is the Added Value of the Concept of the "Essence" of EU Fundamental Rights?' (2019) 20 Ger Law J 767

de Boer N, 'Addressing Rights Divergences Under the Charter: *Melloni*' (2013) 50 CMLRev 1083

de Búrca G, 'The Drafting of the EU Charter of Fundamental Rights' (2001) 26 ELRev 214

—— 'The Road Not Taken: The European Union as a Global Human Rights Actor' (2011) 105 AJIL 649

—— 'After the EU Charter of Fundamental Rights: The Court of Justice as a Human Rights Adjudicator' (2013) 20 MJ 168

de Cecco F, 'The Trouble with Trumps: On How (and Why) not to Define the Core of Fundamental Rights' (2023) 60 CMLRev 1551

de Mol M, 'The Novel Approach of the CJEU on the Horizontal Direct Effect of the Principle of Non-Discrimination' (2011) 18 MJ 109

de Schutter O and de Jesús Butler I, 'Binding the EU to International Human Rights Law' (2008) 27 YEL 277

de Witte B, 'The Legal Status of the Charter: Vital Question or Non-Issue?' (2001) 8 MJ 81
Deakin S, 'Contracts as Capabilities. An Evolutionary Perspective of the Autonomy-Paternalism Debate' (2010) 3 Erasmus Law Review 141
—— 'Brexit, Labour Rights and Migration: Why Wisbech Matters to Brussels' (2016) 17 Ger Law J 13
Delledonne G and Fabbrini F, 'The Founding Myth of European Human Rights Law: Revisiting the Role of National Courts in the Rise of EU Human Rights Jurisprudence' (2019) 44 ELRev 178
Derlén M and Lindholm J, 'Goodbye *van Gend en Loos*, Hello *Bosman*? Using Network Analysis to Measure the Importance of Individual CJEU Judgments' (2014) 20 ELJ 667
Dougan M, 'When Words Collide! Competing Visions of the Relationship between Direct Effect and Supremacy' (2007) 44 CMLRev 931
—— 'The Treaty of Lisbon 2007: Winning Minds, Not Hearts' (2008) 45 CMLRev 617
—— 'Judicial Review of Member State Action under the General Principles and the Charter: Defining the "Scope of Union Law"' (2015) 52 CMLRev 1201
Douglas Scott S, 'The European Union and Human Rights after the Treaty of Lisbon' (2011) 11 HRLRev 645
Eeckhout P, 'The EU Charter of Fundamental Rights and the Federal Question' (2002) 39 CMLRev 945
Eliasoph IH, 'A "Switch in Time" For the European Community? *Lochner* Discourse and the Recalibration of Economic and Social Rights in Europe' (2007) 14 Colum J Eur L 468
Elliot M, 'Beyond the European Convention: Human Rights and the Common Law' (2015) 68 CLP 85
Evju S, 'Labour is not a Commodity: Reappraising the Origins of the Maxim' (2013) 4 ELLJ 222
Ewing K and John Hendy J, 'New Perspectives on Collective Labour Law: Trade Union Recognition and Collective Bargaining' (2017) 46 ILJ 23
Foster SR and Bonilla D, 'Symposium on the Social Function of Property: A Comparative Law Perspective' (2011) 80 Fordham L Rev 101
Fox O'Mahony L and Roark ML, 'Operationalising Progressive Ideas About Property: Resilient Property, Scale, and Systemic Compromise' (2024) 10 Tex A&M J Prop L 38
Jacobs FG, 'Human Rights in the European Union: The Role of the Court of Justice' (2001) 26 ELRev 331
Frantziou E, 'The Horizontal Effect of the Charter of Fundamental Rights of the EU: Rediscovering the Reasons for Horizontality' (2015) 21 ELJ 657
—— '(Most of) the Charter of Fundamental Rights is Horizontally Applicable' (2019) 15 EuConst 306
—— 'Constitutional Reasoning in the European Union and the Charter of Fundamental Rights: In Search of Public Justification' (2019) 25 EPL 183
—— 'The Horizontal Effect of the Charter: Towards an Understanding of Horizontality as a Structural Constitutional Principle' (2020) 22 CYELS 208
—— and Craig S, 'Understanding the Implications of Article 2 of the Northern Ireland Protocol in the Context of EU Case Law Developments' (2022) 73 NILQ 65
Fraser Butlin S, 'The CJEU Confused Over Religion' (2017) 76 CLJ 246
Frese A and Palmer Olsen H, 'Spelling It Out— Convergence and Divergence in the Judicial Dialogue between the CJEU and ECtHR' (2019) 88 Nord J Intl L 429
Fudge J, 'The New Discourse of Labour Rights: From Social to Fundamental Rights?' (2007) 29 Comparative Labor Law and Policy Journal 29

Gabel P and Kennedy D, 'Roll Over Beethoven' (1984) 36 Stan L Rev 1
Garben S, 'The European Pillar of Social Rights: An Assessment of its Meaning and Significance' (2019) 21 CYELS 101
—— 'Balancing Social and Economic Fundamental Rights in the EU Legal Order' (2020) 11 ELLJ 364
Gardner J, '"Simply in Virtue of Being Human": The Whos and Whys of Human Rights' (2008) 2 Journal of Ethics and Social Philosophy 1
Gerstenberg O, 'Fundamental Rights and Democratic Sovereignty in the EU: The Role of the Charter of Fundamental Rights of the EU (CFREU) In Regulating the European Social Market Economy' (2020) 39 YEL 199
Gillman H, 'De-Lochnerizing *Lochner*' (2005) 85 BULRev 859
Gill-Pedro E, 'Freedom to Conduct a Business in EU Law: Freedom from Interference or Freedom from Domination?' (2017) 9 European Journal of Legal Studies 103
—— 'Whose Freedom is it Anyway? The Fundamental Rights of Companies in EU Law' (2022) 18 EuConst 183
Giubboni S, 'Freedom to Conduct a Business and EU Labour Law' (2018) 14 EuConst 172
Goldsmith QC L, 'A Charter of Rights, Freedoms and Principles' (2001) 39 CMLRev 1201
Goodrich P, 'Critical Legal Studies in England: Prospective Histories' (1992) 12 OJLS 195
Gordon RW, 'Critical Legal Histories' (1984) 36 Stan L Rev 57
Grier Stephenson D, 'The Supreme Court and Constitutional Change: *Lochner v New York* Revisited' (1976) 21 Vill L Rev 217
Grogan J, 'Rights and Remedies at Risk: Implications of the Brexit process on the Future of Rights in the UK' (2019) PL 683
Guðmundsdóttir D, 'A Renewed Emphasis on the Charter's Distinction between Rights and Principles: is a Doctrine of Judicial Restraint more Appropriate?' (2015) 52 CMLRev 685
Hancox E, 'The Meaning of "Implementing" EU Law under Article 51(1) of the Charter: *Åkerberg Fransson*' (2013) 50 CMLRev 1411
—— 'The Relationship Between the Charter and General Principles: Looking Back and Looking Forward' (2020) 22 CYELS 233
Harvey D, 'The Essence of EU Fundamental Rights – Reflections in Light of the UK Experience' (2023) 5 EHRLR 438
Hawley JD, 'The Intellectual Origins of (Modern) Substantive Due Process' (2014) 93 Tex L Rev 275
Hepple B, 'A Right to Work' (1981) 10 ILJ 65
—— 'The EU Charter of Fundamental Rights' (2001) 30 ILJ 225
Herzfeld Olsson P, 'Possible Shielding Effects of Article 27 on Workers' Rights to Information and Consultation in the EU Charter of Fundamental Rights' (2016) 32 Int J Comp LLIR 251
Hesselink MW, 'EU Private Law Injustices' (2022) 41 YEL 83
Hofmann HCH and Mihaescu BC, 'The Relation between the Charter's Fundamental Rights and the Unwritten General Principles of EU Law: Good Administration as the Test Case' (2013) 9 EuConst 73
Hogan H, 'The Origin and Development of Article 16 of the Charter of Fundamental Rights' (2023) 2 European Law Open 753
Hohfeld WN, 'Some Fundamental Legal Conceptions as Applied in Judicial Reasoning' (1913) 16 Yale L J 16
—— 'Fundamental Legal Conceptions as Applied in Judicial Reasoning' (1917) 26 Yale L J 710.

Howard E, '*LF v SCRL* and the CJEU's Failure to Engage with the Reality of Muslim Women in the Labour Market' (2023) 52 ILJ 997
Hunt A, 'The Theory of Critical Legal Studies' (1986) 6 OJLS 1
Iglesias Sánchez S, 'The Court and the Charter: The Impact of the Entry into Force of the Lisbon Treaty on the ECJ's Approach to Fundamental Rights' (2012) 49 CMLRev 1565
Jizeng Fan B, 'Convergence, Compatibility or Decoration: The Luxembourg Court's References to Strasbourg Case Law in its Final Judgments' (2016) 2 Pécs Journal of International and European Law 38
Judson FN, 'Liberty of Contract under the Police Power' (1891) 25 Am L Rev 871
Katz CJ, 'Protective Labour Legislation in the Courts: Substantive Due Process and Fairness in the Progressive Era' (2013) 31 Law & Hist Rev 275
Kennedy D, 'Form and Substance in Private Law Adjudication' (1976) 89 Harv L Rev 1685
—— 'The Structure of Blackstone's Commentaries' (1979) 28 Buff L Rev 205
—— 'Critical Labor Law Theory: A Comment' (1981) 4 Berkely Journal of Employment & Labor Law 503
—— 'Distributive and Paternalist Motives in Contract and Tort Law' (1982) 41 Md L Rev 563
Král R and Mádr P, 'On the (In)Applicability of the EU Charter of Fundamental Rights to National Measures Exceeding the Requirements of Minimum Harmonisation Directives' (2021) 46 ELRev 81
Krisch N, 'The Open Architecture of European Human Rights Law' (2008) 71 MLR 183
Krommendijk J, 'Principled Silence or Mere Silence on Principles? The Role of the EU Charter's Principles in the Case Law of the Court of Justice' (2015) 11 EuConst 321
Kuijer M, 'The Challenging Relationship between the European Convention on Human Rights and the EU Legal Order: Consequences of a Delayed Accession' (2020) 24 IJHR 99
Laagland F, 'Member States' Sovereignty in the Socio-Economic Field: Fact or Fiction? The Clash between the European Business Freedoms and the National Level of Workers' Protection' (2018) 9 ELLJ 50
Lazzerini N, '(Some of) the Fundamental Rights Granted by the Charter may be a Source of Obligations for Private Parties: *AMS*' (2014) 51 CMLRev 907
Leczykiewicz D, 'Horizontal Application of the Charter of Fundamental Rights' (2013) 38 ELRev 479
—— 'Prohibition of Abusive Practices as a "General Principle" of EU Law' (2019) 56 CMLRev 703
—— 'The Judgment in *Bauer* and the Effect of the EU Charter of Fundamental Rights in Horizontal Situations' (2020) 16 ERCL 323
Lenaerts K, 'Limits on Limitations: The Essence of Fundamental Rights in the EU' (2019) 20 Ger Law J 779
—— and Gutiérrez-Fons JA, 'The Constitutional Allocation of Powers and General Principles of EU Law' (2010) 47 CMLRev 1629
Lindeboom J, 'Thelen Technopark and the Legal Effects of the Services Directive in Purely Internal and Horizontal Disputes' (2022) 7 European Papers 305
Lindsay MJ, 'In Search of "Laissez-Faire Constitutionalism"' (2010) 123 Harv L Rev 56
Lock T, 'The Future of EU Accession to the ECHR after Opinion 2/13: Is It Still Possible and Is It Still Desirable?' (2015) 11 EuConst 239
—— 'Human Rights Law in the UK after Brexit' (2017) PL 117
—— 'Rights and Principles in the EU Charter of Fundamental Rights' (2019) 56 CMLRev 1201

Lourenço L, 'Religion, Discrimination and the EU General Principles' Gospel: *Egenberger*' (2019) 56 CMLRev 193
Lubens R, 'The Social Obligation of Property Ownership: A Comparison of German and U.S. Law' (2007) 24 Ariz J Int'l & Comp L 389
Madison J, 'Property' National Gazette (27 March 1792)
Mantouvalou V, 'Are Labour Rights Human Rights?' (2012) 3 ELLJ 151
Marella M, 'The Old and the New Limits to Freedom of Contract in Europe' (2006) 2 ERCL 257
Markakis M, 'Can Governments Control Mass Layoffs by Employers? Economic Freedoms vs Labour Rights in Case C-201/15 *AGET Iraklis*' (2017) 13 EuConst 724
Marmor A, 'On the Limits of Rights' (1997) 16 Law & Phil 1
Mast T and Ollig C, 'The Lazy Legislature: Incorporating and Horizontalising the Charter of Fundamental Rights through Secondary Union Law' (2023) 19 EuConst 462
Mayer DN, 'Substantive Due Process Rediscovered: The Rise and Fall of Liberty of Contract' (2009) 60 Mercer Law Review 563.
McMullen J, 'Takeovers, Transfers and Business Re-organisations' (1992) 21 ILJ 15
Mensch B, 'Freedom of Contract as Ideology' (1981) 33 Stan L Rev 753
Meyerson D, 'Fundamental Contradictions in Critical Legal Studies' (1991) 11 OJLS 439
Micklitz HW, 'On the Intellectual History of Freedom of Contract and Regulation' (2015) 4 Penn State Journal of Law & International Affairs 1
Mitchell G, 'Libertarian Paternalism is an Oxymoron' (2005) 99 Northwest U L Rev 1245
Moyn S, 'Reconstructing Critical Legal Studies' (4 August 2023) Yale Law School, Public Law Research Paper, 5
Muir E, 'Of Ages in—and Edges of—EU Law' (2011) 48 CMLRev 39
—— 'The Fundamental Rights Implications of EU Legislation: Some Constitutional Challenges' (2014) 51 CMLRev 219
—— 'The Horizontal Effects of Charter Rights Given Expression to in EU Legislation, from *Mangold* to *Bauer*' (2019) 12 Review of European Administrative Law 185
Mundlak G, 'The Right to Work: Linking Human Rights and Employment Policy' (2007) 146 Int'l Lab Rev 189
Murray CRG and Rice CAG, 'Beyond Trade: Implementing the Ireland/Northern Ireland Protocol's Human Rights and Equalities Provisions' (2021) 72 NILQ 1
Nic Shuibhne N, 'The Resilience of EU Market Citizenship' (2010) 47 CMLRev 1597
—— 'Settling Dust? Reflections on the Judgments in *Viking* and *Laval*' (2010) 21 EBLR 681
Nicol D, 'Europe's *Lochner* Moment' (2011) 2 PL 308
Nourse VF, 'A Tale of Two Lochners: The Untold Story of Substantive Due Process and the Idea of Fundamental Rights' (2009) 97 CLR 751
O'Connor N, 'The Impact of Positive Action on Private Law Freedoms—Proposed EU Directive on Gender Balance in the Boardroom' (2015) 18 TCLR 128
—— 'Interpreting Employment Legislation through a Fundamental Rights Lens: What's the Purpose?' (2017) 8 ELLJ 193
—— 'Whose Autonomy is it Anyway? Freedom of Contract, the Right to Work and the General Principles of EU Law' (2020) 49 ILJ 285
—— '"UnChartered" Waters: Fundamental Rights, Brexit and the (Re)Constitution of the Employment Law Hierarchy of Norms' (2021) 12 ELLJ 52
—— and Harvey D, 'Freedom of Movement and the Normative Value of the Right to Work in the United Kingdom Post-Brexit' (2024) CYELS Online First
O'Higgins P, '"Labour is not a Commodity"—an Irish Contribution to International Labour Law' (1997) 26 ILJ 225

Oetken JP, 'Form and Substance in Critical Legal Studies' (1991) 100 Yale L J 2209
Oliver P, 'Companies and their Fundamental Rights: A Comparative Perspective' (2015) 64 ICLQ 661
Peers S, 'The "Opt-Out" that Fell to Earth: The British and Polish Protocol Concerning the EU Charter of Fundamental Rights' (2012) 12 HRLR 375
Phelan W, 'The Role of the German and Italian Constitutional Courts in the Rise of EU Human Rights Jurisprudence: A Response to Delledonne & Fabbrini' (2020) TRiSS Working Paper Series TRiSS-WPS-02-2020
Pinto du Albuquerque P and Lim H-S, 'The Cross-Fertilisation between the Court of Justice of the European Union and the European Court of Human Rights: Reframing the Discussion on Brexit' (2018) 6 EHRLR 567
Pirker B, 'Mapping the Scope of Application of EU Fundamental Rights: A Typology' (2018) 3 European Papers 133
Pound R, 'Liberty of Contract' (1909) 18 Yale L J 454
Prassl J, 'Freedom of Contract as a General Principle of EU Law? Transfers of Undertakings and the Protection of Employer Rights in EU Labour Law' (2013) 42 ILJ 434
—— 'Business Freedoms and Employment Rights in the European Union' (2015) 17 CYELS 189
Rawls J, 'Justice as Fairness' (1958) 67 Phil Rev 164
Reed L, 'Departing from Precedent: The Experience of the UK Supreme Court' (International Conference on Implementation of the Rule of Law, 20 January 2023)
Reich N, 'Free Movement v Social Rights in an Enlarged Union—the *Laval* and *Viking* Cases before the ECJ' (2008) 9 Ger Law J 125
Rossi LS, 'Same Legal Value as the Treaties? Rank, Primacy, and Direct Effects of the EU Charter of Fundamental Rights' (2017) 18 Ger Law J 771
Rudden B, 'Ius Cogens, Ius Dispositivum' (1980) 11 Cambrian Law Review 87
Rutgers JW, 'The European Economic Constitution, Freedom of Contract and the DCFR' (2009) 5 ERCL 95
Safjan M and Mikłaszewicz P, 'Horizontal Effect of the General Principles of EU Law in the Sphere of Private Law' (2010) 18 ERPL 475
Sales L, 'EU Retained Law: Purposive Interpretation when the Constitutional Architecture Changes', Annual Lecture of the UK Association for European Law, 20 November 2023
Sarmiento D, 'Who is Afraid of the Charter? The Court of Justice, National Courts and the New Framework of Fundamental Rights Protection in Europe' (2013) 50 CMLRev 1267
Scarcello O, 'Preserving the "Essence" of Fundamental Rights under Article 52(1) of the Charter: A Sisyphean Task? (2020) 16 EuConst 647
Schiek D, 'Towards More Resilience for a Social EU—The Constitutionally Conditioned Internal Market' (2017) 13 EuConst 611
Sciaraffa S, 'Critical Legal Studies: A Marxist Rejoinder' (1999) 5 Legal Theory 201
Spaventa E, 'A Very Fearful Court? The Protection of Fundamental Rights in the European Union after Opinion 2/13' (2015) 22 MJ 35
—— 'Should we "Harmonize" Fundamental Rights in the EU? Some Reflections About Minimum Standards and Fundamental Rights Protection in the EU Composite Constitutional System' (2018) 55 CMLRev 997
Stone M, 'Roberto Esposito and the Biopolitics of Property Rights' (2015) 24 Social & Legal Studies 381
Strauss DA, 'Why Was *Lochner* Wrong?' (2003) 70 U Chi L Rev 373
Sunstein CR, '*Lochner's* Legacy' (1987) 87 Colum L Rev 873

—— 'Against Positive Rights: Why Social and Economic Rights Don't Belong in the New Constitutions of Post-Communist Europe' (1993) 2 EECR 35
—— and Thaler RH, 'Libertarian Paternalism is not an Oxymoron' (2003) 70 U Chi L Rev 1159
Syrpis P, 'The Relationship Between Primary and Secondary Law in the EU' (2015) 52 CMLRev 461
—— 'The Influence of the EU on UK Labour Law – Before and After Brexit' (2022) 51 ILJ 802
—— and Novitz T, 'Economic and Social Rights in Conflict: Political and Judicial Approaches to their Reconciliation' (2008) 33 ELRev 411
Tecqmenne M, 'Minimum Harmonisation and Fundamental Rights: A Test-Case for the Identification of the Scope of EU Law in Situations Involving National Discretion?' (2020) 16 EuConst 493
Thielberger P, 'The "Essence" of International Human Rights' (2019) 20 Ger Law J 924
Tridimas T, 'The Court of Justice and Judicial Activism' (1996) 21 ELRev 199
—— 'The General Principles of Law: Who Needs Them?' (2016) 52 Cahiers de Droit Européen 419
—— and Gentile G, 'The Essence of Rights: An Unreliable Boundary?' (2019) 20 Ger Law J 794
Tuominen T, 'Reconceptualizing the Primacy-Supremacy Debate in EU Law' (2020) 47 LIEI 245
Tushnet M, 'Critical Legal Studies and Constitutional Law: An Essay in Deconstruction' (1984) 36 Stan L Rev 623
—— 'Critical Legal Studies: An Introduction to its Origins and Underpinnings' (1986) 36 J Legal Educ 505
—— 'Some Current Controversies in Critical Legal Studies' (2011) 12 Ger Law J 290
Unger RM, 'The Critical Legal Studies Movement' (1983) 96 Harv L Rev 561
Usai A, 'The Freedom to Conduct a Business in the EU, its Limitations and its Role in the European Legal Order: A New Engine for Deeper and Stronger Economic, Social, and Political Integration' (2013) 14 Ger Law J 1867
Van Drooghenbroeck S and Rizcallah C, 'The ECHR and the Essence of Fundamental Rights: Searching for Sugar in Hot Milk' (2019) 20 Ger Law J 904
Walker N, 'The Idea of Constitutional Pluralism' (2002) 65 MLR 317
Weatherill S, 'Use and Abuse of the EU's Charter of Fundamental Rights: On the Improper Veneration of "Freedom of Contract"' (2014) 10 ERCL 167
Wedderburn L, 'Inderogability, Collective Agreements, and Community Law' (1992) 21 ILJ 245
Weiler JHH, 'Eurocracy and Distrust: Some Questions Concerning the Role of the European Court of Justice in the Protection of Fundamental Human Rights Within the Legal Order of the European Communities' (1986) 61 Wash L Rev 1103
—— 'Does the European Union Truly Need a Charter of Rights?' (2000) 6 ELJ 95
White GE, 'Revisiting Substantive Due Process and Holmes's *Lochner* Dissent' (1997) 63 Brook L Rev 87
Whittaker S, 'The Optional Instrument of European Contract Law and Freedom of Contract' (2011) 3 ERCL 372
Whitten LC, 'Post-Brexit Dynamism: The Dynamic Regulatory Alignment of Northern Ireland Under the Protocol on Ireland/Northern Ireland' (2022) 73 NILQ 37
Whittington KE, 'Congress Before the *Lochner* Court' (2005) 85 BULRev 821
Wilhelmsson T, 'Varieties of Welfarism in European Contract Law' (2004) 10 ELJ 712

Wynn-Evans C, 'TUPE, Collective Agreements and the Static-Dynamic Debate' (2010) 39 ILJ 275
Yackle L, '*Lochner*: Another Time, Another Place' (2005) 85 BULRev 765
Yeung K, 'Nudge as Fudge' (2012) 75 MLR 122
Young KG, 'The Minimum Core of Economic and Social Rights: A Concept in Search of Content' (2008) 33 Yale J Int'l L 113
Youngdahl J, 'Solidarity First Labour Rights are not the same as Human Rights' (2009) 18 New Labour Forum 30
—— 'Youngdahl Replies' (2009) 18 New Labour Forum 46
Zahn R, 'The Court of Justice of the European Union and Transfers of Undertakings: Implications for Collective Labour Rights' (2015) 6 ELLJ 72
Załuski W, 'On Social Rights from an Analytical Perspective' (2016) 2 Archiwum Filozofii Prawa i Filozofii Społecznej 76
Zuleeg M, 'Fundamental Rights and the Law of the European Communities' (1971) 8 CMLRev 446
von Bar C and others (eds), 'Principles, Definitions and Model Rules of European Private Law Draft Common Frame of Reference' (DCFR) Outline Edition 2009

iii. Chapters in edited volumes

Adams M and others, 'Introduction: Judging Europe's Judges' in M Adams and others (eds), *Judging Europe's Judges: The Legitimacy of the Case Law of the European Court of Justice* (Hart 2013) 1
Albors-Llorens A, 'Edging Towards Closer Scrutiny? The Court of Justice and its Review of the Compatibility of General Measures with the Protection of Economic Rights and Freedoms' in A Arnull and others (eds), *A Constitutional Order of States? Essays in Honour of Alan Dashwood* (Hart 2011) 245
Alemanno A and Sibony A-L, 'The Emergence of Behavioural Policy-Making: A European Perspective' in A Alemanno and A-L Sibony (eds), *Nudging and the Law* (Hart 2015) 1
—— and Sibony A-L, 'The Legitimacy and Practicability of EU Behavioural Policy-Making' in A Alemanno and A-L Sibony (eds), *Nudging and the Law* (Hart 2015) 325
Arden L and Tridimas T, 'Limited But Not Inconsequential: The Application of the Charter by the Courts of England and Wales' in M Bobek and J Adams-Prassl (eds), *The EU Charter of Fundamental Rights in the Member States* (Hart 2020) 331
Ashiagbor D, 'The Right to Work' in G de Búrca and B de Witte (eds), *Social Rights in Europe* (OUP 2005) 241
Atkinson J, 'Human Rights as Foundations for Labour Law' in H Collins, G Lester, and V Mantouvalou (eds), *Philosophical Foundations of Labour Law* (OUP 2018) 122
Barnard C, 'The "Opt-Out" for the UK and Poland from the Charter of Fundamental Rights: Triumph of Rhetoric over Reality?' in S Griller and J Ziller (eds), *The Lisbon Treaty: EU Constitutionalism Without a Constitutional Treaty* (Springer 2008) 257
—— 'The Protection of Fundamental Social Rights in Europe After Lisbon: A Question of Conflicts of Interest' in S de Vries and others (eds), *The Protection of Fundamental Rights in the EU After Lisbon* (Hart 2013) 37
—— 'The Calm after the Storm: Time to Reflect on EU (Labour) Law Scholarship Following the Decisions in *Viking* and *Laval*' in A Bogg, C Costello, and A Davies (eds), *Research Handbook on EU Labour Law* (Elgar 2016) 337
—— 'Social Policy Law' in C Baudenbacher (ed), *The Handbook on EEA Law* (Springer 2016) 809

—— 'The Worker Protection Justification: Lessons from Consumer Law' in P Koutrakos, N Nic Shuibhne, and P Syrpis (eds), *Exceptions from EU Free Movement Law* (Hart 2016) 108
—— 'EU "Social" Policy: From Employment Law to Labour Market Reform' in P Craig and G de Búrca (eds), *The Evolution of EU Law* (3rd edn, OUP 2021) 678
Bartl M and Leone C, 'Minimum Harmonisation and Article 16 of the CFREU: Difficult Times Ahead for Social Legislation?' in H Collins (ed), *European Contract Law and the Charter of Fundamental Rights* (Intersentia 2017) 113
Baudenbacher C, 'The Relationship Between the EFTA Court and the Court of Justice of the European Union' in C Baudenbacher (ed), *The Handbook on EEA Law* (Springer 2016) 179
Bell M, 'Constitutionalization and EU Employment Law' in HW Micklitz (ed), *Constitutionalization of European Private Law* (OUP 2014) 137
Bogg A, 'Only Fools and Horses: Some Sceptical Reflections on the Right to Work' in V Mantouvalou (ed), *The Right to Work: Legal and Philosophical Perspectives* (Hart 2017) 149
—— 'Article 31' in S Peers and others (eds), *The EU Charter of Fundamental Rights: A Commentary* (2nd edn, Hart 2021) 875
—— 'Default Norms in Labour Law: Form Private Right to Public Law' in B Hacker and J Ungerer (eds), *Default Rules in Private Law* (forthcoming, Hart)
Brodie D, 'The Autonomy of the Common Law of the Contract of Employment from the General Law of Contract' in M Freedland and others (eds), *The Contract of Employment* (OUP 2016) 124
Brownsword R, 'The Theoretical Foundation of European Private Law: A Time to Stand and Stare' in R Brownsword and others (eds), *The Foundations of European Private Law* (Hart 2011) 159
Cameron I, 'Competing Rights' in S de Vries, U Bernitz, and S Weatherill (eds), *The Protection of Fundamental Rights in the EU After Lisbon* (Hart 2013) 181
Cherednychenko OO, 'Fundamental Freedoms, Fundamental Rights, and the Many Faces of Freedom of Contract in the EU' in M Andenas, T Bekkedal, and L Pantaleo (eds), *The Reach of Free Movement* (Asser 2017) 273
Collins H, 'Theories of Rights as Justifications for Labour Law' in G Davidov and B Langille (eds), *The Idea of Labour Law* (OUP 2011) 137
—— 'Social Dumping, Multi-level Governance and Private Law in Employment Relationships' in D Leczykiewicz and S Weatherill (eds), *The Involvement of EU Law in Private Law Relationships* (Hart 2013) 223
—— 'Implied Terms in the Contract of Employment' in M Freedland and others (eds), *The Contract of Employment* (OUP 2016) 471
—— 'Is There a Human Right to Work?' in V Mantouvalou (ed), *The Right to Work: Legal and Philosophical Perspectives* (Hart 2017) 17
—— 'Progress Towards the Right to Work in the United Kingdom' in V Mantouvalou (ed), *The Right to Work: Legal and Philosophical Perspectives* (Hart 2017) 229
—— and Mantouvalou V, 'Human Rights and the Contract of Employment' in M Freedland and others (eds), *The Contract of* Employment (OUP 2016) 188
Craig P, 'General Principles of Law: Treaty, Historical and Normative Foundations' in KS Ziegler, PJ Neuvonen, and V Moreno-Lax (eds), *Research Handbook on General Principles of EU Law* (Edward Elgar 2022)
—— 'Legal Structure, Rights and Enforceability' in C McCrudden (ed), *The Law and Practice of the Ireland—Northern Ireland Protocol* (CUP 2022) 31

de Vries S, 'The Charter of Fundamental Rights and the EU's "Creeping" Competences: Does the Charter Have a Centrifugal Effect for Fundamental Rights in the EU?' in S Douglas-Scott and N Hatzis (eds), *Research Handbook on EU Law and Human Rights* (Edward Elgar 2017) 58

Deakin S, 'Article 15' in F Dorssemont and others (eds), *The Charter of Fundamental Rights of the European Union and the Employment Relation* (Hart 2019) 331

—— 'In Search of the EU's Social Constitution: Using the Charter to Recalibrate Social and Economic Rights' in F Dorssemont and others (eds), *The Charter of Fundamental Rights of the European Union and the Employment Relation* (Hart 2019) 52

Di Porto F and Rangone N, 'Behavioural Sciences in Practice: Lessons for EU Rule Makers' in A Alemanno and A-L Sibony (eds), *Nudging and the Law* (Hart 2015) 29

Dickson B, 'The United Kingdom' in P Popelier, C van de Heyning, and P van Nuffel (eds), *Human Rights Protection in the European Legal Order: The Interaction between the European and the National Courts* (Intersentia 2010) 343

Dorssemont F, 'The Right to Bargain Collectively' in N Bruun and others (eds), *The European Social Charter and the Employment Relation* (Hart 2017) 249

Dougan M, 'In Defence of Mangold?' in A Arnull and others (eds), *A Constitutional Order of States? Essays in EU Law in Honour of Alan Dashwood* (Hart 2011) 219

—— 'The General Principles of EU Law and Private Relationships' in D Leczykiewicz and S Weatherill (eds), *The Involvement of EU Law in Private Relationships* (Hart 2013) 71

Douglas-Scott S, 'The Court of Justice of the European Union and the European Court of Human Rights after Lisbon' in S de Vries, U Bernitz, and S Weatherill (eds), *The Protection of Fundamental Rights in the EU After Lisbon* (Hart 2013) 153

Dworkin R, 'Rights as Trumps' in J Waldron (ed), *Theories of Rights* (OUP 1984) 153

Everson M and Correia Gonçalves R, 'Article 16-Freedom to Conduct a Business' in S Peers and others (eds), *The EU Charter of Fundamental Rights: A Commentary* (2nd edn, Hart 2021) 463

Frantziou E and Mantouvalou V, 'Article 15 The Right to Work' in S Peers and others (eds), *The EU Charter of Fundamental Rights: A Commentary* (2nd edn, Hart 2021) 449

Fredman S, 'Scepticism Under Scrutiny: Labour Law and Human Rights' in T Campbell, KD Ewing, and A Tompkins (eds), *Sceptical Essays on Human Rights* (OUP 2001) 197

Freedland M, 'Ius Cogens, Ius Dispositivum, and the Law of Personal Work Contracts' in P Birks and A Pretto (eds), *Themes in Comparative Law: In Honour of Bernard Rudden* (OUP 2002) 165

—— 'The Involvement of EU Law in Personal Work Relations: A Defining Issue for European Private Law?' in L Leczykiewicz and S Weatherill (eds), *The Involvement of EU Law in Private Law Relationships* (Hart 2013) 279

—— and Prassl J, '*Viking*, *Laval* and Beyond: An Introduction' in M Freedland and J Prassl (eds), *Viking, Laval and Beyond* (Hart 2016) 1

Garben S, 'Balancing Fundamental Social and Economic Rights in the EU: In Search of a Better Method' in B Vanhercke and others (eds), *Social Policy in the European Union 1999–2019: The Long and Winding Road* (ETUI 2020) 57

Gerards J, 'Who Decides on Fundamental Rights Issues in Europe? Towards a Mechanism to Coordinate the Roles of the National Courts, the ECJ and the ECHR' in S de Vries, U Bernitz, and S Weatherill (eds), *The EU Charter of Fundamental Rights as a Binding Instrument: Five Years Old and Growing* (Hart 2015) 51

Gray K, 'Land Law and Human Rights' in T Tee (ed), *Land Law: Issues, Debates, Policy* (Willan 2002) 211

Groussot X, Pech L, and Petursson GT, 'The Reach of EU Fundamental Rights on Member State Action' in S de Vries U Bernitz, and S Weatherill (eds), *The Protection of Fundamental Rights in the EU After Lisbon* (Hart 2013) 97

—— Pétursson GT, and Pierce J, 'Weak Right, Strong Court—The Freedom to Conduct Business and the EU Charter of Fundamental Rights' in S Douglas-Scott and N Hatzis (eds), *Research Handbook on EU Law and Human Rights* (Edward Elgar 2017) 326

Herdegen M, 'The Origins and Development of the General Principles of Community Law' in U Bernitz and J Nergelius (eds), *General Principles of European Community Law* (Kluwer 2000) 3

—— 'General Principles of EU Law—The Methodological Challenge' in U Bernitz and others (eds), *General Principles of EC Law in a Process of Development* (Kluwer 2008) 343

Herresthal C, 'Constitutionalisation of the Freedom of Contract in European Union Law' in KS Ziegler and PM Huber (eds), *Current Problems in the Protection of Human Rights* (Hart 2013) 89

Hesselink MW, 'If You Don't Like Our Principles We have Others: On Core Values and Underlying Principles in European Private Law: A Critical Discussion of the New "Principles" Section in the Draft Common Frame of Reference' in R Brownsword and others (eds) *The Foundations of European Private Law* (Hart 2011) 59

Imamović S, 'The Role of the Court of Justice in the Fragmented European Union Fundamental Rights Landscape' in L Violini and A Baraggia (eds), *The Fragmented Landscape of Fundamental Rights Protection in Europe: The Role of Judicial and Non-Judicial Actors* (Edward Elgar 2018) 73

Jääskinen N, 'Fundamental Social Rights in the Charter—Are They Rights? Are They Fundamental?' in S Peers and others (eds), *The EU Charter of Fundamental Rights: A Commentary* (2nd edn, Hart 2021) 1855

Jacobs A, 'Article 11: The Right to Bargain Collectively' in F Dorssemont, K Lörcher, and I Schömann (eds), *The European Convention on Human Rights and the Employment Relation* (Hart 2013) 309

Kenner J, 'Economic and Social Rights in the EU Legal Order: The Mirage of Indivisibility' in T Hervey and J Kenner (eds), *Economic and Social Rights under the EU Charter of Fundamental Rights* (Hart 2003) 3

Kilpatrick C, 'The Human Rights Puzzle of the Euro-Crisis: Why Massive Breaches of Human Rights but None of the EU Charter of Fundamental Rights?' in M González Pascual and A Torres Pérez (eds), *Social Rights and the European Monetary Union: Challenges Ahead* (Edward Elgar 2022) 121

Konstadinides T, 'The Rule of Law as the Constitutional Foundation of the General Principles of EU Law' in KS Ziegler, PJ Neuvonen, and V Moreno-Lax (eds), *Research Handbook on General Principles of EU Law* (Edward Elgar 2022) 287

Kosta V and de Witte B, 'Human Rights Norms in the Court of Justice of the European Union' in M Scheinin (ed), *Human Rights Norms in Other International Courts* (CUP 2019) 263

Lazzerini N, 'The Horizontal Application of the General Principles of EU Law: Nothing Less than Direct Effect' in KS Ziegler, PJ Neuvonen, and V Moreno-Lax (eds), *Research Handbook on General Principles of EU Law* (Edward Elgar 2022) 173

Leczykiewicz D, 'Conceptualising Conflict between the Economic and the Social in EU Law after *Viking* and *Laval*' in M Freedland and J Prassl (eds), *Viking, Laval and Beyond* (Hart 2016) 307

Lenaerts K, 'The Role of the EU Charter in the Member States' in M Bobek and J Adams-Prassl (eds), *The EU Charter of Fundamental Rights in the Member States* (Hart 2020) 19

—— and Gutiérrez-Fons JA, 'The Role of the General Principles of EU Law' in A Arnull and others (eds), *A Constitutional Order of States? Essays in EU Law in Honour of Alan Dashwood* (Hart 2011) 179

—— and Gutiérrez-Fons JA, 'The Place of the Charter in the European Legal Space' in S Peers and others (eds), *The EU Charter of Fundamental Rights: A Commentary* (2nd edn, Hart 2021) 1711

Lewis Siegel R, 'The Right to Work: Core Minimum Obligations' in AR Chapman and S Russell (eds), *Introduction to Core Obligations: Building a Framework for Economic, Social and Cultural Rights* (Intersentia 2002) 21

Mayer FC and Wendel M, 'Multilevel Constitutionalism and Constitutional Pluralism' in M Avbelj and J Komárek (eds), *Constitutional Pluralism in the European Union and Beyond* (OUP 2012) 127

McCrudden C, 'Human Rights and Equality' in C McCrudden (ed), *The Law and Practice of the Ireland—Northern Ireland Protocol* (CUP 2022) 141

Moeckli D and White ND, 'Treaties as "Living Instruments"' in D Kritsiotis and M Bowman (eds), *Conceptual and Contextual Perspectives on the Modern Law of Treaties* (CUP 2018) 136

Mundlak G, 'The Right to Work, the Value of Work' in D Barak-Erez and A Gross (eds), *Exploring Social Rights: Between Theory and Practice* (Hart 2007) 341

Neuvonen PJ and Ziegler KS, 'General Principles in the EU Legal Order: Past, Present and Future Directions' in KS Ziegler, PJ Neuvonen, and V Moreno-Lax (eds), *Research Handbook on General Principles of EU Law* (Edward Elgar 2022) 7

O'Cinneide C, 'The Right to Work in International Human Rights Law' in V Mantouvalou (ed), *The Right to Work: Legal and Philosophical Perspectives* (Hart 2017) 99

—— 'The Present Limits and Future Potential of European Social Constitutionalism' in KG Young (ed), *The Future of Economic and Social Rights* (CUP 2019) 324

O'Leary S, 'The Charter and the Future Contours of EU Social and Employment Law' in P Cardonnel, A Rosas, and N Wahl (eds), *Constitutionalising the EU Judicial System: Essays in Honour of Pernilla Lindh* (Hart 2012) 317

Oliver P, 'What Purpose does Article 16 of the Charter Serve?' in U Bernitz, X Groussot, and F Schulyok (eds), *General Principles of EU Law and European Private Law* (Kluwer 2013) 281

Pech L, 'Article 7 TEU: From "Nuclear Option" to "Sisyphean Procedure"' in U Belavusau and A Gliszcynka-Grabias (eds), *Constitutionalism Under Stress* (OUP 2020) 157

Peers S and Prechal S, 'Article 52' in S Peers and others (eds), *The EU Charter of Fundamental Rights: A Commentary* (2nd edn, Hart 2021) 1611

Pollicino O, 'Common Constitutional Traditions in the Age of the European Bill(s) of Rights: Chronicle of a (Somewhat Prematurely) Death Foretold' in L Violini and A Baraggia (eds), *The Fragmented Landscape of Fundamental Rights Protection in Europe: The Role of Judicial and Non-Judicial Actors* (Edward Elgar 2018) 42

Smismans S, 'Fundamental Rights as a Political Myth of the EU: Can the Myth Survive?' in S Douglas-Scott and N Hatzis (eds), *Research Handbook on EU Law and Human Rights* (Edward Elgar 2017) 13

Spaventa E, 'The Horizontal Application of Fundamental Rights as General Principles of Union Law' in A Arnull and others (eds), *A Constitutional Order of States? Essays in EU Law in Honour of Alan Dashwood* (Hart 2011) 199

Sunstein CR, 'The Ethics of Nudging' in A Alemanno and A-L Sibony (eds), *Nudging and the Law* (Hart 2015) v

Tasioulas J, 'On the Nature of Human Rights' in G Ernst and J-C Heilinger (eds), *The Philosophy of Human Rights* (De Gruyter 2012) 17

Toth AG, 'Human Rights as General Principles of Law, in the Past and in the Future' in U Bernitz and J Nergelius (eds), *General Principles of European Community Law* (Kluwer 2000) 73

Tuori K, 'The Pluralism of European Fundamental Rights Law' in S Douglas-Scott and N Hatzis (eds), *Research Handbook on EU Law and Human Rights* (Edward Elgar 2017) 35

van der Donk B, 'Restricting Access to Legal Content in House Rules: The Platform's Freedom to Conduct a Business as a Counterargument to Limit Users' Freedom of Expression' in S Hindelang and A Moberg (eds), *YSEC Yearbook of Socio-Economic Constitutions 2021: Triangulating Freedom of Speech* (Springer 2022) 33

Veneziani B, 'Article 16—Freedom to Conduct a Business' in F Dorssemont and others (eds), *The Charter of Fundamental Rights of the European Union and the Employment Relation* (Hart 2019) 351

Wahl N, 'Uncharted Waters: Reflection on the Legal Significance of the Charter under EEA law and Judicial Cross-Fertilisation in the Field of Fundamental Rights' in The EFTA Court (ed), *The EEA and the EFTA Court: Decentred Integration: To Mark the 20th Anniversary of the EFTA Court* (Hart 2014) 281

—— 'The Freedom to Conduct a Business: A Right of Fundamental Importance of the Future of the European Union' in F Amtenbrink and others (eds), *The Internal Market and the Future of European Integration* (CUP 2019) 273

Ward A, 'Remedies under the EU Charter of Fundamental Rights' in S Douglas-Scott and N Hatzis (eds), *Research Handbook on EU Law and Human Rights* (Edward Elgar 2017) 162

—— 'Article 51—Field of Application' in S Peers and others (eds), *The EU Charter of Fundamental Rights: A Commentary* (2nd edn, Hart 2021) 1553

Weatherill S, 'Article 38—Consumer Protection' in S Peers and others (eds), *The EU Charter of Fundamental Rights: A Commentary* (2nd edn, Hart 2021) 1065

Weiler JHH, 'Epilogue: The Judicial Après Nice' in G de Búrca and JHH Weiler (eds), *The European Court of Justice* (OUP 2001) 215

Wollenschläger F, 'Article 17(1) Right to Property' in S Peers and others (eds), *The EU Charter of Fundamental Rights: A Commentary* (2nd edn, Hart 2021) 489

Ziegler KS, 'Autonomy: From Myth to Reality—or Hubris on a Tightrope? EU Law, Human Rights and International Law' in S Douglas-Scott and N Hatzis (eds), *Research Handbook on EU Law and Human Rights* (Edward Elgar 2017) 267

2. OTHER SOURCES

Alston P, 'Report of the Special Rapporteur on Extreme Poverty and Human Rights' 73 UN Doc A/HRC/34/51 (18 January 2017) 22

Commission Communication COM(2000) 559 final on the Charter of Fundamental Rights of the EU (13 September 2000)

Communication from the Commission to the European Parliament and the Council, 'European Contract Law and the Revision of the Acquis: The Way Forward' COM (2004) 651, Annex I, 15

Communication from the Commission Guidelines on the application of Union competition law to collective agreements regarding the working conditions of solo self-employed persons [2022] OJ C374/2

Department for Exiting the European Union, 'Legislating for the United Kingdom's Withdrawal from the European Union' CM 9446 (March 2017)

Department for Exiting the European Union, 'Charter of Fundamental Rights of the EU: Right by Right Analysis' (5 December 2017)

ECNI and NIHRC, 'Working Paper: The Scope of Article 2(1) of the Ireland/Northern Ireland Protocol' (December 2022) 11

EU Report on 'Protection of Fundamental Rights Post-Lisbon', FIDE Conference 2012

European Agency for Fundamental Rights, 'Freedom to Conduct a Business: Exploring the Dimensions of a Fundamental Right' (2015)

European Commission, 'Facts About the "Social Chapter"', MEMO/97/13 (5 February 1997)

House of Commons European Scrutiny Committee, 'The Application of the EU Charter of Fundamental Rights in the UK: A State of Confusion' HC 979 (2 April 2014)

House of Lords Constitution Committee, 'European Union (Withdrawal) Bill' HL Paper 69, (29 January 2018)

Joint Committee on Human Rights, Legislative Scrutiny: The EU (Withdrawal) Bill: A Right by Right Analysis, First Report of Session 2017–2019, 24 January 2018 HL Paper 70, HC 774

Joint Declaration of the Parliament, Council and Commission of the European Communities concerning the protection of fundamental rights and the European Convention for the Protection of Human Rights and Fundamental Freedoms [1977] OJ C103/1

Miller V, '"Ever Closer Union" in the EU Treaties and Court of Justice Case Law', House of Commons Library Briefing Paper Number 07230 (16 November 2015)

Ministry of Justice, 'Government response to the House of Commons European Scrutiny Committee Report 43rd Report, 2013–2014, HC979, 'The Application of the EU Charter of Fundamental Rights in the UK: A State of Confusion' CM 8915 (July 2014)

NIHRC and ECNI, 'Submission of the NIHRC and ECNI to "Retained EU Law: Where Next?"—An Inquiry by the European Scrutiny Committee' (11 April 2022)

Northern Ireland Assembly, 'Report of the Ad Hoc Committee on a Bill of Rights' 156/17-22 (4 February 2022)

Northern Ireland Office, 'UK Government Commitment to "No Diminution of Rights, Safeguards and Equality of Opportunity" in Northern Ireland: What does it mean and how will it be implemented?' (NIO 2020)

Stewart JB, 'Did the Supreme Court Open the Door to Reviving One of its Worst Decisions?' *New York Times* (2 July 2022)

United Kingdom Government, 'Smarter Regulation to Grow the Economy' (10 May 2023)

United Nations Committee on Economic, Social and Cultural Rights, 'General Comment No 23 on the Right to Just and Favourable Conditions of Work', E/C.12/GC/23, 27 April 2016

United Nations Committee on Economic, Social and Cultural Rights, 'Concluding Observations on the Sixth Periodic Report on the United Kingdom of Great Britain and Northern Ireland' E/C.12/GBR/CO/6, 14 July 2016

United Nations Committee on Economic, Social, and Cultural Rights, 'General Comment No 3: The Nature of States Parties' Obligations' E/199/23, 14 December 1990

United Nations Committee on Economic, Social and Cultural Rights, 'General Comment No 18 on the Right to Work, 24 November 2005 concerning art 6 ICESCR' E/C.12/GC/18, 6 February 2006

Index

For the benefit of digital users, indexed terms that span two pages (e.g., 52–53) may, on occasion, appear on only one of those pages.

Tables are indicated by an italic *t* following the page number.